Aviation's Great Recruiter

Cleveland's Ed Packard

H. L. (Herm) Schreiner

The Kent State University Press   *Kent and London*

Frontis: Edward T. Packard (a.k.a. Pachasa), founder and president of Cleveland Model and Supply Company, at age eighty-one at his 10307 Detroit Avenue location, 1987. Modelers from seventy-two countries worldwide formed a continuous pilgrimage to their "shrine" in Cleveland from 1929 on. The model is a ¾-inch scale, eight-foot-wingspan 1935 Martin 130 China Clipper, originally built in 1937 by Col. Robert Hawkins of Ashley, Indiana. It was double-tissue covered and silver doped, as shown. In 1990 Dan Scherry, Cleveland volunteer model engineer, refurbished it with aluminum covering. It is on display at the Treasure Island Museum, San Francisco, California. *Photo by Ralph Mroch. E. T. Packard Collection.*

© 2005 by The Kent State University Press, Kent, Ohio 44242
All rights reserved

Library of Congress Catalog Card Number pending
ISBN-10: 0-87338-821-6
ISBN-13: 978-0-87338-821-4
Manufactured in the United States of America

09 08 07 06 05   5 4 3 2 1

Library of Congress Cataloging-in-Publication Data pending

British Library Cataloging-in-Publication data are available.

Aviation's Great Recruiter

To my daughter
Kathryn Amelia Schreiner Greene
Who took her last one-way flight on February 10, 2004

⤳

This narrative is respectfully dedicated to the spirit of Edward Thomas Packard and his lifelong effort to provide authentic plans and kits of model airplanes so as to allow the youth of America and the world to experience the satisfaction of the hobby of exhibitions, scale flying, and freelance models and the exhilaration of their controlled flight.

Edward T. Packard dedicated his story to his wife, Kay Kreitzer Packard, whose professional expertise at Cleveland Model and financial support from outside the company made it possible for the business to exist until 1996; to his children, Robert, Doris, Cheryl, Donald, and Nancy; and to his four brothers, Andy, Albert, Fred, and Will, whose dedicated service was instrumental in the success of Cleveland Model and Supply.

Contents

Preface and Acknowledgments

⚜ MY INITIAL CONTACT with Ed Packard was made in 1971 in Cleveland at the 10301 Detroit Avenue site. This visit and others resulted in an article I published in the *American Aviation Historical Society Journal* 17 (Fall 1972). There followed continued correspondence between us and other visits until December 1989, when I enjoyed a three-day visit with Packard at Cleveland Model and Supply. During that time I taped interviews with him and received a thorough tour of the facility, which provided the basis for this book. Our correspondence and interviews continued until his death in 1992.

This book was not written—it was assembled. It is a vehicle for the long over-due recognition of the spirit that lived within Master Model Engineer Edward T. Packard, since it was that indomitable, resolute dedication to providing "wings for everyone" that created a lifelong hobby for so many of us, a hobby that made it possible for us to dream dreams of flying—of building or flying our own planes, of being test pilots, or of serving in the military. Dreams are the fabric of which Ed Packard was made. Had he not had dreams, there would never have been a Cleveland Model and Supply Company, and millions of us would never have experienced the satisfaction of the accomplishment of model construction and the euphoria of flight, one of the great joys of life.

Dreams come first, then goals, then accomplishments. They are the propelling force behind greatness. In the 1930s kids could go to the corner candy or news shop, the dime store, or a department store and for about ten to twenty-five cents buy their choice of airplane kits that included an all-important construction plan plus that dramatic photo or sketch of a finished model—a passport into the "magic world of argosies of wings and pilots of the purple twilight."

The kids who could not afford a kit or who as yet were unable to build one could in 1932 for five cents buy the first issue of *Cleveland Model Engineers*

News, and they could pore over the how-to illustrations and photos of modeling techniques and drool over the ads for the latest C-D (Cleveland-Designed, synonymous now with the Cleveland Model and Supply Company) realistic scale models. Another passport to dreams.

When most model airplane manufacturers were turning out toy-type airplanes with only a vague resemblance to the prototype, C-D was producing ¾-inch (¹⁄₁₆ size) accurate scale miniatures. And, if the plan was for a World War I model, such as the famous French Spad XIII Pursuit flown by America's ace-of-aces, Capt. Eddie Rickenbacker, it would have an instrument panel shown; the red, white, and blue roundels on the wings and stripes on the rudder and the fuselage; and then the world's most famous squadron insignia, the great "hat in the ring" of America's 94th Aero Squadron. Of course, there was a photo of the ace with his uniform and with those wings on the tunic. There was even a special C-D offer with World War I kits, making it possible for the kids to get an autographed copy of Rick's famous book about his twenty-six victories in the Great War, *Fighting the Flying Circus* (1919). Who is to say how many youths were influenced by factors such as these at an early age, formulating a deep desire to be in aviation?

Packard's first commercial venture, selling five Skylarks, 20-inch-wingspan twin pushers, retailing for $3.75 in 1919, became the inception of the world-famous Cleveland Model and Supply Company. (The development of the nascent business was somewhat erratic because Packard had to make time available after fulfilling his priorities of education, part-time employment, and supplementary income-producing business enterprises.) He grappled with a choice of careers in the civil aviation industry as a light plane manufacturer or starting a model airplane and hobby company. However, after several years of summer employment with some of the then-famous airframe manufacturers such as the Glenn L. Martin Company in Cleveland, Fokker's Atlantic Aviation in Hasbrouck Heights, New Jersey, and Woodson Aircraft Company in Bryan, Ohio, he discovered that the economic reality of the fledgling industry was highly cyclical and labor-intensive and that quality, safety, and performance were yet to be proven. Despite the fact that he had designed plans for several light planes and had three different concepts under construction in the family basement, he arrived at the conclusion that it would be far shrewder to further develop his hobby business, from which he could possibly generate adequate funding for his ambitious light plane venture.

However, the foremost characteristic of the Master Model Engineer that emerges is his lifelong intense passion for aircraft. The result was his absolute, complete dedication to producing the most realistic, practical, scale flying models possible, and in the process he became "aviation's great recruiter."

In the span of a six-decade model design engineering career, Packard had brushes with many of the famous greats in and out of aviation. At an early juncture in his career (1930), he initiated the National Advanced Model

Engineers (NAME) to encourage youthful participation in the building and flying of scale models, preparatory for careers in aviation. It climaxed with a national contest held in conjunction with the annual Cleveland National Air Races. The great Cliff Henderson, flamboyant promoter of the National Air Races, a sponsor and an effective booster of Packard's efforts, insisted on early air-race-model contests in conjunction with Packard's NAME. The amazing Jimmy Doolittle was president, and Col. Billy Bishop, Canada's top World War I ace (seventy-two victories), and ace William K. Thaw (five victories), of the famous Lafayette Escadrille, were vice presidents.

In 1931 at a Cleveland Chamber of Commerce luncheon honoring Doolittle, Packard was introduced to Billy Bishop, and they became great friends. Subsequently, Bishop furnished the photos and data making possible the C-D reproduction in 1:16-size (¾-inch scale) kit SF-12 of his famous World War I Nieuport 17 Scout, complete with markings and authentic insignia. It was later in that same year that Packard contacted Rickenbacker, the future president of Eastern Airlines, to request his personal assistance for C-D to produce the authentic scale model of "Captain Eddy's" famous French Spad XIII Pursuit (SF-13).

Packard was a skilled craftsman for aviation pioneers Glenn L. Martin in Cleveland and the famous Dutch aircraft designer Anthony H. G. Fokker, who had become an American manufacturer of the famous Fokker Universals and tri-motors at the Atlantic Aircraft plant in Hasbrouck Heights, New Jersey. Packard's expertise in cabin upholstering and his early experiences at the Martin factory and at Woodson Aircraft Factory in Bryan, Ohio, qualified him to work elbow-to-elbow with Fokker on the assembly floor at "Uncle Tony's" (as he was respectfully called).

Some of the daredevil National Air Race pilots seeking record-breaking top speeds got to know Packard through early Cleveland airport superintendent Maj. Jack Berry; among them were Doug Davis, Roscoe Turner, Jimmie Weddell, and Benny Howard. Hence, his line of National Air Race kits—beginning with the 1929 Travel Air Mystery Ship, the Lairds, the Gee-Bees, Howard's, Weddell-Williams, and Severskys—scooped others in the model industry thanks to his access to the racers hangared at Cleveland.

Notable former U.S. Navy captain Holden C. "Dick" Richardson, Naval Aviator No. 13, was the hull designer and pilot of the 1919 NC-3 flying boat. As director of engineering at Cleveland's Great Lakes Aircraft Company, he became C-D's first vice president. He was also the first stockholder and acted as adviser to C-D over a span of seventeen years until his death. Through his access to Great Lakes factory drawings, in 1929 Packard released the SF-1 kit of the greatly acclaimed 2T-1 Great Lakes Sport Trainer, complete with factory insignia, authentic details, and color scheme, which brought international recognition to C-D almost overnight. His center-page spreads and color back cover ads in national model aviation magazines in the 1930s and 1940s were classics of realism and the envy of the industry. Such early outstanding results could be attributed in part to utilizing top artistic talent like Charles H. Hubbell of TRW calendar fame; James D. Powell, newspaper and magazine artist; and later retired University of Wisconsin art professor, Ken Sniffen, who had graphically dramatized most of the Golden Era designs.

When America found itself engulfed in World War II after the attacks on Pearl Harbor on December 7, 1941, the American people undertook a Herculean effort to tap their resources—human as well as industrial. Since the enemy's major spearhead was air power, the U.S. air armada had to undergo a massive expansion virtually overnight. From every walk of life, men and women came, heeding the call. Some were absorbed by industry to further the production effort. Others became the technicians and mechanics who maintained the power, armament, and avionics. The most compelling response came from those who were destined to pilot the thousands of aircraft that would comprise an ultimately invincible air force.

There was a common trait that evidenced itself throughout a significant share of the raw recruits. It was discovered that, in many of them, there existed an understanding of the basic principles of flight—primary aerodynamics— which proved to be an invaluable foundation on which flight instructors and ground school administrators could build. It was invariably learned that those youthful fledglings, potential flight mechanics and aerial gunner candidates, had previously been exposed to the hobby of building and flying model airplanes. Some had advanced to gas-powered types, and a select few had experimented with radio-controlled gas models. As a result, they could more readily absorb their class expertise in recognition silhouettes (small-scale black views of military aircraft) that distinguishes friend from foe, so vital in combat. Since they had learned to make the appropriate adjustments on the components of their own craft, they more aptly absorbed their courses in flight instruction. When it came to learning construction and field repairs, they found a commonality with the assemblies of the prototype to their miniatures.

But the most significant effect of their exposure to the addictive hobby was the kindling of an irrepressible, enthusiastic desire to fly, and they would settle for nothing less. Packard's greatest contribution to the war effort resulted when the boys and young men who had built models from his C-D kits during the decade prior to World War II became the recruits that the Air Corps and Naval Aviation so sorely needed. More C-D kits were flown across the Atlantic via unofficial military ferry to England than the total of their full-scale prototypes, providing many hours of constructive relief from utter boredom for AAF and British airmen at remote bases. He eventually filled his largest order ever, 30,000 kits for the War Department, and shipped planeloads of P-38, SBD, B-17, Spitfire, Hurricane, Wildcat, Focke-Wolfe, and Messerschmitt kits to servicemen, especially to outlying bases in the Aleutians. Thus Ed Packard, whose formal education had been interrupted in the ninth grade so that he could become co-breadwinner of the family of seven, influenced millions of young men to pursue a career in military or civil aviation.

Now when the airlines face a serious shortage of available pilots, there is no significant pool of aviation-oriented youth from which to draw for jobs, since today's youth have grown up in an era of quick fix, plastic-oriented, mass-produced models. Consequently, they have missed the opportunity to develop an understanding of the principles of flight, the satisfaction of working with their hands, and the comradery of constructive and friendly competition of flying model contests and recreational flights.

Likewise, with many of his former young model builders entering the ranks of retirees, Packard received a multitude of letters from the senior citizens who built his kits forty, fifty, or sixty years ago. Seeking to relive those glorious memories and wishing to acknowledge Packard's influence on their careers and lifestyles, they wrote emotional and impressive testimonials and still continually make purchases from his vast line of some 1,400 plans. The following excerpt is from a letter written by Don Clancey of Edinburg, Texas, and is representative of the many testimonials he received:

> It was that little dark-blue Austin with the Travel Air Mystery Ship on top that got me started as a Cleveland modeler back in 1930 at the corner of Derbyshire and Clarkson in Cleveland Heights. My first kit was a Rickenbacker $2 Spad [he cut grass to earn the money]. I became an aviation cadet in 1942 and flew B-24s and B-29s. I flew thirteen B-29 sorties in North Korea and got shot down.

Paul Poberezny, founder of the Experimental Aircraft Association (EAA), credits the existence of that organization, to a large extent, to his exposure at a young age to C-D models. The EAA, with a 2004 membership of 170,000 members, has long been the driving force behind aviation "home-builts." Currently, it finds itself in the midst of a boom in home-built kits, which make it possible to build a light plane with costs anywhere from $4,995 to $100,000 or more. The plans are available for as little as $200. The FAA registered some 25,000 of such amateur-built aircraft in 2004.

Many home-built owners are former model builders, and many credit C-D kits for kindling their interest and honing their ability to build flyable aircraft. Burt Rutan, the innovative designer who created the famous 1986 around-the-world nonstop *Voyager,* has also been in the limelight for his popular home-built kits called the Long-Ez. Rutan, along with thousands of other such enthusiasts of personal "dream ships," also began his career as a model builder.

No model aircraft manufacturer or prototype manufacturer, with the possible exception of the late Sir Thomas Sopwith, can match Edward T. Packard's seventy years of continuous participation. At age eighty-six he completed a fifteen-year-long project, with the aid of many knowledgeable people, to produce the most complete, accurate museum scale (1/16 size) model plan, as well as 1/32, 1/24, and 1/8 scale, of the famous 1903 *Wright Flyer,* the world's first successful, powered, heavier-than-air aircraft. This effort required utilizing the extensive resources of his library, reports, and 130 various aviation periodicals, plus the able assistance of several artists and engineer volunteers. The result was the most detailed, authentic scale plan of the historic, canard-type pusher, which will be recognized as the crowning achievement of his model-design-engineering career. Now it is possible for institutions, associations, and individual modelers around the world to construct a historically correct scale replica for flying scale (or display) of this most important aircraft.

On November 11, 1978, at the fifth annual Tournament of Champions (a contest for radio-controlled gas-powered models) in Las Vegas, Packard's peers presented him with the highest award in his industry. He was inducted into the Model Aviation Hall of Fame by the Academy of Model Aeronautics, now located in Muncie, Indiana, where in their museum an impressive array of approximately twenty of his Cleveland-Designed models and memorabilia are on display as an enduring testimonial to his role as "aviation's great recruiter."

The compilation of this biographical narrative was a long and significant undertaking, one that involved many people and therefore much grateful thanks.

Thank you to the Pachasa brothers: Will, who was instrumental in the success of C-D from the beginning until he left in 1958 to found his own wholesale hobby business, who provided numerous photos for this book, especially of the early Lorain Avenue store; Fred, Albert, and Andy, all of whom worked in the C-D enterprise early in their careers.

Grateful acknowledgment also goes out to Kay Kreitzer Packard, who joined C-D after high school and quickly became part of its management team. As Ed's wife, she continued her role in the company (as well as having three children) and, later, contributed her own outside earnings to make it possible for the company to continue.

J. Ken Sniffen's aviation art enlivened the New Era plans and catalogs as well as this book. He made innumerable and significant contributions to all graphic arts and is credited by Ed Packard with much of the success of the later C-D years. Similarly, C-D artist James D. Powell underscored Packard's role as "aviation's great recruiter."

Dan Scherry, the company's leading model engineer, produced many plans and offered engineering assistance and was instrumental in keeping C-D afloat. Other talented C-D model engineers include Dick Gates and Paul Kirk.

I thank Sid Bradd for his generous loan of photos. As a member of the Board of Directors of the Crawford Auto/Aircraft Museum, Western Reserve Historical Society, he led the effort to induct Packard into its Hall of Fame.

Thanks to the various publishers and artists of *Model Airplane News,* who helped inspire youth to build flying scale model aircraft.

In my research and writing, I thank Ellen Gossett for her expertise in word processing; noted modeler, artist, and KAPA president Jim Alaback for his contribution of C-D cartons, photos, and other invaluable information; Jack Deveny, for providing me with many flying pulps; John J. Sloan, for the loan of his illustrations and magazines and photos of WWI-era aircraft; R. S. Hirsch, for his expertise in aircraft and piloting as well as the use of his photos and other memorabilia; John Grabowski, of the Western Reserve Historical Society, who supported the publication of this book; and Ray Schreiner, my brother, for his generosity in providing storage space and assistance in preserving C-D memorabilia.

Special thanks is extended to Thomas Yanowski, for his efforts to restore C-D exhibition models for display at the AMA museum; NASM curator Paul Garber, who helped establish the ¾ scale as a standard for museum scale flying models and for his exhibition of many C-D plans in the Smithsonian; Paul Poberezny, the chairman and founder of the EAA, for his endorsement of the authenticity of the Cleveland plans and their influence on his organization; Mike Fulmer, AMA museum curator, for his outstanding C-D exhibit; and John Jacox, for acquiring C-D and preserving and continuing its traditions.

Finally, I thank the magnificent cadre of C-D volunteer model engineers whose professional expertise and unselfish efforts provided plans that made the New Era Phase II of C-D possible.

Abbreviations

AMA	Academy of Model Aeronautics
ATC	Approved Type Certificate (Department of Commerce)
CMN&PH	*Cleveland Modelmaking News and Practical Hobbies*
EAA	Experimental Aircraft Association
FAI	Federation Aeronautique Internationale
IGMAA	International Gas Model Airplane Association
MAN	*Model Airplane News*
NAA	National Aeronautic Association
RC	radio control
ROG	rise off ground
ROW	rise off water
NACA	National Advisory Committee for Aeronautics
SAM	Society of Antique Modelers

Aviation's Great Recruiter

PART I

The Birth of a Successful
Cottage Industry

CHAPTER 1

Origins

Still faintly visible on the drab, eroding brick facade of a century-old structure on Cleveland's densely developed West Side is the once-proud logo of the White Chewing Gum Company. The 34,000-square-foot building, located adjacent to the twin-ribboned steel artery of the New York Central, near where it crosses Detroit Avenue, was erected in 1890 by company founder William J. White. A pioneer entrepreneur in the marketing of the national fad for a popular chewing confection under the Yucatan label, he subsequently became mayor of West Cleveland and still later a member of Congress.

Relegated to obscurity in 1920 as a result of the declining fortunes of White's parent company, American Chicle, the Detroit Avenue facility went through several owners until recently, when it was designated as a city landmark by Cleveland's city council. There is no more appropriate locale for the site of another equally famous industry leader, a legend in his own time, Cleveland's Ed Packard, "Aviation's Great Recruiter."

When I was invited by Packard to write an article for *American Aviation Historical Society Journal* and showed up for the tour he was to give me as part of my research, I discovered that there was no sign or other identifying features on the building. I arrived at the run-down industrial structure, the then-anonymous location of the Cleveland Model and Supply Company, and parked near the loading dock. I cautiously tried the heavy fireproof door and, on entering, found myself hesitating at the base of four flights of massive, imposing stairs.

The manually operated elevator was broken, and I could only marvel at Packard's ageless agility and stamina, since it was part of his daily routine at age eighty-six to negotiate the intimidating staircase at least four times. As I rounded the sturdy balustrade of the staircase, I was literally stopped in my tracks. Confronting me was an array of impressive mahogany and glass display cases, featuring a lineup of gas-powered, profile, control-line Thompson

Above: Packard holding the Curtiss Hawk P6-E flagship of C-D fleet, 1987. *Author's Collection.*

Above right: This five-story 10307 Detroit Avenue building was built in 1890 by William J. White and later declared a city landmark. Modern chewing gum had its origin at White's Candy Shop on Lorain Avenue near West 25th Street. The building was C-D's third home, from 1968 to 1993, occupying the entire 7,800-square-foot top floor (1993). *Sid Bradd Collection.*

Trophy winners—a series of ¾-inch scale SF (scale flying) display models and an arrangement of Cleveland-Designed (C-D) kits representative of the entire line. The awe-inspiring scene combined the realism of the professional-appearing scale models with the impact of the colorful silver, red, white, and blue C-D cartons.

Inside the museum-warehouse, and somewhat isolated on the expansive fifth floor, I found Ed Packard, founder and president of the Cleveland Model and Supply Company, in the midst of his 7,800-square-foot domain, with its largesse of huge planks of bulk balsa wood and shelves stacked to the breaking point with all manner of model airplane printwood, dies, patterns, tooling, equipment, machinery, and supplies; drawer upon drawer of original drawings and prints of model plans; stacks and bookcases full of aviation publications; hundreds of unused flat model cartons; fliers and window advertising banners of the past beckoning from the walls; and an endless array of dust-laden, ¾-inch scale assembled aircraft display models, mute testimony to a once halcyon past when the Cleveland Model and Supply Company was the most famous name in the model airplane business. In short, everything was in order, almost as it was in 1968 when Packard vacated his most famous location, the 9,000-plus-square-foot facility at 4506 Lorain Avenue, after the model industry postwar bubble finally burst for Cleveland.

Operating at its peak during World War II and until 1945, his burgeoning enterprise ultimately consisted of 100 employees—many for this type of business. Later in 1945, after the end of the war, incoming orders slowed abruptly to a trickle, and the handwriting was on the wall that the model business would never be the same. (Over C-D's forty-two-year existence in the kit manufacturing business, Packard estimated that there had been a total of

Mildred Filsinger, assistant to Ed Packard, was hired a the Detroit Avenue facility in 1970 as a typist. She ultimately assumed responsibility for typing captions and specifications on C-D "new era" plans and processing orders. She became an invaluable asset to C-D and remained a loyal employee until she retired in 1996. *Stephen Kanyusik Collection.*

more than 2,000 employees hired.) Reluctantly, the employee roster had to be trimmed to a bare minimum of ten to fifteen workers until his final move to Detroit Avenue. C-D manufactured more than fifty million kits over its forty-two years of full-time production, with 1944 sales of approximately $7.5 million (current inflationary dollars).

Then Packard and his loyal assistant, Mildred Filsinger, and a cadre of dedicated and talented volunteer model engineers located throughout the country carried on the Cleveland tradition, with one significant difference—the elimination of kit production. Instead, Packard's company now provided the most authentic, detailed, and extensive line of model aircraft scale flying construction plans available worldwide. In the lower righthand corner of every plan produced, as had been the practice of the Master Model Engineer from the very beginning, was the hallmark to the simple humility of Cleveland's origin, its unbelievable growth, its innumerable achievements, and its worldwide recognition: "A Design Incorporating the Experience of This Concern as Model Engineers Since 1919."

What sparked Ed Packard's creative drive, and how did Cleveland outlast all other similar enterprises in this business?

His many fans, customers, and admirers are unanimous in their appraisal of his longevity, commenting that he had not only survived but had prevailed. Even at the age of eighty-seven he continued to put in a full day every weekday, and some weekends, in the midst of his museum warehouse, plus additional time spent in the creative atmosphere of his office in his Westlake, Ohio, home.

I found Ed Packard at his drawing board, answering mail and phone calls, filling orders, finalizing plans, and giving instructions to his devoted associate in his relentless pace to produce additional museum-scale (which are highly accurate) model plans through several dozen volunteer model engineers. His response to my questions enabled me to develop a frame of reference within which his career, spanning so many decades, can be described.

My impression of Packard coincided with that of the many others who had spoken with him. Namely, that his mien belied his chronological age, since his visage and demeanor were those of one twenty to twenty-five years his junior. An erect figure in his business suit, Packard, his face devoid of wrinkles, with earnest brown eyes, appeared more like a banker than a highly skilled, creative designer and artisan. His dexterous hands on the inclined drawing board designing, lettering notes, and answering the phone were as steady and as well coordinated as if he were in his fifties or sixties.

His animated responses and enthusiasm for his ambitious objectives further confirmed my expectation that the fascination and dedication for his lifelong hobby-turned-career had perpetuated the boy in the man. He believed that there will always be those modelers, or buffs, young and old, who, because of their passion, will seek a source of plans and kits to build their favorite aircraft. Over the years, Packard had been asked nearly every possible question pertaining to his craft. His unrelenting ardor and determination to produce the ultimate authentic plans and specifications for particular aircraft made it easy for him to treat each interviewer as though they were the first. He was never known to have been discourteous, unfriendly, or arbitrary with those who interviewed him. Packard had assumed that those who sought his counsel and insight shared his zeal for flying machines and their genealogy. It was only a few moments after engaging him in conversation before I realized that this visionary artisan, this delightful, mature, dignified human being, was in reality an enduring youthful model builder in disguise.

Ed Packard's pleasant voice began his narrative: "I can never forget Newark, New Jersey, the city where I first grew up after my birth on January 13, 1906, as Edward Thomas Pachasa." (Pachasa is the Anglo version of his unpronounceable, unspellable Austro-Hungarian family name, arbitrarily chosen by his mother and having no actual language derivation; he later changed his name to Packard.) I realized that he had been born a scant three years after the Wrights' epoch-making flight. Little did I know then that their *Wright Flyer,* the world's first successful heavier-than-air, man-carrying flying machine, was to play such an important role in his later life.

During my first years we lived at 200 Howard Street, within sight of the inspiring Statue of Liberty, and then moved to 241 Walnut Street. Lady Liberty held a special significance to our family, for my father's, Andrew

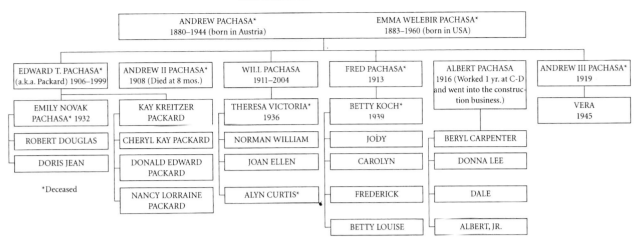

The Pachasa-Packard family tree.

Pachasa, and my mother's, Emma Susan Welebir, parents emigrated from Austria at the turn of the century.

The Welebir clan on my mother's side came from a long line of fine linen weavers and posh leather producers in Austria. The Welebirs had emigrated from Vienna where they were generations of leather tanners. However, they became "hatters" in their newly adopted land, and their custom-crafted hats were sold for $25 to $50 in some of the finest shops on Fifth Avenue in New York City.

As was customary in the many relatively small monarchies coexisting border-to-border within densely populated Central Europe during the nineteenth century, most young men served a compulsory hitch in the military, for border disputes and confrontations between rival neighboring factions were legendary. In due course, Ed's father was drafted into the then-proud Austro-Hungarian army, where he ultimately attained the rank corresponding to a U. S. first lieutenant. When he was discharged in 1901, he learned that his father had died, and one of his first priorities was to visit the gravesite, for he had had great respect and admiration for him. He came from a family of eight generations of fine linen weavers, but this craft, though well respected, did not appeal to his father. His army service had prepared him to serve in the capacity of a courier for a count engaged in international commerce, and he was soon making regular crossings of the Atlantic to New York City.

During these trips to America, the senior Pachasa visited with relatives and friends in Newark, New Jersey, who were enthusiastically outspoken about the unlimited job possibilities and freedom for immigrants in this young, rapidly developing new land.

After giving his employer due and proper notice, Andrew Pachasa succumbed to the lure of the land of opportunity, and he made the critical decision that he would not return to his homeland on his next trip to America. Consequently, Newark, where Andrew settled with relatives, became the American city for the humble beginnings of the immigrant Pachasas. Shortly afterward, relatives and friends in Pittsburgh, which had become famous for the blast furnaces, slag hills, and sprawling factories of its steel empire, urged him to move there to take advantage of the job opportunities in the thriving coal industry, and he soon found himself attempting to adapt to the underground environment of mining.

However, it did not take long to convince the ambitious Pachasa that this dark, confining, unhealthy, and dirty work was not for him, so he bade his relatives and friends goodbye and quickly returned to familiar and pleasant surroundings in Newark. Now that he felt a kindred relationship in Newark, his adopted home in the new world, he seriously considered his options for a more permanent type of employment. However, symptomatic of the millions of foreigners comprising the uninterrupted tide of immigrants, he was handicapped to some extent by a language barrier. He had not yet learned to speak English.

Again, the network of fellow countrymen came to his aid, and he located a job on the bottom rung of the ladder as a sweeper in a machine shop in Newark, which was a supplier to Thomas A. Edison. There were two offsetting perks included in the new slot, namely, that they would give him the skills to become a machinist and, most wonderful of all, that he would be able to learn English.

The machine shop owners found in Andrew not only a willing and eager-to-learn apprentice but also one whose family had been gifted with manual dexterity and the pride of workmanship he soon demonstrated. The Pachasas were typical of the many Europeans in their new land in that they espoused a deep religious conviction and their families were close-knit, with autocratic leadership of the breadwinner fathers, who customarily worked ten and twelve hour days, six days a week.

It was not surprising that Andrew should meet his future wife, Emma Susan Welebir, whose family had emigrated from Vienna, in the Lutheran Slovak church in Newark, where her father was a lay minister. After Andrew and Emma were married and settled in Newark, they reared a family. Edward was their first son, and there were to be five more sons, which would turn out to be beneficial in the establishment of the part-time cottage-based enterprise known initially as A. Pachasa and Sons (managed by Ed).

Continuing the narrative, Ed added, "When a World War I job opportunity for my father with Brakeshoe Manufacturing, maker of field guns for the U.S. Army, necessitated that the family move to Erie, Pennsylvania, it afforded an opportunity for me to see my first military aircraft. It was an impressive Handley Page 0/400, a giant, 100-foot wingspan World War I bomber, which roared overhead during one of the many frenzied, patriotic Liberty Bond drives throughout the country in 1918, and I pondered the likelihood of my ever flying during my lifetime."

After the war ended in 1919, the senior Pachasa was able to realize his greatest job opportunity. The vast General Electric plant at Nela Park in Cleveland, Ohio, the major manufacturer of Mazda electric light bulbs, needed machinists to make the equipment used in the manufacturing of the carbon filaments and beckoned him with a job offer.

Andrew Pachasa, overjoyed at his good fortune, gathered up his meager possessions and moved his family to Cleveland. Andrew soon distinguished himself as an expert machinist, designing and building the tooling required for spinning the vital and delicate lamp filaments, and remained employed at General Electric for several years. In fact, Andrew was later able to arrange a job for Ed in the tool department, affording him a golden opportunity to accumulate some savings to finance his interim model airplane business, from which he hoped to go into manufacturing light aircraft. None of the family could have foreseen then how Andrew's peerless expertise as a machinist was to prove to be the linchpin in the development of the famous Cleveland line of aircraft models.

While these moves to various cities were necessary to keep bread on the table for the growing Pachasa family, it meant that Ed attended the eighth grade in three different cities. As the educators at each school insisted he start all over again, he became quite disillusioned. Further, as immigrants in the rapidly developing industrialized eastern United States, the Pachasas faced difficulties with the number of rules and regulations of the country's growing bureaucracy, which they were forced to comply with in order to start their own business.

Since he was the oldest in the family of six brothers, as was often the custom in large families during the time, the responsibility to be the co-breadwinner fell on Ed's shoulders. Thus Edward T. Pachasa's formal education abruptly ended while he was enrolled in the ninth grade at Lincoln High in Cleveland. He had excelled in his drafting classes, however, and he enrolled in night-school classes to further improve his ability, as well as to seek out other courses, which he continued for several years. It is interesting to consider whether his exposure to further traditional education would have negated the development of Cleveland Model and Supply Company had his formal schooling not ended in the ninth grade. Ed knew instinctively that his future lay in the infant aviation industry, and he envisioned himself as an aeronautical engineer, designing and building light planes.

CHAPTER 2

Destiny: Aviation

A BURNING QUESTION had to be asked of this man who had devoted the better part of his existence to a single vocation: "How did it all begin and what has been the driving force that has kept you at it longer than anyone else in the industry?" The question elicited a turning of his head, a setting aside of the drafting pencil, and sparkling eyes as an animated smile spread across his face. Obviously this had been asked of him before. "It was my mother who initiated the development of my manual dexterity," Packard began, "providing me with all manner of paper cutouts, which were so popular during my youth. As I recall, this occurred about 1910, when I was nearing my fifth birthday. As a result, I became rather capable of neatly shearing cutouts of every variety available, except airplanes. For there were none available at that time, since this was only seven years after the Wright brothers' first flight. Perhaps my very first interest in airplanes occurred at age five, when I became enthralled with the illustration on the 1911 sheet music of 'Come Josephine in My Flying Machine.'"

He remembered, "I saved my pennies for craft items of all types rather than for sweets. Simulated toy tin twisted helicopter-type blades that would shoot into the air on a twisted metal strip called 'whizzers' also fascinated me until I was about ten." (Interestingly, in addition to carefully observing how the gulls were able to control their flight, the Wright brothers were also motivated by experimenting with models. In 1878 their father, in their Dayton living room, released a helicopter made of cork and bamboo, which formed two blades driven in opposite directions by rubber bands under tension. In 1879 he surprised them with a model of a flying paper Dandrieux butterfly.) But then, when it became accepted thinking that "heavier-than-air powered, man-carrying flying machines were here to stay, I began seeing pictures of those primitive crafts, and I marveled at their ability to fly. Undoubtedly, although I was not aware of it then, there was developing within me such an

intense, insatiable curiosity to learn everything possible about what made man-carrying powered flight possible, that it would endure lifelong. The result of this almost instinctive feeling then was that I had to see and observe a real 'aeroplane' fly. Obviously, at this time there were few flying machines on the scene, so it would be a number of years before I could satisfy that desire."

I asked when this overpowering curiosity led to his actual involvement with building model airplanes. Packard reflected momentarily and then enthusiastically responded, "Oh, it really began in my eleventh and twelfth years, when I built a few stick models, which could hardly fly. However, when we finally settled in Cleveland at age thirteen, I really went at it in earnest." At that time Cleveland had a well-developed public library system with several branches, and Francis A. Collins's *The Boys Book of Model Aeroplanes* (1910), which had many photos of beginners' models, was one of his inspirational references.

In March 1919, at age thirteen, young Pachasa originated the business aspect of the company at a time in his life when most modelers are barely able to begin making models. However, Ed already started out with the mindset of an entrepreneur. The origin of the enterprise occurred in the fall of 1919. He enthusiastically described his initial effort:

In keeping with the trend at that time, the Skylark was a 28-inch-long twin pusher with no balsa wood. Balsa was not readily available then and was virtually unknown for model construction in this country. Instead, ¼-inch-square white pine sufficed for the frame, with the 24-inch-span bird-shaped wing and stabilizer made of .005-inch white fiber. It was hand

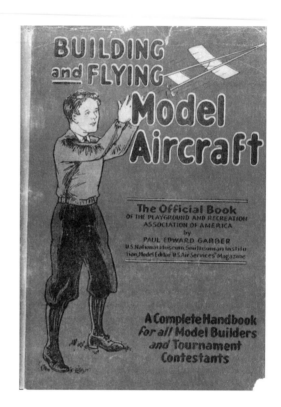

Cover of *Building and Flying Model Aircraft* by Paul Edward Garber, who would later become curator of the National Air and Space Museum (1929). *Author's Collection.*

painted with red, white, and blue roundels, inspired by those of Rickenbacker's Spad. Twin 6-inch bent holly wood rubber-powered props provided the thrust. [Each model was guaranteed to fly.]

I made eight models, which retailed for $3.75 assembled. Five were sold at $2.50 each to dealers (one-third discount), and three were sold to friends for their children's Christmas presents at $3.75 each. It flew well. I can still feel the sales resistance I encountered from merchants reluctant to do business with a lad my age.

All of this expertise from a thirteen-year-old!

The details of this ambitious project were noted and documented with drawings in a five-by-eight-inch bound notebook-catalog, *National Aero Company-Model Aeroplanes and Supplies.* For the following year, 1920, there is this entry in the notebook: "National Aero Company, operated by the partnership of Edward T. Pachasa (age 14) and John Catzan (age 12)," a schoolmate of Ed's. Their slogan: "Keep prices as cheep [*sic*] as possible."

Apparently young Pachasa envisioned a business that would bear the name of National Aero, no doubt because it sounded impressive and conveyed the image of a company national in scope engaged in manufacturing airplane models and supplies. His younger partner's singular contribution to the fledgling partnership consisted of carving a few propellers, and then his family

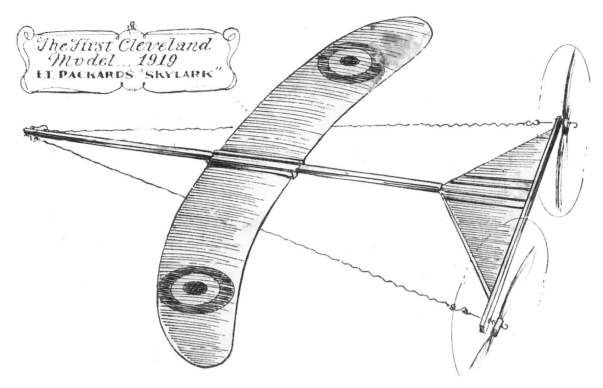

The First Cleveland Model... 1919 E.T. PACKARDS "SKYLARK"

The Skylark twin pusher. Packard built a total of eight models at a retail price of $3.75 each, guaranteed to fly. This accomplishment marked the official founding beginning of Cleveland Model and Supply Company (1919). *E. T. Packard Collection.*

moved away. Shortly afterward, the young modeler discovered another National Aero Company located in Lincoln, Nebraska, and the further use of that company name was abandoned. The name of Cleveland Model and Supply Company probably would never have come into existence had he not discovered the other National Aero.

In reminiscing about a most fragile, distant past, Ed added an entry in 1986 into this well-preserved 1920 notebook: "At this period of the 1920s, one of the few model airplane factories that advertised, Ideal Aeroplane and Supply Company's catalog, contained illustrations which were clipped by me and pasted in this notebook to become the first ever C-D catalog." Ed drew the balance of the illustrations himself.

Within the twenty pages of this first-ever C-D catalog were listed three types of models:

(1) Loop the Loop Glider No. 1.—This glider is shot with a rubber band and has our fibre indestructible planes. This glider is good for beginners and experimenters to study air currents and "waves," price: 20 cents.
(2) Type "A" Racers—Single-Prop Tractor. No. 2, one-foot racer, price: 38 cents; No. 3, two-foot racer, price: 65 cents; No. 4, three-foot racer, price: one dollar.
(3) Type "B" Racers—Twin Pushers. No. 5, three-foot racer, price: $1.50; No. 6, giant racer (50 inches), price: $3.75.

Packard constructed this seven-foot scale hook-and-ladder fire engine as a present to his younger brother. After making several trips to Cleveland Fire Station No. 1 to take measurements, he constructed it from memory over a period of a year. It was exhibited in the window of the Lorain Avenue store and is now preserved by his son Don Packard. After witnessing the attention it received, he vowed to have the same degree of authenticity in his aircraft models (ca. 1924). *E. T. Packard Collection.*

Ed subsequently noted in 1966: "Rudders were not believed necessary on models in 1919 and the early 1920s." Twin pushers' counter-rotating props neutralized torque.

This humble inception of what was to become an internationally known enterprise is evidenced on most all C-D plans to this day: "This Design Incorporates the Experience of This Concern as Model Engineers Since 1919" appears on the title block of each his plans for all to see. Enlightening me, he said, "In the course of experimenting with over a hundred models to determine what the best materials were, and to learn about the proper adjustments to ensure long and stable flights, I had honed my skills to the point where I felt I was capable of making them well enough to sell to others."

In that period it was more typical for fathers, older brothers, uncles, or other relatives to be involved in projects such as kite building and, eventually, model airplanes. C-D was well aware of this factor, and in its advertising and house organs the father was often pictured in a way similar to how the Lionel organization sold their trains. And an aspiring modeler's enthusiasm was severely challenged because he often had to garner his wood from cigar box lids, orange and apple crates, and from bamboo split from fishing poles. Since balsa wood still had to make its debut in America for model building at this time, an extensive variety of other wood was offered by suppliers.

Silver spruce, birch, basswood, sugar pine, and poplar were stocked in various sizes for structural members. Bamboo and rattan reed were used for curved surfaces, such as wing tips and empennage surfaces. White holly was steamed and placed in a form that became a bent-wood propeller as an alternative to laboriously carving a prop blank out of wood much more difficult to handle than balsa.

Adhesives, which were sold by the pound as a powdered substance, were mixed with water and then became known as hide glue. Some types of glues had to be heated, and, to make matters worse, some joints subject to higher stress had to be glued, wrapped, and, in some instances even fastened with brads. Obviously, not only was the building process a chore, but there was

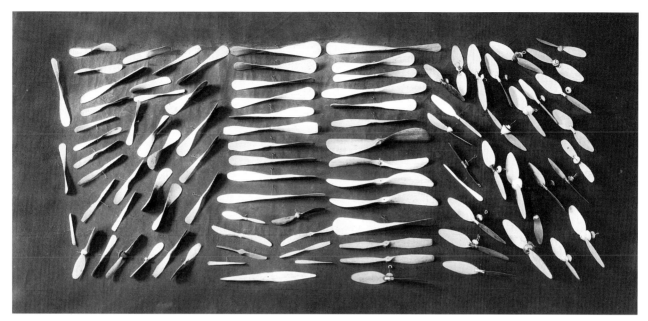

also not much of a chance to make quick, remedial repairs in the field in case of minor flight damage. (Before the advent of balsa the spruce or pine longerons first had to be boiled or steamed before being fitted to any curvatures in the fuselage.) "Every hobbyist of that day either carried a sharp pocket knife or had access to another sharp cutting instrument of some type," Ed remembered. "Jack knives were a standard item for most boys to carry, whether for modeling or not, and there were games such as mumblety-peg in which the players flipped a pocket knife from various positions so that the blade would stick into the ground." Although most of these construction requirements made on the modeler were challenging, nevertheless a generation of boys with many self-developed handicraft skills evolved, and it kept them busy and out of trouble and gave them the priceless, undeniably visual, satisfaction of personally creating projects, not to mention the supreme euphoria of watching something they had built take wing.

At the beginning, C-D procured supplies from firms in the New York area, and the challenging experience involved in doing business with them left an indelible impression on the young entrepreneur, which had a profound effect on how he would do business with his future modeling customers. Packard vividly recalled, "Construction materials and the necessary hardware and accessories had to be procured via mail order from a few sources on the East Coast, since there were no hobby shops elsewhere in the country established before the early 1930s." In short, boys either had to be older, outstanding craftsmen, or have the benefit of parental guidance or other assistance.

Because of Louis Bleriot's great epic flight crossing of the English Channel on July 25, 1909 (that prompted a smaller version of the unbridled enthusiasm for modeling that would follow after Lindbergh's flight), model airplane

A display of more than 100 propellers, hand carved by Ed to test the effects of varying the size and pitch. Ed standardized the hub and fiber or wood blade types, since they were not prone to shatter as easily as balsa wood and could be replaced (1932). *E. T. Packard Collection.*

The Ideal Supply Company was a major industry leader at the time and Packard's major competitor. *Author's Collection.*

IDEAL Model Aeroplanes and Supplies

1925

PRICE 5 CENTS

IDEAL AEROPLANE & SUPPLY CO.
165-167 Spring Street
Corner of West Broadway
NEW YORK CITY

supply companies became established in the greater New York City area. They included the Wading River Manufacturing Company (that became U.S. Model Aircraft Corporation), established in 1909 in Brooklyn; the White Aeroplane Company, established in 1911, also in Brooklyn; the Ideal Aeroplane and Supply Company, 1911, New York; and Broadfield Model Aeroplanes and Supplies, 1919, Hempstead, Long Island.

Later, when it became necessary for him to leave school to support his family, he found part-time employment in the Cleveland Public Library system. It is important to realize that this was the period preceding 1927, because before Lindbergh's epoch-making flight, Ed was involved in attempts to organize model builders' clubs through the Cleveland Public Library and the public schools. However, the reliability and popularity of the airplane had not yet been sufficiently established to create an adequate demand for models. Model building as such had not quite caught on, and aside from the meteoric effect of the Lone Eagle's achievement, the hobby was too much of a chore. Full-size plans were not commonplace, and this void necessitated

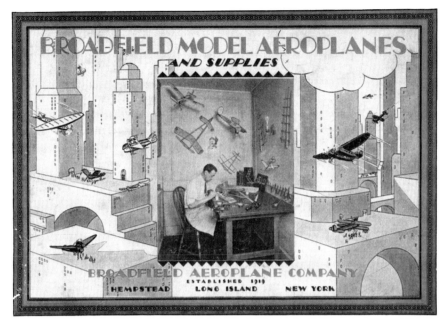

Broadfield's was one of the most complete lines of the era, including several "Ready to Fly" models, supplies, balsa fuselages, wing ribs (Clark Y, a popular air foil), power tools, and compressed air motors in its 44-page catalog, and it offered design consultation. *Author's Collection.*

Cover of *Flying Model Airplanes* handbook by the U.S. Model Aircraft Corporation in Brooklyn, New York. The expanded company had dropped the "aeroplane" reference and used the contemporary term "airplane" (1928). *Author's Collection.*

that the enthusiast draw his own plans, for which many of the boys simply did not have the ability. This glaring shortcoming represented a great opportunity of which C-D would take full advantage when the company launched its initial sales and advertising campaign.

Two concepts of Packard's single-seat sport plane design. He had the fuselages of three light plane designs in the family basement that he hoped to complete and eventually fly but never found the time to do so (1924). *E. T. Packard Collection.*

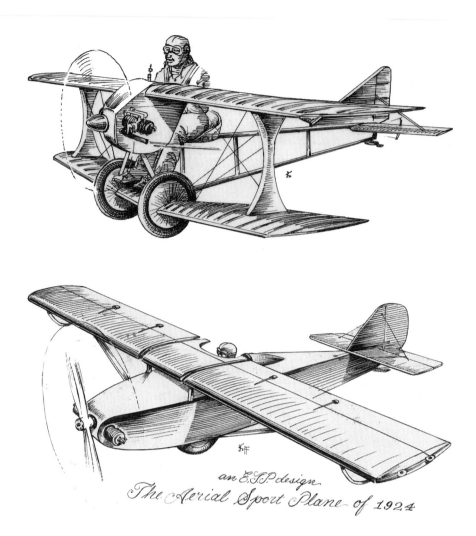

an E.T.P. design
The Aerial Sport Plane of 1924

The initial progress of C-D was somewhat erratic since Ed could not pursue his entrepreneurship on a fulltime basis because he was attending school. And there was a lack of capital, due in part to having the fuselages of three lightplanes under construction, on which he finally had to give up. (The three lightplane types he had under construction in the family's basement were a de Pischof monoplane, an Antoniette, and a design resembling a Sperry Messenger.)

Ed's destiny in aviation was greatly influenced by his Lincoln High School eighth- and ninth-grade English teacher, Stella Broadwell. She understood his complete devotion to airplanes and flying, allowing him to write compositions and do research around his compelling interest. However, she outdid herself when she arranged a field trip to the Glenn L. Martin Company plant on Ed's behalf.

In the process of the tour, he was introduced to the president, Glenn L. Martin. Martin was a famous pioneer builder-aviator who, on August 1, 1910,

Glenn L. Martin and his mother, Minta Martin, at Balboa Beach, California. Martin was the first U.S. aviator to take his mother for a flight. Martin was a pioneer builder-aviator who made one of the first heavier-than-air powered flights in California. On November 22, 1910, 2,000 people in Santa Ana witnessed his first flights in his own 30 hp pusher. He held U.S. Pilot License No. 56 (1912). *Author's Collection.*

made one of the first heavier-than-air powered flights in California (Glenn Curtiss, in January 1910 at the Dominguez meet, was the first to fly), and since it was his own 30 hp designed and built pusher aircraft, he became the first airframe manufacturer in the state. Thus, he was quite possibly only the fifth U.S. civilian to fly in the United States after Charles Willard, who was taught by Glenn Curtiss and soloed on July 18, 1909. (Lt. Thomas Selfridge, who on March 12, 1908, first flew in the Red Wing, had preceded him, but he was military; J. A. D. McCurdy, a Canadian, on February 23, 1909, first flew in the Silver Dart at Baddeck, Nova Scotia. For further reading, see William A. Schonebeger's *California Wings* [Woodland Hills, Calif.: Windsor, 1984].) Martin received U.S. Pilot License No. 56 and in 1913 had delivered seventeen dual-control Martin "TT" tri-cycle tractor biplanes to the Army Signal Corps at Rockwell Field, North Island, San Diego.

In 1917, after the 1916 merger with the Wright Company of Dayton, Ohio, which then became the Wright-Martin Aircraft Company (which owned all of the Wright patents; Simplex Automobile Company; the Wright Flying Field, Mineola, Long Island; and the exclusive U.S. rights to the Hispano Suiza aircraft engine), Martin, who was then producing ten planes per month for the military, accepted an offer too good to turn down from Cleveland maverick industrialist and aviation buff Charlie Thompson. Thompson, who had lined up $2.5 million in funding from local Cleveland investors, owned Steel Products, an engine-parts company (later Thompson Products Company, and ultimately it became TRW Incorporated). He had acquired a cow pasture on the East Side of Cleveland on St. Clair Avenue—the site of the Glenn L. Martin Company that would by 1926 comprise a 71-acre flying field, a 61,000-square-foot plant, and 800 employees.

In 1918, during World War I, Martin won a contract for six MB-1 twin-Liberty-engined 800 hp 105 mph Army bombers (the army's first American-designed bomber). In October the order was increased to fifty, but with the sudden signing of the Armistice in November, the quantity was reduced to four. The ingenuity of the Martin staff, which consisted of three later company CEOs—Donald Douglas, chief engineer (Douglas Aircraft Company, DC-3); "Dutch" Kindleberger, chief draftsman (North American Aircraft, P-51); and Larry Bell, factory manager (Bell Aircraft, P-39 Aircobra, Bell Helicopter, X-1)—converted the canceled bombers into a mail plane contract.

In 1920 an order for twenty MB-2 second-generation MB bombers was received from air power advocate Gen. Billy Mitchell. By 1928 a $3 million contract for 103 T4M-1 "74" 525 hp Hornet powered carrier based observation-bomber-torpedo aircraft had further swelled the back order total. However, growing dissension within the staff had precipitated the departure of Donald Douglas, Larry Bell, and Kindleberger. In 1928 Martin, always grousing about wanting a plant site near the water to build seaplanes, announced that he was moving to Baltimore, near Chesapeake Bay, where he would later build the famous M-130 China Clipper flying boat. (A plan set CD-300 would be issued later by C-D.) As a consequence, the St. Clair Avenue plant was sold to Great Lakes Aircraft Company for $1 million later in 1928.

As Martin and the air-minded future entrepreneur conversed during the plant tour, Ed's grasp of aviation was apparent to the great airman, and they hit it off well. The young son of an immigrant father made up his mind then and there that some way, somehow, he must get a job with this great aviation pioneer.

How could the aspiring entrepreneur remotely foresee how his future and the destiny of C-D would be intertwined with not only the Glenn L. Martin Company but even more so with its successor, Great Lakes Aircraft Company?

CHAPTER 3

Building a Nest Egg in the "Soaring Twenties"

The decade of the 1920s, characteristically referred to as the Roaring Twenties, was an unsavory era in America's history, dominated by a rash of lawlessness and organized crime run by gangster mobs with the prolific speakeasies (10,000 in Chicago alone) incumbent with the enactment in 1920 of the Eighteenth Amendment. Prohibition, as it came to be known, was a time famous for rum ships, smugglers ("just off the boat"), hijackings, Thompson submachine guns ("typewriters"), illegal stills ("alky cooking"), hip flasks, "Joe sent me," being "taken for a ride" or "rubbed out," thugs, torpedoes, heisters, and hoodlums. In 1927 the income for the Capone gang was $105 million. By 1929 there were ninety-one different rackets in Chicago, with an estimated total cost to the citizenry of $150 million a year. But when viewed from an aviation perspective, this decade might aptly be designated as the "Soaring Twenties."

The meteoric growth of aviation at the beginning of the 1920s was hampered by those who saw aviation as an industry that was unregulated, labor intensive, and too economically dependent on military contracts. Sales were highly cyclical, and aircraft quality, safety, and performance were yet to be proven.

This era would witness unprecedented progress in airmail, originated in 1918 by the U.S. Postal Service, with a scant fleet of obsolete, inefficient Army Signal Corps surplus DH-4s and Curtiss Jennys, which by 1925 would be superseded by 12 CAM (civil airmail) routes awarded to private carriers authorized by Congress in the Kelly Bill, which awarded twelve air mail contracts to private air carriers.

Aircraft speeds barely exceeding 125 mph in 1920 would be bested by daring American airmen such as Cyrus Bettis, Jimmy Doolittle, and Al Williams, nearly cracking the 250 mph barrier with their record-shattering performances in the Gordon Bennett, Pulitzer, and Schneider Cup Races, which presaged the subsequent decade of the National Air Races. By the 1929 Schneider Cup

Races, the 300 mph barrier would be shattered by the Spitfire's predecessor, the Supermarine S-6, flown by RAF Lt. Officer Waghorn at 328.63 mph. With the passing of the Air Commerce Act of 1926, the Department of Commerce would be created, establishing five-year aviation development plans for the Army and Navy and the implementation of aviation regulatory requirements, inaugurating an age of safety and reliability for aircraft manufacturers and airlines. Thus the ATC—Approved Type Certificate—came into existence.

Superimposed over this aerial panorama, Edward T. Pachasa honed his business acumen as well as his model engineering expertise, serving as family breadwinner while in the process accumulating a nest egg to launch the Cleveland Model and Supply Company full time.

The Budding Entrepreneur

As Ed's endeavors as an entrepreneur in various home-based enterprises are traced through his subsequent exposure as an apprentice aircraft metal fitter and fabric-dope and upholstering craftsman, it becomes apparent that his participation in such diverse and challenging jobs prepared him well to survive the Great Depression. This regimen also provided him with insight into the design, construction, and fabrication of prototypes that would ultimately be reflected in the outstanding realism of the C-D line. Ed led this double life of his founding C-D and moonlighting with various enterprises and aircraft manufacturing jobs all between the ages of fourteen and twenty-one.

During this period a business could be started virtually overnight, since there was no permit process as such and no jungle of bureaucratic obstacles that are so intimidating and frustrating to contemporary businessmen. Un-

Cleveland Model and Supply Company, a real cottage industry at 1866 West 57th Street on Cleveland's West Side. The company was started in this converted horse barn. Brother Fred Pachasa can be seen through the window, waiting on a customer in the small retail store, one of the very first hobby stores nationally (1926). *E. T. Packard Collection.*

C-D's second retail store was located at the corner of West 57th and Bridge Avenue, just a few doors from the first store and C-D headquarters. This store was probably one of the very first such hobby stores in the United States. Fred Pachasa is seen in the back room's shipping department. After the move, Fred took over the woodshop and youngest brother Andy managed the factory retail store (1934). *E. T. Packard Collection.*

doubtedly, this great freedom of enterprise contributed mightily to the formation of many small businesses, giving further rise to the period's appellation of the Roaring Twenties.

Capitalizing on the day's craze for breeding and racing carrier and homing pigeons, Ed showed further evidence of his inclination for entrepreneurship by making his first acquisition, the E. Houck Company, which he renamed Loft Supply Company, for $75. He and his brother Will operated it as a mail-order business out of the family residence until 1926, supplying a line of traps, nest fronts, and other accessories to the pigeon-raising market. Although not a pigeon fancier himself, he developed an adequate product line and a clientele built largely as a result of his impressive catalogs, brochures, flyers, and glib advertising copy. At such an early age, he already had an appreciation and respect for the power of graphic arts and advertising. It would be one of the vital links in the future success of C-D.

Cleveland Airport: Springboard for Airmail

Ed's infatuation and fascination with aviation's budding development grew as he witnessed the dawn of airmail service at Cleveland's airport. Among the first to benefit from daily service to Detroit and Pittsburgh, Cleveland's proximity to the Great Lakes, Detroit, and Canada and the city's role as a major industrial center positioned it to become a key air transportation hub.

Before the 1926 authorization of CAM (civil airmail), Maj. Ruben Fleet, in charge of U.S. Army Air Service pilots, inaugurated airmail in 1918 using surplus modified 170-hp "Hisso" (Hispano-Suiza)-powered Curtiss JN-4H aircraft with a 150-pound-mail capacity. Ed's neighborhood friend, Elmer Leonhardt, former test pilot for Glenn L. Martin and an airmail pilot of a Jenny as well as a DH-4, made the Jenny a familiar sight and was primarily responsible for it becoming the subject of the future SF-4 C-D kit. Supplementing the Jenny was the 180-hp "Hisso"-powered former Standard J-1, modified as a Lincoln Standard LS-5 with an increased 200-pound mail-load capacity. It became the Standard JR 1B when modified with a 150-hp Wright "Hisso."

Because the postal service could procure the 400 hp Liberty DH-4 with an increased mail load of 500 pounds as surplus from the War Department, in 1921 it became the standardized aircraft. Modifications to the DH-4 and to the Liberty power plant made it a reliable, increased-payload aircraft.

"I often witnessed the DH-4 mail planes landing with their precious cargo at night, their 150,000-beam candle-power wing-mounted landing lights illuminating the blackness of the night sky," Ed remarked. "Later, I was absolutely enthralled to see the converted Martin MB-2 twin-Liberty-powered mail plane lumbering into the landing traffic pattern of the airport with its payload of 600 pounds of mail. Of course I had seen it previously when it was originally developed at the Glenn L. Martin plant in Cleveland as a World War I bomber."

However, in 1924, when transcontinental service was inaugurated, both improved service and greater payload became compulsory. So in 1926 the postal service purchased fifty-one Douglas M-1 and M-2 mail planes, which had a mail-load capacity of 1,000 pounds and a faster cruising speed.

With the passing of the Kelly Bill in 1926, which authorized twelve civil airmail routes, Cleveland was served by CAM 6; the Ford Motor Company was the contractor with three Stout 2AT all-metal single-engine monoplanes, flying one round trip daily from Detroit. CAM 11, with Clifford Ball as the contractor, using three Waco "9" OX-5-powered biplanes, operated daily from Cleveland to Pittsburgh and back. As the demand for airmail service increased, his fleet was supplemented with a Ryan Brougham, a Whirlwind Travel Air, and Pitcairn Mailwing.

Major Berry: Gateway to Cleveland Airport

With the increased concentration of air traffic in Cleveland, the air-minded, aircraft-infatuated, would-be entrepreneur became a habitué of the rapidly expanding Cleveland municipal airport and was to develop a lasting relationship with Maj. John Berry, airport manager, who later became airport commissioner. In large measure, as a result of the foresight and aggressive financial organizing and planning of Bill Hopkins, city manager, and with

Maj. Jack Berry, Cleveland's airport manager and, later, airport commissioner, had the foresight and planning skills that helped make Cleveland's airport the largest municipality-owned facility in the country in 1937 (ca. 1935). It was capable of hosting most of the National Air Races. *E. T. Packard Collection.*

the resultant combined talents and expertise of this duo of visionaries, the Cleveland airport emerged in 1925 as the first major city-operated facility. It was fully equipped with well-lighted, all-weather runways and with state-of-the-art navigation and communications, offering maximum safety to operators and passengers alike.

It would become the terminal for ten major airlines as well as the base of operations for the private, sport, and executive general aircraft of innumerable businesses and major corporations such as Sohio, General Electric, Ford, and Thompson Aeronautical. In the 1930s the famous National Air Races held there would make Cleveland Municipal Airport world renowned, with its 1,040 acres and parking for 36,000 autos. It was designed not to interfere with airport traffic during the air races. By 1937, with significant assistance from the Works Progress Administration (WPA) Cleveland Municipal was the world's largest airline terminal. During that time, Cleveland and Newark, New Jersey, were neck-and-neck for first place in air traffic, with Chicago following.

His bond with Major Berry exposed Ed to all aspects of aviation—civil, military, and airline—plus afforded him virtually unlimited access to the most advanced aircraft, the idolized pilots, and the behind-the-scenes operations. In his inimitable and discerning manner, the young aviation enthusiast took advantage of his access to nearly every element of operations and absorbed the many aspects of the care and maintenance of the winged craft. He thus acquired the valuable trade secrets of aircraft mechanics as he observed them plying their unique expertise in the art of covering, doping, and finishing the fabric-covered components. These various segments of the aviation experience funneled into what was Ed's master plan for penetrating the aircraft manufacturers' barriers; these acquired trades would prove to be his passport into the emerging aircraft plants with which he was about to cast his occupational lot.

As a greater variety of aircraft types were being used by the expanding air carriers, Ed was becoming thoroughly indoctrinated with aviation's entire spectrum of aircraft types then in vogue. It was to have a most significant, lasting effect on the founding and development of the future C-D enterprise.

Friend of the Barnstormers

As the early barnstormers, initially known as gypsy fliers, made their appearances with their war-surplus "crates," Standard J-1s, Curtiss Jennys, and DH-4s, the news of any such errant fliers commandeering an isolated pasture on the outskirts of Cleveland traveled fast, and Ed took bicycle, streetcar, motorcycle, and other various means to seek out and reach the adventurous airmen ahead of the crowd. He was drawn to the dramatic spectacle of aviation and its aircraft like a bumble bee to a rosebush.

Ed clearly recalled, "I developed a routine of services I could offer, including to volunteer to protect the precious aircraft from careless spectators likely to poke a finger or foot through the plane's worn fabric, assist in the refueling process, do the tie-downs, pull the chocks, but, most importantly, offer my services to repair and dope any existing tears or perforations in the bird's vital fabric covering. Fortunately I had early on developed an expertise in the art of covering and doping fabric, as well as the installation of the upholstering and linings of cabin interiors." In the process, the aero artisan simply became intoxicated with the pungent, aromatic vapors of doped fabric, well-worn leather, deteriorating rubber, and the mixed smells of oil and petrol emanating from the heated radiator and overworked engine, which made aircraft of that era animated things to ensnare men's souls.

"A few years hence, a budding friendship flourished between myself and a local barnstormer, Duke Fox, with whom I was associated when we were employed at the Glenn L. Martin Company," Ed said. "Fox had swapped a Jenny for a 'Hisso'-powered Standard J-1, a faster and more reliable aircraft, and it was rumored that some of his flying buddies might be supplying transportation to nearby Canada for bootleggers. His promise to teach me to fly never materialized as he made an unscheduled departure from the area to avoid any further involvement in the clandestine flights to Canada."

As a result of his involvement with the aerial gypsy pilots, Ed developed affection for the popular, durable surplus JN-4D used by the numerous barnstormers and early mail pilots, which would further influence him to designate it as the SF-4, the fourth in his series of the extensive line of scale flying famous aircraft when C-D became operative full time.

The Martin Organization Beckons

Driven by his insatiable desire to be a part of this emerging undeveloped but promising industry, Ed began his quest in 1922 by capitalizing on his previous contact with Glenn L. Martin in Cleveland. Barely sixteen years old, he was able to demonstrate his multifaceted craftsmanship when he landed a job there assisting in the labor-intensive production of the MO-1 scout monoplane, one of a series of designs for which Martin had a navy contract. The pioneering Cleveland aircraft manufacturer had developed a reputation for sound engineering and reliability with the navy and would become a major contractor, producing additional types such as the SC-1 (1925), SC-2 (1926), T3M-1 (1927), and the T4M-1 Martin 74 (1928), equipped with the recently developed 525 hp Pratt and Whitney Hornet.

Ed found himself assigned to work with major fittings maker Tony Tucci, a former employee of Caproni, the famous Italian aircraft manufacturer, where he earned 30 cents an hour; but, because of his mechanical ability and budding relationship with Tony, he soon received a raise to 35 cents. (Tony was paid 65 cents per hour.) Initially, Ed made the No. 1020 metal fittings so prevalent

Glenn L. Martin was the CEO of Glenn L. Martin Aircraft after his plant was acquired by Great Lakes Aircraft for $1 million. Ed worked at his plant when it was located in the outskirts of Cleveland.

The Martin T4M-1, or "74," was described both as a Navy Torpedo bomber and commercial transport (1928). *Author's Collection.*

during that era and then graduated to filing fittings and doing special assignments.

During his tour of duty at Martin, he became an expert at covering and hand-brushed doping the unbleached cotton muslin predominately used in aircraft. Perhaps his crowning achievement was hand spraying the wood pontoons that used strips of Honduras mahogany for the three Navy MS-1 Spotters that Martin produced. An all-metal wing pontoon float and a safety flotation gear were also developed, which further strengthened Martin's relationship with the Navy.

Many friendships were initiated, cultivated, and nurtured with associates at the Martin Company during his tours of duty in 1922, 1925, and 1926. About the only application of balsa wood in these years was for flotation in naval aircraft or for similar applications on ships. Edwin Bielfelt of Martin arranged for Ed to have three pieces of 1-by-4½-by-28-inch balsa for experimentation. Balsa then was almost unheard of in the United States and not readily available for modelers, so this small supply enabled Ed to begin to familiarize himself with the characteristics of balsa wood, with which he would soon revolutionize modeling. Another Martin associate, George Razmer, would later in 1932 draw the formal title block for the SF drawings when C-D went national.

When the Martin plant was in between contracts, Ed managed to find a slot at O. L. Woodson Aircraft Engineering Company in Bryan, Ohio, where the Woodson Air Express 2-A, Woodson Transport 3-A, and the Woodson M-6 Low Wing were manufactured, ingeniously utilizing modified surplus DH-4 wings in the process. Many early American aircraft manufacturers found it expedient and more profitable to acquire surplus planes, such as Jennys and DH-4s, and modify, improve, and ultimately transform the major components, such as wing panels and tail surfaces, from what had been slow, inefficient military and training types into much more reliable, utilitarian, fast, and attractive new designs with much greater payloads.

During this expansive era in aircraft manufacturing, Eddie Stinson, whose name would become synonymous with sportsman-type aircraft as well as airliners, had become a nationally known barnstormer. His air shows often included a race between his Horace Keane Ace biplane and Barney Oldfield's racecar, which produced a thick "rooster tail" of dust around a typical county fairground horseracing track. Stinson was paid lucratively for his fifteen or so minutes of daredevil flying, a non-negotiable fee of $1,500 that, coupled with the fees he commanded from Pathé Films for delivering newsreel footage by air, generated $100,000 annually, which was a fortune then.

After Stinson introduced in 1926 his first Detroiter SB-1, a revolutionary 200 hp Wright J-6-powered 128 mph enclosed-cabin biplane with brakes and starter (priced at $12,500), the visionary airman gained entry into the airline business via Northwest Airlines, Florida Airways, Braniff, and Ludington Airlines.

The enterprising Pachasa, lured by the stories of the rapidly developing Stinson Aircraft Company, journeyed to the Detroit area in 1926 with a reference from a friend of Stinson. Ed boldly looked Stinson up at his home, and the great airman acknowledged the referral from his friend; however, he politely asked Ed to come back in about a month since "things were a little slow right then."

Atlantic Fever

The year 1927 was rapidly becoming subject to "Atlantic fever," with several famous and adventuresome fliers seeking the renowned $25,000 Raymond Orteig prize for the New York–Paris flight. Tense drama was being enacted near Teterboro Airport, Tony Fokker's Atlantic Aircraft Company's location in Hasbrouck Heights, New Jersey. Frenzied preparations were under way to meet the deadlines imposed on Fokker's plant by several of the Atlantic-spanning challengers. On the flight line was *Old Glory* (NX-703), a modified 63-foot span extended range of 5,000 miles Fokker F-VII, with a single-engine 450-hp E. W. Bliss Bristol Jupiter radial power plant, scheduled for a New York–Rome flight (the F-VII was normally a tri-motor).

Richard E. Byrd (left) with his pilot Floyd Bennett at the Atlantic Aviation Teterboro, New Jersey, flight line after testing the Fokker F7–3M that was being groomed for the flight to the North Pole (1926). *Author's Collection.*

Commander Byrd's (NX-206) tri-motor America, a modified Atlantic C-2, was another special aircraft being prepared for the 3,600-mile New York–Paris flight in competition with Lindbergh, Chamberlin, and several other daring birdmen all vying for the same $25,000 prize. Rodman Wanamaker, the department store tycoon, was underwriting Byrd's aerial contender.

"At that time Bernt Balchen, Byrd's pilot, was in Fokker's employment office when I walked in to ask for a job," Ed recalled. "I was really looking for a crack at a woodworking or final assembly slot. However, as soon as it became known that I had covering, upholstering, and doping experience with such well-known firms as Martin, Balchen urged me to take them up on their offer, when who should walk in but Commander Byrd, and he backed him up.

"With the added enticement of 65 cents per hour, a fair wage at that time, I agreed to the terms, and I was immediately assigned to the flight line. In addition to instrument covers, which I made, I often worked side-by-side with the great Tony Fokker himself on the cabin upholstering and other plush interior furnishings. When the famous airman discovered my special extra sharp pocketknife I used for my tasks, he was constantly borrowing it for various special jobs in which he was involved.

Anthony H. G. Fokker, holder of the Federation Aeronautique Internationale (FAI) certificate No. 88 (1934). He was the hands-on CEO of Atlantic Aircraft when Packard worked for him and with him on the Fokker assembly line in 1927. He was the author of the book *The Flying Dutchman* and introduced the tri-motor design, with a steel tubing, fabric-covered fuselage, and plywood-covered wing to the United States in 1925. His four-engine Fokker-F-32 was his largest airliner during the 1930s. Fokker had perpetuated the myth that he had invented the interrupter gear in 1915–16 during World War I, which allowed a German pilot to fire his Spandau machine gun bewteen his plane's propeller blades. In fact, the gear had been designed by Robert Morane and Raymond Saulnier of the French aircraft company Morane-Saulnier. Fokker, by chance, acquired it from Roland Garros's downed Morane fighter, where it was inoperative from a failed test. Of course, Fokker modified it for his Fokker Eindekker E.II pursuit, which resulted in the infamous "Fokker scourge" until the Allies designed their own gear. His D-VII was the most famous and Germany's most effective fighter. *Author's Collection.*

"While at the Fokker plant I saw Lindbergh's *Spirit of St. Louis* parked inside the hangar and learned that Slim had been there just the day before to leave his plane, so a special canvas oil sump cover could be fabricated for him."

When he was assigned to upholstering duties in the final assembly of Fokker F-7 tri-motors and Universals, Ed saw Commander Byrd on several occasions. He was always attired in his official Navy dress white uniform and would usually arrive after lunch to await Tony Fokker's return from General Motors executive meetings, often observing him at work.

"During one of the numerous occasions when I was working side-by-side on the line with Uncle Tony, as he was called, I happened to mention that I belonged to a primary glider club in Cleveland. In his typical exuberant manner, he threw his arm around my shoulder and said, 'Do you like gliding too? Oh, that is the only way to fly. I love it,' and then he went on telling me about his experiences in European motorless flight.

Atlantic Aviation Fokker F-7–3M *Josephine Ford,* named after major sponsor Edsel Ford's daughter (1926). The BA-1 marking indicates the first Byrd Arctic expedition. Powered by three Wright J4 200 hp Whirlwinds, it was flown by Floyd Bennett and Richard E. Byrd from Spitzbergen to the North Pole and back in fifteen hours (making it the first aircraft to fly over the North Pole). Retired Air Force colonel Bernt Balchen revealed in the *Chicago Daily News* (Dec. 14, 1971) that Floyd Bennett, Byrd's pilot on the May 9, 1926, flight to the North Pole, told him that Byrd never reached the Pole. (Balchen reported this in his book *Come North with Me,* but the publishers would not print it.) The F-7–3M was derived from an F-7 single-engine Fokker and flew in the 1925 Ford Reliability Tour. After its modification, the aircraft became Charles Kingsford-Smith's *Southern Cross,* flown across the Pacific to Australia. Young Pachasa considered plans to produce a kit of the famous aircraft; however, he felt the wing construction would be too difficult for the average modeler of that era. *Author's Collection.*

"During this period in 1927, the Fokker Universal, a single-engine, 220 hp, Wright J-6–powered, open-cockpit, four-passenger-cabin monoplane, had established a solid reputation for rugged construction and reliability with several airlines. The metal fuselage framework and empennage were fabric-covered and I covered several Universals for Fokker. One in particular I remember was No. 696 for the Aero Corporation of California, which provided three round-trips weekly between Los Angeles and Phoenix, with fare that was about the same amount as rail travel."

Also coming off the Fokker assembly line at that time were the Super Universal, a five-passenger, single-engine, 410 hp, P&W Wasp–powered, enclosed-cabin monoplane; the F-7 tri-motor, an eight-passenger, enclosed-cabin monoplane powered with three 220 hp Wright J-6s; the F-10 tri-motor, a ten-passenger, enclosed-cabin monoplane with three P&W 410 hp Wasps; and the C-2A Army tri-motor transport powered with three 220 hp Wright J-6s.

Old Glory was a Fokker aircraft. One of the pilots in the Atlantic Air Derby was Lloyd Bertaud, a twenty-one-year-old airmail stunt pilot and World War I air service lieutenant. He had been signed as a co-pilot and navigator for Clarence Chamberlin, who would fly the Charles Levine–owned Wright-Bellanca Columbia on their attempt for the New York–Paris flight that Lindbergh won. However, the temperamental Levine was constantly making changes in the proposed flight crew to include himself until, finally, Bertaud, his patience exhausted, quit in a huff.

Ed was to learn that Bertaud later boasted that he would fly the ocean "in spite of Charles Levine." Teaming up with James DeWitt Hill, a fellow airmail pilot and a student of Glenn Curtiss with 5,000 hours, Bertaud secured the financial backing of the famed publishing magnate William Randolph Hearst to underwrite the cost of *Old Glory.* Their ill-fated flight to Rome, not undertaken until September 6 from Old Orchard, Maine, ended tragically as evidenced by a 34-foot section of the wing that was identified in wreckage recovered 700 miles east of Cape Race, Newfoundland, one week later.

"I have a vivid memory of the sadness all of us felt at the Fokker plant about the outcome of *Old Glory*'s Atlantic flight," recalled Ed. "It was particularly sensitive to me, for I had put in many hours covering the fuselage and empennage plus upholstering the cabin. I still have a roll of blue interior fabric given to me by Uncle Tony."

The Education Gap

After his forced exodus from Lincoln High in the ninth grade to help support his family, Ed was constantly striving to bridge the education gap. The aspiring model engineer, along with thousands of other ambitious American workers, enrolled in an International Correspondence School (ICS) course in mechanical engineering. The Ohio Department of Education awarded him one full year of academic credit in English for his 35,000-word, elaborately illustrated study, "Aerodynamics and the Model Airplane." This effort involved extensive research of data from National Advisory Committee for Aeronautics (NACA) reports garnered from wind-tunnel testing and test pilots' reports. Ed's brother Will, woodshop superintendent, assisted him in building the models involved, and he also acknowledged the further assistance of E. S. Brown and his friend and publisher of the modeling manuals, W. Edmunds Spon. (Several years later Packard bought out Spon's business and sold model trains.)

The Cleveland Public Library Model Airplane Club was directed by Edward Pachasa (1929). The model on the lower right, the C-D SF-1 Great Lakes Sport Trainer 2-T-1, was built by Ed from the first kit released in late 1929. Note the difference between the realistic scale appearance of the C-D model and the other models, which were typical of those popular at the time. *E. T. Packard Collection.*

Above: Cleveland Model and Supply Company's staff of nine at the first backyard store (1932). Father Andrew and mother Emma are not shown, though both worked nearly full time. Front row from left: Ed Pachasa, general manager; Fred Pachasa; Margaret Kender; Marie Zuccola; Rudy Germain, draftsman; and John Zivco, draftsman. Back row from left: Albert Pachasa; Tom Lindow; Will Pachasa, shop foreman and later vice president. *E. T. Packard Collection.*

Right: Beloved mother, Emma Susan—role model as mother, receptionist, and bookkeeper (ca. 1927). *E. T. Packard Collection.*

A labor-intensive routine began emerging for Ed during this period, consisting of his intermittent fulltime employment for three major aircraft manufacturers. Evenings and weekends were devoted to filling orders for his Loft Supply Company as well as constructing stick models and twin pushers to fill orders for C-D, in addition to the constant designing and experimenting with new model construction techniques and mastering the nuances of model stability to ensure consistent flights of longer duration.

With the conquest of the Atlantic by Lindbergh's historic 1927 nonstop flight, the attention of not only America but of the entire civilized world was caught, and public recognition and confidence in aviation seemed to happen overnight. In the eyes of millions of people, the greatest man in the world was a pilot, and not until the first astronauts came along would the aviator as the modern hero be displaced from that pedestal. (But, even so, an astronaut is only another form of pilot.)

The result of Lindbergh's singular solo achievement in crossing the Atlantic in a single-engined monoplane, produced by a relatively unknown manufacturer, coupled with the perception that Slim personified the world's vision of a modest, courageous American boy of twenty-five, perhaps explains why the resultant idolatry was so impassioned. Consequently, the early fliers achieved renown and provoked a kind of awestruck reverence in the public that now seems almost incredible. Girls swooned in the very presence of a pilot, or so it seemed.

At this point in his odyssey, Edward T. Pachasa, endeavoring to pursue both his careers of model manufacturer and aircraft craftsman, could not know how soon the decision of which career to follow would be made for him. Lindbergh idolatry was about to ignite an era of aviation frenzy.

CHAPTER 4

The Lindbergh Phenomenon and the Pachasas

✳ How could the feat of a solitary, heretofore-unknown airman become the catalyst that would propel A. Pachasa and Sons into a fulltime business and ultimately into national and international prominence as the Cleveland Model and Supply Company?

The 1920s appeared to many living then as a time of unparalleled lawlessness, sensationalism, political corruption, and commercialism. Then there flashed unheralded before the jaundiced public eye a slim, clean-cut, single-minded youth who seemed to be many things the Jazz Age appeared to have lost. In an era of synthetic public personalities, he was clearly authentic. Americans, by identifying themselves with him, could regain some of their lost self-respect. Understanding and interpreting the extent to which the public had embraced the Lone Eagle and the feat that inspired the explosive, unprecedented growth of aviation worldwide will help explain the impact Lindbergh had on the fortunes of A. Pachasa and Sons.

The Lindbergh Phenomenon

It was Lindbergh's 1927 epic solo flight across the Atlantic that almost overnight propelled the aviation industry into an unparalleled growth worldwide. To further evaluate this accomplishment in the context of the infancy of aviation, it is meaningful to list the reaction of America, and the rest of the world, to this great feat.

- Lindbergh received publicity offers totaling $5 million, including a $1 million movie offer and a $300,000 phonograph company offer. He turned down all of them.

Lindbergh's solo flight across the Atlantic generated a plethora of aviation-oriented pulp magazines and books: the September 1933 10-cent *Lone Eagle* hero pulp featured WWI aerial combat scenes by artist Eugene Frandzen, starring fighting ace Lt. Scott Morgan; and *We,* Lindbergh's book describing his collaborative relationship with his Ryan monoplane, the *Spirit of St. Louis. Author's Collection.*

- He received 14,000 packages, 100,000 telegrams, 3.5 million letters, 5,000 poems, and innumerable proposals of marriage.
- In Paris, he received the Cross of the Legion of Honor. The American flag flew all day over the French Foreign Office. At his press conference there were twenty-five movie cameramen, fifty news photographers, and 200 reporters.
- In Belgium, King Albert presented him with the Chevalier of the Order of Leopold.
- In London, he was received by Prime Minister Stanley Baldwin and presented to the king and queen in Buckingham Palace, where he received the rare Air Force Cross.
- On his arrival in Washington, D.C., on the cruiser *Memphis,* he received a twenty-one-gun salute, which was reserved only for presidents. The House of Representatives and the Senate passed bills awarding him the Medal of the Congress of the United States, making him the second aviator, after the Wright brothers, to be so honored. President Coolidge presented him the Distinguished Flying Cross. At the Press Club, he was presented with the first of a new and unprecedented issue of the Lindbergh airmail stamp and informed that never before had a living man been so honored. The Smithsonian awarded him the Langley Medal. He was promoted to the rank of colonel in the Officers' Reserve Corps, but he did not wear the uniform.
- In New York City, his ticker-tape parade down Broadway and Fifth Avenue generated 1,800 tons of paper, which cost the city $16,000 to remove; 500 boats in the harbor welcomed him; Mayor Jimmy Walker

presented the Special Medal of the City of New York; Governor Al Smith presented the State Medal of Valor; he received an ornate, hand-lettered, multicolored check drawn on Bryant Park Bank for $25,000 from Raymond Orteig, the wealthy Frenchman who had sponsored the New York–Paris flight challenge; at the Commodore Hotel, 4,000 people attended the dinner to honor Lindbergh; the *New York Times* gave him the first sixteen pages of their special edition, which required 25,000 pounds of newsprint; and the crowd of 4–5 million gave him the greatest welcome in the city's history.

- Curtiss Wright stock, Wright Aeronautical, manufacturer of Lindy's J-5C engine, surged from $29¾ to $34⅜, with 13,000 shares traded immediately after his flight.
- Airmail usage swelled from 97,000 pounds in April, before his flight, to 146,000 pounds in September.
- His personal description of the flight in his book *We* sold 190,000 copies in eight weeks and firmly established him as "the Lone Eagle."
- He appeared on the cover of *Time* magazine as their first Man of the Year. In addition, he received 15,000 gifts from sixty-nine countries with an aggregate value of $2 million.

Lindberg loosed the greatest torrent of mass emotion ever witnessed in human history. From August through October 1927, he embarked on an air tour of the forty-eight states, jointly sponsored by the Guggenheim Fund and the U.S. Department of Commerce to stimulate popular interest in aviation while demonstrating the safety and punctuality of truly professional flying. Lindbergh's itinerary included eighty-two cities; 22,350 miles accomplished in 260 flying hours; and he was late only once. He made 147 speeches, attended sixty-nine dinners, and traveled 1,285 miles in parades, having been seen by 30 million people.

Perhaps one of the most appropriate examples of his influence in aviation was his endorsement of Transcontinental Air Transport, which would be known as the Lindburgh Line and would later become TWA and for which he received 25,000 shares of stock at $10 per share.

He was worshiped by his fellow countrymen as no other private individual had ever been while still a contemporary of his worshipers. He was Rickenbacker, Fonck, Bishop, and Jimmy Doolittle all rolled into one. His every word, his slightest gesture, became invested with symbolic meaning. His glorification became ritualistic.

The ongoing national and international honors, the popularity of his book *We*, and the ultimate public relations coup from the eighty-two-city, 30-million-citizen exposure resulted in the public's preoccupation with aircraft and the idolatry of their pilots. The Lone Eagle mass mania created an unprecedented market outpouring, offering an array of an infinite variety of "Lindy" memora-

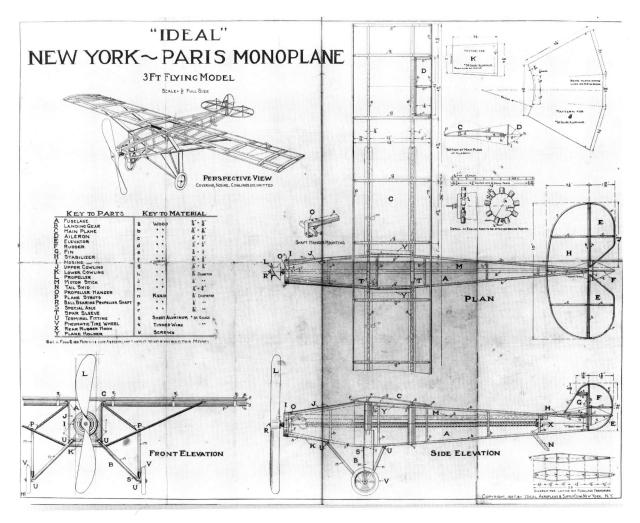

The Ideal plan for a 36-inch-wing-span scale flying model (1927) did not use balsa and required bamboo to be bent to form the curved surfaces. Worst of all, the non–balsa wood structure was laborious to construct and unnecessarily heavy. Many of the details were missing from the prototype, such as the Wright Whirlwind engine, the license number NX-211 on the rudder, and the name *Spirit of St. Louis* on the cowling. These authentic details were typical of the model plans then available and created a great opportunity for Ed Packard. *Author's Collection.*

bilia to American consumers. Included in this copious profusion of Lindy souvenirs were "Lucky Lindy" coins, numerous pin-backs, Lindy sheet music, Lindy children's coloring books, auto radiator ornaments with whirling propellers, boys' pedal push cars with stub wings, and all manner of whirling, propeller-like toys, culminating in boys' aviator-like flight jackets, helmets, and goggles.

However, it was the *Spirit of St. Louis* element of the innovative *We* partnership—Lindy and his plane—that was emulated prolifically, from crude toy representations sold in the dime stores to kits from which boys could build flying scale models. Ideal Aeroplane and Supply Company of New York was among the first to offer a complete construction outfit of the famous plane, advertised in the July 1927 issue of *Aero Digest*. Priced at $7.50, it was a 3-foot-span, rubber-powered model with a hand-carved prop, formed wing ribs, and rubber-tired disc wheels. But since balsa wood was not yet generally available in the infant model industry, building a scale *Spirit* replica with the spruce, pine, or basswood then available represented a challenge for most air-minded youth, and the added weight reduced the possible flight duration.

Compounding the task, the plans that were first offered, unfortunately, bore poor resemblances to their famous prototype. Furthermore, because the Ryan NYP had been designed primarily with weight-saving and fuel capacity standards for maximum range, the empennage configuration of the predecessor Ryan M-2 had been adapted and lacked the necessary area to provide the desirable inherent stability for the larger 46-foot *Spirit*'s wingspan. Thus, without adding considerable area to the vertical and horizontal stabilizers, it was not the kind of flying model that would quicken the pulse of the typical American boy.

The Boy Scouts of America, innumerable boys' clubs, and youth publications such as *American Boy Magazine,* which sponsored the Airplane Model League of America (Detroit), plus *Popular Mechanics* and a few hardcover books, such as Francis A. Collins's *The Boys Book of Model Aeroplanes*, had been instrumental in involving boys in the construction and flying of kites, gliders, tractor-type stick models, and the universally popular twin pushers. Various retailers, such as dime stores, hardware stores, and, in particular, department stores, were the chief sources where the Lindy-crazed youth sought their plans and supplies. In many instances they were compelled to send away to a New York supplier when there was no source in their area.

The Role of Cleveland's Halle Bros. Department Store

Cleveland was fortunate to have had an outstanding example of the American department store in Halle Bros., which offered a wide variety of goods and services and had sponsored an active Halle Bros. Model Club. The venerable store provided model airplane supplies plus other hobby materials and Erector sets and periodically staged boys' model airplane contests.

Ever since the Lone Eagle's feat and his subsequent lionization, the store had been deluged with air-crazed youth who had visions of building and flying a model airplane to emulate their new role model. A. Pachasa and Sons had been supplying Cleveland retailers, including Halle Bros., with several different stick models. The models had established a reputation for sturdy construction and stable flights.

And then it happened—the single most dramatic event to change the course of Edward T. Pachasa's life that would cast his lot for the future in the direction of entrepreneurship in the model airplane business.

It was July, some two months after Lindbergh's triumph, when Ed was contacted by Katherine Gifford, a toy buyer for Halle Bros., who placed an order for 360 C-2 Wasp 14-inch-wingspan ROG (rise off ground) stick models, which retailed for $1. (Halle Bros. initially received a 33.33 percent discount, which later was increased to 40 percent.)

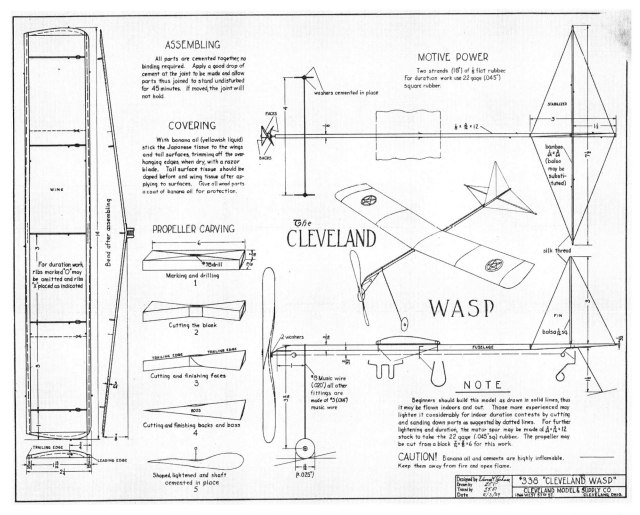

The following text appears within the construction plan diagram:

ASSEMBLING

All parts are cemented together, no binding required. Apply a good drop of cement at the joint to be made and allow parts thus joined to stand undisturbed for 45 minutes. If moved, the joint will not hold.

COVERING

With banana oil (yellowish liquid) stick the Japanese tissue to the wings and tail surfaces, trimming off the overhanging edges, when dry, with a razor blade. Tail surface tissue should be doped before and wing tissue after applying to surfaces. Give all wood parts a coat of banana oil for protection.

PROPELLER CARVING

Marking and drilling
1

Cutting the blank
2

Cutting and finishing faces
3

Cutting and finishing backs and boss
4

Shaped, lightened and shaft cemented in place
5

MOTIVE POWER

Two strands (18") of ⅛ flat rubber. For duration work use 22 gage (.045") square rubber.

The
CLEVELAND

WASP

NOTE

Beginners should build this model as drawn in solid lines, thus it may be flown indoors and out. Those more experienced may lighten it considerably for indoor duration contests by cutting and sanding down parts as suggested by dotted lines. For further lightening and duration, the motor spar may be made of ¼ × ¼ × 12 stock to take the 22 gage (.045 sq) rubber. The propeller may be cut from a block ¼ × ⅝ × 6 for this work.

CAUTION! Banana oil and cements are highly inflamable. Keep them away from fire and open flame.

Designed by Edward H. Pachasa
Drawn by
Traced by
Date 11/3/29

#338 "CLEVELAND WASP"

CLEVELAND MODEL & SUPPLY CO.
1866 WEST 57th ST.   CLEVELAND, OHIO.

At first awestruck yet elated at his good fortune to have cracked the big-time department store market, Ed recovered his composure and, as had become established practice with the Pachasas (as in so many other close-knit American families), a family council was called. The Pachasas, from father Andrew and mother Emma Susan down to the youngest of the five sons, had all assisted in various roles to fill orders as their business grew. This household epitomized what has come to be recognized and accepted as a part of the great American institution, the cottage industry.

The family caucus resulted in a consensus to gamble a bit and produce 1,000 Wasp ROG models, not only to anticipate additional demand but also to incorporate more economical quantity production, which was to be a hallmark of C-D's operational strategy. The relatively simple packaging, which was a two-color no. 10 envelope that included instructions, die-cut wing ribs, strip balsa, propeller hub and hook, nose bearing, and rubber strands, contributed to brisk sales at the Halle Bros. Model Club, resulting in many reorders.

CD Wasp—the 14-inch ROG all-balsa model, ordered by the Halle Bros. Department store, that jump-started the C-D business (1927). Wasp construction plan for modelers. It could be flown both indoors and outdoors. An initial run of 1,000 kits was produced, packaged in a no. 10 two-color envelope and priced at $1.00. *E. T. Packard Collection.*

There was yet another meaningful by-product of this department store breakthrough: the euphoric recognition and realization that, if this humble, incipient, home-based business could command orders of this size with a so-called freelance, non-scale, unrealistic type of model such as the diminutive Wasp, what possibilities could be realized by being able to offer a realistic scale model of a popular prototype properly designed so that it would also have outstanding flying characteristics?

So, the seed was sown in the entrepreneur's fertile mind, for Ed was determined to be one of the first to penetrate and dominate the flying-scale market with a line of models that left no doubt which real aircraft the model emulated. He had carefully examined the kits and plans of the various models offered by Ideal Aeroplane and Supply, then the market leader. Ideal's models of the NYP *Spirit of St. Louis,* the Fokker Tri-motor, the DH-4, and the Curtiss JN-4 Jenny bore crude resemblances to their prototypes and also imposed on the young modeler a struggle with the difficulty of construction and added weight characteristic of non-balsa kits.

As 1927 faded into 1928, the demand and youthful enthusiasm for model airplanes only increased, in part due to Lindy's continued exploits, for he was now on his six-week tour of fourteen Latin American countries and the Canal Zone, flying his famous Ryan NX-211 through all types of challenging weather and managing to land in a myriad of far-flung airfields, continually making the headlines. The world's most famous aircraft had its final flight on April 30, 1928, when Slim flew it to Bolling Field, Washington, D.C., to be delivered to Paul Garber of the Smithsonian Institution, who had personally asked Lindy for it immediately after his record flight.

During this formative stage of C-D, it would not have been cost effective to hire on outside adult labor at even the nominal prevailing rates, for a significant repeat sales volume had not as yet been realized. Furthermore, the prices being charged to the trade for the models were relatively low, as market acceptance of the fledgling company was being developed. However, as the business grew, Ed realized that there was another way to solve part of the labor problem, and the solution was to be found within the ranks of the local modelers.

Because of his many years of experience at General Electric in Nela Park, Andrew Pachasa, who had worked up to a salary of $35 per week, respectable for the time, had become familiar with the operational procedures of manufacturing to meet production schedules. Hence, he was able to introduce to the members of the Pachasa family a method to expediently fill the large order from Halle Bros. In the process, being a machinist, Andrew introduced some tooling and used power equipment to produce parts such as thrust bearings, propeller and tail hooks, wheels, and numerous die-cut balsa parts, as well as precision power sawing of balsa wood, which required extremely sharp saw blades.

This initial automation was a revelation to Ed, and it opened his eyes to

Will Pachasa Sr. on the Cincinnati No. 2 milling machine (1932). Each member of the Pachasa family was able to participate in more than one function of the business. *E. T. Packard Collection.*

the possibility that, when the volume of the business could justify it, he would ask his father to consider leaving General Electric and formally become a full-time member of the C-D staff. Andrew was actually making plans to do just that, and he was formulating a layout in his mind of what additional power equipment he would need, since he was looking forward to such a time and was growing weary of the daily two-hour grind of streetcar commute and the company hierarchy and bureaucracy with which he had to cope.

With the continued increase in demand for models, there was no difficulty in organizing model clubs through the Cleveland library system. There Ed was able to demonstrate to eager air-minded boys not only construction techniques but also the somewhat delicate art of flight adjustments for both outdoor and indoor types, for the long and arduous wintry blasts of Canadian arctic air sweeping across Lake Erie kept all but the hardiest indoors for nearly half of the year insofar as model flying was concerned.

Consequently, in conjunction with the *Cleveland Press,* an agenda was implemented for indoor flight contests that were held in the cavernous confines of

Above: The machine shop in the family's enlarged basement, which could compete with many industrial shops, totaled 1,400 square feet (1932). *E. T. Packard Collection.*

Right: The 25-FL105-Alexander *Bullet* 14⅝-inch span, profile-fuselage, semi-scale flying model, priced at $1.25 (1930–31). This plan was typical of the eleven different profile types offered, all of which were reported to be excellent flyers because of their light weight and ample wing and stabilizer areas. *Author's Collection.*

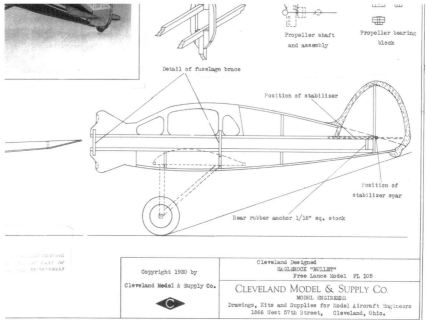

Propeller shaft and assembly

Propeller bearing block

Detail of fuselage brace

Position of stabilizer

Position of stabilizer spar

Rear rubber anchor 1/16" sq. stock

Copyright 1930 by
Cleveland Model & Supply Co.

Cleveland Designed
EAGLEROCK "BULLET"
Free Lance Model FL 105

CLEVELAND MODEL & SUPPLY CO.
MODEL ENGINEERS
Drawings, Kits and Supplies for Model Aircraft Engineers
1866 West 57th Street, Cleveland, Ohio.

the huge Cleveland Auditorium. The versatile Wasp, with its 14-inch cambered wingspan, could be flown either indoors or outdoors. When flying contests were not possible, there were standoff-scale events to further encourage interest in the art of model building. The impressive, spacious interior of the auditorium in the downtown department store of the Higbee Company was the scene for Cleveland's annual model airplane show.

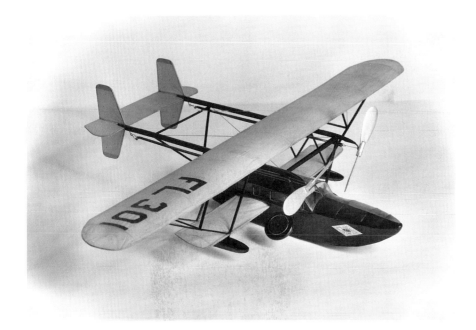

The 1930 F1-301 Cleveland Amphibion [*sic*] spanned 27 inches and sold for $3.30. It was modeled after the famous Sikorsky S-38. While not to exact scale, it was a remarkable ROW flyer and one of the very few such types in kit form at this time (1930). *Author's Collection.*

Numerous model clubs, such as Scripps-Howard, the American Boy, the Airplane Model League of America, and Junior Birdmen of America, began sponsoring contests. (The nation's news press, such as Scripps-Howard, the Hearst publications, and innumerable local papers such as the *Cleveland Press* and, later, the *Cleveland Plain Dealer,* played a significant role with their daily and weekly aviation journalists' columns and their sponsorships of model airplane contests.) To further encourage the formation and participation in these clubs, Ed offered a club discount on quantity purchases.

The Genesis of the C-D Trademark

As 1928 ended, the C-D stable included a complete line of supplies and accessories rivaling that of the Ideal Company, plus the following line of models:

C-1. Cleveland Moth, 9-inch wingspan (beginners, indoor and outdoor)
C-2. Cleveland Wasp ROG, 14-inch wingspan (indoor and outdoor)
No. 311. Cleveland Bee, 24-inch-wingspan Pusher
No. 313. Cleveland Tractor, 37-inch wingspan
No. 314. Cleveland Twin Canard, 37½ inch wingspan
C-6. Cleveland Twin Pusher, 24-inch wingspan
Large Toy Parachute, 36-inch diameter

The Halle Bros. order was the catalyst that elevated C-D into a position in the marketplace that enabled it to lay the groundwork for the major marketing growth plan that the Pachasas were hatching.

The front cover of the first bound Cleveland Model and Supply catalog to use the diamond "C" trademark, the No. 5 catalog at 10 cents. *E. T. Packard Collection.*

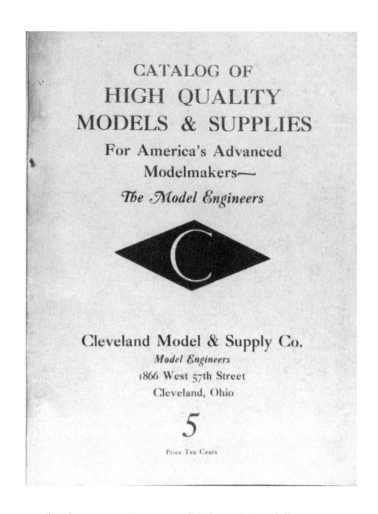

CATALOG OF
HIGH QUALITY
MODELS & SUPPLIES
For America's Advanced
Modelmakers—
The Model Engineers

Cleveland Model & Supply Co.
Model Engineers
1866 West 57th Street
Cleveland, Ohio

5
Price Ten Cents

"Perhaps most important," Ed reminisced, "it was apparent to me and to my customers, who had suggested that for us to compete successfully in the major retail marketplace the company must have a recognizable name and trademark. So, on the threshold of imminent growth at the end of 1928, officially we became known as the Cleveland Model and Supply Company, and since the diamond had a high-quality image, initially the trademark displayed a 'C' inscribed inside the diamond."

Subsequently they added the slogan, "Cleveland Blue Diamond, the Mark of High Quality and Rapid Service." In an effort to further establish an identity unmistakably different from the other model airplane industry companies, they began publicizing the slogan "Model Engineers."

"To facilitate the acceptance by the modelers of the engineering concept, we then produced a notebook entitled 'Notebook and Catalog of the Latest and Most Progressive Model Aircraft Engineering Developments,' admittedly quite a mouthful. As we introduced new items, they were designed on catalog sheets, which were to be placed in this notebook, which we hoped would become a repository for the modelers' plans, building hints, catalogs, and all manner of related items, and further entrench the Cleveland brand identity."

The linchpin in promoting this concept at this time was C-D's first bound catalog, a sixteen-pager with a blue cover emblazoned with the diamond C and called "Catalog of High Quality Models and Supplies . . . For America's Advanced Modelmakers—The Model Engineers." Near the bottom of the cover, the company name and address were listed as well as the number (5) and price (10 cents). Ed recalled, "On the rear cover was my first move for the dealer market in print, with the following copy: 'Does your dealer display this card? Watch for it!' Then we illustrated the card, which stated, 'This is an authorized Cleveland Model Supply Store. We carry high-quality Cleveland models and supplies.'

The cover of the Great Lakes Aircraft Corporation factory official brochure issued in 1928 with the acquisition of the Glenn L. Martin plant. *Author's Collection.*

"And, of course, our slogan, which appeared on the title block of all of our SF line kits' official plans, later stated, 'A Design Incorporating the Experience of This Concern as Model Engineers Since 1919.' Then, as a final lockup with the engineering concept, on all of our kit cartons appeared the copy 'Cleveland Designed,' which became popularized simply as C-D."

As 1929 dawned for America, a year forever etched in the minds of its contemporary citizens, corporate American aviation, oblivious of the bloodbath to come, would be involved in a frenetic progression of mergers, acquisitions, and consolidations. General Motors would acquire 40 percent of Atlantic Aircraft Company (Fokker Aircraft Corporation of America), to become known as Fokker–General Motors, with C. F. "Boss" Kettering as vice president and general manager. It would become the springboard for General Motors employee Eddie Rickenbacker's move into airline management.

Leading aircraft manufacturers, such as Walter Beech's Travel Air Company of Wichita, would become a division of Curtiss-Wright. E. L. Cord, the automobile tycoon and industrialist, would acquire Eddie Stinson's famous company and add Lycoming Engines to his lineup of aviation enterprises.

And in 1928 at St. Clair Avenue in Cleveland, site of the 71-acre flying field and the 61,000-square-foot, 800-employee plant of the Glenn L. Martin Company, a changing of the guard had occurred. The recalcitrant, eccentric Martin, who had lost the invaluable assistance of his vice president and general manager, Larry Bell, in 1925, along with Donald Douglas and Dutch Kindleberger, had decided he would enter into the design and production of seaplanes and flying boats in Baltimore. The Martin facility was sold to Great Lakes Aircraft Company for a reported $1 million.

Edward Pachasa, who had befriended the great Glenn Martin as well as become his dedicated employee intermittently during three years, profoundly felt the loss of the famous and influential aviation pioneer-manufacturer. However, he could not possibly foresee how the influx of the new cast of management characters at Great Lakes would be so instrumental in the transformation of the C-D cottage industry into a thriving, nationally and internationally known hobby enterprise.

CHAPTER 5

The SF-1, Springboard to Greatness

STOCK AND COMMODITY exchange malaise . . . frenetic, runaway, free-wheeling, near-unregulated brokerage trading . . . wild speculation on newly formed aviation conglomerates.

Such typical daily financial happenings describe the preoccupation of the 1929 America in which Edward Pachasa, general manager and designer of the newly named corporation, Cleveland Model and Supply Company (he would not become president until 1931), found himself, poised on the threshold of his emerging company's expansion into a family-operated, full-time manufacturer.

The New York Stock Exchange that year presided over a financial circus of dubious securities, many of which were unregistered, questionably financed enterprises, ruthless consolidations, takeover mergers, leveraged acquisitions, and wild-eyed, opportunistic, and often unethical stock brokers and traders. From the entry-level office boy to the chairman of the board, from blue-collar laborer to the echelons of administrative labor union executives—even the man on the street—all had "hot tips" on stocks bound to make them rich. And, to make it almost painless, margin requirements were unrealistically low, which was to spell doom for millions of would-be investors near the end of the year.

The shares of many aviation companies, including an assortment of aircraft and engine conglomerates, mirrored the burgeoning airlines, the civil and military airframe manufacturers, and the engine builders, such as the already famous Wright Aeronautical and Pratt and Whitney (1926), with its Wasp and Hornet powerful, efficient, radial power plants—all were being aggressively touted on the street. How could someone lose? Big business had climbed aboard aviation's bandwagon, which had assumed the role of the wave of the future in transportation, flying schools, commercial flyways, and the relatively new fad of sport flying. The familiar cry was voiced repeatedly:

"Get aboard now before another surge of wild-eyed, free-spending speculators drives the share prices up still higher."

Below are some examples of speculative stock prices in the aviation industry in 1929:

Company	Initial Offering Price	March 1929 Price
Curtiss Airplane	$3	$153½
Douglas Aircraft	13½	26
National Air Transport	100	550
Warner Aircraft	20	220
Western Air Express	5.40	67
Wright Aeronautical	6	273

Big business had formed four major aviation conglomerates: United Aircraft and Transport Corporation (Boeing), Aviation Corporation (Fairchild), the Curtiss Aeroplane and Motor Company, and the Hoyt Group (Wright Aeronautical). Lindbergh's fame and his image of dependable and safe flying were being used and manipulated in every possible way but most particularly to pioneer the expansion of new routes for Transcontinental Air Transport (TAT) and Pan American Airways. In Cleveland, Chicago's Allied Industries' Benjamin F. Castle, new president of Great Lakes Aircraft Corporation headquarters (formerly the Glenn L. Martin Company), in May 1929 announced contracts for fifty Trainers, forty Sportplanes, and ten Amphibians, totaling $610,000 (a significant number for 1929).

On the periphery of this chaotic myriad of financial transactions and manipulations occurring daily on the nation's relatively unregulated stock and commodity exchanges, the founder of C-D, oblivious to much of the seething financial caldron, was seeking to launch his fledgling enterprise into a significant commercial presence. With all the prolific financial mania in the land, it was no particular wonder, therefore, that it occurred to Edward Pachasa that perhaps aviation executives could become shareholders in his enterprise, which was dedicated to produce exact-scale miniatures of their aircraft, superior to any other such models then offered, and thus capitalize on the current aviation craze.

Middlemen, brokers, and all sorts of agents were customarily involved in arrangements to bring entrepreneurs, promoters, and businessmen—those who had the connections to open the doors to deal making—together with capital sources And then, inexplicably and without forewarning, Ed was introduced to just such an agent. His eyes sparkled and his entire countenance became animated as he related, "I can clearly picture him in my mind; a suave, urbane gentleman impeccably attired in an expensive-looking jet-black greatcoat with a felt collar, black Homburg, and carrying a pair of pigskin gloves as he offered a handshake. He casually introduced himself as Henry Condor. "Whether he had been sent by someone at my bank who knew I had a search on for equity capital or by some other friend, I never learned. After he quickly gained from me my financial requirements, which were highly specialized and much less than he was normally accustomed to, he certainly pressed all the right buttons. For I soon found myself at my former employer, Glenn L. Martin's plant, now known as Great Lakes Aircraft Corporation, in the office of Capt. Holden C. 'Dick' Richardson, vice president of engineering. The company now occupied 80 acres and consisted of 90,000 square feet, with 750 employees."

Fate could not have been kinder or more clairvoyant in its choice, for Captain Dick, as Ed soon came to know him, had in his dossier all the trappings of an aviation icon. He was a 1901 graduate of the U.S. Naval Academy, a Navy constructor, and Naval Aviator No. 13, and he was regarded as the ultimate authority of navy-flying-boat hull design. In 1919 he had sailed and taxied the crippled NC-3 Navy flying boat for 209 miles into Ponta Delgado Harbor, Azores, after it had been forced down in treacherous weather into the storm-tossed Atlantic thirty-seven miles out from Fayal Island. At the time, he was involved with the veteran test pilot Charlie Meyers of the Waco 10 fame in the design and flight testing of the spirited, highly maneuverable Great Lakes Sport Trainer 2T-1A. This innovative sportplane trainer attracted multitudes of flying fans who became boosters for the compact craft, and at one time there was a backlog of 700 orders at Great Lakes.

"I visited Captain Dick on three occasions at that period in my planning, and it became readily apparent that ours was an ideal, productive relationship," Ed continued. "Our personal chemistries clicked, and this chance relationship, engineered by the phantom Henry Condor, who thereafter vanished, was to coalesce into a winning combination for C-D. My newfound, ideal, relationship with Captain Dick was the deciding factor influencing us to incorporate."

After Captain Dick learned of Ed's plans for C-D's expansion and incorporation, he volunteered to be the first stockholder and on the spot produced his personal check for $500. He also agreed to serve as the first vice president, and from then on he became Ed's personal financial adviser and confidant on many matters pertaining to the designing, marketing, and strategic planning for C-D's growth. At the same time he handed over his check, he also provided a complete set of blueprints for the construction of the 2T-1A.

"To cap the arrangement, he took me into the president's [Col. Benjamin F. Castle] office. Captain Dick and I had thoroughly explored most of the elements of producing the plans for a kit of the 2T-1A. In my youthful enthusiasm I had exclaimed to Captain Dick how great it would be if we could duplicate the official Great Lakes insignia in the form of a decal, to be included in the kit. Without hesitation he approached Colonel Castle with the idea, and with no deliberation whatsoever, Castle authorized 2,000 decals [two for each of 1,000 kits] and said, 'Send me the bill.' Thanking both of them profusely, I bounded out of the Great Lakes offices that day in high spirits and vowed to immediately implement my plans on a nonstop schedule until the kit was ready to market."

Prior to his meeting with Richardson, Ed had spent several sleepless nights agonizing over decisions such as which aircraft should this first kit be; how would he secure the necessary prototype plans on which to base the kit design; how would he arrange for the financing of the initial material, supplies, and other expenses; and what quantity should be manufactured of this first, all-important model.

His new, providential relationship with the impressive Captain Dick had solved many of those perplexing concerns. Consequently, at the next meeting of the Pachasa family, he had much new information and progress to share. Needless to say, the Pachasas reacted to the good news as enthusiastically as had Ed. In an outstanding example of the close-knit loyalty so typical of the families of that era, they pledged their total combined ingenuity, creativity, and resources in support of Ed's effort for success—particularly the senior Pachasa, Andrew.

While the pledging of $500 by the Great Lakes "veep" would not solve the initial financial requirements by any means, Richardson's fame and his association with Great Lakes Aircraft enabled Ed to refer to him as an outstanding testimonial for C-D, and in short order additional stockholders were recruited, such as A. H. Tinnerman, president of Tinnerman Range Company and president of Lorain Street Savings and Trust, where C-D banked. Tinnerman Range later became Tinnerman Products Company, famous for the ubiquitous "speednut," an aircraft metal fastener used extensively in World War II. Another luminary, James Hartshorn, aviation journalist for the *Cleveland Press,* pledged his support as a stockholder with promises for future commitments from many other of Cleveland's prominent citizens, such as Roy Robinette, president of the Tropical Paint and Oil Company and the president of the Cleveland Chamber of Commerce. (See Appendix B.)

Since the ball was now in Ed's court, he initiated a series of priorities that were part of his marketing plan, chief of which was to arrive at a plant layout, converting both levels of the garage and adjacent space of the Pachasa residence into an efficient engineering, production, and shipping facility. This task fell to Andrew and to the eldest of Ed's brothers, Will, as well as the younger brother, Fred, all of whom were to distinguish themselves in their accomplishments far exceeding Ed's fondest expectations.

Since the Master Model Engineer was already familiar with the pricing and quality of the top-of-the-line flying scale kits then available at retailers, it

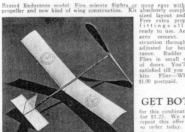

The ad on the back cover of the June 1930 *Model Airplane News* was for Moskito Flier Company. Their models bore no resemblance to prototypes; they were most likely all freelance types. *Author's Collection.*

was more a matter of deciding if, even with a superior product, he would dare to set a higher price than his major competitor, Ideal Aeroplane and Supply. In 1929 Ideal's four most popular 3-foot span kits ranged in price from $7.50 to $8.50 and bore a poor resemblance to their respective prototypes.

Among his other versatile accomplishments, Ed had taken a night school drafting class at Cleveland's West Tech High School, and because for several years he had been drawing model plans and various other construction and design details, he was further advanced than the other students. In fact, his instructor soon realized this and permitted him a great deal of latitude in his selection of projects. Consequently, a rough layout had already been begun and, by finalizing some structural details, he was able to develop a bill of materials and an estimated final cost of materials for the Great Lakes kit.

However, to be doubly sure that this first C-D effort would set a desirable precedent insofar as accuracy and realism were concerned, Ed secured approval from Captain Dick to scale off key dimensions and, in particular, engine and cowling details from a recently assembled 2T-1A awaiting its flight test. In so doing, a practice was established that was repeated on every one of his future kit designs wherever possible. As a result of his experience with aircraft companies such as Glenn L. Martin and Anthony Fokker's, Ed learned that prototype factory drawings used for model airplane plans, and particularly three-views, left much to be desired insofar as completeness and accuracy were concerned.

After a hasty conference with Andrew, Will, and Fred to get their input on labor costs using state-of-the-art power production techniques, as well as their young, inexpensive part-time helpers to perform the relatively menial tasks, a final total cost of labor and materials was estimated.

Then, taking advantage of some sound advice from his major retailers and other customers, a key marketing decision was made to use the time-honored, successful technique of establishing a retail price with a special introductory lower price for a limited time to encourage initial sales. Hence, the Great Lakes kit was to hit the market and be advertised at a retail price of $6.25, with an introductory price of $4.95, which kept it below the psychological barrier of $5. One final element of the marketing plan was to identify the soon-to-be-famous line of C-D kits with the prefix "SF" (for "Scale Flying"), and hence the trail-blazing antecedent of many designs to follow was designated "SF-1," by which it is still known to this day.

The euphoria that engulfed young Pachasa as a result of these fortunate developments further motivated him to seek perfection, because the entire Pachasa clan knew that the fate of their enterprise hung in the balance. He became immersed in a relentless pace in the final phases of completion of the ¾-inch scale (¹⁄₁₆ size) plans and organizing the remaining steps required before marketing the SF-1 kit. On completion, the set of plans incorporated four plates, each drawn meticulously as a labor of love by the aeromodelist himself. Wisely, he incorporated many photographs in the instructions, unprecedented by the competition. The detailed construction of the engine and cowling in seven steps was clearly shown, as well as the assembly of the simplified slab-sided, ¹⁄₃₂-inch, balsa-sheeted fuselage. Photographic views clarifying the model's assembled framework and the proper color scheme, decal placement, and rigging details were also included.

The informative, realistic, step-by-step instructions, as could have been formulated only by a master model engineer, completed the "plan package." Critical evaluation of the plans by contemporary standards would most likely result in superlative marks, even with the many improvements in model construction components achieved since then. The final plan was a masterpiece and certainly qualifies it to be exhibited today at the AMA museum headquarters in Muncie, Indiana.

The title block on the plans had not yet acquired its final design; however, it was impressive considering it was a first effort, and it incorporated the "C" inside a diamond, with the following text:

Cleveland Model & Supply Co.
Model Engineers
Supplying Drawings, Kits
& Supplies to Aeromodelists

To complement Ed's 34-by-44-inch plan and the detailed instructions, the contents of the kit included the following:

ambroid cement
die-cut wing ribs
lower and upper nose blocks
fibre prop blades and slotted hardwood spinner (eliminating the need for a laboriously hand-carved prop)
propeller shaft bearing and washers
finished, turned balsa scale wheels
spools of no. 5 and no. 8 music wire
Japanese tissue
windshield celluloid
precut sizes of top-grade balsa
clothes snap fasteners (for removable nose to facilitate winding)
patterns for the scalloped designs on the wings, tail surfaces, and fuselage trim
ballast material
banana oil
Great Lakes official company decals
clear dope
bottles of international orange and black dope
several strands of flat rubber
patterns for all parts clearly shown separately to be traced onto balsa (prior to C-D's introduction of printwood)
sandpaper

"C-D, being a home-based enterprise, incorporated many advantages," commented Ed, "but, perhaps the most important one was the fact that I did not have to commute to my work. The tasks were always at hand, and I can

Left: January 1929 was the first issue of *Model Airplane News* as published by Sal Messina of Brooklyn, New York. It was only a two-color cover, and the overall impression of the magazine was somewhat unprofessional. *Author's Collection.*

Right: July 1929 *Model Airplane News,* with a full-color cover from Macfadden Publications, a publishing house with some seventeen magazines. This initial issue and subsequent issues glorified the American boy in pursuit of his wholesome hobby of model airplane building and flying. *Author's Collection.*

remember how, late at night while I was trying to meet an advertising deadline, when the hunger pangs finally got to me, I could quietly slip into the kitchen and always find some delicious leftovers sufficient to replenish my depleted energy level. My intense concentration on the priorities which I had set for myself did not include regular hours or time for meals. There seemed to be an inner warning system, which kept reminding me that I must keep going to finish the project. Not only were all of our time and meager financial resources at stake, but I strove to vindicate the trust of my stockholders, my suppliers, employees and many friends and relatives who were supportive of our efforts."

In his attempt to keep abreast of the developments within the modeling business, to purchase supplies, and to monitor current and new publications with some information of model airplane contests and construction improvements, Ed found it necessary to visit New York City as often as possible. He always visited Ideal's offices, although they were rather tightlipped about their operations. Wading River Manufacturing Company in Brooklyn and its derivative, U.S. Model Aircraft Corporation; White Aeroplane Company; and Broadfield Model Aeroplane and Supply in Hempstead, Long Island, were also on his hit list, if for no other reason than to obtain their latest catalogs.

"It was on one such trip that I was fortunate to obtain the first issue of *Popular Aviation* of August 1927, which was the first to devote a section of the magazine to modeling. [Bertram Pond, a pioneer modeler and inventor of a three-cylinder, compressed-air-driven engine for models, became the model editor.] Prior to that, *Aero Digest* and *Aerial Age* were two of the few national aviation publications featuring a model airplane department of which I was aware."

In addition to acquiring these publications for modeling information and trends, Ed made an informal, off-the-cuff evaluation to determine which publications would provide the best returns on his future advertising expenditures. Ed was a dedicated believer in the power of advertising and would become one of the most visible advertisers in his industry.

However, an industry breakthrough occurred in January 1929 when gutsy Brooklyn creative entrepreneur Sal Messina introduced his publication, *Model*

October 1929 of *Model Airplane News*. The cover brings the American boy and his grandfather together through the hobby of model aircraft building. *Author's Collection.*

This December 1929 cover featured a holiday theme. The issue featured C-D's first ad (at right) in this publication, offering two choices of "stick models." In one short year, Cleveland Model and Supply would become the publisher's number-one advertiser. *Author's Collection.*

Airplane News, as a two-color, twenty-six-page, rather amateurish magazine to be devoted almost entirely to model building. Featured were the crudely drawn plans for a ¹/₂₀-size model of the Dornier Super-Wal Flying Boat with ¼-inch-square longerons of basswood, which had to be boiled in hot water to conform to the plan outline. It was powered with rubber strands through gears to the pusher-tractor propellers. Modeldom could not fathom why Messina would choose such a complicated, heavy, foreign, obscure aircraft for the national debut of the magazine. However, while issue 2 included the Ideal Company's ¹/₂₁-size plans for a Fokker Trimotor in a much more professional manner, the publication lasted for only these two issues. In retrospect, it is somewhat understandable why.

Only four months later in July, Bernaar McFadden, president of MacFadden Publications, introduced his forty-eight-page publication with the same title, *Model Airplane News*. It featured full-color covers on slick stock with the plans for a ½-size, 3-foot span Ideal Model Company Fokker Trimotor, plus two action-packed, fictional, fully illustrated stories involving flying, which would be a part of the standard monthly package. Also introduced, as an attraction for young readers, was the *MacFadden Sky Cadets,* which would offer contests and prizes for young model builders. The publication would endure decade after decade, through many ownerships, and today remains the longest running such publication with the same title. What excited Ed the most, however, was the abundance of ads from all types of enterprises involved in aviation, including several model airplane manufacturers. Assuming that the publication could be successful and continue, it could represent a prime outlet for his future advertising.

While many famous names of prototype manufacturers, such as Travel Air, Detroit Aircraft, Alexander Aircraft, Verville, American Eagle, New Standard, Great Lakes, Buhl, Berliner-Joyce, Loening, Keystone, Lincoln Page, and many others, disappeared, directly or indirectly as a result of the Great Depression, in 1929 Cleveland Model and Supply, Incorporated, was launched and has operated ever since. As 1929's financial juggernaut, personified by Wall Street's daily convolutions, sped relentlessly toward its incomprehensible October debacle, Ed's élan was reinforced by further stock pledges from such Cleveland business luminaries as Walter Halle of Halle Bros. Department Store. His stockholder largesse at this point had attained a total of $2,750, which in 1929 was significant for a small business.

While the final steps of the master plan to introduce the SF-1 were evolving, on September 2, 1929, an epochal event transpired at the Cleveland National Air Races and Exposition that would have a profound effect on the progress of air racing's role in aviation development, as well as have a major influence on the destiny of C-D. In an event called the "Free for All," subsequently to be known as the Thompson Trophy Race, a five-lap, 10-mile course around pylons, Douglas Davis, an Atlanta Travel Air dealer, startled the aviation world. He won the event in a Wright J-6–powered Travel Air Model "R" Mystery Ship at a speed of 194.90 mph, even eclipsing the top speeds of U.S. military aircraft. "The low-wing monoplane, beautifully streamlined with an NACA cowling and drag reducing wheel pants, was such an improved, clean design over contemporary aircraft that it stole the show," Ed recalled. "Had we not been so far along with the SF-1 Great Lakes, we could well have been tempted to make a switch. However, it had left its mark on me. I inherently knew that this design would have to be C-D's next effort if all went well with the SF-1, for it would have a built-in demand."

As if decreed by fate, the stock market seemed to have delayed its horrendous plummeting course until after the air races. The stock market crash—a

Charlie Meyers, Great Lakes Aircraft test pilot, in his Great Lakes Sport Trainer demonstrator (1930). Meyers became a test pilot after leaving Waco Aircraft in Troy, Ohio, where he was instrumental in the development of the Waco 10. *R. S. Hirsch Collection.*

tremor on Black Thursday (October 24), was followed by an even more disastrous quake on October 29, triggering the Great Depression. By November 13, $30 billion had been blown into thin air, a staggering devaluation that was as much as the U.S. cost of World War I and twice the national debt. Common stock for RCA, which had attained a peak of $540 per share in early 1929, had dropped to $28 by November 13 and would see its price further eroded to $2.50 by 1930. The Dow Jones average lost nearly 90 percent of its value, and it would take until 1954, twenty-five years later, for it to recover. While aviation stocks would take a hit along with the rest of them, 1929 was a high-water mark of overproduction for aircraft, with 6,034 units produced that year, up 26.7 percent from the 4,761 units of 1928.

What effect would this economic collapse have on the well-orchestrated market plan of C-D? "While I was fully aware of the crash and its unfortunate effects," Ed explained, "I was so totally involved with the myriad of details necessary to ensure a professional introduction of the SF-1 that I did not have time to worry. Perhaps it would be difficult for most people to understand my state of mind then, but I had invested so much time in planning, designing, drawing, and flight testing the SF-1 model that I had become almost overconfident. I just had a gut feeling that it would go over."

However, it did hit him in the pocketbook in another way. Several of his friends and associates in business, such as a vice president of a major oil company, who had made commitments to become C-D stockholders, had to renege. They were either seriously financially clobbered by this economic misfortune or were just wiped out. As a result, several thousand dollars were unrealized.

An ad for the Great Lakes Sport Trainer prototype, 2-T-1, extolling the merits of its agile maneuverability and the reliability of its American Cirrus 4-cylinder 95 hp power plant with a No. 167 ATC (June 1929). *Author's Collection.*

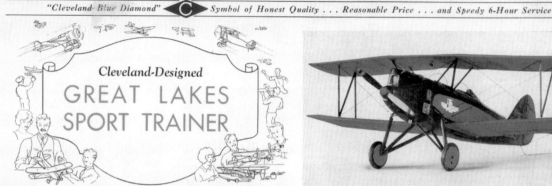

Catalog sheet No. 6, which was a two-color layout showing the authentic international orange (used for visibility) and black color scheme of the SF-1 (1930). The twelve specific features of the kit were enumerated, and the story of the ¾-mile flight of an SF-1 (ROG) by J. E. Powlaski of Cleveland was also featured. *Author's Collection.*

Advertising was a hard sell in the context of the Great Depression and suffered greatly when budgets had to be slashed by entrepreneurs and businesses. However, Ed had other opportunities to validate his strong feelings about its effectiveness. Even though C-D was relatively unknown, Ed had been solicited by James LeBaron, who was a representative for *Model Airplane News,* which after its colorful introduction in July with forty-eight pages had survived six issues and grown to fifty-six pages. C-D history was made when its first ad appeared in the December 1929 issue, a single-column, ⅓-page ad offering a three-foot span, No. 313 Tractor stick model at $1.50 and a 14-inch span ROG Cleveland Wasp at 80 cents.

The December issue also featured an ad for the Selley Company of Brooklyn on the inside front cover, with four poor representations of well-known aircraft scale models, with prices up to $7.75, backed by Ideal Aeroplane and Supply's full-page, black-and-white, inside back cover ad that showed two nonscale models and two almost unrecognizable scale models of famous aircraft, at prices of $2.50 to $8.50. Never in their wildest dreams would the employees at the *Model Airplane News,* C-D's competitors, or Ed himself anticipate that C-D would become the publication's most prolific and outstanding advertiser in just a very short time.

There was a degree of premature elation in the Pachasa family as the senior Pachasas and the brothers observed the implementation of a marketing plan for their first major venture. The copyright bureaucracy had been successfully navigated with the capable and learned assistance of Captain Dick. The Pachasas reflected with justifiable pride on the realistic and attractive appearance and the stable flight characteristics of their test model. Now they anxiously awaited sales results.

A small quantity of kits had been prepared and packaged in an attractive red hobby tube that enabled the plans to be shipped rolled as well as to circumvent the prohibitively high additional expense of a printed carton, which would have had to be produced in much larger quantities. Halle Bros. Department Store and their Boys Club were again involved, as were Higbee's Department Store and the May Company. Initially, a few dealers were billed

The Cleveland SF-1¾-inch scale 2T-1A Great Lakes Sport Trainer flying model, the first complete all-balsa model offered nationally by Ed Packard (1929). Its realism was enhanced by his having measured and sketched the prototype at the factory to ensure maximum authenticity. *E. T. Packard Collection.*

The Cleveland SF-2 in profile, uncovered and unpainted to illustrate its slab-sided fuselage. It was the only model in the line constructed this way and was so designed in order to make this first model as easy to construct as possible. *E. T. Packard Collection.*

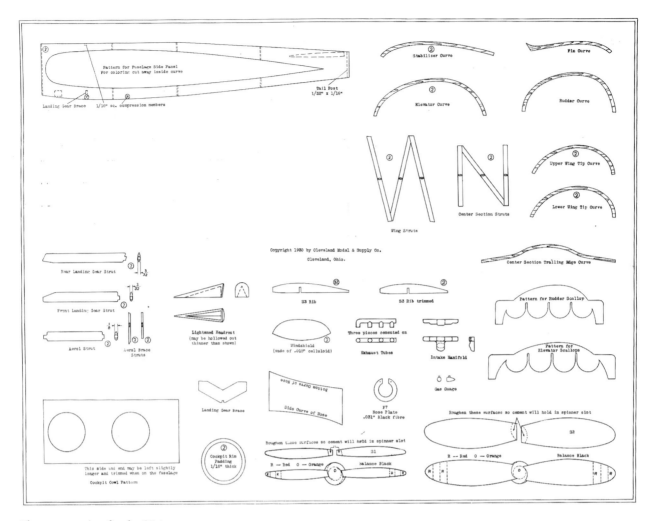

The construction for the SF-1 1929 Great Lakes Sports Trainer 2T-1 was listed in twelve steps and was extremely detailed. When the kit was first introduced to Cleveland model dealers in late 1929, there was no model kit plan on the market comparable to this advanced flying technology. The kit contained patterns for all parts, thus eliminating the need for tracing parts or cutting up the main plan. It was the first step in C-D providing printwood, which would occur shortly thereafter. *E. T. Packard Collection.*

at a one-third discount, but later C-D was forced to offer 40 percent to meet competition, which became standard practice in the industry, including the smallest outlets.

The marketing plan called for a modest ad campaign kickoff in the February 1930 *Model Airplane News,* featuring a return cutout coupon for purchasing a ¼-inch scale outline drawing of the Great Lakes Trainer for ten cents, plus two cents for postage. This was an attempt to offer modelers an opportunity to begin the inexpensive hobby of collecting accurate scale drawings and photos of real aircraft, thereby developing a following for C-D. The modest one-column, ⅓-page ads, with various cutout coupon offers, would climax in the spring with an exciting two-column ad announcing the spectacular SF-1 kit, coinciding with the youthful urge to be liberated from the confines of winter's cabin fever.

"It was about this time that Frank Lamorelle, an account representative from the Carpenter Advertising Agency, located me and painted a convincing picture of how his agency could inject a high degree of professionalism into

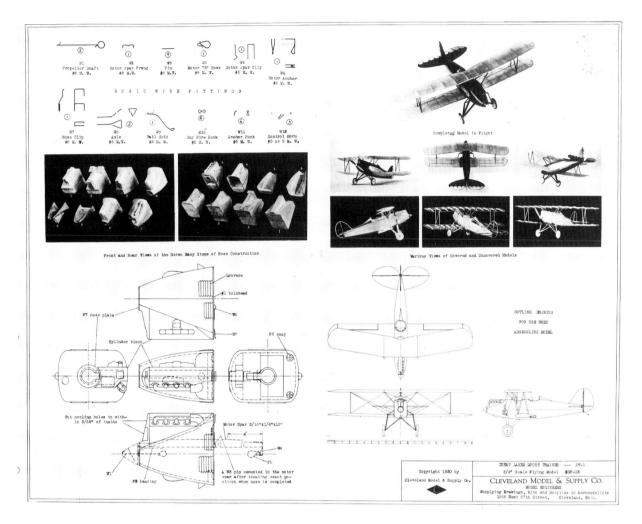

the design, timing, and placement of our contemplated advertising plans," Ed mused. "In the process our ads would be more effective, enabling us to realize greater sales, and by utilizing the most productive publications save us money in the long run. This became another one of those fortunate, informal partnerships, for the Carpenter organization entered into our marketing and advertising then and there and were an instrumental element of our success right up until shortly after World War II."

After the first few conferences with the Carpenter people, Ed came away with a feeling of solid confidence that they were on the right track. "I would develop the preliminary copy for the ads and then Carpenter would refine the text and make suggestions concerning the layout and graphics. My mentor in Lincoln High printing class, Mr. Flascamp, had advised me to buy various different point types and do my own layouts for fliers, catalog pages, and forms, which I had begun doing. Consequently, I had an above-average feeling for what constituted an effective printed page and kept my standards high for all of our ads and other graphics." The kickoff for the SF-1 was scheduled

A three-view drawing of the SF-1 Great Lakes Sports Trainer ready for final assembly (as well as seven photos of the model before and after construction). Note that all wire parts were also shown. *E. T. Packard Collection.*

Travel Air Model R Mystery Ship R614K as it appeared at the Wichita, Kansas, plant in 1929—the same model that won the 1929 Cleveland "Free for All" pylon race. The great Jimmy Doolittle called it one of the most forgiving airplanes he ever flew. *R. S. Hirsch Collection.*

for the 1930 *MAN* (*Model Airplane News*) May issue, which meant it would be on the newsstands and in the mail on April 23, when the modelers were itching to get outside and fly their models. C-D had received repeat orders from a few of the Cleveland retailers to whom they had made preliminary sales, so they knew it was selling.

"When we received our copy of the May issue with our ⅔-page ad on page forty-nine, we collectively caught our breath. Our ad was dynamite compared to the competition's ads: Its headline read, 'Great Lakes Flying Model Which You May Now Build.' With the exception of a half-page ad by Independence Model and Airplane Supply, which featured a Vought Corsair and the Curtiss Army Hawk, all the rest were showing unrealistic-appearing models—yes, toys. Even the inside-front-cover ad by Hawthorne Model Aero, which promoted two Lockheed toy-type models, could not remotely compare with the obvious superior appeal of our beautiful Great Lakes Sport Trainer." Before the advent of C-D on the modeling scene, the existing companies could be best characterized as woebegone purveyors of toy-like offerings passing as replicas of realism. "In our ad copy we took a calculated risk to flat-out state, 'We emphatically advise beginners against attempting construction of the Trainer, but to start with our simpler models.'"

Based on the preliminary sales results and comments from retailers, plus those that filtered in via the mail and word of mouth, they knew they had a hit. However, what astounded them the most was that orders were coming in from Canada, Mexico, Australia, and Europe. Ed recalled, "Consequently, I began feeling uneasy about the possibility of having back orders and not being able to ship orders within three to six hours of receipt, a C-D caveat. Therefore, my eldest brother, Will, and my father began making plans to place orders for more materials so we could continue our outstanding record of filling orders and shipping the same day received."

The *MAN* June issue ad had a smashing headline: "Takes Off in Three Feet." In addition, out of deference to the wretched state of the economy, an offer was included for an assortment of twelve ¼-inch scale outline drawings at 15 cents each or all twelve for $1.50. Wisely, a cutout coupon was included, which listed all the choices.

"We went for broke in the July issue with our first two-color, rear-cover ad. Facing the reality of the dire economic situation nationally, our headline read, 'For three and one-third cents per day you may now buy your C-D Great Lakes Sport Trainer, and offering the C-D Time Payment Plan: $1.00 down and $1.00 each month.'"

The ad had said it all. In effect the Pachasas were serving notice on the trade and to modelers from coast to coast that C-D was now a contender in this industry. To bolster this challenge, the Pachasas had produced a second round of 2,000 red SF-1 hobby tubes after the original round of 750 sold out. Although both the trade and modelers enthusiastically accepted the SF-1, Ed was alert to new opportunities. Capitalizing on the heightened enthusiasm for air racing that followed the National Air Races held in September, he redirected the collective efforts of Pachasa family into an intensive marketing plan for the second C-D SF kit. The record-breaking performance of the Travel Air Mystery Ship, which won the "Free for All" event of the National Air Races, stimulated demand for the model and provided C-D with a prototype for their second design choice.

Fortunately, since the plane's debut in September 1929, the great Frank Hawks had been breaking record after record in the Texaco 13–sponsored

Travel Air Model R Frank Hawks's Texaco NR1313 version. This variation featured an enclosed cockpit as required for Hawks's 1930 intercontinental dash between Los Angeles and New York, which he flew in twelve hours and thirty-five minutes, averaging 215 mph. *R. S. Hirsch Collection.*

Cleveland-Designed
TRAVEL AIR MYSTERY SHIP

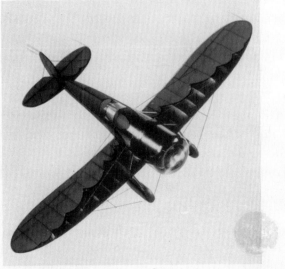

Span, 22"; length 15⅜". Colored: A Brilliant Red and Black.

EVER since that exciting day at the National Air Races in Cleveland, when a brilliant red and black daringly designed, mysterious looking ship took off and pointed its nose almost straight up in the air and kept on climbing in the most breath-taking ascent ever witnessed, thousands of model makers have wanted to build a model of this *original* Travel Air Mystery Ship. In all honesty it has been one of the toughest assignments our Engineers have ever tackled. But it was done—and done well—for *here it is in Kit form ready for you to build.*

Except for a very slight modification (which even an expert might not discover) it's an exact ¾" scale model of its mystifying prototype—the type of plane flown by Capt. Hawks, Lt. Jimmy Doolittle, Dale (Red) Jackson, and many other famous aviators. Like the big plane itself, it dis-

plays spirit, verve and zip in its every movement. Experienced aeromodelists marvel at its breath-taking climb, slashing speed, and surprising distance. With a scale speed well over 200 miles per hour, this remarkable little model has easily flown at 30 m. p. h. to a height of 25 to 50 feet, and for distances of 500 feet and over. There is no reason why you cannot do the same or even better with your model.

Despite its appearance of being a very difficult model to build, our super-detailed drawings and easy-to-follow instructions make the Travel Air Mystery Ship actually easier to build than our famous Great Lakes Sport Trainer. This will be one of your most highly coveted models—one that will bring you many exciting moments in building as well as flying it. There is nothing like it—anywhere—at any price. *Be sure to get it.*

MOST REALISTIC SCALE MODELS HE'S EVER SEEN

"Since I read the new Cleveland catalog, I have flung out all the rest, and am going to do business with a dependable company that can produce the most realistic scale models I've ever seen."

FEATURES

1. Kit contains an extra large drawing—everything full size—and crammed with photographs and super-detailed instructions.
2. All balsa construction. Main wing ribs supplied.
3. All possible details reproduced.
4. Perfectly and completely turned balsa N. A. C. A. Cowl and Ring (something new—an exclusive Cleveland-Designed feature).
5. The Fillet (between Wings and Fuselage) and complicated curved fuselage, easy to build.
6. Very efficient wing section employed.
7. Many of the usual wire fittings eliminated.
8. New Cleveland-Designed nose bearing.
9. It is a flying or exhibition model (change only propellers).
10. Simplified construction throughout (simple even for beginners).
11. New simple method of Cleveland-Designed propeller making (indestructible propellers).
12. Colored like its prototype, a brilliant red beautifully scalloped batlike in black, with the use of patterns cut from our pattern sheet.
13. Adjustable control surfaces and removable parts. Flight adjustment simple.
14. Very well stressed. Will even power dive into the ground from a moderate altitude without crashing. (Flattening out often comes into play due to "ground effect," in which case the model makes a beautiful 3-point landing.)
15. Wings do not slide for balancing. It always looks like the real original Mystery Ship.
16. Wheel shoes easily made.
17. Perfectly proportioned to ¾" scale, the standard set by Cleveland Model Engineers.
18. Travel Air nameplate to place below pilot's cockpit, realistic Cleveland Air Line labels, and many other advanced Cleveland-Designed features which you will discover yourself when you get your kit.

TRAVEL AIR MYSTERY SHIP
Kit SF-2C, Price *_____

*See latest Price Sheet. Before ordering, be sure to read Inside Back Cover. . . . **CLEVELAND MODEL & SUPPLY CO., INC.,** *Model Engineers,* 1866 West 57th St., CLEVELAND, O.

When the Travel Air Model R Mystery Ship kit was introduced, there were few low-wing aircraft to model. The Travel Air was not only a famous racer but was one of the most beautiful designs and remained a best-seller for many years. The summary of construction had detailed instructions, down to specifying 6–8 strands of ⅛-inch flat rubber and advising 400 turns with a winder. *E. T. Packard Collection.*

version of the Travel Air, smashing transcontinental flight times, while James Haizlip had come in second with his Travel Air Model R at the 1930 Thompson Trophy Race. That meant that the kit would have to be ready to fill orders in late October when the November announcement in *Model Airplane News* would be mailed and on the newsstands for its 50,000 readers.

The contacts that Ed had made and cultivated when he was on the payroll at Glenn L. Martin paid off, because he was able to tap one or more of the draftsmen, such as Bob Nightengale and Charles Mandrake, from their engineering department to do some moonlighting, since the aeromodelist himself could not carve out the time needed. Fortunately, Captain Dick's great rapport with associates in the aviation industry was such that he was able to obtain plans for the Travel Air and, combined with the photos and measurements taken when it was hangared in Cleveland during its triumphant win in 1929, the best possible authenticity was thus ensured.

C-D's October 1930 *Model Airplane News* full-page ad set precedents in the industry. A C-D modeler, Joe E. Powalski of Cleveland, set, in front of witnesses, a record flight of 3,608 feet (¾ mile) after an ROG takeoff with his Great Lakes model, which was no doubt the first such specifically documented testimonial to appear in *Model Airplane News*. The ad also offered twelve flate-profile (no cross-section) models for beginners, and, to further dramatize the Airline of FL-100 Profiles, their debut showed realistic cardboard pilot heads in the cockpits of all of the non-cabin types, which created a mild sensation. Inspired and motivated by this innovation, William Brothers and other contemporary manufacturers have since offered scale, full-figure pilots for radio-controlled models, a development begun by C-D in 1930. To incorporate further dramatic appeal and engineering documentation to the introduction of the spectacular, flashy, red and black Mystery Ship in the November 1930 full-page ad, a photo of Captain Dick was included along with the caption: "Boys, meet Captain Richardson, chief engineer of C-D . . . formerly chief of design section, Bureau of Aeronautics, U.S. Navy."

Cleveland used a fiber blade prop from the beginning to avoid the need of carving a balsa prop (before machine-made props were available). Also, the fiber blades were less likely to crack or break than balsa during winding or in crashes. The company provided excellent photos of the assembled uncovered model, such as this SF-2 1930 Travel Air Model R, to help the modeler in his final assembly. *E. T. Packard Collection.*

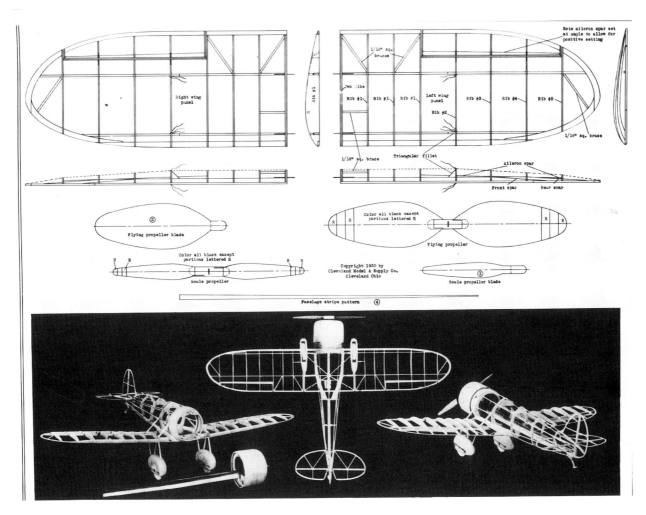

An outstanding feature of the SF-2 Travel Air Kit was a fully turned, balsa, scale NACA engine cowling and cowl ring engineered by Will Pachasa. Ed proudly proclaimed, "It was the first ever in the industry. Of course, all of these production specials were the result of my father Andrew's building and operating expertise on our hand-tooled special equipment. The cowling made an ideal anchor for the motor spar, which was our standard practice to take the stress of the rubber power and save the fuselage. The Travel Air was a win-win situation, for we had had back orders for many months from air racing crazed modelers, including grown men, who were swept up in the mania for this streamlined beauty. Along with the Great Lakes Sport Trainer, it was an outstanding seller for years."

What more impressive way to end 1930, the first full year of the Depression and C-D's first year as a national contender, than to be represented by a strategic double-page center spread in *Model Airplane News*'s December issue? The layout treated the Great Lakes and the Travel Air as equals, so each had their

The empennage, fuselage, and center section with cowl and motor unit of the SF-2 1930 Travel Air Model R. This assembly was required since C-D furnished a turned balsa cowl (the first in the industry) designed by Will Pachasa. Dress snaps were supplied to facilitate cowl removal for winding. *E. T. Packard Collection.*

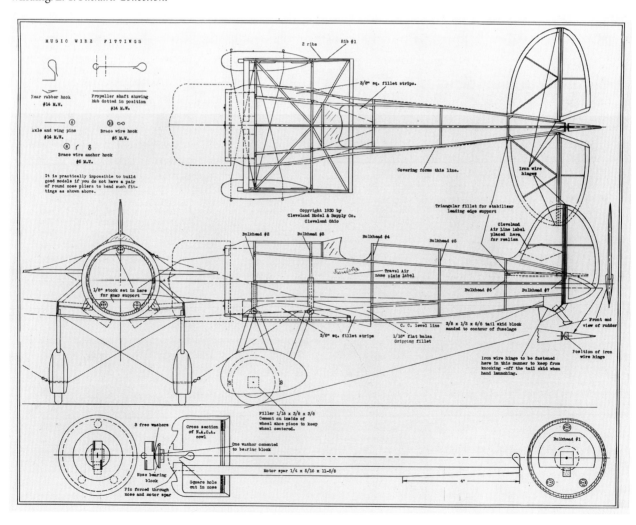

SF-2 1930 Travel Air Model R uncovered front three-quarter view, showing the removable (with dress snaps) turned NACA cowling. It was one of the very first kits to offer the construction of a low-wing type, which would be capable of flights of above-average duration. *E. T. Packard Collection.*

This is the famous Cleveland 1930 Baby Austin automobile with the 1929 Travel Air Mystery Ship solid model perched on top. The Mystery Ship is 1½-inch scale with revolving propeller. According to Ed, "It was intended to tour the country to further encourage boys and men in model airplane building but because of the rush of business in the early days, we were unable to follow through" (ca. 1931–34). *E. T. Packard Collection.*

respective page, with an appropriate heading, "Christmas Comes but Once a Year," and was obviously bent on influencing modelers, retailers, or modelers' parents to pick a C-D model for their Christmas gift. Another documented testimonial was included, attesting to the outstanding contents and engineering of the SF-1 kit compared to others. Captain Richardson's photo was again shown, but there was yet another element of C-D's merchandising and showmanship that would characterize this company throughout its early years.

Ed had purchased a brand new 1930 Baby Austin Coupe automobile for about $475 and cleverly fitted it with a 1½-inch scale, 44-inch-span solid model of the Travel Air, beautifully constructed by brothers Will and Ed, complete with spinning propeller and striking red and black color scheme, featuring a unique professionally lettered sign on its base that asked, "Have you a hobby? Why not build model airplanes?" The diminutive auto was a show stealer wherever it went and soon became a trademark of C-D. As a tribute, a large, full-size photo of it is currently mounted on the wall adjacent to the C-D exhibit in the headquarters of the Academy of Model Aeronaurtics.

A 7-by-11-inch flyer handed out to passersby by Ed Packard from the window of his colorful 1930 Austin coupe with the 1½-inch scale solid Travel Air Model R mounted on the roof. Model airplane building was a new hobby, and he was promoting it (1930). *E. T. Packard Collection.*

The extent to which the details surrounding the entry of C-D into the model industry on a national scale have been described is justified for many reasons. C-D's ads were not just a series of unrelated announcements. The marketing and ad campaign were orchestrated to serve notice to dealers, modelers, and competitors that the bulk of the manufacturers in the industry were at best offering unrealistic toys and that C-D would offer realistic-appearing scale models that could unquestionably be identified with their real aircraft counterparts. The campaign was a professional effort, a product of the partnership of a visionary entrepreneur and a qualified advertising agency that was successful despite the Great Depression and an economically shell-shocked populace, at a time when the unemployment rate hit a peak of 25 percent and never fully recovered until the World War II military buildup primed the economy. Of course, part of the scenario that made it possible for C-D to achieve its success in such short order was its ability to piggyback on the avid interest in and fascination with the expanding role of the airplane in the rapid development of civil, military, and commercial aviation, not only domestically but worldwide. This factor was so influential that it negated a great deal of the effect of the devastated economy.

The C-D spread in the December 1930 *Model Airplane News* issue reminded readers that "Christmas Comes but Once a Year" and dedicated a page to the SF-1E and SF-2C. The ad was impressive for its size and was an outstanding symbol of the first-year success of Cleveland Model and Supply. *Author's Collection.*

C-D succeeded and would continue to succeed for years to come because several needs were fulfilled:

- The need for a simpler way to construct models so that young people could enjoy the art of building rubber-powered scale flying or display models without parental or adult assistance;
- The use of balsa extensively to make it easier for modelers to build lighter, better-flying models without special tools (only razor blades, sandpaper, and glue were needed);
- The need to supply authentic scale models with movable control surfaces and important structural details to educate young America about aviation, thus motivating millions to seek careers in the airlines, military air force, or related industries;
- The need to provide a hobby to the youth of America to keep them constructively occupied and out of trouble;
- The need to provide young people with the opportunity to experience the satisfaction of building something with their own hands, thus possibly leading to a career in the trades rather than one in a profession to which they would not be as well suited;
- The need to provide modelers with the opportunity to experience the satisfaction and motivation that comes from competing with their peers for exhibition honors and awards from participating in flying contests.

Perhaps one of the most important reasons the degree of success described could be achieved in such a short time is that the Pachasa family backed up the ad promises with top-quality plans and materials, accurate scale realism, innovative structural design simplification, and the kind of top-notch service on orders that only a dedicated, family-run, cottage-based business could deliver.

Reminiscing about his relationship with the Carpenter ad agency, Ed recalled, "We most likely would not have been able to swing such an ambitious campaign in our first major year if it had not been for their generous credit policy. They scheduled the ads and handled the billing from the publications. I can remember at the beginning of the Depression, when we were reminded by owner A. C. Carpenter that our balance amounted to about $1,300. Of course, at that time, because the 1929 Depression closed many banks, we had no checking account, so I asked them if they would accept cash. I shall never forget arriving at the agency with a cigar box loaded with cash, including many coins, which were a part of our retail business, and humbly counting out the amount necessary to pay off the bill. Our early practice of paying by cash was particularly appreciated, for during the Depression bank closings were common and many larger firms could not pay their bills."

The ad campaign was an expensive, calculated risk for a fledgling company striving for success in a depression-plagued era, ultimately costing around

$1,800, based on *Model Airplane News*'s rate schedule for 1930. It took guts on the part of Ed Pachasa, but after witnessing firsthand as an employee of two major airframe manufacturers the emergence of a fledgling industry ushering in the air age to America with their pioneering "aeroplanes," he had become enthralled with the romance of the early birds. Consequently, his resulting confident, positive outlook for aviation's future led him to believe implicitly that, if he had "done his homework," so to speak, he had every chance to succeed.

Within a year of the introduction of the SF-1 by C-D in 1930, followed closely by the SF-2, model making had been transformed from pine, reed, bamboo, wire, cloth, and nailed and thread wrapped joints to a more simplified all-balsa glued construction. Perhaps unrealized at the time, C-D had begun a precedent-setting tradition with the introduction of the Travel Air Mystery Ship. C-D would become famous for its stable of Thompson Trophy–winner kits that were produced through 1939 (it was the only company to offer all the Thompson Trophy winners), after which the event was terminated because of war clouds over Europe.

CHAPTER 6

The Legacy of the War Birds

As we learn what was involved in the initial expanding and flourishing growth of C-D, we should see that this success should be given additional recognition since it occurred during the foreboding, omnipresent Depression.

It had become apparent that the economic collapse of America's free-enterprise system was not endemic to the expansion of U.S. businesses so prominent during the Roaring Twenties. The enormity of the financial calamity had its roots, to some extent, in the complex structure of the tariffs and duties in place in a burgeoning world trade as well as in rampant financial speculation. This international overregulation had escalated to the point where it was rapidly becoming a deterrent to free trade among major worldwide trading partners. Many felt the Smoot-Hawley tariff bore a significant responsibility. Consequently, as reality set in, economists and business and government leaders became aware that the financial cancer would become a global phenomenon and, most unfortunately, would not be of short duration.

The economy hit rock bottom in 1932, the year of Franklin D. Roosevelt's election. To further assess the extent of the Depression, a comparison by year of the degree of unemployment that resulted might serve to emphasize the challenge the incipient C-D organization faced.

Year	Unemployment as % of Labor Force
1928	3.9
1929 (a year of aviation overproduction)	.9
1930	7.8
1931	16.3
1932 (FDR and the New Deal elected)	24.9
1933 (the bottom)	25.1

Year	Unemployment as % of Labor Force
1934	20.2
1935	18.4
1936 (an economic revival begins)	14.5
1937	12.0
1938 (auto industry sales off 48%)	18.8
1939 (the influence of World War II buildup)	16.7

It would finally take the massive lend-lease program and conversion to military production of World War II to pull us out of the deepest depression in history.

The Auto Industry Takes Its Lumps

As another barometer of the extent of the economic crisis, the Ford Motor Company saw its sales go from $1 billion in 1929 to a low of $259 million in 1932. The capacity of the Ford Motor Company annually was 2 million cars. By 1932 twenty-six out of thirty-two plants were closed, and only 400,000 cars were produced. The turnaround began in 1933 with the introduction of the 75 hp new V-8 engine models, with prices ranging from $475 to $610.

The fallout from the economic debacle was even more dramatically evident as it impacted the fortunes of one of the leaders of the luxury car market, the legendary Packard Motor Car Company. From the introduction by the two Packard brothers of their first passenger car model in 1899, the company evolved into a most successful, profitable, and astoundingly diversified enterprise, laying claim to being leaders in aircraft, automobile, and boat production.

Packard established a line of impressive, high-quality, prestigious automobiles and racers; six 350 hp Packard engines powered the USS *Shenandoah* dirigible; twin Packards propelled the Navy (NAF) PN-9 Seaplane; an aircraft radial diesel powered a Stinson Detroiter, a Bellanca Pacemaker, and a Waco biplane, thus garnering the Collier Trophy; a marine engine drove Gar Wood's speedboat to a record 102.256 mph, the first to break the 100 mph barrier; and during World I it was the pragmatic engineering acumen of Packard's engineer, Jesse Vincent, in concert with Hall Scott's engineer Elbart Hall, that developed America's 400 hp Liberty V-12 of which ultimately 20,476 were built to power the DH-4 Battleplane. In 1926 Lt. John Macready established a 38,704-foot altitude record in a supercharged Liberty-powered U.S. Army Le Pere Pursuit and was awarded the Mackay Trophy.

For the four years prior to the Depression, Packard outsold its major rival, General Motors' Cadillac-LaSalle, three to one. Next to GM, Packards were the most widely owned passenger cars. During the first years of the Depression, Packard stock declined from a double-digit price range to below $2. Packard's marketing strategy was to introduce the lower-priced model "120" at $1,000, in contrast to their former price range of $2,000 and up. After the 1938 economic decline, which resulted in a 48 percent decrease in auto industry sales, Packard suffered a $1.6 million loss. Packard attempted a comeback with the new model "110" Six at $795, thus entering the medium-priced market.

Packard's demise was hastened by the Depression, but it fell behind in engine development and suffered from decadent styling.

While Packard never fully recovered from the effects of the Depression and had to merge with Studebaker in 1956, with the marque disappearing in 1962, the Ford Motor Company recovered and went on to greatness as a member of the "Big Three" automakers. As in the aircraft industry, many other famous auto marques disappeared, including Marmon, Pierce-Arrow, Peerless, Stutz, and Duesenberg.

Despite the Great Depression, the aircraft division of the Ford Motor Company, which had introduced the famous "Tin Goose" twelve-passenger, 110 mph tri-motor transport in 1926, produced 199 of the 77-foot wingspan aircraft costing $55,000 to $68,000 each until 1933, when it was displaced by the faster, greater-passenger capacity, all-metal twin engine Boeing 247. Ford's aircraft division lost from $1 to $3 million. Remarkably, Ford had been able to finance the reliable, durable, noisy airliner from its enormous automotive capital reserves.

C-D Loses Stockholders

Buoyed by the welcome flush of C-D's initial success of its first two SF models, in what was to be a long line of successive types, Ed Pachasa had a few meetings with the core of his stockholders to share his 1931–32 strategic plans. "Each of them had been painfully impacted, to some extent by the economic fallout, and could only marvel at the relative success of my fledgling enterprise," Ed remarked. "Several initial shareholders had to request that I return their financial commitments, most embarrassing for them, of course."

The year 1931 was destined to leave its imprint through the giant strides being made by C-D as its product line was rapidly expanded to nearly twenty SF models, plus the Profile Series and the beginner stick types, miscellaneous plans, and a growing line of supplies. The result was enhanced market penetration and increased sales.

In late 1929, underwritten by the Guggenheim Fund, a close knit father-and-son team of Elmer Sperry Sr. and Jr., instrument designers, together with Lt. James H. "Jimmy" Doolittle, combined their expertise, talent, and determination to develop instrumentation capable of enabling aircraft pilots to overcome the crippling menace of fog, which held aviation at is mercy. Airborne commerce was abruptly brought to a halt in foggy conditions.

On September 24, 1929, at Mitchel Field, Long Island, Lieutenant Doolittle, "under the hood" in the cockpit of their Navy Consolidated NY-2 (NX7918) biplane, and with Lt. Ben Kelsey in the front cockpit acting as safety pilot, made a fifteen-minute flight in the fog. After takeoff, the plane was flown on a given course, and a landing was made at the point of departure through the use of instruments exclusively. Thus was demonstrated for the first time the ability to fly safely under foggy conditions.

To commemorate this achievement in flight, on April 7, 1931, the Cleveland Chamber of Commerce held a luncheon at the prestigious Winton Hotel (later to be known as the Carter Hotel), a favorite hostelry and watering hole of the aviation fraternity, particularly during the National Air Races. The occasion also was also a tribute to Myron T. Herrick, the U.S. ambassador to France who hosted Lindbergh in Paris. The Diplome d'Honneur award was posthumously presented to his son, Parmely Herrick, in recognition of the ambassador's support for the 212 brave Americans who, before America's entry into World War I , flew in the Lafayette Flying Corps and, in particular,

On September 24, 1929, Mitchel Field, Long Island, Lt. J. H. (Jimmy) Doolittle, while under the hood in a Consolidated NY-2 (NX7918) with Lt. Ben Kelsey as observer, took off, flew over a 15-mile course, and landed at the same takeoff location in fog with the aid of specially developed blind-flying instruments. The NY-2 was a composite of an NY-1, NY-2, PT-1, and a Vought UO-1. The power plant was a Wright J-5, the landing gear had special oleos, and the 40-foot wingspan had additional dihedral. The project was directed by Navy captain Emery S. Land. Initially Doolittle approached father-and-son Sperry team to design a single instrument incorporating directional control and wing attitude positioning. The Sperrys wisely determined that since the attitudes of the aircraft involved were by separate controls, two separate instruments would provide a cross-reference under the hood. Hence, the artificial horizon (for wing positioning) and the directional gyro (for compass course indication) were the result. *Robert Mikesh–National Air and Space Museum Collection NASM through Nut Tree Association.*

Jimmy Doolittle Jr., age nine, with his famous father, Maj. J. H. "Jimmy" Doolittle, admires a model of a Lockheed Vega sponsored by Shell Oil Company, in which his father would later fly in the National Air Tour starting from Detroit, Michigan, on July 5, acting as referee (1931). *Underwood and Underwood Collection.*

to the "Valiant 38," fearless, daredevil American pilots who flew in the L'Escadrille Lafayette (Escadrille No.124).

Col. William Bishop presented the Harmon Trophy, named in honor of Clifford Harmon, a pioneer balloonist and aeronaut and holder of pilot's license No. 6, and the Medaille d'Honneur, and the Diplome d'Honneur of Ligue Internationale des Aviateurs to Doolittle for his blind flying achievement in the fog. As a tribute to Doolittle, whom they cherished as their role model, the pilots of the 17th Squadron of the 1st Pursuit Group, in their distinctively marked Great Snow Owl–insignia Boeing P-12s, had flown in from Selfridge Field, Michigan, and were in the audience of famous aviation personalities.

SF-21B C-D Curtiss Hawk P6-E. This photo was used in many ads and was often confused with the real thing. *E. T. Packard Collection.*

Notably present were two World War I celebrated aces: Canadian Col. William Avery Bishop, commanding officer of RAF Squadron 85, Victoria Cross, Distinguished Service Order, and Distinguished Flying Cross with seventy-two victories; and Lt. Col. William Thaw, America's five-victory ace, Lafayette Escadrille No. 124, commanding officer of the 103d Squadron and of the 3d Pursuit Group. Thaw was one of the seven key Americans of the "Valiant 38" who founded the Escadrille Americaine, those pilots who in 1916 volunteered to fly and fight for France before the United States entered the war. His awards included the Distinguished Service Cross, with Bronze Oak Leaf; the Legion d'Honneur (Rosette); the Croix de Guerre (four palms and two stars), and numerous citations.

Young Pachasa had arranged with the hotel for a display of C-D World War I models, which were ingeniously suspended from the hotel's decorative lobby ceiling. "I could never have dreamed that I would ever be invited to be present at such a gathering of famous fliers," commented Ed, "for I was truly in awe of them. I had relived Bishop's telling of his own aerial exploits and victorious dogfights in his nimble, highly maneuverable Nieuport XVII, as described in his book, *Winged Warfare.* Fortunately, I was put at ease somewhat by good old Captain Dick, who introduced them to me, for he knew them all."

And so the twenty-five-year-old entrepreneur struck up a lasting friendship with Colonel Bishop, who then was a vice president with the McColl Frontenac Oil Company of Montreal, Canada. Subsequently, Bishop, as well as Thaw, agreed to serve as vice presidents of NAME (National Advanced Model Engineers), with Jimmy Doolittle accepting as president. In his quest to organize this association to further the advancement of youth in model building, Ed had reasoned that to initiate such an activity successfully would

A view of the lobby of the Winton Hotel in Cleveland, April 1931, with a display of World War I C-D models suspended from the decorative ceiling. *E. T. Packard Collection.*

require famous aviation personalities as officers. As an exponent of showmanship and merchandising, he went for the most impressive names. Orville Wright had been asked to serve as president; however, he politely and understandably declined since he was already contest chairman for the National Aeronautic Association.

Cliff Henderson and the First Major National Air Races

NAME had one of its strongest boosters in Cliff Henderson, the flamboyant, hard-driving managing director of the National Air Races along with Clifford Gildersleeve, a Cleveland Chamber of Commerce executive. Its big annual event was centered around a national contest held concurrently with the National Air Races, which Henderson had requested Ed direct.

When the promotionally oriented Henderson arrived in Cleveland in March 1929 to initiate the planning for the city's first National Air Races, he was already a staunch advocate of model building for youth. In World War I, after a brief stint as an ambulance driver, Henderson transferred to the air service. While awaiting flight training he served as a "sandbagger," acting as ballast strapped in the rear cockpit of the imbalanced DH-4s being ferried to air fields along the Western front. In 1919 he was founder and president of the American Legion Post in Santa Monica, California. Next he acquired a Nash automobile agency, where he honed his marketing and promotional talents. He served as a lieutenant in the 476th Pursuit Squadron Reserve at Santa Monica's Clover Field and was appointed chairman of the Chamber of Commerce Aviation Committee.

After he had sunk $317 into a surplus Jenny, which he flew at Clover Field, he cultivated friendships with aviation personalities, including many movie stunt pilots. His initial brush with fame occurred as a result of a request from Donald Douglas, whose plant was located nearby, to organize a reception for the departure and arrival of the four Douglas DWC round-the-world cruisers, their pilots, and their crews at Clover Field, beginning April 6, 1924.

This exposure to commercial and military aviation VIPs led to Henderson's zealous endeavor to organize the most ambitious effort in aviation up to that time, which has been chronicled as the "romance of a barley field." In just fifty-eight days, the talented Henderson, under the auspices of the California Air Race Association, created Mines Field in Inglewood, California—the site of the first National Air Races, September 8–16, 1928. The new facility, immense for its day, consisted of three 7,000-foot runways, a 200,000-square-foot exposition building, parking for 38,000 cars, and was surrounded with seven miles of fence.

The colorful promoter was aided in accomplishing the seemingly impossible because he had on his advisory committee an impressive roster of southern California captains of industry: Harry Chandler (*Los Angeles Times*), Donald Douglas (Douglas Aircraft), Sid Grauman (Grauman's Chinese Theater), Harris Hanshue (Western Air Express), Allan Lougheed (Lockheed Aircraft), Jack Maddux (Maddux Air Lines), B. F. Mahoney (Ryan Aircraft), Maj. C. C. Mosley (Grand Central Air Terminal), Joseph Schenck (Hollywood movie mogul), and W. E. Gilmore (Gilmore Oil Company).

The bottom line of the air extravaganza included a pragmatic proposition that provided that the entire package would then become the official, sorely needed Los Angeles Municipal Air Terminal. Henderson was then engaged as the first director of airports in Los Angeles for a brief period of time after the National Air Races.

Henderson had an impressive portfolio with which to ballyhoo the 1928 event. Los Angeles County, with its year-round flying climate, could lay claim to being the "air capital of the nation," with 30 percent of air activity and 40 percent of the nation's aviation personnel (it was the home port of the carriers *Lexington* and *Saratoga* and the zeppelin USS *Los Angeles* and boasted

The 1928 National Air Race was the first of twelve years of the event under the direction of Cliff Henderson. At this time he had not secured either Thompson Products or Vincent Bendix as sponsors, who would make it possible for the Thompson Trophy Race (closed course) and the Bendix (Los Angeles to Cleveland) Race. *Author's Collection.*

fifty local private and municipal airports). Four airlines served the metro area, together with five airframe and engine manufacturers.

In his quest to boost the popularity of model building for youth, Henderson listed prominently in the thirty-page air race program Special Event Nos. 3 and 4: "Airplane Model Building and Flying Contest," with Don Grubbs as the chairman. There were seven special events total and fifteen other events for both civil and military planes. The transcontinental race from New York to Los Angeles, on September 10, would later in 1931 be known as the Bendix, sponsored by Vincent Bendix, wealthy industrialist CEO of Bendix Aviation.

The 1928 National Air Races' (from left) Cliff Henderson, managing director; Lt. Al Williams, racer and aerobatic pilot; Charles A. Lindbergh; and Maj. James H. "Jimmy" Doolittle. Henderson, master showman, was able to attract the stars of aviation, both civilian and military, to these events, and thereby draw in fans. *R. S. Hirsch Collection.*

There was no major sponsor such as Thompson Products for the closed-course races events. The emphasis was on military competition, since, at that time, their aircraft had the edge in performance statistics. The Pan American race from Mexico City to Los Angeles and the International Race from Windsor, Canada, opened two event races to Latin Americans and Canadians exclusively. More than 200 exhibitors, with a value of $2 million, participated in the show, and seventy airmen flew in the aerial spectacle.

Cleveland's First National Air Races, 1929

When the National Air Races—"a symphony of the sky," as Cliff Henderson termed it—were staged at the Cleveland Airport in 1929, a precedent was set for closed-course speed and cross-country records to be shattered annually. Cleveland would become the home of the "air classic of the century" for most of the remaining years through 1939, except for the 1930 event in Chicago and the 1933 and 1936 races in Los Angeles.

Maj. Jack Berry's baby, the Cleveland air terminal, was then the role model for aviation events. In 1925 it became the first such municipally owned facility in the country. Berry could boast state-of-the-art services, including a weather bureau, customs and immigration processing, radio control, and a modern restaurant and sleeping quarters for pilots. Its space-age lighting consisted of a 150 mm arc flood with 500 million candlepower, 80–600 lumen lamps for general lighting, and a utility floodlight of eight 3 kw lamps. Its

The 1929 National Air Races winner, Doug Davis, who flew in a Travel Air "Mystery Ship." *E. T. Packard Collection.*

family of airlines included United, American, Pennsylvania Airlines, and Transport and Central Air Lines. Cleveland and Newark were nearly always neck-and-neck for first place in arrival and departure statistics, with Chicago next.

After Major Berry introduced Ed Pachasa to Cliff Henderson, Ed was asked to direct a model airplane activity that Henderson hoped would become a repeat event every year. The formal director of the model airplane contest was listed as Fred Thomas, because Ed was too involved with launching C-D nationally and releasing the SF-1 Great Lakes Sport Trainer kit to oversee the contest. The Miniature Aircraft Show at 10 A.M. was listed on the agenda in the smashing sixty-four-page program for Tuesday, August 27.

A quarter-page ad for Cleveland Model and Supply in the program, embellished with Cleveland's diamond "C" trademark and with copy identifying C-D as "model engineers" and the punch line, "When you want the very best, send ten cents for a catalog," was the very first model airplane ad ever placed in a National Air Races program. A final touch of merchandising magic by the master promoter was a souvenir coin commemorating the air races and exposition, of which thousands were sold for twenty-five cents. Anthony (Uncle Tony) Fokker gave an address, "Gliding as an Aid to Aviation," on Tuesday, and a National Air Race theme song, "Wings of Love," with lyrics by none other than Cliff Henderson, was featured in an evening musical production at the Cleveland Public Auditorium on Saturday.

The 1929 Cleveland National Air Races established Cliff Henderson as a most capable managing director of the aerial races as well as of the event's diverse entertainment. As testimony, the Chicago Air Racing Corporation made it known that it wanted to host the 1930 event at the Wright-Curtiss-Reynold Airport.

Ed Pachasa as Modelers' Mentor

Ever attuned to the whims and fickleness of American youth, Pachasa contrived to keep a flow of a variety of activities for his following of modelers in Cleveland. Through his relationship with Jack Berry, whose memorial at the Cleveland-Hopkins Air Terminal attests to his significant role in the city's airport development, he was provided with an area designated for flying models on the Grayton Road side of the airport—now the site of the NASA laboratory. Ed, followed by a retinue of his devoted aero enthusiasts holding their precious models, became a familiar sight around the Cleveland airport as they made their way to an empty hangar or en route to the Grayton Road flying area. Pachasa seemingly assumed the role of a modern Pied Piper.

With his many years of experience involving adjustments of all kinds to his experimental flying models, he was able to guide many modelers through the initial test flights of their models, thus probably avoiding unnecessary damaging crashes and ensuring a successful positive first exposure to the hobby. During the onslaught of inclement weather, typical of Cleveland's infamous climate influenced by its proximity to Lake Erie and the Canadian border, he had an agreement with Berry that if any of the cavernous airport hangars were empty, his modelers were permitted to fly their cherished fragile aircraft under Ed's direction and were thus protected from the vagaries of nature.

Ed became identified as a prime mover in the planning in the early 1930s of the city's annual flying model contests, both indoors and outdoors. Each year, as the fall dates for the National Air Races approached, movie theaters, hotel lobbies, department stores, and hobby retailers hosted avid enthusiasts for model display contests to capitalize on the popular aviation craze that engulfed Cleveland. He devoted untold hours at the air races airport site, providing properly displayed C-D exhibition models for enterprising businesses as well as arranging for modelers to have the glorious satisfaction of seeing their own personal creations exhibited.

Recognition of the War Birds

Meanwhile, the beleaguered American populace, negatively impacted by the deepening Depression, more than ever needed heroes, icons, and role models to admire. Perhaps this was why there seemed to be a rediscovery of the thrilling events of the Great War and its War Birds—the aces and their aerial chargers.

While Lindbergh idolatry continued, Americans had begun to realize that their own young, brave, and intrepid airmen, whose fighting prowess would become near-legendary, had established an outstanding record of heroism with aerial exploits and victories on the Western front. Their valiant, challenging,

Eddie Rickenbacker's *Fighting the Flying Circus* (1919), which offered readers detailed descriptions of his dog-fighting episodes over the Western Front in WWI, no doubt influenced the "flying pulps" that followed. Rickenbacker's twenty-six victories in just seven months made him America's ace of aces. Similarly, *Winged Warrior* was the story of the brash, intrepid Canadian WWI ace, Maj. W. A. Bishop. *Author's Collection.*

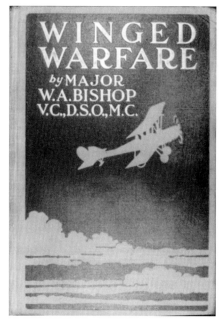

War Birds: Diary of an Unknown Aviator (1938), by Elliot White Springs, was taken from the diary of his flying buddy, the 85th Squadron's John McGavock Grider. Springs later published a series of WWI books lampooning aviators and their aerial exploits and social escapades. *Der rote Kampfflieger* (*The Red Battle Flyer;* 1919), by Manfred Freiherr von Richthofen, was the story of Germany's greatest eighty-victory ace during WWI. *Author's Collection.*

high-flying encounters were colorfully chronicled in a series of books, feature magazine articles, movies, and syndicated newspaper series that established a hero-worship culture for the war's "aces"—those airmen who had five or more confirmed victories.

In the forefront was RFC Maj. Billy Bishop, who in his 1916 book *Winged Warfare* documented his seventy-two victories as Canada's top ace, with thrilling encounters as a lone challenger until he was made commanding officer of the 85th Squadron. In 1919 there followed Eddie Rickenbacker's thrilling volume *Fighting the Flying Circus,* relating his account of twenty-six victories in seven months over the front, which established him as America's ace of aces.

In 1926 American ace Elliot White Spring's (twelve victories) smashing, widely read book *War Birds: Diary of an Unknown Aviator,* taken from the diary of the 85th Squadron's fallen member, John McGavock Grider, was followed by a series of his related volumes, and in 1927 Floyd Gibbons's revealing narrative of *The Red Knight of Germany,* Baron Manfred von Richtofen, vividly portrayed the encounters of the war's greatest ace, with eighty victories.

William Wellman, a World War I sergeant who flew a Nieuport 27 in the N.87 Squadron of the Lafayette Flying Corps and who had three confirmed victories before America entered the war, in 1927 directed Paramount's *Wings,* the first major silent motion picture version of American exploits in the air service at the front. Charles "Buddy" Rogers, later married to Mary Pickford; Richard Arlen; and the "It" girl, Clara Bow, were the stars, with a cameo appearance by Gary Cooper in his film debut. It was filmed at San Antonio's Brooks and Kelly Fields and won the first Oscar awarded by the Academy.

The pilots and stars of *Hell's Angels,* Howard Hughes's WWI aviation epic, pose in front of an authentic British WWI Sopwith "Snipe." From left: Ralph Douglas, exhibition parachute jumper; Leo Nomis, actor; Frank Clarke, stunt pilot; James Hall, actor; Ben Lyon, actor; Frank Tomick, stunt pilot; and Roy Wilson, key aerial photographer. This 1930 film is famous for its realistic aerial battle scenes. *Hugh Wynne Collection.*

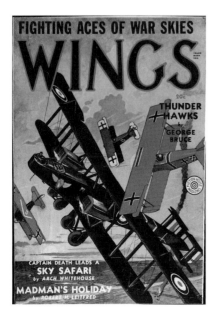

[a] The December 1931 issue of *Aces* flying pulp with a dramatic cover by artist Rudolph Belarski, one of the best such artists. Here the gunner is being bandaged by the pilot. In the [b] February 1933 issue of *Sky Birds,* with cover art by Frank Tinsley, an American Nieuport 28 is on the attack. [c] *G-8 and His Battle Aces,* with cover art by Frederick Blakeslee and narrative by Robert Hogan, was one of the most acclaimed hero pulps and was published well into World War II. [d] The Fall 1939 issue of *Wings,* with cover art by Rudolph Belkarski, illustrates a British Handley Page bomber being attacked by German Fokker D-7s. Another Belarski cover, [e] here *War Birds* shows a British RAF RE-8 observation aircraft being rescued by several British fighters. This pulp featured its hero, Terrence X. O'Leary, who would later command his own pulp, in its feature narrative, "Terrence X. O'Leary and His War Birds." [f] The 1933 famous "hero pulp" *G-8 and His Battle Aces,* with cover art by Frederick Blakeslee, featured WWI-related aerial adventures. *Author's Collection.*

In 1930, after two years in the making, Howard Hughes's $4 million *Hell's Angels* premiered at Grauman's Chinese Theater in Hollywood, featuring the debut of "the platinum bombshell," Jean Harlow. More than 100 pilots were used in the film, supported by 87 aircraft, 26 cameramen, and a 150-man aircraft maintenance crew, experiencing three fatalities. It would spawn a series of copycat movies, all of which further glorified World War I American aces versus the enemy (*Dawn Patrol, Ace of Aces, The Eagle and the Hawk,* and *Hell in the Heavens*, for example).

To capitalize on this revived interest in the Great War's aces, the April 1931 issue of *Model Airplane News*, now with new publisher Harold Hersey of Magazine Publishers, a veteran of the lurid pulps, had sported a cover not unlike those on the "flying pulps" (*Aces, Battle Birds, Dare-Devil Aces, Flying Aces, G-8 and His Battle Aces, Sky Birds, War Aces, War Birds,* and *Wings*) and featured an aerial dogfight scene with an American 94th Squadron Nieuport 28 versus the fabled German Fokker D VII. In the previous winter months, Packard had already had in process model plans for the Nieuport XVII (Bishop's mount), the Albatross D-III, the Fokker D VII, and, most significant, Rickenbacker's Spad XIII. To cap off Ed's opportunistic planning, the issue contained a full-page editorial on C-D's line of World War I models on back of a full-page C-D ad featuring Rickenbacker's Spad, with a special offer of a free copy of Rick's book with the purchase of any three of the World War I kits at $4 each.

The "Flying Pulps"

Examples of the "flying pulps"—the 7-by-10-inch, 120-plus-page magazines printed on coarse, pulpy paper—were sold in the C-D hobby store beginning in 1931. The covers were created as 21-by-30-inch oil paintings by such outstanding commercial artists as Rudolph Belarski (who painted for *Aces* and *War Birds*), Frederick Blakeslee (*Battle Aces, Dare-Devil Aces*), and Frank Tinsley (*Sky Birds, Squadron*). Packard, ever attuned to the whims and fantasies of young modelers, knew that these flying pulps attracted the boys and lengthened their stays in the store.

Initially these adventure magazines did not feature plans to build solid scale or flying scale models. In 1932 C-D did some advertising in *Flying Aces* when it published plans supplied by U.S. Model Aircraft Company. It was in 1932 and in 1933 when several titles, such as *Flying Aces,* moved to a slick 8½-by-11-inch format magazine with full-size plans included in every issue. Of course, *Model Airplane News,* never a pulp, had begun publishing this format in July 1929, and it always included plans for some type of solid scale and/or flying scale model.

The plots of the pulps' stories seemed to revolve around a hero being trapped in some insurmountable situation from which he extricated himself through indomitable courage, superhuman strength, *and,* of course, amazing flying skills. And he was ready to go through a similar ordeal next month. The narratives did not feature a love interest; swear words were never used, and the Allied hero pilot and his trusty aircraft always saved the day. The hero was sure to escape his imprisonment, somehow regain his downed plane (or commandeer an enemy aircraft), and, with his master flying and marksmanship, emerge victorious.

So the dramatic art on the covers of these magazines was influential in attracting readers to the daredevil antics of the characters as well as to the models of the planes featured.

Rickenbacker and His Famous Spad

"It was in late 1930," Ed recalled, "after a diligent search of all the manufacturers and many dealers, that I was quite surprised to come to the realization that there did not exist a construction plan or kit of the World War I Spad, the most famous plane of America's ace of aces, Eddie Rickenbacker." This void in the marketplace of such a world-famous pursuit ship represented another opportunity on which C-D could capitalize. So, with some encouragement from Captain Dick, Ed decided to seek out the source and track down the ace himself.

In early 1931 Captain Eddie Rickenbacker was deeply involved in the management of Tony Fokker's Atlantic Aircraft Company, at that time an acquisi-

Lieutenant Rickenbacker with his Spad XIII, serial number 4523, in which he achieved fourteen of his twenty-six victories, making him "America's Ace of Aces" (1918). When he took delivery of his Spad on July 5, 1918, at Orly, the American Experimental Aerodrome, he commented, "Inside ten minutes I was strapped in the seat of the finest little Spad that ever flew French skies. I have it to this day and would not part with it for all the possessions in the world." *Hugh Wynne Collection.*

This SF-13 Spad XIII shows the intricate details of the engine and cowling, the wing bungs and tubes from the center section into the engine compartment, and the engine shutters in front of the radiator. C-D improved the plan after researching details. This model was a faithful ¾-inch scale reproduction of Rickenbacker's plane and, with its colorful markings, was a great contest winner. *E. T. Packard Collection.*

tion of General Motors. Rick had switched positions from GM's Cadillac LaSalle division to the aircraft subsidiary as a stepping-stone into the airline industry. Rickenbacker not only replied to Ed's letter of request for information on the Spad in the affirmative but also sent a 1919 photo of himself in uniform, as well as photos of his famous Spad XIII (serial number 4523, delivery date July 10, 1918) with the numeral "1" on the fuselage, plus details of the 94th Squadron's famous "hat in the ring" insignia, camouflage coloring, and other markings.

The name of the famous French pursuit airplane, Spad, was an acronym of the initials of the manufacturer Society pour l'Aviation et ses Derives (the Company for Aviation and Its Derivatives). Louis Bleriot, CEO of the French aircraft manufacturer, persuaded Louis Bechereau, designer of the famous Deperdussin monoplanes, which had won the Gordon Bennett and Schneider Trophy Races, to remain with the firm, which was at the time embroiled in a financial scandal. Bechereau ingeniously mated the rugged structure of the Spad with Swiss engine designer Mark Birkigt's modified automobile Hispano-Suiza, 90-degree V-8 engine, which in its ultimate refined Model 8BEc developed 235 hp. This resultant design combination made it possible for Rick to perfect a strategy for the "chasseur" to dive out of the sun from above the enemy aircraft, fire one or two quick bursts from the twin .30s, and zoom with acquired speed into a spiral climb, for virtually no enemy aircraft could out climb or out dive the powerful Spad.

In a flashback Ed recalled, "When we had the SF-13 Spad plan finished and the components of the kit designed, my brother Will, shop superintendent, and I breathed a sigh of relief and felt a resultant surge of great pride. We shared the feeling that we had done justice to America's ace of aces in producing a C-D product of which he also could be proud. I think that may have been a motivating force, a patriotic obligation to develop a truly authentic replica of this famous ace's plane.

"Rick had come through with photos and valuable data. I had sought all the library file data, magazine photos, plus the 1917–18 issues of Fred T. Jane's *All the World's Aircraft* and any prototype plans available. Will had likewise developed a remarkable balsa nose turning which required only a minimum of sanding to prepare it for painting."

The plans clearly detailed all the structural components, including the lower wing aileron bellcrank, which Spad model plans seldom revealed. This feature was a part of the push-pull control system that was one of the Spad's endearing piloting advantages, and it moved a vertical control arm along the outer L. H. and R. H. wing struts, which in turn actuated the upper wing ailerons.

If there ever was a scale flying model built for static scale competition, this was it. And one with which many C-D model engineers won their share of contests, with all of its red, white, and blue patriotic markings; its colorful camouflaging, including "starred insignia wheels"; an outstanding detailed engine cowling with radiator shutters; twin .30 cal. Vickers machine guns with gun sight and ring sight; and with the bungs for the auxiliary gas tank and water tank protruding from the top of the center section. When the Spad was equipped with a geared engine, it sported an L. H. propeller, which was shown.

"There seemed to be only one final element missing to complete the cycle. Captain Eddie had, in a sense, initiated the project with his personal approval, his endorsement of his book offer, and his cooperation in supplying information. It seemed only right that in return he should be able to see the fruits of our mutual efforts. Forthwith, we had one of our best model engineers construct a model painstakingly and professionally accurate down to the last detail, of which we were all very proud. It was carefully padded, packed, crated, and shipped off to the ace."

It was gratifying to Packard to note that the C-D Spad appeared prominently on Rickenbacker's desk in magazine photos and newsreel footage from 1935 on when he became general manager for Eastern Airlines. (This initial SF-13 was superseded by a revised plan, the SF-13B, which incorporated many refinements added by Ed and draftsman John Zivco to make it unquestionably the most authentic such plan available.)

Colonel Bishop and His Nieuport Remembered

Ed's last brush with one of the Great War's aces was the result of his meeting Billy Bishop at the Cleveland Chamber of Commerce luncheon honoring Jimmy Doolittle in April 1931. Despite the fact that the ace's Nieuport XVII Scout kit had been advertised in a most impressive full-page ad in the April 1931 issue of *Model Airplane News,* featuring four World War I models, Ed

RAF Col. Billy Bishop with his Nieuport XVII in 1917. Note that the numerals on his rudder were censored out of the photograph. C-D's ¾-inch scale model of the SF-12 Nieuport XVII displayed the simplified construction that was designed for flying, not exhibiting; therefore, there are not as many details. *E. T. Packard Collection.*

wanted to benefit from Bishop's input to be able to include the special details and markings in order to offer the SF-12 as Colonel Bishop's personal plane, à la Rickenbacker's Spad.

Bishop, of course, proved to be of the "tough generation" with a cast-iron constitution, having the distinction of serving in two World Wars as a result of his appointment as Honorary Air Marshall in the RCAF in World War II. He had the distinguished honor of pinning his son's RCAF wings on his tunic. Bishop's presence and previous military and combat experience were a great asset to Canada's war effort.

There ensued several months of correspondence from April to November 1932 between Bishop in Montreal and Ed in Cleveland. Initially, the colonel was offered a professionally built model Nieuport XVII, for which he wanted to pay, but Ed, of course, refused. The ensuing correspondence resulted in Bishop's supplying structural and marking details.

Bishop offered the following suggestions in an effort to provide Ed with the maximum possible authenticity:

1. The spinner should be about twice its present size, the same color as the cowling and quite round and blunt.
2. There was a red, white, and blue circle [cockade] just aft of the cockpit, and behind that came the letters "C5," exactly as you have them only slightly reduced to fit the fuselage size at that point.
3. The colors on the rudder were in reverse order—the blue forward and the red at the stern. Within the blue area was the letter "B" in white. In the white portion of the rudder were the numerals "1–5" in blue. In the red stripe were the numerals "6–6" painted in white.

Bishop suggested that the Lewis machine gun should be mounted on the wing to fire at an angle of approximately 15 degrees to clear the tip of the prop. He also indicated that the angle of the Aldis sight mounted on the fuselage should also be mounted at the same 15-degree angle. Ed was also advised that on the underside of the lower starboard wing was the letter "C" with the figure "5" correspondingly located on the underside of the lower port wing. Bishop finally told Ed that the wheel discs were painted blue on the outside and silver on the inside.

On November 1, 1932, when Bishop received the professionally built ¹⁄₁₆-size C-D model of his World War I Nieuport XVII, he replied by letter to Ed, "I have just received today the model of my Nieuport, and I want to thank you more than I can say for it. It gives me a great thrill to see the little machine again. I also want to congratulate you on the accuracy of your reproduction. There are only a few points on it where I could possibly suggest a more accurate reproduction, and they are all unimportant; so if you do not feel inclined to alter them, please do not bother to do so."

In closing, Bishop commented, "I do sincerely hope that you have success in selling the kit, as you have today given an old-time pilot a great thrill." His last comment: "Heartiest congratulations on the undercarriage, which is really the most beautiful work."

For C-D the year 1931 had heralded an impressive array of SF series of World War I models—ten, to be exact—that comprised an impressive tribute to the Great War, enabling model builders and institutions, such as museums, to indulge in the preservation of authentic aviation history. The timing of the introductions of the World War I SF line coincided with the country's reawakening to the significant role of America's airmen in the Great War. Consequently, interest in the line of the ten SF kits was keenly heightened and added prestige to C-D's standing in terms of its effort to recognize the aircraft of American and allied airmen as well as those of the central powers.

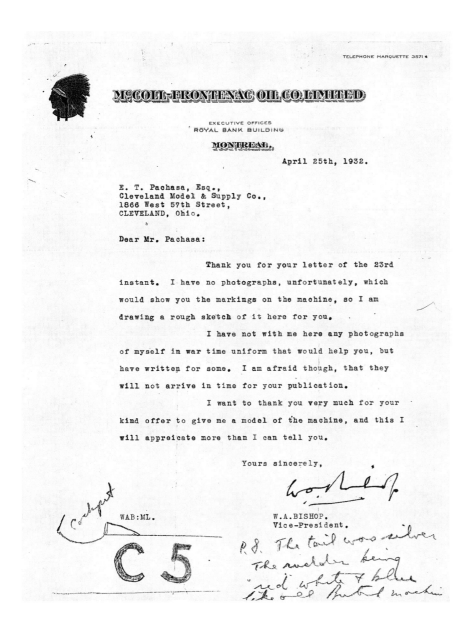

One of a series of letters from W. A. Bishop, Canadian ace, providing Packard with details of his Nieuport XVII as well as thanking him for the final delivery of the model so painstakingly constructed by Packard's model engineers (1932). *E. T. Packard Collection.*

The 1930 Chicago National Air Races Promotes Modeling

After the outstanding results of Cleveland's 1929 epic air extravaganza, Col. Robert McCormick, chairman of the board of the Chicago Air Race Corporation, made it known that they wanted a piece of the action. The Windy City's desire was not to be denied, and so Chicago's Curtiss-Wright-Reynolds Airport, with a $525,000 budget (50 percent more than Cleveland's), certainly deserved the right to roll out their red carpet.

Although Thompson Products had sponsored the "Free for All" closed-course race at Cleveland, it was not known there as the Thompson Trophy Race. The Thompson name was first applied to that event when the National

The 1930 Chicago National Air Races was the first of the races to stage the official Thompson Trophy Race, to be won by Charles "Speed" Holman in his Laird Speedwing Solution. Chicago's Curtiss-Wright-Reynolds airport had a $525,000 budget, 50 percent more than Cleveland's. *Author's Collection.*

Air Races were held in Chicago, and Charles "Speed" Holman had the distinction of being the first so-named official Thompson Trophy winner in his Laird Solution, barely nosing out Jim Haizlip in his Travel Air Model R by a scant average speed of 2 mph. Holman just cracked the 200 mph barrier at 201.90 mph, versus Haizlip at 199.80 mph.

The tragedy of the event was that accomplished Marine speed pilot Captain Page was overcome by engine fumes in the cockpit of his Curtiss Racer, fatally crashing, though safely away from the crowd.

Cliff Henderson, in making good on his promise to continue his quest to boost modeling for youth, locked in as model-event sponsors the *Chicago Daily News;* Ajax Balsa Wood Company, distributor for Lata balsa wood; Fleischman Transportation; A. G. Spaulding; and Aero Model Company (Silver Ace "ARF" flying models). Joseph Lucas was appointed chairman of the Model Airplane Contest Committee, with two assistants who were to become luminaries in modeldom: Joseph Ott, model editor for *Popular Aviation* magazine, and Bertram Pond, model editor for *Aero Digest.* Four modeling events were scheduled, each with an impressive trophy, with a Sweepstakes Trophy offered by the *Chicago Daily News.*

NAME Is Curtailed

Ed, in recalling how the NAME organization fared, remarked, "After the Cleveland Chamber of Commerce Doolittle Harmon Trophy luncheon in April 1931, we were fortunate to have the following volunteer leadership as the

1931 National Air Races Model Airplane Contest flyer by Harvey's Toy Shop in Cleveland's Terminal Building. Contestants had their choice of building a Howard Pete, a Laird Solution, or a Travel Air Mystery Ship, flying scale or solid. There were four prizes offered, and the contestants' entries would be displayed in the store's windows. *E. T. Packard Collection.*

national officers of NAME: James H. Doolittle, president; Col. William Avery Bishop, Col. William Thaw, Capt. Holden C. Richardson, Louis F. Ross (glider contest expert), Edward T. Pachasa, and Capt. Loftus Price (formerly of the Royal Air Force), vice presidents."

In Dayton he had met premier modeler Donald F. Chase, who had asked him to be an agent for C-D (at that time they had not thoroughly established their dealer organization). Since Jimmy Doolittle was based at McCook Field in Dayton (before Wright-Patterson Air Force Base), Ed appointed Donald national director of NAME. "I was completely swamped with my administrative, design and marketing responsibilities as C-D was developing," Ed said. "Consequently, there was no way I would be able to find the time for administering the NAME organization.

Dayton, Ohio, McCook Field. Fourth from left: Maj. "Jimmy" Doolittle, president of the National Association of Model Engineers, accepts the C-D SF-5 Laird Super Solution exhibition model from National Director Donald Chase in recognition of the association's first anniversary and Doolittle's Bendix Trophy victory in the Laird (1932). *E. T. Packard Collection.*

"One of the first things Donald accomplished was to plan and execute an informative mailing on our first letterhead with the impressive listing of our famous NAME national officers. An established nickel membership card was provided, plus a ten percent discount on C-D kits and supplies to members was offered. A beautiful NAME rose gold lapel pin was also available at a nominal price of 50 cents. He promptly organized a Dayton chapter of NAME, and Maj. Jimmy Doolittle agreed to be the speaker at their first meeting. Chase made several excellent contacts in Dayton and surrounding areas, which resulted in some sales for C-D."

As the date neared for the first anniversary of the organization, Chase came up with an excellent promotional plan. Since Jimmy Doolittle had become an even more famous personage in 1931 after winning the first Bendix Trophy Race in the Laird Super Solution, Chase prevailed upon Ed to have a C-D SF-5 special model of the Laird constructed. Ed remembered, "At the anniversary banquet in Dayton, Donald presented the excellent model during his cutting of the 'birthday cake.' Jimmy was really appreciative, and I learned that it was the first accurate, realistic scale model he had ever received. Don had the occasion recorded on film so that I was able to include a photo of the event on the front page of volume 1, number 1 of the *Cleveland Model Engineers News* 1932 with the heading, 'Doolittle Cuts a Piece of Cake for Himself.' The photo showing him cutting the cake also showed the C-D Laird model prominently."

There was no question in the Master Model Engineer's mind that Donald Chase used every opportunity to remind prospective dealers, modeling organizations, and schools of his relationship with Jimmy Doolittle. And, of course, by having the photo of Doolittle in the first issue of *Cleveland Model*

Engineer's News, the forerunner of *Cleveland Modelmaking News and Practical Hobbies,* which was mailed to the dealers, C-D was obviously capitalizing on this association with the famous airman.

However, as 1932 progressed, with the Depression only worsening, all aspects of business and society became so negatively impacted that it became apparent that to make NAME succeed, more time and effort would be required—more than both Donald Chase and he could muster. The whole country was just trying to survive, so after about a year of coping, it became necessary for him to conclude that NAME would have to be disbanded.

Ed sent his apology to all of the officers as well as to Chase. "It was a most embarrassing and difficult action for me," he remembered. Donald did, however, continue to act as an agent for C-D for some time and succeeded in generating new business from time to time.

Despite the need for the cessation of NAME, its demise was not due to lack of purpose, objectives, or organization; it was a result of the increasing severity of the Depression. Its objective was noble: to contribute to the development

The Variety Theater in Cleveland with a display of Cleveland models for a contest—a tie-in with an aviation movie *Devil Dogs of the Air*, starring James Cagney and Pat O'Brien. When an aviation movie was booked, theater owners would often contact Ed to arrange a model contest for displays in their lobbies. It was the Great Depression, and they had to resort to all types of showmanship to entice the customers (1935). *E. T. Packard Collection.*

of youth through an interest in aviation by the building and flying of model airplanes.

This was really the first such activity initiated by the Master Model Engineer that was not successful. His earlier leadership in the branches of Cleveland's Carnegie Library that had model airplane clubs capitalized on the eager interest of Cleveland youth in aviation ignited by Lindbergh's epic flight. It was, however, another in a lifelong series of involvement by the ever-young entrepreneur with America's youth that would justifiably earn him the appellation "aviation's great recruiter."

The year 1931 marked the retirement of the Schneider Trophy Races, with England winning the last three consecutive races (during the 1931 race the Supermarine S6B attained a speed of 414.08 mph). The year also saw the inauguration of the Bendix Trophy Race, with the colorful, daring, and accomplished Jimmy Doolittle as the first winner of the Los Angeles to Cleveland race. He flew his Laird Super Solution at a then-amazing speed of 233 mph, making it to Cleveland in only 11 hours and 15 minutes. In the December 1931 issue of *Model Airplane News,* C-D announced the SF-5 kit of the Laird with a 15½-inch wingspan, for $2.50. It enjoyed brisk sales that Christmas season. And, more tragically, 1931 witnessed the death of the daredevil stunt airman and the first winner of the Thompson Trophy, Charles "Speed" Holman, who died in a crash while performing in his Laird biplane at an Omaha, Nebraska, airshow.

The continued growth of C-D would result in an increasing market share in spite of the depths of the Great Depression. As aviation's seemingly inexorable expansion and technical development defied all odds, C-D would be enabled to offer even more attractive, authentic designs, plus the added colorful winners of the Thompson and Bendix Trophy winners. The decade of the 1930s was about to witness the rise of Cleveland Model and Supply as the undisputed leader of the industry.

CHAPTER 7

C-D Takes Off

⌘ AMERICA CAME CLOSE to rock bottom in 1932. Crude oil sold for 10 cents per barrel, wheat for 25 cents per bushel, and General Motors common stock was quoted at less than $8 per share, with no buyers.

The entire aviation industry produced a total of only 549 commercial aircraft valued at $2.2 million, down from $6.7 million in 1931. Waco Aircraft Company of Troy, Ohio, one of the most successful civil and military aircraft manufacturers to survive the Depression without bankruptcy, a takeover, or selling out, shipped $923,000 in annual sales more than 41 percent of the total annual national commercial aircraft sales.

Not so with Ed and the Pachasa family at C-D. As though orchestrated by a Madison Avenue "suede shoe" advertising agency, Ed would pragmatically and effectively direct a series of strategic, innovative measures that would prove 1932 a high-water-mark year in terms of new, prestigious model design, further improved quality of plans, and kits with resultant increased sales. The company's destiny would be further molded and shaped, and its growth would soar on the "power of superior graphics"—conceivably the most influential ingredient of C-D's marketing plan.

The dramatic accomplishments of the growth plan, as well as the expansion of the physical facility, were observed with awe and a certain degree of envy by the industry suppliers and competitors, as well as by the nation's modelers, and appeared to have been staged with strategic planning more characteristic of a Fortune 500 company. It took superior confidence and courage to implement the plan, despite the deepening national and worldwide economic malaise. However, each of these steps in C-D's evolutionary emergence emanated from the fertile mind of the single entrepreneur, Ed Pachasa, headquartered in the unpretentious residence and barn complex at 1866 West 57th Street on Cleveland's West Side.

While the aviation industry itself was negatively impacted by the economic straightjacket imposed by lack of adequate commercial and military funding, the doom-and-gloom economy could not totally throttle aviation design progress. In fact it could be argued that many small, struggling aircraft companies, soon to become famous, worldwide suppliers of desirable, dependable, high-performance aircraft, cut their eyeteeth during the challenging depression-plagued years of the 1930s. Subsequently, many of these companies became sufficiently developed by the end of the decade to form a stable, reliable, and powerful manufacturing base for the capabilities necessary to fuel America's pivotal aircraft-supplier role in World War II. There still existed pockets of capital in various fields, such as in oil, movies, publishing, and exporting, as well as in wealthy sportsmen, all of whom seemed to appear on the scene propitiously as "sugar daddies" to bankroll crucial aviation designs. Thus was the progress of America's aviation development propelled ever forward, despite the threatening economic shackles of the Depression.

Examples abound, such as Walter Beech's return to Wichita in April 1932 to found Beech Aircraft after having resigned from the Travel Air Division of Curtiss Wright. His revolutionary negative staggerwing 420 hp Beech 17-R and its successors would find a market with the Ethyl Corporation.

Clayton Brukner, financially astute president of Waco Aircraft, had fortunately taken his company public before the market crash and had a reserve of capital of $500,000. He wisely and prudently diversified his sales in the Latin American–export market with the successful development of the 190 mph Waco Model D military series. Eddie Stinson's lines of Reliants and Model U trimotor executive and feeder line transports were financed by the Cord-Lycoming conglomerate.

With a continuing "binge" of aerial achievements typified by Wiley Post and Harold Gatty's 1931 eight-day circumnavigation of the globe in their Lockheed Vega, sponsored by oil money, and with Doolittle's cross-continental eleven-hour, fifteen-minute speed dash in winning the first Bendix Trophy in Matty Laird's Super Solution, the stage was set for 1932 to eclipse the existing established speed and distance records and set blazing new marks of performance, harnessing American entrepreneurship and ingenuity and its airmen's bold and daring courage. Many of these heady, headline-making serial exploits were a fertile field from which C-D could select and expand its already impressive SF line of more than fifteen different models of famous aircraft.

Vying for leadership in sales to dealers and the patronage of America's model enthusiasts, C-D's 1932 kickoff featured an impressive outside back cover ad in the January issue of *Model Airplane News*, promoting membership in NAME before its demise later that year, and a repeat offer of kit SF-5 of the Bendix Trophy–winning Laird Super Solution at $2.50.

C-D had by now established itself as the industry leader in the exclusive modelers' niche with the most complete stable of National Air Race winners. With the introduction of the SF-2 1929 Travel Air Mystery Ship, the SF-46 1930 Thompson Trophy winner Laird Solution, and the SF-5 1931 Bendix Trophy winner Laird Super Solution, the lineup was current with the announcement in the inside-front-page ad in the April 1932 *Model Airplane News* for the 1931 Thompson Trophy winner SF-17 Lowell Bayle's Gee-Bee Z.

With its distinctive, contrasting yellow-and-black color scheme, streamlined wheel pants, and unorthodox compact, stubby, closely coupled design, expressly for "pylon polishing" (banking close to the pylons), the model was an instant hit with air race fans. It was to win many exhibition prizes for C-D modelers. The Gee-Bee Z made the racers' builders, the Granville brothers of Springfield, Massachusetts, famous almost overnight, and their subsequent revolutionary designs would be among the leading contenders in the early 1930s National Air Race classics.

In deference to the chilling economic climate, C-D made a bold marketing decision to offer both the Gee-Bee Z and Benny Howard's "Pete" racer kits available at $1.00 each for a limited time. Talk about bargains—an SF kit for a buck was unheard of.

Quite possibly, the multifarious elements of C-D's all-important graphic design program were anchored in highly developed professional photography, planned and personally directed by Ed Packard. These were dramatic

Designer-builder Matty Laird of E. M. Laird Company, Chicago, himself a former model builder of the Illinois Model Club, congratulates Maj. Jimmy Doolittle in the cockpit of his Laird Super Solution after Doolittle's winning the first Bendix Trophy dash from Los Angeles to Cleveland. Doolittle flew on to Newark to eclipse Frank Hawk's cross-country record (1931). *R. S. Hirsch Collection.*

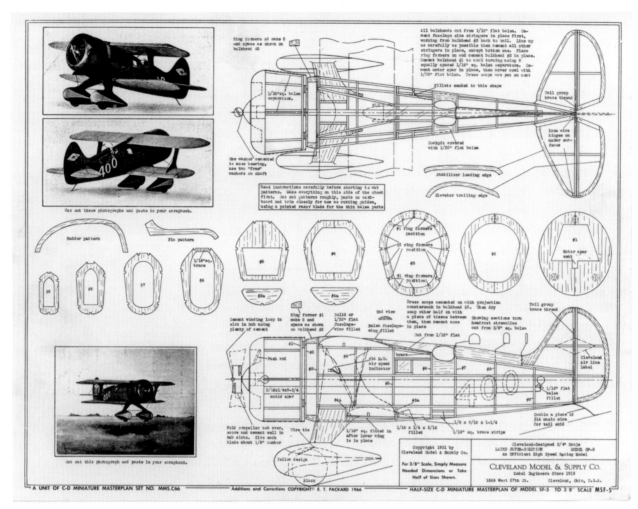

The SF-5 Laird Super Solution plans featured a turned cowl nose ring and semi-finished wheel pants and authentic markings. The 15⅞-inch span kit sold for a reduced price of $2.50. *E. T. Packard Collection.*

photos—realistic, inflight scenes and closeups of construction details; movable flight controls; flying and landing wires; engine components; insignia markings, and company logos. From the very first 1930 ad for the SF-1 Great Lakes Sport Trainer in *Model Airplane News,* Ed made the use of every aspect of photography in his graphics an integral part of his ads to dramatize, to the maximum, the appeal of C-D models.

Richardson Photography in Cleveland was a capable and willing partner in this important practice, and C-D ads were far and away the most compelling, attention-getting, and outstanding examples in the 1930s issues of *Model Airplane News.* Many had the impression that retouched photos of the prototypes had been used in the ads to achieve the desired effect; however, it was not the case. Richardson and Ed experimented with every possible type of backdrop to portray the model in flight. Various methods of propping up the model were involved to pose the model in dynamic, in-flight attitudes. Not many C-D ads would show the model in the typical "on the shelf," static position. Propellers were either left off or airbrushed or otherwise appeared to be spinning. When necessary, to further educate the novice as well as the

Lowell Bayles by his Gee-Bee Z 236.2 mph Thompson Trophy winner, with Jimmy Wedell a close second. Designed by Robert Hall, it established the Springfield Racing Association and the Granville brothers as racing contenders. Unfortunately, shortly after his victory, Bayles was killed during a crash while attempting to establish a new land plane speed record. Note the one-piece metal Curtiss-Reed fixed pitch propeller (1931). *R. S. Hirsch Collection.*

seasoned modeler, flying and landing wires, control cables, bracing, and flight control surfaces would be retouched to emphasize the many details of the particular model.

Every one of the photographs of the entire SF series went through this exhaustive routine to discover what pose, what flight attitude, what lighting against which backdrop would best portray the élan of a particular model. Ed had breathed so much realism and scale accuracy into each design that he was able to project the personality of each model to such an extent that in most cases the buffs found them irresistible.

In its relentless pursuit of industry leadership, C-D dominated the advertisers in the June 1932 issue of *Model Airplane News* with an inside-back-cover, blue-toned ad, featuring a smashing photo of the Supermarine S-B Schneider Trophy winner, plus a full-page ad announcing a model that would join the SF-1 Great Lakes Sport Trainer kit as the all-time "flagship design" of the C-D fleet—the Curtiss Hawk P6-E, a breathtakingly beautiful, taper-winged biplane with a striking olive drab and chrome yellow color scheme, streamlined cowled 600 hp Curtiss Conqueror liquid-cooled engine, and slick single strut cantilever landing gear, with wheels housed in sleek owl-talon-decorated wheel pants. A later, modified kit would be offered with the addition of the distinctive markings and the "great snow owl" insignia of the 17th Squadron of the First Pursuit Group, based at Selfridge Field, Michigan. When this squadron flew in formation and performed aerobatics in military precision at the 1932 National Air Races in Cleveland, they left the crowd spellbound, and every kid who saw them had to have a model of the thrilling P6-E Hawk.

May 1932 saw the introduction of the first of a series of publications that, in addition to the outstanding appeal of C-D advertising, would establish the company unequivocally as the industry leader in graphics—the first issue of the *Cleveland Model Engineers News,* at five cents, "Devoted to the Interests of Cleveland Model Engineers for the Building of Fewer but Better Models."

Its first headline, "Model Aircraft Is Cheapest Hobby," was in keeping with the Depression. The impressive tabloid, a 5½-by-8⅝-inch self-mailer that unfolded to a 17⅜-by-22-inch, four-page broadside, was an instant hit with its newspaper format and small type, bolstered by many dramatic photos of Cleveland models in flight and the liberal use of boldface type for emphasis. Ed labored long and unceasingly to write the copy and do the layout to achieve maximum impact.

He had mastered the art of space management, and in every ad and subsequent promotional graphic arts publication he was able to squeeze an unbelievable amount of copy in such space as was available. Volume 1, no. 1, is certainly a collector's item today, and its message and advertising still send the clarion call that "Cleveland models are the best." Another characteristic of his publications was the inclusion of numerous testimonials, always a powerful, effective way to convey the message.

To capitalize on some daring merchandising promotion, the SF-18 Howard "Pete" racer was offered for $1, postage free. Ed confided that this particular kit, offered in subsequent direct mail and other advertising media, was his most successful, albeit not the most profitable. It was only made direct to modelers for that price; there was no way a dealer discount could be included (however, later discounts were allowed in dozen lots).

In recalling the concept of *Cleveland Model Engineers News,* Ed remarked, "It began basically as a house organ, which I felt our young, relatively less-known company needed to promote our extensive line and report on important aviation events such as the Harmon Trophy–Doolittle Chamber of Commerce luncheon. C-D's rapport with famous airmen such as Captain Dick, Doolittle, Bishop, and Rickenbacker could be dramatized, and in the process it also became an important adjunct to our marketing program to boost our acceptance with our embryonic dealer organization, for none of the other large manufacturers such as Ideal had anything to equal it during that era."

Cleveland Modelmaking News and Practical Hobbies *Announced*

"It was while I was racking my brain to dream up some compelling copy for a subsequent issue of *Cleveland Model Engineers News,*" mused Ed, "that I had a 'brainstorm.' Modelers were having a tough time coming up with the money to buy our kits. However, we knew there was a demand out there, because our dealers kept reordering, we received inquiries and orders from foreign countries, and the kids themselves kept telling us that our models were the most realistic and, yes, they did fly as well as we said. So, why not make it possible for them to get the plans as painlessly as possible and then let them buy the supplies on their own, piecemeal, as they could afford it?"

Secretly, he had always harbored the concept of C-D ultimately becoming a complete hobby business, where hobbyists could purchase their plans, supplies, and tools to build not only airplane models but ship models, trains, autos, and other hobby projects, plus helpful "how to" hints. So, why not expand the *Cleveland Model Engineers News* into a magazine format? C-D already had more than enough plans to get started, and Ed's draftsman friends

Vol. I, no. 1 (1933) of *Cleveland Modelmaking News and Practical Hobbies* featured the SF-27 Gee-Bee plans on the cover and included some six projects—all for only a quarter. With its full-sized plans, data, and low price, *CMN&PH* set an unrivaled precedent for hobby magazines at that time. *E. T. Packard Collection.*

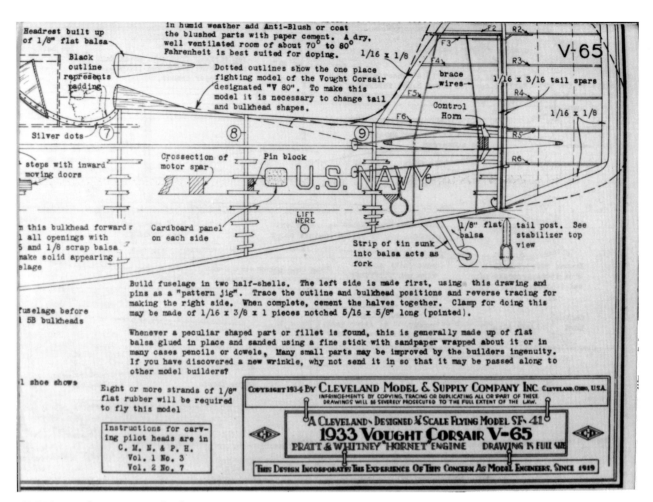

CMN&PH, vol. I, no. 7, contained plans for an SF-41 Vought Corsair V-65, Packard Phaeton, a Union Pacific 3/16-inch scale streamlined train, and other hobby projects. *E. T. Packard Collection.*

from the former Glenn L. Martin Company engineering department were capable of drawing more.

With the insight of a Solomon, Ed marshaled his meager but capable, competent, and dedicated forces and announced to the ever-faithful Pachasa family that C-D was about to publish its own magazine. And, since his hope was to eventually build a complete hobby business, why not call it *Cleveland Modelmaking News and Practical Hobbies (CMN&PH)*?

As the plan unfolded, it was projected to have ten issues appearing bimonthly, beginning with volume 1, no. 1, as the January–February 1933 issue at 25 cents, or six issues for a dollar. Of course, the creative and print resources of the ever-dependable Carpenter ad agency were extremely important elements in making this dream a reality. By including design plans in *CMN&PH*, C-D offered a new line of kits without plans (N kits), making these kits available at a substantial price reduction.

When the first issue made its debut in December 1932 in time for the holidays, it consisted of twenty-four pages, not including the separate ¾-inch scale plans for the Gee-Bee R-1 and the Heath Parasol, having a total of seventeen items to build. All for 25 cents. Could Madison Avenue ingenuity have equaled this phenomenal accomplishment in 1932? As further testimony to the entrepreneur's gutsy optimism, he decided on an initial print order of 25,000.

In retrospect, 1932 was indeed a pivotal year for C-D's mercurial growth in so many ways that it had to be extremely challenging for its twenty-six-year-old president. Before the year was out, he would manage to keep abreast of the many milestones in new aircraft designs by announcing the JSF-1005 kit of the Boeing B-9, a radically revolutionary low-wing twin engine bomber that, with its nearly 200 mph top speed, exceeded that of most of its escort pursuit contemporaries.

Ed, never to shirk his dedication to authenticity, reproduced the multi-engine configuration by having the motive rubber power housed in the fuselage, with a pulley transmission to each nacelle. This power feature had never before been offered by any other model manufacturer. His prior multiengine-powered models, the FL-301 Cleveland Amphibion [*sic*], the FL-302 Cleveland Trimotor, and the F1–304 Commodore Flying Boat, had all utilized rubber-powered motor spars outboard of the fuselage.

Since the Lockheed Vega had been involved in so many record-making flights by famous aviators such as Wiley Post and Amelia Earhart, by the end of the year it made its debut as the SF-24, along with the SF-25 Curtiss A-8 Attack. It was the latest addition to the U.S. Army Air Corps winged armada in the conversion of its fleet of aging, outmoded biplanes to the innovative, speedier low-wing, mostly all-metal monoplane designs.

It is indeed difficult to visualize Ed as having a semblance of a normal domestic life with the many long hours he kept in the process of starting C-D. However, love always finds a way, and on June 2, 1932, he was married to Emily Novak. They would have two children: a daughter, Doris Jean, and a son, Robert Douglas, who was named after Ed's role model, Donald Douglas. Robert would become an expert model builder and ultimately became the proprietor of an impressive hobby shop in Cleveland.

Behind the Flight Line at the Cleveland National Air Races

As already related, over the years Ed had developed a close relationship with the Cleveland airport superintendent, Maj. Jack Berry, who was most always able to alert Ed whenever any new military type, air racer, experimental test type, or otherwise unusual aircraft would land. This unique arrangement enabled Ed to scamper out the nine miles to the field in his conspicuously marked Austin Coupe and quickly scale off dimensions and make copious notes of construction, markings, and color-scheme details. The result was that C-D usually scooped its competitors by not only being first to introduce

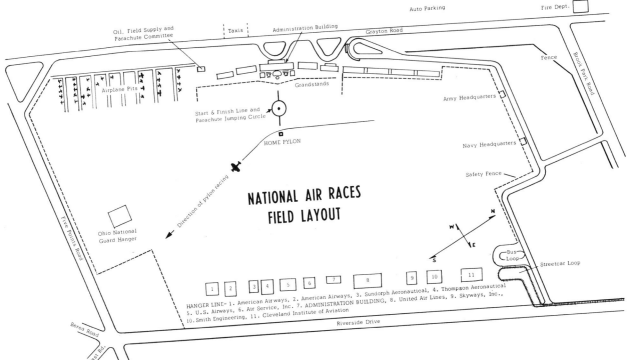

NATIONAL AIR RACES
FIELD LAYOUT

HANGER LINE- 1. American Airways, 2. American Airways, 3. Sundorph Aeronautical, 4. Thompson Aeronautical
5. U.S. Airways, 6. Air Service, Inc. 7. ADMINISTRATION BUILDING, 8. United Air Lines, 9. Skyways, Inc.,
10. Smith Engineering, 11. Cleveland Institute of Aviation

Above: The field layout for the Cleveland Municipal Airport for the 1932 National Air Races. The area at the top of the layout, along Grayton Road, was the area where Packard's modelers were allowed to fly their models. Charles Mandrake, *National Air Races 1932: A Pictorial Review.*

Below left: The official program for the 1932 Cleveland National Air Races, with cover art by Thompson Products (TRW) artist Charles Hubbell. *Author's Collection.*

Below right: Charles Thompson (left), president of Thompson Products and sponsor of the Thompson Trophy, presents the trophy to Jimmy Doolittle as the 1932 winner at the Cleveland National Air Races. *Author's Collection.*

a new National Air Race winner, but the plan would be the most detailed, complete, authentic reproduction available.

C-D's next model illustrates the success that resulted from the careful attention paid to producing these plans. Partly because of his friendship with the flamboyant Jimmy Doolittle, Ed felt obligated to offer Doolittle's Gee-Bee R-1 as the next model kit, the SF-27. Capitalizing on its unorthodox design and the appeal of its record-breaking performance (winning both the Thompson

Left: SF-17 Gee-Bee Supersportster R-1 1932 Thompson Trophy winner. This kit became a landmark identification for C-D. The model was really one of the first of the super-detailed series for which Cleveland Models were famous. This posed scene would easily pass for the real thing, and the modelers loved it. It was a top seller for many years. Span: 18½ inches, at $2.50. *E. T. Packard Collection.*

Below: SF-27 Gee-Bee miniature master plan, showing the half-shell method and the many details to make this model a real C-D milestone (1933). *E. T. Packard Collection.*

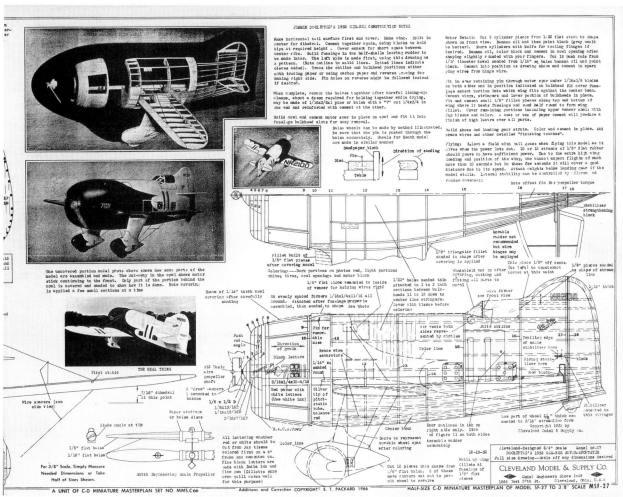

Trophy at 252.86 mph and the Shell speed Dash at 296.28 in 1932), the R-1 was featured on the cover of the first issue of *CMN&PH*. It was also the headliner in the January 1933 *Model Airplane News* full-page ad offering the N2 kit (without plans) at $1.00, only sold direct. As a testimony to its authenticity, to this day aging modelers, veteran pilots, and National Air Race fans of the 1930s often associate the Gee-Bee R-1 with Cleveland Model and Supply.

C-D's Emergence as a Cottage Industry and Hobby Store

C-D's ambitious marketing development, which included a panoply of dramatic, arresting graphics, required not only the creative leadership that the young president brought to bear but also necessitated an adequate, functional physical facility. With economic restraint imposed more or less on most businesses during the early 1930s, for C-D to have assumed the added financial liability of an industrial plant site was out of the question. The heart of C-D's expansion, therefore, was dependent on the Pachasas' determination and ingenuity to modify and develop their residence and premises to the needs of their budding enterprise. In view of the subsequent spectacular success that C-D realized, I had to ask the Master Model Engineer just how it was accomplished.

Ed enthusiastically began: "The Pachasa family occupied the original home at 1866 West 57th from 1924 to 1937, with its garage converted from a former horse-and-buggy barn. Initially I kept my 1923 Harley-Davidson twin motorcycle with sidecar [$368 new] and later, when I could afford it, my 1929 Essex in one half of the garage, and our tiny retail store comprised the other half. This hobby store, small though it was, actually was the first, or nearly so the first, such enterprise in the entire country, for hobby stores did not exist yet.

"A 28-inch-wide stairway led to the loft above, which became my office and engineering department above the store. The shipping room was located in the other half of the loft above the garage, separated by a wall. Four of us worked amazingly compatibly and effectively in this compact second-floor area."

For C-D to become an effective competitive manufacturer, it had to have a certain degree of automation, and that meant power equipment. The only feasible way to develop the necessary space was to excavate and enlarge the existing basement area beneath the home. This was accomplished via an expenditure of $700, a formidable amount during the Depression.

"In 1931, Ed explained, "I had had the kitchen roof raised to provide a second story for office space, where we employed three to four clerical people. It was there where I dictated every word of *CMN&PH*, while sitting at my huge 300-pound walnut desk, which I still have.

"Including my father, mother, and four brothers, we employed as many as fourteen people, all males, during busy periods without getting in each other's way.

"Adequate shelving to sell kits and supplies plus display space to exhibit each finished model of our twenty-five-unit SF line, as well as the simplified FL [freelance, not exact scale] designs, was a must; so, fortunately, we were able to rent at $25 per month the former small grocery store at the corner of West 57th and Bridge."

When C-D was able to move its kits and supplies, and finished display models into the rented store, it began a new era for C-D, for Ed was able to witness the reactions of young and old alike as their eyes expressed their amazement and delight at seeing the beautifully constructed and finished SF line of models acting as a silent salesman for C-D. Similarly, when a dealer or a future dealer was able to see firsthand the thoroughness of construction and scale realism of the entire line, it became the lynchpin, clinching the deal. Ed recalled, "I was telling myself that, then and there, if we were to take C-D into the big leagues, we would ultimately need a much larger display room, which would in itself be an attraction, a sort of museum for modelers, dealers, parents of future modelers, and all types of hobbyists. Through the maximum utilization of space, ingenious display arrangements, and the absolute dedication of my brother Fred, who wanted to run the store, we successfully operated and occupied this location until 1937, when C-D was moved to the Lorain Avenue site."

Appropriately timed to appear before Christmas, C-D's center-spread ads in the 1932 November and December issues of *Model Airplane News* carried an announcement of "Cleveland's new hobby store," listing directions for its location and advising the reader that all forty-five flying model kits comprising the entire C-D line would be on display.

These humble facilities, epitomizing the often overdramatized American "cottage industry," hosted thousands not only from all corners of America but from Canada and Europe as well, including modelers, dealers, aviation and model airplane journalists, competitors, families, youth leaders, teachers, and the curious—all of whom expressed astonishment that C-D was able to accomplish so much in such limited space. Perhaps it further impressed them that, with a highly professional finished product line, it was able to create the illusion that C-D must be a manufacturer of much greater magnitude.

Ed said, "Had I deliberated longer before committing the investment money needed to expand our residential site in light of the critical economy, I may have had second thoughts. However, new model designs, advertising, new publications, new carton designs, advertising reps, and new aviation industry breakthroughs provided constant challenges, and I enthusiastically embraced the continual decision-making process necessary to the company's success."

Under a boldfaced "Features" block in the December 1932 issue of *Model Airplane News* was a most important notice: four of the latest SF kits (SF-22, -23, -24, and -25) all contained printwood, which meant there was no more tracing patterns onto balsa for all the curved parts. This feature was one of the greatest developments to simplify model construction and made it possible for much more rapid and accurate building techniques. Ed had been experimenting with John Poly, a nearby printer, and a technique was perfected using 2-by-18-inch and 3-by-18-inch zinc "cuts," which produced sharp, dark images consistently.

C-D enforced rigid specifications on the balsa purchased from Balsa Wood Company of New York and International Balsa Company of New Jersey. Prem Gary, their contact representative, was instructed to ship only Triple A, kiln-dried balsa, which they were soon purchasing in carload lots to get the lowest prices and to ensure an adequate supply. With this select quality of balsa for sheets, the printer was able to improve the resultant quality of the printwood, and C-D was most likely the first major model manufacturer to offer it as a standard item. (The 1933 mailer catalog 12B folder listed the following kits with printwood: SF-1G, -17B, -18B, -22B, -23, -24, -25, -34, -36, -37, -38, -39, and -40.)

Ultimately, Ed was able to purchase his own printing equipment and was no longer dependent on outside printers for delivery. It was only during the early years of World War II, when large orders were received from the military, that C-D had to resort to outside assistance for printwood, and it was then that a longterm relationship with Bob Tufts, who had leased the Poly Printing plant, came in handy, for he had the capability to deliver printwood almost on demand.

The world of retail merchandising exacts certain requirements on those entrepreneurs, manufacturers, and distributors who would qualify for "facings" of their products on the retailers' much-sought-after counters, gondola shelving, display cases, and featured endcap promotions. Companies such as Hawk, Aurora, Monogram, Revell, and Hasegawa have wisely resorted to having the top aviation artists, such as Joseph Kotula, John Amendola, and John Batchelor, create full-color paintings of accurate, in-flight scenes of the actual prototype aircraft on their packaging. The illustrations have become so realistic and compelling that the modeler or buff collector anxiously believes that one must be bought for his collection before the current run is sold out. Thousands of these kits are thus purchased daily, transactions that otherwise would not have caused the cash register to ring had it not been for the colorful, artistic, arresting design of these cartons. Often, the kits are purchased but never constructed. Otherwise somewhat drab, unappealing hobby shops and hobby departments in retail stores and mass merchandisers have been converted into appealing, attractive display areas by these uniquely designed kit boxes, in many cases negating the need for any clerk sales assistance.

The sweet smell of success that C-D experienced with their unprecedented national introduction of the SF-1 and SF-2 kits was accomplished despite the unconventional packaging in a red and silver cardboard tube (called "hobby tubes") that accommodated the outstanding rolled plan, strip and sheet balsa, rubber strands, cement, and miscellaneous parts. However, this tube hardly lent itself to the needs of the retailer when it came to displaying the kit on the shelves of the department stores, one of the most important outlets then.

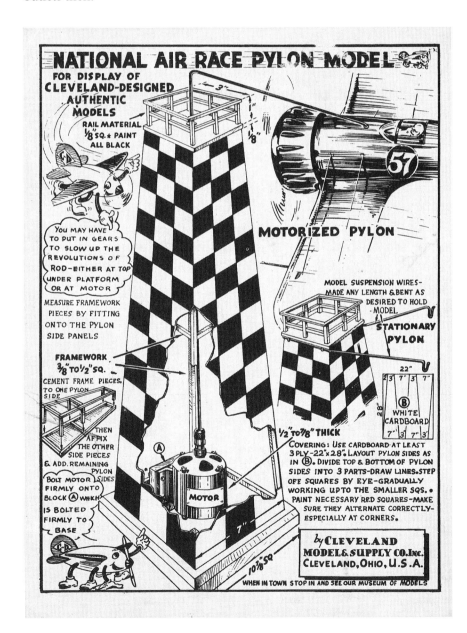

The National Air Race Pylon model instruction sheet illustrating how the modeler could use a small electric motor hidden in a pylon to have a whirling model, simulating the real air races. Some of these pylons were used in window displays in retail stores. *E. T. Packard Collection.*

The boys' departments, boys' clubs, model clubs, or toy departments in America's famous department stores, such as R. H. Macy, Gimbels, Stearns, May Company, Bambergers, Hahnes, Wanamakers, Marshall Field, Higbees, Halle Bros., the Emporium, Bullocks, and the Broadway, were the target markets for C-D. It was in these prestigious retailers that the American boy was king and C-D's ticket to fame and fortune.

The twenty-five-year-old zealous entrepreneur of C-D was much more sophisticated in the ways of the world of business than his chronological age belied. Hence, he impressed on the Pachasa family and the staff at Carpenter Advertising the dire need for switching the packaging design of the SF line to a more conventional carton design. Ed had been astutely observing the progress of his major competitor, Ideal, and how they had developed a standard company image on their cartons, albeit not particularly attractive or outstanding. Several of his retail customers were offering carton design suggestions, and he also shrewdly sought out shelf carton designs from the staff at some well-known carton manufacturers in Cleveland, such as J. Poly and Sons and United Paper Box Company, who collectively had several outstanding, successful clients.

Because of the higher priority of developing printwood and the time required to create and write the first issue of *CMN&PH,* the carton design change was delayed. In the interim, the prosaic, existing red tube was dressed up with a photo of the specific model and imprinted with a message, "Slit here," to make it easier for the modeler to open.

C-D had established a token identity with its two-color, dark-blue diamond with a white "C" in reverse on light blue, the Cleveland blue diamond signifying "quality made." The Pachasa family, typical of many American families with immigrant origins, felt deeply loyal to their new country and all it represented, and this patriotism may have influenced C-D's decision to adopt the colors of the American flag in its design graphics wherever appropriate.

Approximately three years of C-D's initial corporate operation would have swiftly passed before it was possible to phase in chipboard cartons for the SF line.

The New C-D Carton

The choice of silver for the basic color of the carton design was effective and with minor exceptions remained throughout the evolution of the carton graphics until cost considerations forced the background color to become the natural white or off-white of the chipboard stock. However, the attractive combination of red, white, and blue colors was to be the image of C-D and, indeed, gave it an identity entirely unto itself.

The first arrangement used in the sequence of carton design incorporated on the silver background twin jet-black stripes at either end of the label

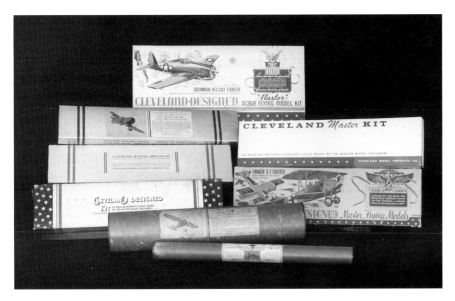

Development of cartons from mailing tubes to Master Flying Kits. From bottom, clockwise: Eaglerock Alexander Bullet FL 105; PZL-SF-6 mailing tube with pictorial label; 1935 "All American Carton" in red, silver, and blue, by James Powell; the first carton (1933–34), with blue stripes but no picture-descriptive label; the second carton (1934), with black stripes and red, white, and blue stripes on a picture label; red, white, and blue master kit with removable lid and center space for furnished liquids; red, white, and blue master kit with no descriptive label; red and blue with white stars master kit with background of natural paper. *Ruth Chinn Collection.* July 1979 *Sport Aviation* (EAA), showing the Brown *Miss Los Angeles* followed by Bill Turner's Gee-Bee Z, owned by Disney Industries, that appeared in the movie, *The Rocketeer.* Both the Brown *Miss Los Angeles* and the Gee-Bee Z were originally built for Bill Turner by Ed Marquardt. *Author's Collection.*

on the face of the box. The label bore no illustration of the specific SF model, which was designated on the end flap.

The next step in the carton evolution coincided with the announcement of the SF-17 kit Gee-Bee Z in 1932. The twin stripes had now become an attractive royal blue, and the label was enlarged, printed in red and blue on white, and incorporated an in-flight photo of the aircraft. The nomenclature was separated from the photo by red, white, and blue stripes. This example might have been the first carton with the patriotic color scheme. Ed related that as each carton design evolved, a certain quantity of cartons was reserved for the SF-1 Great Lakes Sport Trainer. It was such a perpetually solid seller that placing it in the latest carton could always ensure another spurt in its sales.

The development of the C-D carton design continued on when James D. Powell, an outstanding artist from Boston whose artistic ability was to have a major influence on the carton and promotion graphic designs from 1934 on, joined the C-D staff.

Suffice it to say that with its new carton designs, Cleveland Model and Supply Company further qualified for access to the space and visibility on the shelves of the nation's major department stores to slug it out with the competition.

The elements of the C-D marketing plan were unquestionably customer driven. The impetus given to the growing company by the power of superior graphics was evident in the sensational *CMN&PH* magazine, the dramatic and realistic ads, the introduction of printwood, the switch from tubes to cartons, and the development of the physical facility with a separate retail store.

If Ed had had a script or blueprint precisely listing and defining each step of his marketing plan, C-D's progress for the years immediately following 1928 could not have evolved more logically, effectively, or sooner, particularly in context of the depressed economy and the extremely limited staff.

CHAPTER 8

The Era of the C-D "Giants" versus the Pylon Polishers

 WHILE THE NATION'S 1933 unemployment rate inched up slightly to the highest ever of 25.1 percent (12.7 million unemployed), the following years would witness a gradual decrease in the rate and a mini–economic recovery from 1935 to 1937.

Commercial aircraft manufacturing produced a significant upward trend in 1933, with a tripling of its unit value to $6.2 million from the $2.3 million at the bottom in 1932. Units had only a slight increase from 549 to 596. However, 1934 would experience a surge of demand, driving units produced up 30 percent, from 591 to 772, and unit values up 66 percent from $6.2 million to $10 million

During the years following 1934, unit production would increase by degree and remain in four digits. However, manufacturing units would never achieve the 5,357 units at $33.6 million attained during the overproduction year of 1929 until military demand swelled because of the lend-lease agreement with the future Allies in Europe, begun in 1939.

Aviation's development juggernaut would continue to disavow the constraints of the economy by etching the pages of its history with major milestones of design in both military and civil aircraft. Consequently, in fulfilling his destiny as "aviation's great recruiter," C-D's president would have the increased opportunity to offer aeromodelers outstanding choices of miniatures of revolutionary new aircraft as America's designers bent to the task of creating innovative craft to accommodate the expanding airlines, to meet the demands of the speed seekers and the pylon polishers, and to make it possible for the U.S. military to be able to meet the challenge of the formidable worldwide opponents of democracy. It was Ed's passion to chronicle aviation's historical development by producing the most significant aircraft in the most accurate designs possible.

The "Peashooter"

The February 1933 issue of *Model Airplane News* introduced the C-D SF-23 version of the Boeing P-26A, the first production, all-metal, Army Air Corps monoplane fighter (230 mph). The P-26A diminutive fighter ("peashooter") was another trendsetting aircraft from the Boeing engineering powerhouse led by Bill Boeing and Clair Egtvedt, who had startled the aviation world with the all-metal 135 mph Monomail 221A with retractable landing gear in 1930, followed by the all-metal 160 mph B-9 bomber in 1931. It would also be the last open-cockpit type, the last with fixed gear and externally braced wing, and the last Boeing production fighter. Its high landing speed of 82.5

A C-D mailing broadside from 1932 listed the complete line at that time. *E. T. Packard Collection.*

William Winter, a modeler and editor of *Air Trails, MAN, American Modeler,* and *Model Aviation,* here flies his Wakefield type model. *Author's Collection.*

The 1933 SF-23 Boeing P-26A, span 20¾ inches, was sold for $1.95. It featured a chrome-yellow and olive-drab color scheme with printwood, drag ring, machine guns, moveable control surfaces, flying and landing wires, detailed cockpit layout, pilot bust, plus insignia and markings of the 34th Pursuit Squadron. *E. T. Packard Collection.*

mph was reduced to 73 mph with the addition of wing flaps. The SF-23 kit at $1.95 included printwood with super detailed plans of the P&W Wasp drag ring, crankcase cover plate, supercharger, exhausts and breathers, machine guns and sight, movable control surfaces, flying and landing wires, and a detailed cockpit layout, pilot bust, plus insignia and markings of the 34th Pursuit Squadron.

In his further assessment of the advertising value of the aviation/model airplane publications, Ed had been urged to further consider *Popular Aviation*'s greater circulation. *Popular Aviation* magazine debuted in August 1927, riding the wave of Lindbergh euphoria, and had a two-year lead time on *Model*

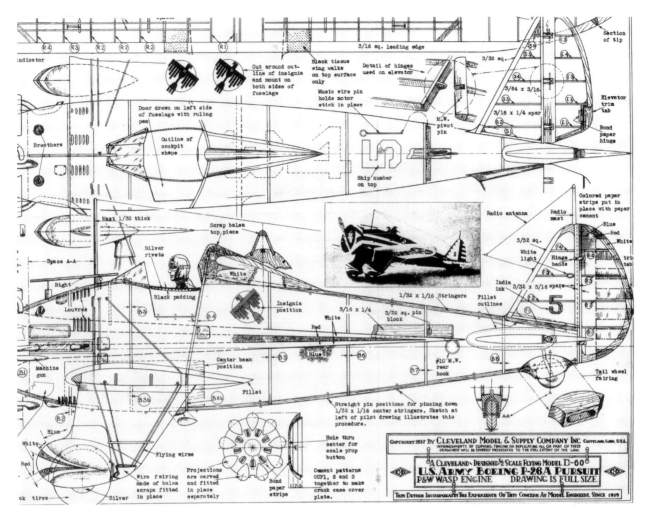

Airplane News, published in July 1929. It could boast of a greater and more diverse circulation. In conjunction with his ad agency, Ed began a modest program with *Popular Aviation* in March 1929 and relatively small ads in 1930. In the June 1931 issue, C-D took the inside back cover to promote Rickenbacker's Spad and the other C-D World War I designs. From then on, C-D would maintain a significant presence in the publication, in contention with Comet of Chicago, which locked in the back cover on most issues. Other competitors were Ideal and Scientific of Newark.

Consequently, *Popular Aviation*'s March 1933 issue had a ⅓-page C-D ad promoting the feisty P-26A. A definitive comparison could be made by evaluating model editor Joseph Ott's scale flying model plans in the early issues of *Popular Aviation* to C-D plans. The polarity was especially evident in the August 1932 issue. Ott's Great Lakes Sport Trainer plan was a vague, unrealistic-looking version, with no control surfaces shown and no flying or landing wires. It also handicapped the modeler with the outmoded use of bamboo for curved surfaces. Ott apparently felt young modelers to be incapable of mastering the

The SF-49 Curtiss F11C-2, also known as the "Goshawk," was one of the most detailed of the Curtiss fighters, with a span of 23½ inches. Packard received a letter from the Navy commending its authenticity. *E. T. Packard Collection.*

The SF-49 Curtiss F11C-2 uncovered exhibition model shows the scale rib spacing and detailed armament as well as the realism of the radial engine. *E. T. Packard Collection.*

technicalities involved. The difference—Ed's regard for modelers was visceral—was that at C-D "model engineers" were eager to learn all the design details of the prototype, and every one of the SF plans was literally an education in aviation design.

The Flying Pullmans

The airlines were sorely in need of a more modern, faster, increased-passenger-capacity replacement for the venerable "Tin Goose," Ford 4AT Trimotor that served the passenger and cargo carriers reliably from 1926 to 1930, albeit with the limitations imposed by its 107 mph cruise, ten-passenger capacity, and limited 570 mile range—with abundant noise and vibration. Since Boeing's empire included United Air Transport, they conveniently had a captive market for any of their new airline designs to replace the aging, outmoded Boeing 80-A trimotored biplane transport.

In the race for the emerging lucrative airline transport market, Boeing drew first blood when their 247D prototype first flew in February 1933. Subsequently, United Transport, which became UAL, received the first sixty delivered to them and thus could enjoy a tremendous competitive edge over Jack Frye's TWA, Rickenbacker's Eastern, and C. R. Smith's American Airlines.

However, when Frye first evaluated this imbalance of competition posed by the interlocking relationship between Boeing and UAL, he fired off a letter to five major airframe producers, requesting their bids on a three-engined transport to cruise at 150 mph with other specifications. Douglas Aircraft Company was the first to reply. Douglas's chief engineer James "Dutch" Kindleberger, who would later become North American Aviation's CEO, and assistant chief engineer Arthur Raymond convinced TWA to accept the plans for their twin-engined 200 mph fourteen-passenger version to be known as the DC-1 (Douglas Commercial) in September 1932.

With a prodigious and resourceful management effort, Donald Douglas, who had cut his eyeteeth in engineering at Glenn L. Martin's Cleveland plant on the MB-1, fielded his all-star engineering team at their modern Santa Monica, California, plant and produced the DC-1 prototype that had its rollout and first flight in July 1933, just six months after the 247D rollout.

The press announced the 247D with a great deal of publicity, since it was the first all-metal, streamlined transport equipped with retractable landing gear, trim tabs to ease pilot fatigue, and the first such monoplane powered

Boeing 247D prototype shown on takeoff from Chicago Municipal Airport. It was the first all-metal streamlined transport equipped with retractable landing gear and trim tabs to ease pilot fatigue and was the first such monoplane powered with twin engines and Hamilton all-metal variable pitch props to provide maximum takeoff and cruising performance (1933). *Author's Collection.*

with twin engines and Hamilton all-metal variable pitch props to provide maximum takeoff and cruising performance.

TWA, as well as Eastern, was to have sweet revenge on United when, on February 18, 1934, Rick and Frye teamed up in the cockpit of the newly delivered DC-1 and set a new record for transports of thirteen hours, two minutes from Los Angeles to Newark. Until United finally received the DC-2s they were forced to order to remain competitive, it was United's turn to be stuck with a fleet of airliners experiencing rapid obsolescence.

Ironically, Douglas Aircraft Company assumed the lead in the air transport market when it introduced its fabled DC-3 in 1935, maintaining its dominance over Boeing until 1958. In August 1958 Boeing engineered a four-engined, jet-powered 707, 600 mph, 189-passenger capacity transport, regaining the lead in an absolutely marvelous coup. Nearly a year elapsed before the Douglas DC-8 jet would be delivered.

The First of the C-D "Giants": SF-35-247D

Ed and the Pachasa family faced the decision of whether their growing company, with a well-deserved reputation for authentic designs, should take the risk involved in producing a large-size, ¾-inch scale design, since the 247D model would have a 55-inch wingspan. Competitively, there was really no choice, because C-D had to maintain its hard-fought position of leadership in the scale flying field, and since it had been learned via the industry grapevine that Comet would be offering a smaller version of the plane with about a 2-foot wingspan, the die was cast.

In recalling the gravity of this decision, Ed remarked, "I gathered my draftsmen together to evaluate their input—Rudy Germain, George Ratzmer, and John Sinko. They were intrigued by the prospect of creating the largest rubber-powered scale flying kit then on the market and were almost feeling honored to have the opportunity to be a part of such an undertaking. They felt that it was almost like being a part of the design of a real aircraft. I further

The kit for the 1933 F-35 Boeing 247, with a 53-inch span, for sale at $6.50, was the first of the C-D "giants" (shipped in a 40-inch wooden box at a total weight of 10 pounds). The kit's plans consisted of four 17-by-44-inche panels. The finished model weighed 16 ounces and had turned engine nacell cowls, a partially finished nose block, cabin details, detailed engines, and retractable landing gear. *E. T. Packard Collection.*

contacted some of my friends who were in the drafting department of Martin, plus my mentor, Captain Dick. It was a strong consensus that we waste no time nor allow Comet or any other modeling company to jump in and have a scoop of the market."

Aside from the strong support of the C-D staff, there was the matter of price; something with a 55-inch wingspan and the incumbent design considerations of the rest of the structure meant that this was a much larger undertaking. With the ominous Depression still very much in evidence, a price of $9–10 was out of the question. So, with the able assistance and wise counsel of Will, who functioned as general superintendent and woodshop foreman as well, Ed began the laborious task of estimating, realizing that the costs of all that balsa and other materials, plus the large plans needed, were formidable. Finally they began getting the price down into the $7–10 dollar ballpark."

Once again his draftsmen were at their boards. and Ed was in his office until the wee hours for many nights until the construction plans and kit components were mastered. To capitalize on all of the effort involved and further entrench itself in the catbird seat of scale flying modeling, C-D committed to the first inside page in the October 1933 issue of *Model Airplane News,* and, simultaneously, the same full-page ad was placed in the October issue of *Popular Aviation.* The ad layout featured two dramatic, realistic photos of the SF-35 247D, one in flight and one static, with a price of $6.50. The ad copy advised the modeler that the finished model would weigh 16 ounces, powered with a motor spar protruding from the rear of each nacelle, including a finished nose block, finished cowlings, finished wheels, and all the necessary tissue and colored dopes required. It was also stated that the SF-35 would be shipped in a 40-inch wood box, express only. (Ed confided that he was pleasantly surprised during the test flights of the first finished model when it rose to a height of thirty to forty feet and flew remarkably well.) An initial run of 100 kits was cautiously fabricated.

As had been expected, Comet Model Airplane and Supply was going all out to position itself in the scale flying market with this prestigious aircraft and

The 1932 Martin B-10B all-metal bomber, with a span 70 feet 6 inches, was powered with two 750 hp Wright "Cyclones" and reached a top speed of 207 mph, making it the world's fastest bomber. It also featured retractable landing gear, the first powered transparent gun turret on a U.S. bomber, sliding cockpit enclosures, and an internal bomb bay and had a capacity of 2,260 pounds, all of which contributed to its receipt of the prestigious Collier Trophy. *Author's Collection.*

opted for the outside back cover of *Model Airplane News* for the October, November, and December issues, advertising their 23-inch wingspan, rubber-powered pulley transmission-driven version at $1.50. Likewise, Comet further committed itself in *Popular Aviation* for a combination of inside-front and outside-back cover ads. C-D's strategy was to place full-page ads in the October and November issues of *Popular Aviation,* and then in the December issue C-D made its presence further felt with a double-page center spread.

Radial Engine Renaissance

At the opposite end of the aviation spectrum from the military, civil aircraft were experiencing a renaissance to meet the more demanding specifications imposed by the rapidly expanding commercial market. No longer acceptable to businessmen were the open cockpit, drafty, cold, noisy, wet, uncomfortable, and often unreliable OX-5 powered models.

With the introduction of the more powerful, more economical, more reliable radial power plants by commercial aviation, business began to realize that valuable travel time could be saved by switching to private air transportation. Major commercial aircraft companies such as Stinson, Fairchild, Travel Air, and Curtiss had wisely converted a substantial portion of their production to cabin types.

In the shadow of Dayton's Wright-Patterson Air Force Base, Waco Aircraft Company had been located in a modern, new plant in Troy, Ohio, since 1928. Clayton Brukner, cofounder and president, had prudently and effectively managed Waco into one of the most financially sound and successful commercial aircraft firms, with a diversified cadre of Waco owners domestically and worldwide in thirty-five countries. The Waco name had become synonymous with the popular Waco 10 and its ATO J-5 Taperwing had been

Renowned aviation artist, historian, and author Charles H. Hubbell at his easel, where he painted more than 350 scenes describing the history of man in flight. The scenes shown are from Thompson Products' (TRW, Inc.) annual calendars, which he began in 1939. *Author's Collection.*

SF-37 Waco C cabin with its beautiful elliptical wing tips and tail configuration. Wing and landing gear fillets and the absence of rigging (except for wing struts) made this C-D model a highly desirable kit. Francis Arcier, the Waco designer, was responsible for the outstanding lines of the aircraft. *E. T. Packard Collection.*

made famous by Waco test pilots and aerobatic champions "Fearless" Freddie Lund and Johnny Livingston.

In 1931, aware of the trend to enclosed models, Brukner wisely introduced their first cabin type, the QDC-1, powered with a 165 hp radial Continental. Based on its success, in 1933 the model UIC 210 hp cabin type was unveiled and was quickly hailed as the most attractive cabin biplane on the market. With its streamlined full skirt "bump cowl," wing root and landing gear fairings, and sleek wheel pants, its lines were further enhanced by its elliptical wing tips and graceful "tail feathers," plus Waco reliability.

C-D needed a hot commercial-type model at this time to offset the bevy of military and multi-engine SF types introduced throughout 1933. Reacting to the many requests that had been received for a model of the Waco C, Ed's cadre of dedicated draftsmen and shop and office personnel concentrated their efforts to design the SF-37 Waco C to coincide with the upcoming Christmas market. The prototype's graceful lines were faithfully reproduced in the kit, which also included printwood, finished cowling front ring, partially finished wheel pants, and cabin details, at $3.00.

The December 1933 issue of *Model Airplane News* featured the SF-37 in a center-spread ad, with the same center spread in the December issue of *Popular Aviation*. The kit enjoyed immediate popularity and continued generating sales for many years because the Waco name had a great domestic and international following of owners and doting admirers.

From Pulps to Slicks

An example of the degree of product and service diversification that Ed resorted to from about 1930 on was the sale of modeling and aviation magazines. Many such publications began as "flying pulps," the 7-by-10-inch magazines characterized by a colorful, action-oriented aerial World War I dogfight scene or an otherwise captivating aviation-oriented cover, with 128-plus thrill-packed pages of World War I yarns printed on coarse, pulp stock. *Flying Aces,* known today as *Flying Models* (Carstens), began as a pulp in October 1928, becoming an 8½-by-11-inch "slick" magazine in November 1933. *Air Trails* (Street and Smith) also began as a pulp in October 1928, ceased publication in October 1931, became *Bill Barnes Air Adventurer* in February 1934, and finally emerged as an 8½-by-11-inch slick in October 1935 under the title *Bill Barnes Air Trails*. The *Bill Barnes* part of the title was deleted in December 1937, and it became *Air Trails* exclusively.

"My merchandising concept involved in stocking the magazines was based on my reasoning that, if modelers could find their favorite flying pulp or aviation publication while at C-D, and if the publication contained plans which appealed to the modeler, the bill of materials could be purchased right then and there," Ed explained. "*Model Airplane News* [Jay Publications] and *Popular Aviation* [became *Flying,* published by Ziff] were early favorites for plans, later followed by *Flying Aces* and *Air Trails.* Of course there was a profit for us on the magazines as well, and it enabled us to also display the current C-D ads running.

"Possibly the only negative of the practice was that modelers would thumb through all of the magazines and not buy any. However, I had come to feel that during the dark days of the Depression, if our stocking the magazines brought some sunshine into the otherwise dreary, somewhat discouraging,

less-fortunate modelers' existence, then it was not a total loss. I also later discovered that some of these young lads without any spending money then grew up into fine young adults with jobs and later on came in to patronize our Lorain Avenue store." It was just another example of how Ed was ever playing the role of aviation's great recruiter.

The Pylon Polishers

In maintaining the position C-D occupied as the leader in providing the most authentic, complete line of kits of Thompson Trophy–winning miniature pylon polishers, Ed was fortunate in being able to establish relationships with many of the famous air-race pilots and designer-builders during his many visits to Cleveland Municipal Airport. On one such occasion, prior to the 1933 National Air Races, he met the famous Jimmie (James Robert) Wedell, of Wedell-Williams racer fame. It was shortly after Wedell, on his final approach flareout, bounced in his *Miss Patterson* racer (named after Patterson, Louisiana, home field of Wedell-Williams Air Service Corporation) from about fifteen feet. This type of landing was not uncommon for the agile racer aircraft. Because of the poor pilot visibility resulting from the cockpit location aft of the wing trailing edge, leveling off correctly was difficult. Don Young, famous race pilot Roscoe Turner's mechanic, best summarized the flight characteristics of the nimble No. 44 racer: "That airplane had no flaps and a fixed gear, no shock absorber whatsoever. No one could grease it onto the runway to save his soul. It was a murderous airplane to fly, no question about it!"

Pilots of the 1920s and 1930s learned to fly in slow-speed biplanes with the common technique of three-point landings, making the plane stall about

Jimmie Wedell in his 1933 Thompson Trophy–winner Williams No. 44, which was powered by a 550 hp P&W Wasp Jr. and attained an average speed of 237.95 mph to win first place. At the Chicago International Air Races in 1933, Wedell set a new land speed record of 316 mph. *R. S. Hirsch Collection.*

the time of touchdown. The sleek monoplane racers, being so much faster, had uniquely different stall characteristics. Consequently, most racers usually bounced three or four times before a stall kept them on the runway. So Jimmy's flareout was not much different from that of any of the other racers, such as Howards, Chesters, Folkerts, or Gee-Bees.

During the National Air Races from 1931 to 1935, Wedell-Williams racers took more than their share of firsts. In the Thompson Air Races, they took two firsts, three seconds, and two thirds. They had three firsts, three seconds, and one third in the Bendix.

The year 1933 was a particularly great one for Wedell-Williams racers. Roscoe Turner took first place at the Bendix; Jimmie Wedell took second place in No. 44. At the Chicago International Air Races Wedell set a new world record of 305.33 mph. Jimmie Wedell, again in No. 44, took first place in the Thompson, which was a fitting tribute for the great air racer. On June 24, 1934, he was killed with a student pilot while he was instructing the student at his home field in Patterson, Louisiana.

When Wedell died as a result of the accident, a great wealth of knowledge and racing know-how went with him, because it was generally known that there were no formal blueprints for the line of racers. Contrary to the popular impression that Wedell was strictly an "eyeball designer," not only could he read blueprints, but he had learned stress analysis as well.

After the previous near-fatal crash in the racer he was building for Roscoe Turner, Turner had wisely arranged for an MIT professor to teach Jimmie how to calculate the stresses involved in racer design. The popular conception of Wedell's racer outlines being designed from chalk lines on the hangar floor evolved when he was designing his 1931 No. 44 with a modified wing to replace

The 1933 Thompson Trophy winner: SF-47 Wedell-Williams, with a 19½-inch span and sold for $2.95. Trimmed with black on red with silver numerals and a bump cowl, it was striking in appearance. Packard scaled measurements while the racer was hangared at the Cleveland Municipal Airport. *E. T. Packard Collection.*

Frank Hawks in his Texaco 13 Travel Air Model R, in which he established several cross-country records and toured Europe as well (ca. 1932). *R. S. Hirsch Collection.*

No. 91's wings. He was asked by his parachute rigger and draftsman, Charles "Frudey" Fortune, "How much span do we want on this new configuration?"

Ed had had adequate opportunity to measure, sketch, and photograph the winning No. 44 while it was housed in the Cleveland airport hangar. From his meticulously gathered data emerged C-D's SF-47 Wedell-Williams No. 44 *Miss Patterson* in the configuration of the 1933 Thompson Trophy 237.98 mph winner, at $2.95. The plan was a most outstanding authentic miniature of the famous racer, right down to the authentic stringer and rib spacing with the proper sponsor and racing numeral decals. A vertical layout center-page spread

Above: The C-D ad in the 1934 National Air Races program showed the SF-27 Gee-Bee R-1 at $1.75, a Depression-era price. Directions were also given to the 57th and Bridge hobby store location. *Author's Collection.*

Right: The 1933 National Air Races (Los Angeles) official program. Each year the program became more of a "show" publication. The event's managing director, Cliff Henderson, knew the value of professional artwork in these promotional efforts, so each cover was a winner. *Author's Collection.*

in the December 1934 issue of *Model Airplane News* displayed this star as the newest addition in the SF line in a dramatically posed flight photo. Jimmie Wedell must have been smiling.

With Wedell thus a nonparticipant in the 1934 Thompson, Roscoe Turner, in his J. H. Heintz-sponsored No. 57, all gold-colored, 1,000 hp Wedell-Williams racer, without his usual competitor hot on his tail, took first place, which would prove to be the first of his three wins in the Thompson. It would also be the last year that a Wedell-Williams would be in the Thompson Trophy winner's circle.

With Roscoe's great wave of popular adulation from National Air Race fans for their colorful role model, it was a must for C-D to follow up with the SF-48 version of the all-gold No. 57 Wedell-Williams, which was featured in the January 1935 *Model Airplane News* center-spread ad in another vertical layout that dominated the issue. The unique color scheme of the flashy racer, with its large bump cowl and streamlined landing gear, was authentically reproduced, and C-D National Air Race fans snapped up the first run of the kits.

Sales and Marketing Problems

America's leaders of commerce and industry could seek solace, to a degree, with the beginning of 1934, because at last the relentless escalation in the nation's rate of unemployment reversed its direction and decreased to 20.2 percent,

Above left: Roscoe Turner at the 1934 National Air Races at Cleveland in his No. 57 Wedell-Williams—winning speed: 248.1 mph. Turner emerged from World War I and embarked on a meteoric aviation career as a test pilot, flying-school operator, movie stunt pilot, and star of a flying circus. In 1929 he operated Nevada Air Lines, had a one-man route of Los Angeles-Reno-Tonapah-Las Vegas and became famous for his *Honeymoon Express,* a sleek Lockheed Air Express in which he flew eloping movie stars to Las Vegas. *R. S. Hirsch Collection.*

Above right: SF-48, Turner's No. 57 Wedell-Williams all-gold racer, with its bump cowl and markings, was a great favorite of the modelers.

Below: H. J. Heinz Company, famous for their "57" varieties, was Turner's sponsor during the 1930s, hence the "57" insignia on the fuselage. Heinz offered a Modern Aviation series of cards, which required three box tops of Rice Flakes to obtain and had full-color cards packed in the boxes of cereal. *E. T. Packard Collection.*

down 2.3 million from a total of 12.7 million. The welcome downtrend halved the maximum rate of 25.1 percent of 1933 to 12 percent by 1937.

Coinciding with the ravages of the Depression, various examples of criminal behavior occurred throughout heretofore unblemished areas of society.

The post offices in Cleveland were no exception. During the period from 1931 to 1933 C-D experienced a loss in excess of $20,000 (a tremendous sum then) through letter pilferage.

Due to the failure of so many banks, people could not trust them as before, so as a consequence there were many more cash transactions sent through the mail. Apparently, unscrupulous postal employees apparently soon learned to recognize letters destined for C-D, not only by the name but by the youthful-looking handwriting of modelers. It was tragic that so many model builders who had sacrificed and saved so they could ultimately afford a C-D kit would send their order with cash, only to have it intercepted at the post office. Ed advised that no more than 10 percent of the lost funds was ever recovered. Unfortunately, many customers of C-D were lost who felt that their money was being purposefully kept by the company and the orders just never filled.

In discussing his relationship with C-D dealers, I had apparently discovered a sensitive area, for Ed responded: "From the humble inception of the company, I often overextended my resources to provide our dealers with every possible sales aid: *Engineering News, Cleveland Model News and Practical Hobbies,* catalogs, flyers, attractive cartons, and even window banners and other display and advertising copy. Much of this expensive promotional material was never used.

"One of the most flagrant abuses of disreputable dealers was their so-called 'bait and switch' tactics, which was just out-and-out misrepresentation. This type of dealer would stock just a few of the most desirable C-D kits, representing himself as a full-fledged C-D dealer and even displaying C-D banners and flyers. Then, when the modeler would come in and request a particular C-D item, the dealer would tell him that he was temporarily out of stock but that he had the same plane in a competitor's line [Comet, Megow, Scientific, or Ideal] and for less money. With this tactic he would switch the purchase to another brand. I learned about this practice from loyal C-D aeromodelers who would write me or tell me personally about such an experience.

"In weighing the pros and cons of this dilemma, it meant many sleepless nights for me, for I realized there were many loyal and dedicated dealers who made every effort to expand C-D sales and to develop the image of the hobby business. I simply had to make up my own mind or forget it, for it was beginning to sap too much of my creativity.

"Therefore, in the March 1934 issue of *MAN* and *Popular Aviation,* a center-spread ad with a vertically read layout in large type declared: 'Effective February 1, 1934, C-D discontinues selling to dealers, thereby making possible sensational price reductions on all kits and supplies.' Near the bottom of the ad were examples of price reductions, most notably the Boeing 247 kit was slashed from $6.50 to $4.95. Near the lower edge of the ad was shown the SF-1G 1933 Great Lakes Sport Trainer redesigned with the price reduced to $1.75."

Great Lakes Cleveland SF-1G 1936 "Flagship of the Fleet." The actual plane was a 2T-1A with upright Cirrus or a 2T-1E with inverted Cirrus. This modified design was the company's last attempt to overcome the Depression and sold for $29.85. With rounded cowl and enlarged fin and rudder, with airwheels, it was impressive in appearance. A terrific exhibition model, the C-D kit contained 68 pieces and was finished in orange and cream. (Note the realistic pilot figure in the cockpit.) *E. T. Packard Collection.*

Actually, this variant of the prototype Great Lakes Trainer was their 1931 2T-1A (upright Cirrus) and 2T-1E (inverted Cirrus), featuring rounded cowl with larger fin and rudder area and low pressure air wheels. Its factory price had been dramatically reduced from $4,990 to $2,985. With such inducements as this the great aerobatic pilot and instructor Tex Rankin ordered 200 for his dealership and flying school. Cirrus engines were used exclusively since the company was a part of Allied Motors Industries, parent company of Great Lakes. However, the effects of the Depression were so widespread that many orders had to be cancelled. Sadly, over its eight years of existence, Great Lakes never showed a profit and regrettably in 1936 the company was liquidated.

In contrast, however, the SF-1G C-D model, with its sporty, attractive, eye-catching cream and international-orange color scheme, with simulated air wheels, was a perennial success. It was a consistent scale display contest winner. With the enlarged tail surfaces and lower center of gravity, the model was a superior flyer.

However, C-D's decision to "go it direct," without dealers, on February 1, 1934, was a most strategic move. Dealers were forced to pay full list to buy the C-D models that were demanded by their customers. After receiving letters, phone calls, and personal visits from former C-D dealers requesting their reinstatement, as the Christmas holiday buying season approached, Ed received a call from a well-established dealer in Cleveland who appealed for a return to the former policy. He couched his appeal in an enticing offer for an exceptionally large order. The Christmas season represented a large portion of C-D's annual sales, likewise for the dealers, so if there was to be a change, now was the time.

As a result, the December 1934 issue of *Model Airplane News* featured a center spread C-D ad announcing "A New Deal for Dealers" and advised them to rush their orders if they expected delivery in time for holiday gift buying.

In retrospect, Cleveland had sent a message to the country's toy and modeler retailers that a certain degree of loyalty was expected from them to be a C-D dealer.

Another Prestigious "Giant"

Ed's former employer, Glenn L. Martin, had the distinction of producing the first U.S.-built bomber, the twin engine MB-1, in 1918, which was intended for the U.S. World War I effort.

While Boeing delivered their successful all-metal 160 mph B-9 low wing bomber in 1931, the Army Air Corps in their 1932 bomber specifications was seeking performance capability of "a ton of bombs and a range of 2,000 miles."

Martin's all-metal B-10B bomber had an internal bomb bay with a capacity for a 2,260-pound bombload and a range of 590 miles, powered by two 750 hp Wright Cyclones at a top speed of 207 mph, making it the world's fastest bomber—faster than any pursuit in service. Its outstanding design features included retractable landing gear and the first transparent rotating powered nose gun turret on a U.S. bomber. Pilot, radioman, and rear gunner were protected from the 200 mph windstream by sliding transparent canopies. No surprise then that Martin walked off with the 1932 Collier Trophy, an annual national award presented to the most outstanding plane of the year by president. As further proof of its performance reliability, Lt. Col. "Hap" Arnold in 1934 led a flight of ten B-10s from Washington, D.C., to Alaska and back, a distance of 7,360 miles, with only one plane experiencing a forced landing.

Although the Martin plant was located in Baltimore, through his connections with the Martin organization Ed was able to procure the necessary information to begin designing a faithful ¾-inch scale miniature that would become another addition to the line of C-D "giants," since it would measure a whopping 53-inch wingspan.

In describing the efforts to develop the B-10 kit, Ed explained, "With the experience gained from our producing the SF-35 Boeing 247 kit, many production shortcuts and design construction improvements were incorporated in the SF-45 Martin Bomber. Our final price was $6.50, with the kit tipping the scales at ten pounds. Since I had met Glenn Martin when I worked in his plant at Cleveland, to produce a miniature of one of his aircraft called for an all-out C-D effort. Every avenue and resource for the most current information on the construction and details of the B-10 was utilized. At times we were stonewalled by the airplane's classified status."

The construction plan, which consisted of two 28-inch-by-40-inch plates, was one of the most detailed C-D ever produced. Included were four close-up photos of the finished model with two views of the framework construction before covering. Consequently, when the October 1934 issue of *MAN* appeared, Ed took great pride in C-D's full-page ad, which featured a sharp close-up photo showing the model with the rubber motor spars in place, since he had just successfully flown it. Clearly shown were the movable plastic nose turret; the turned balsa "invisible hub" wheels; detailed plastic enclosures for pilot, radioman, and rear gunner; radio mast and antenna; details of the Wright Cyclone power plants and the official insignia of Wright Field. Ample quantities of olive-drab and chrome-yellow dope, cement, banana oil, and tissue were included. It amazed Ed that they ever made a profit on the kit with the 10 pounds of raw materials included.

Increased Competition

The 1933–34 period was a tumultuous one for C-D, both in additions to its impressive SF line of forty-seven models and its announcement of the seventh issue of *CMN&PH,* with a full-color cover by the noted artist Charles Hubbell, to be followed by issues 8, 9, and 10 at a new price of 40 cents, or all four issues for $1.50.

However, it was in the area of marketing where C-D found itself beginning to feel the effects of increasing competition. C-D had enjoyed an accelerated rise in popularity, acceptance, and success partially because it had boldly introduced the era of simplified, all-balsa construction and a rapidly expanding line of authentic scale flying models with little peer competition.

As established modeling concerns awakened to the fact that dealers and aeromodelers were readily accepting what C-D had to offer and at higher prices despite the Depression, they were forced to offer competitive designs, which they finally did and at lower prices. Competitors such as Comet, Megow, Scientific, and Miniature, who had not advertised nationally at all or only infrequently, began to increase the size and frequency of their ads. Ideal was the last to react, possibly because it had had the industry leadership for so long. For the first time Ideal seemed to have developed a plan which certainly emulated C-D scale realism.

In addition, there were new companies, albeit many even more humbly than C-D's origin, entering the market every month, who wanted a piece of the pie. Locally, in the Cleveland suburb of Lakewood, Peerless Model Airplane Company, who had benefited from the defection of a C-D draftsman, emulated C-D's design features, plans, and construction techniques. In fact, in the December 1934 issue of *Model Airplane News,* Peerless boldly committed for the inside-front cover for their ad. It was even rumored that the company was bent on putting C-D out of business.

The C-D organization knew that their major competitor, Ideal, was truly a "sleeping giant" insofar as competition was concerned. Their initial ads were nondescript, touting Trubild models at 50 cents and featuring unimpressive layouts with the emphasis on flying types. However, the June 1934 issue of *Model Airplane News* began a series of totally new type Ideal full-page dramatic ads announcing "New Super Detailed" models, beginning with the Stinson Reliant at $2.50, featuring movable controls from the cabin or cockpit and guaranteed to fly. The July 1934 issue would similarly offer a Curtiss Goshawk at $2.00; the September issue would feature a P-26A at $1.75, and then, the blockbuster in their full-page November ad—the Martin B-10 ½-inch scale 34½-inch wingspan model at $3.50, approved by the Junior Birdmen of America organization, a national group that promoted model airplane building.

"I will admit," Ed confided, "that there were some apprehensions when I saw their ½-inch-scale version. Way back then and earlier I was sowing the seeds for a move to offer the SF types in a smaller scale and the idea for a 'dwarf' line was germinating.

"It was obvious that Ideal had done their homework for undoubtedly the 'giant' sizes resulting from my criterion of a museum scale of ¾-inch had simply been outpriced and possibly even had intimidated some modelers. Another fact had to be considered for apartment dwellers; where do you find the room to keep a four-and-a-half-foot model?"

The Master Model Engineer again rose to the challenge and the contents of the December 1934 C-D center-spread ad in *Model Airplane News* represented a masterpiece of communications. First, the dealer sales policy was reinstated. Second, The C-D dwarf line was announced at a ½-inch scale, and kits would contain no cements or liquids. This feature enabled C-D to offer the line in a price range from 25–85 cents, thus enabling modelers to have the benefits of most of the SF line at reduced prices, a most appropriate marketing move in view of the Depression. (It had to be viewed as a great competitive marketing strategy and was C-D's answer to the increasingly threatening competition.)

Third was a listing of SF models by degree of difficulty to build. This was a clever step, for it was a boon to both dealers and modelers since there were many SFs too difficult for beginners to build. The designations were given as:

> 1st Class—most difficult (SF-2D, -3, -21, -23, -25, -27, -31, -35, -37, -39, -41, -43, -45, -47, -48, -49, -50)
> 2nd Class—second-most difficult (SF-1G, -4, -13B, -17B, -19, -20, -24, -28, -29, -30)
> 3rd Class—third-most difficult (SF-6, -12B, -14B, -16, -34, -44)
> 4th Class—easiest (SF-9, -10, -11, -18B, -22B, -26, -32, -33, -36, -38, -40, -42)

The fourth marketing strategy was to list and then to offer all six Thompson Trophy Winners at $15.80. These were the1929 SF-2D Travel Air Mystery Ship, the1930 SF-46 Laird Solution, the1931 SF-17B Gee-Bee Z, the 1932 SF-27B Gee-Bee R-1, the 1933 SF-47 Wedell-Williams No. 44 (Jimmie Wedell), and the 1934 SF-48 Wedell-Williams No. 57 (Roscoe Turner).

A 1933 C-D broadside mailer, with the front page announcing new low prices and the inside listing the entire line. *E. T. Packard Collection.*

When a disastrous fire of mysterious origin swept through the supposedly fireproof structure of the Carpenter Advertising printing plant, it spelled the doom of the *CMN&PH* series. Fortunately, most of the No. 7 full-color-cover issues had been removed prior to the fire, so existing orders could be filled. Subscribers who had committed for the quarterly issues Nos. 7, 8, 9, and 10 were notified that they had a choice of either a refund or a credit to be applied to future purchases. It was an unfortunate and costly event for C-D. It brought to an end what had transpired as a turbulent, eventful, and memorable 1933–34 period in the history of C-D.

Yet, if only the Master Model Engineer could have foreseen the unprecedented expansion, increased sales, and success just over the horizon, this loss could have been accepted less painfully.

PART II

The Lorain Avenue Move and War Clouds over Europe

CHAPTER 9

The "All-American" Carton and Gateway to Lorain Avenue

⊗ With positive vibes emanating from segments of the economy in 1935, the stage was set for the American aviation industry to inject an increasing degree of optimism in its marketing and capital investment planning.

Reacting to the encouraging growth indicators in the country's commerce and industry, 1935 commercial aviation would produce 1,109 units, up 43.9 percent from 772 in 1934 with production dollars topping $10.4 million, an increase of 4.5 percent from $9.96 million the previous year.

As a positive indication that the Depression-ridden economy was at last healing, in November Pan American Airways would inaugurate Hawaiian Clipper flights with the innovative, giant Martin 130 flying boat, followed by the Philippine Clipper, and, most famous of all, the China Clipper. The visionary C-D president could not possibly realize at the time that the third and most famous Martin giant 130-foot-span China Clipper would have such a profound influence on him and his company.

Fortunately, for the ever-expanding C-D enterprises, a brief respite from the increasing pressures of lack of space occurred unexpectedly when the residence and garage across the street, which had been harboring a soft drink bottling operation, was suddenly vacated—another victim of the deep Depression. Ed marshaled his resources quickly to take advantage of this opportune situation, signing up for a modest monthly rental that would allow an expansion of C-D's shipping and receiving department, plus accommodate a dope bottle-filling location.

"It was during the early thirties that our family came in contact with Fritz Gasse, a capable, conscientious, bookkeeper who offered to relieve my mother of her increasingly demanding financial chores," Ed related. "Fritz quickly fit in with the C-D family and shortly demonstrated that he was one of those dedicated, completely trustworthy souls who had been born to keep books. He completely assumed the responsibility for our financial record keeping and in short order was guiding our organization on a sound, well-planned financial basis. He would remain a part of the C-D family until his retirement some twenty years later."

In an unrelated series of events, Ed would attract and recruit the services of several outstanding creative artists and draftsmen, each to have a significant effect on C-D's success.

The Recruitment of Artistic Talent

It was through correspondence that the young, creative Moyer Thompson of Portland, Oregon, became a vital part of the *CMN&PH* publication. His humorous and educational cartoons enlivened the pages with his likeable, folksy wit and made heroes out of the typical young modelers to whom Ed was ever appealing. Their initial correspondence blossomed into a productive and harmonious relationship without their ever having met.

Model enthusiasts of all ages were inexorably drawn to the Master Model Engineer because of their admiration for what C-D represented—the ultimate in scale flying models, always the most current, historically significant aircraft. He was their role model, and they followed him because they had a desire to be a part of this growing enterprise that capitalized on this era of the development of aviation.

Moyer's provocative art and copy helped Ed develop the central character of "Modelin' Bill" in the editorials, accompanied by a visual of the real-life archetypal, wholesome relationship between the quintessential American father and son in a model building mode of the 1930s—before television, drugs, and promiscuity. Moyer's first cartoons appeared in the No. 2 issue of *CMN&PH* (1933), where on the back page he demonstrated his insight into modelers' lifestyles by beginning a series illustrating the realism portrayed in the publication, resulting in bringing a father and son together to read *CMN&PH* while mother keeps supper waiting for them. In issue No. 3 (May–June 1933), he adds another dimension to family relationships by showing that "men are just boys grown tall," cleverly illustrating grown men having a glorious time flying C-D models and reading *CMN&PH*.

Ed planned to introduce the young Moyer to his readers in No. 4 with a photo showing him at his desk as a modeler surrounded by some finished C-D models. Identifying with the real life Depression, when jobs were hard to come by, Moyer's artistry created the series, "How Bill landed his job." Young Bill overwhelms a potential employer by showing him his C-D P-26A kit radial engine assembly. But by far his most creative efforts appeared in issue No. 5, where he created an "SF-35 Hangar," in which the recently released Boeing 247 model was housed accompanied by a bevy of small airplane-like animated characters who were measuring, admiring, and extolling its merits.

All airplane pictures on this page are of actual C-D models. Built from kits containing printed out wood.

C-D's columnar ad in the February 1934 issue of *Model Airplane News* was the only such spread in the issue. It headlined the F-41 Vought Corsair, 27-inch span for $3.50, and introduced the Akron & Macon fighter SF-22B, $2.50. Note too that the SF-1G revised Great Lakes Sport Trainer kit, at $2.50, now contained printwood. *Author's Collection.*

To illustrate an outstanding educational series, in Vol. 1, No. 5 he conceived a new character, "DARE," who demonstrated how to properly test fly a new model for the first time.

Another new name had appeared in the credits in issue 5, a name that would become synonymous with the power of C-D's colorful graphic designs—James D. Powell. On page 116 of that issue his artwork demonstrated how to convert a drawing compass into a cutting tool to make accurate circular cutouts in balsa or paper. Powell, a professional artist in Boston, likewise had corresponded with Ed and was given the task to create an appropriate carton design to differentiate the recently announced Dwarf ½-inch scale kit series. Ed was impressed with his carton design submission with its dynamically, aviation-oriented emblazoned graphics and vivid color scheme to differentiate it from the other C-D kits. Ed's instincts told him that here was an artist who not only had top-notch artistic ability but also that his creations disclosed that he possessed a deep feeling and an appreciation for the exciting era of the development of aviation. To some extent this creativity had been nurtured as a result of Powell's fascination with the authenticity of the C-D product line and its resultant growing industry leadership.

Coincidentally, the artist, who had been plagued with a chronic respiratory affliction, had been advised by his doctor to distance himself from the Boston climate. After a brief exchange of phone calls and correspondence, Powell agreed to move to Cleveland and to assume the responsibilities of staff art designer at an agreed salary of $35 per week, an above-average wage for his type of position in 1935.

One of the most famous fans of C-D was Charles H. Hubbell, renowned aviation artist, pilot, member of the OX-5 Pioneers, historian, and author. Best known for his paintings for Cleveland's Thompson Products annual calendars, before his widespread fame Hubbell was an ardent C-D model builder, which enabled him to interject additional realism into his paintings of historical aircraft. There developed a great bond of friendship between Ed and Hubbell. When the series of seven issues of *CMN&PH* began, Hubbell was so impressed that he enthusiastically supported the publication and indicated that he would like to create a painting for one of the covers.

His offer was accepted and in 1933 two outstanding examples of his ability to paint realistic in-flight aircraft appeared in the last two issues of *CMN&PH* The cover of No. 6 pictured the docile, ultra-stable, safe Aeronca C-3 lightplane, illustrated in a black-and-white "wash" scene, winging its way over the picturesque Ohio countryside. The cover of the seventh, and final, issue (Jan.–Feb. 1934) portrayed a sleek, powerful, two-place U.S. Navy Vought Corsair V-65 in full color with an offer for a free color print of the cover suitable for framing with an order placed for any two C-D kits.

Commissioned by Fred Crawford, president of Thompson Products, Hubbell created paintings of more than 500 aircraft, twenty-five of which were OX-5–powered craft, in his studio located for many years on the top floor of the Sweetland Building on Euclid Avenue. From 1939 on, 375 of his paintings depicting the history of flight for the Thompson aviation calendars were continued after the 1953 merger of Thompson with Ramo-Wooldridge under the TRW, Inc., banner. Later Hubbell had his studio located at Cleveland's Frederick C. Crawford Auto-Aviation Museum, to whom Crawford had donated 357 of the original paintings. In appreciation for Ed's valuable assistance to Hubbell and his calendar paintings, he was summoned by Fred Witt, advertising manager of Thompson Products, to be presented with a replica of the famous Thompson Trophy, which he regarded as one of his fondest possessions.

This relationship with Hubbell led to Ed's association with Edwin G. Thompson, son of the Thompson Products founder. Edwin was involved in the management of Thompson Aeronautical Corporation, located at Cleveland Municipal Airport, flying Leoning Amphibians (later known as Keystone Leoning Air Yachts after Grover Leoning sold out to Keystone) between Cleveland and Detroit. "Occasionally I gave a hand to the planes that landed at the foot of Cleveland's East Ninth Street, where I initially became associated with him," Ed recalled. "Edwin became keenly interested in our future expansion plans. I received a phone call from him one evening, and he stated that as soon as he and his wife returned from an air trip to the west coast he would like to discuss his future with C-D. Unfortunately, these plans ended tragically when he and his wife were fatal victims of an airplane crash on their trip to the coast. I often wondered what effect our relationship could have had on the future course of C-D if it had had an opportunity to become business oriented."

Invasion of the Gassies

While 1932 had witnessed America's economy plunge to nearly rock bottom, the stage was being set for a revolutionary technological development that would permanently alter the character of modeldom. In a word, gas power— a new method of powered flight making traditional rubber power-driven models obsolete overnight. In the traditionally ivy-covered environs of the historical city of Philadelphia, a talented model enthusiast had been involved in developing a miniature gasoline two-cycle engine in which he, William Brown, had faith that it would revolutionize rubber-powered flight. In 1932 his latest modified engine, which he called the Brown Jr. and had installed in Maxwell Bassett's four-foot nine-inch-span high wing cabin monoplane, set a world record of 2:55. However, since there did not exist an established, accepted body of principles of flight for gas-powered models, Bassett's model, which was directionally unstable, had to be trimmed to stall and fall off to prevent it from going into a spiral dive. With a modified design, Bassett "wiped out" the opposition at the 1933 Nationals, winning the Texaco, Moffett (28:18) and Mulvihill (14:55) Trophies. By so completely overwhelming the rubber-powered contestants with his gassies, it became apparent that a new class for gas-powered models was needed. Bassett's conclusive demonstration of the superiority of gas-powered flight occurred on May 28, 1934, when his Brown Jr.–powered cabin monoplane took off from Camden, New Jersey, and two hours and thirty-five minutes later landed at Middletown, Delaware.

Enter Charles Hampson Grant, appointed as editor of *Model Airplane News* in 1932 and whose monthly articles chronicling "The Aerodynamic Design of the Model Plane" would exert a profound influence on free-flight model design for a decade. During his more than a decade at the helm of the publication, it had expanded from forty-eight pages to sixty; his articles on design specifications for the model airplane had been incorporated into a 528-page book *Model Airplane Design and Theory of Flight,* which chronicled his thirty years of experience in model building and design, developing an established criteria for the design of rubber and gas powered models. In his designing he returned to the prototype field, where he became intensely involved in the concept of a double-slotted flap that was incorporated and used on the Martin 4-0-4 airliner in August 1947. Grant would be presented with the Frank Brewer Trophy in 1968 by his peers for his many accomplishments, including segmented flaps, airfoils, the delta wing, and V/STOL aircraft. Few men could point to such design accomplishments in both the prototype and miniature model airplane field.

Determined to prove that his design principles could be applied to gas-powered flight, Grant joined forces with a friend and accomplished model builder Joseph Kovel, who constructed the now-famous 10-foot wingspan K-G (Kovel Grant). On May 25, 1935, at Hadley Field near New Brunswick, New Jersey, propelled by a Brown Jr. engine with 1½ ounces of fuel, a world's endurance record of 64½ minutes was established by the K-G before flying out of sight. The errant model was located undamaged two days later, sixty miles away.

Grant's leadership would be instrumental in establishing the International Gas Model Aircraft Association (IGMAA), having six thousand members, which would ultimately evolve into the NAA and finally become the Muncie, Indiana–based Academy of Model Aeronautics (AMA), having more than 175,000 members currently. (Nathan Polk was also identified with the founding of the IGMAA and held its first gas model contest on May 6, 1936, at Hadley Field, New Jersey. He wrote a monthly column in *Model Airplane News* called Gas Lines, which reported on their contest activities. His brother Irwin Polk was a founder of the Metropolitan Model League.)

The masthead of the October 1943 issue of *MAN* listed Robert McLarren as managing editor. Charles Hampson Grant retired after eleven years of distinguished, dedicated service as editor of the Bible of the model industry. However, Grant continued with model design articles and other related modeling projects.

After the "Free for All" initial competition of gas models based on a fuel allotment, so many models flew out of sight of the timers that it was obvious other methods of flight limitations would have to be developed. Fortunately, the IGMAA and, ultimately, the NAA prudently established three classes: A, B, and C, based on engine displacement. Then, after much deliberation and various experimenting, the initial fuel allotment method was discarded in

Charles Hampson Grant, who would later become editor of *Model Airplane News* at his boys' camp in Peru, Vermont, where the curriculum included instruction in the construction and flying of model airplanes (1923). *E. T. Packard Collection.*

favor of limited engine runs. At first it was a forty-second engine run, then it was reduced to thirty seconds, and, finally, twenty seconds, with competition thus established within each class to assure the maximum degree of equality.

"Speculation was rife among my industry associates," Ed confided. "We were all aware that Grant had significant influence in our industry. Hence, it was a cinch that there would be some degree of commercialization of gas models as soon as one key element in the equation was solved—the availability of gas model engines at affordable prices.

"We all knew that Bill Brown, despite his lead on future competitors in the model engine field, could not expect to have a monopoly for long and particularly not at a price of $21.50, an exorbitant price then. I quickly decided it would be a wise move for me to make some contacts with manufacturers who were supplying engines for miniature auto racers and model speed boats.

"At the same time I began thinking about how C-D should enter this new facet of modeldom, which would soon become a battle royal. My gut feeling was that we did not want to throw our hat in the ring, so to speak, with all the freelance designs which were sure to proliferate. We were known for our scale flying capability and that would be the way we should cast our lot in the gas model derby now emerging. I immediately began a search on my own for some popular monoplane designs with inherent stability, coupled with classic design features that would appeal to our following of dealers and modelers."

With an eye to the anticipated heavy demand for a popular-priced, reliable gas model engine, the December 1935 *MAN* issue featured a "surprise

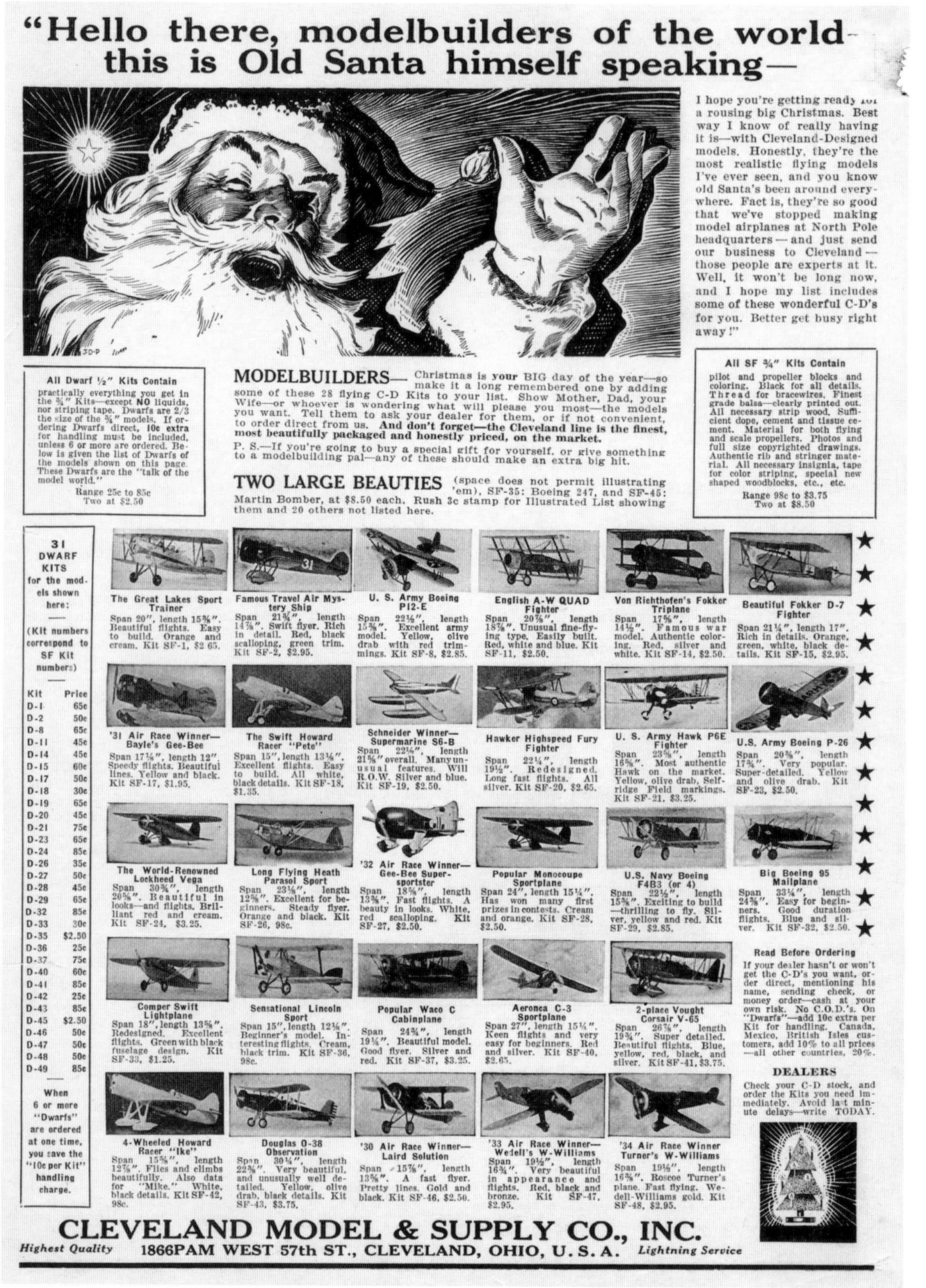

"Hello there, modelbuilders of the world—this is Old Santa himself speaking—

I hope you're getting ready for a rousing big Christmas. Best way I know of really having it is—with Cleveland-Designed models. Honestly, they're the most realistic flying models I've ever seen, and you know old Santa's been around everywhere. Fact is, they're so good that we've stopped making model airplanes at North Pole headquarters—and just send our business to Cleveland—those people are experts at it. Well, it won't be long now, and I hope my list includes some of these wonderful C-D's for you. Better get busy right away!"

All Dwarf ½″ Kits Contain
practically everything you get in the ¾″ Kits—except **NO** liquids, nor striping tape. Dwarfs are 2/3 the size of the ¾″ models. If ordering Dwarfs direct, **10c extra** for handling must be included, unless 6 or more are ordered. Below is given the list of Dwarfs of the models shown on this page. These Dwarfs are the "talk of the model world."
Range 25c to 85c
Two at $2.50

MODELBUILDERS— Christmas is **your** BIG day of the year—so make it a long remembered one by adding some of these 28 flying C-D Kits to your list. Show Mother, Dad, your Wife—or whoever is wondering what will please you most—the models you want. Tell them to ask your dealer for them, or if not convenient, to order direct from us. **And don't forget—the Cleveland line is the finest, most beautifully packaged and honestly priced, on the market.**

P. S.—If you're going to buy a special gift for yourself, or give something to a modelbuilding pal—any of these should make an extra big hit.

TWO LARGE BEAUTIES (space does not permit illustrating 'em), SF-35: Boeing 247, and SF-45: Martin Bomber, at $8.50 each. Rush 3c stamp for Illustrated List showing them and 20 others not listed here.

All SF ¾″ Kits Contain
pilot and propeller blocks and coloring. Black for all details. Thread for bracewires. Finest grade balsa—clearly printed out. All necessary strip wood. Sufficient dope, cement and tissue cement. Material for both flying and scale propellers. Photos and full size copyrighted drawings. Authentic rib and stringer material. All necessary insignia, tape for color striping, special new shaped woodblocks, etc., etc.
Range 98c to $3.75
Two at $8.50

31 DWARF KITS for the models shown here:
(Kit numbers correspond to SF Kit numbers)

Kit	Price
D-1	65c
D-2	50c
D-8	65c
D-11	45c
D-14	45c
D-15	60c
D-17	50c
D-18	30c
D-19	65c
D-20	45c
D-21	75c
D-23	65c
D-24	85c
D-26	35c
D-27	50c
D-28	45c
D-29	65c
D-32	85c
D-33	30c
D-35	$2.50
D-36	25c
D-37	75c
D-40	60c
D-41	85c
D-42	25c
D-43	85c
D-45	$2.50
D-46	50c
D-47	50c
D-48	50c
D-49	85c

When 6 or more "Dwarfs" are ordered at one time, you save the "10c per Kit" handling charge.

The Great Lakes Sport Trainer
Span 20″, length 15⅝″. Beautiful flights. Easy to build. Orange and cream. Kit SF-1, $2.65.

Famous Travel Air Mystery Ship
Span 21¾″, length 14⅞″. Swift flyer. Rich in detail. Red, black scalloping, green trim. Kit SF-2, $2.95.

U. S. Army Boeing P12-E
Span 22½″, length 15⅝″. Excellent army model. Yellow, olive drab with red trimmings. Kit SF-8, $2.85.

English A-W QUAD Fighter
Span 20⅞″, length 18⅞″. Unusual fine-flying type. Easily built. Red, white and blue. Kit SF-11, $2.50.

Von Richthofen's Fokker Triplane
Span 17⅝″, length 14½″. Famous war model. Authentic coloring. Red, silver and white. Kit SF-14, $2.50.

Beautiful Fokker D-7 Fighter
Span 21¼″, length 17″. Rich in details. Orange, green, white, black details. Kit SF-15, $2.95.

'31 Air Race Winner—Bayle's Gee-Bee
Span 17⅛″, length 12″. Speedy flights. Beautiful lines. Yellow and black. Kit SF-17, $1.95.

The Swift Howard Racer "Pete"
Span 15″, length 13⅛″. Excellent flights. Easy to build. All white, black details. Kit SF-18, $1.35.

Schneider Winner—Supermarine S6-B
Span 22¼″, length 21⅝″ overall. Many unusual features. Will R.O.W. Silver and blue. Kit SF-19, $2.50.

Hawker Highspeed Fury Fighter
Span 22¼″, length 19½″. Redesigned. Long fast flights. All silver. Kit SF-20, $2.65.

U. S. Army Hawk P6E Fighter
Span 23⅝″, length 16⅝″. Most authentic Hawk on the market. Yellow, olive drab, Selfridge Field markings. Kit SF-21, $3.25.

U.S. Army Boeing P-26
Span 20⅜″, length 17¾″. Very popular. Super-detailed. Yellow and olive drab. Kit SF-23, $2.50.

The World-Renowned Lockheed Vega
Span 30¾″, length 20⅝″. Beautiful in looks—and flights. Brilliant red and cream. Kit SF-24, $3.25.

Long Flying Heath Parasol Sport
Span 23⅛″, length 12⅝″. Excellent for beginners. Steady flyer. Orange and black. Kit SF-26, 98c.

'32 Air Race Winner—Gee-Bee Supersportster
Span 18⅝″, length 13⅜″. Fast flights. A beauty in looks. White, red scalloping. Kit SF-27, $2.50.

Popular Monocoupe Sportplane
Span 24″, length 15¼″. Has won many first prizes in contests. Cream and orange. Kit SF-28, $2.50.

U.S. Navy Boeing F4B3 (or 4)
Span 22½″, length 15⅝″. Exciting to build—thrilling to fly. Silver, yellow and red. Kit SF-29, $2.85.

Big Boeing 95 Mailplane
Span 33¼″, length 24⅜″. Easy for beginners. Good duration flights. Blue and silver. Kit SF-32, $2.50.

Comper Swift Lightplane
Span 18″, length 13⅝″. Redesigned. Excellent flights. Green with black fuselage design. Kit SF-33, $1.25.

Sensational Lincoln Sport
Span 15″, length 12⅛″. Beginner's model. Interesting flights. Cream, black trim. Kit SF-36, 98c.

Popular Waco C Cabinplane
Span 24¾″, length 19¼″. Beautiful model. Good flyer. Silver and red. Kit SF-37, $3.25.

Aeronca C-3 Sportplane
Span 27″, length 15¼″. Keen flights and very easy for beginners. Red and silver. Kit SF-40, $2.65.

2-place Vought Corsair V-65
Span 26⅞″, length 19¾″. Super detailed. Beautiful flights. Blue, yellow, red, black, and silver. Kit SF-41, $3.75.

Read Before Ordering
If your dealer hasn't or won't get the C-D's you want, order direct, mentioning his name, sending check, or money order—cash at your own risk. No C.O.D.'s. On "Dwarfs"—add 10c extra per Kit for handling. Canada, Mexico, British Isles customers, add 10% to all prices—all other countries, 20%.

4-Wheeled Howard Racer "Ike"
Span 15⅝″, length 12⅞″. Flies and climbs beautifully. Also data for "Mike." White, black details. Kit SF-42, 98c.

Douglas O-38 Observation
Span 30¼″, length 22⅜″. Very beautiful, and unusually well detailed. Yellow, olive drab, black details. Kit SF-43, $3.75.

'30 Air Race Winner—Laird Solution
Span 15⅞″, length 13⅝″. A fast flyer. Pretty lines. Gold and black. Kit SF-46, $2.50.

'33 Air Race Winner—Wedell's W-Williams
Span 19½″, length 16¾″. Very beautiful in appearance and flights. Red, black and bronze. Kit SF-47, $2.95.

'34 Air Race Winner Turner's W-Williams
Span 19½″, length 16⅝″. Roscoe Turner's plane. Fast flying. Wedell-Williams gold. Kit SF-48, $2.95.

DEALERS
Check your C-D stock, and order the Kits you need immediately. Avoid last minute delays—write TODAY.

CLEVELAND MODEL & SUPPLY CO., INC.

Highest Quality **1866PAM WEST 57th ST., CLEVELAND, OHIO, U. S. A.** *Lightning Service*

announcement," full-page ad, offering a ⅙ hp Baby Cyclone engine at $15.75. This ad marked the first major competitive entrant against the Brown Jr. at $21.50 in the national gas model engine derby. The motor's early national presence in the market would enable it to become a well-established, popular brand, and, after improvements and modifications, it would emerge in late 1939 as the Super-Cyclone (Super-cyke), a dual ignition twin spark plug cylinder head design. Although the engine was produced and marketed by Major C. C. Mosley's Aircraft Industries of Grand Central Terminal at Glendale, California, the rotary valve miniature had been designed and perfected by W. E. "Bill" Atwood after years of experimenting with gas powered model speedboats and midget racecars.

Meanwhile, in the model business the buzzword for 1935 was *competition*. C-D's answer was announced in a bevy of *MAN* ads beginning in April and running through July. It was possible to offer the modeler a choice of a Dwarf kit (½-inch scale) or SF ¾-inch scale kit in twenty-nine different aircraft choices. It made C-D the line with the most choices, reflected in the ad's punch line "from 25 cents to 85 cents" in the Dwarf kits. The Dwarf line had become further enhanced with the attractive color scheme of the carton, which was Jim Powell's first major design for C-D.

While the formidable presence of the gassies was in the wings awaiting center stage, C-D's most aggressive marketing campaign to date was unveiled in the 1935 *MAN* August issue. The plan would feature red, white, and blue back cover ads and a black and white center page spread in the last five months of the year. This would prove to be C-D's most ambitious and expensive ad campaign to that point. Each ad had a different, compelling message.

The headline for the August ad, first in the series, "Model Airplane History Has Been Made by Cleveland," was a showstopper. The clean cut, sharp layout in red, white, and blue with a border of stars, and an improved logo featured the six Thompson Trophy winners plus a listing of the "famous 50 SF series." Who else had such an extensive line? What the readers were not aware of was that artist Powell was shrewdly revealing part of C-D's hand— a sneak preview of the 1935 C-D "All American" carton that would feature a field of stars within those patriotic colors.

The August black and white center spread was equally impressive. The character "Modelin' Bill," who had been featured in *CMN&PH* issues, was reactivated by Powell's art and holding the SF-21 Curtiss Hawk P6-E (the unofficial flagship of the SF fleet) along with the message "The whole country's talking about 'em," meaning the thirty-one ½-inch scale Dwarf kits, priced from 25 to 85 cents. A special offer was six Thompson Trophy winner kits, postpaid, for $3.00—quite an offer in 1935's still depressed economy. The C-D campaign, with the back full color ad plus center spread, dominated the August issue and each one of the four subsequent issues, both in space and content.

Facing page: December 1935 *Popular Aviation* magazine ad listing all the C-D Dwarf kits along with the fact that most of them were priced under $1. *E. T. Packard Collection.*

"Modelbuilders: Patronize the Dealer with This Display. It Pays!" was the message in the November *MAN* back cover color ad, illustrating six impressive counter-window display banners to identify a C-D dealer. It was a powerful package of promotional material that a C-D dealer received at no charge with an order of kits. Included in the six banners were two that sent an undeniable message to America's youth: one said, "Break into Aviation—Start as Many Pilots—Fun while Learning," while the other, "Be Prepared for a Successful Career in Aviation . . . Earn while Learning and Further Your Education." For the first time in an ad campaign, Ed Packard had disclosed his deepest passion, identifying his persona, which would further evolve as America approached unavoidable involvement in World War II. The elements of the ad spoke loudly and clearly for his role as "aviation's great recruiter." It is significant that even at this early date in C-D's expansion, Ed had been the recipient of numerous complimentary but true testimonials from those who credited C-D with motivating them and creating an awareness of the possibility of a future career in aviation, a difficult challenge during a depression-plagued economy when jobs were hard to come by. There was no one else in the business end of modeldom that was so obviously sending this message. Furthermore, the national interest in aviation reached a crescendo at the outbreak of America's entry into World War II, continuing until V-E and V-J days.

The ad copy went on to enumerate specific military air bases, colleges, universities, prep schools, and military academies that had become devotees of C-D models and publications. Not listed was the fact that both Royal Frey (at Dayton's Wright Field and later Wright-Patterson's Airforce Museum) and Paul Garber (director of the Air Museum–Smithsonian Institute and the future National Aeronautics and Space Museum [NASM]) were ardent supporters of C-D's ¾-inch museum scale authenticity.

Garber had an arrangement with Ed whereby he would receive the plans for every SF model released, for he himself was an outstanding lifelong model builder and consequently set high standards for exhibition models which the Smithsonian's NASM would accept. (At one time Ed learned that there were some sixty-three models on display made from C-D SF series plans.)

The November *MAN* center-spread ad in the series was absolute dynamite: "Build Real Flying Models . . . First Choice of America's 'Big Shot' Model Builders" headlined the layout, with one half of the spread featuring a smashing Powell illustration of an SF-21 Martin B-10 with props spinning and guns blazing. In the right-hand lower corner Powell had meticulously illustrated all the partially finished components found in C-D kits: turned cowls, cowling and rings, prop hubs, spinners, wheel shoe semi-cut blocks, and so on. No modeler would be able to thumb the pages of that issue without being stopped dead in his tracks with the impact of the dynamic Powell graphics.

The December *MAN* back-cover color ad, appropriately in keeping with the holiday spirit, featured an authentic Powell-created Santa with a gallery of

SF models surrounded by a border of holly and what appeared to be a new C-D carton hot off Powell's drawing board. The accompanying center spread divulged the new design close up—"No Christmas Wrappings Necessary." That said it all. The carton was so attractive and dressed up that gift wrapping was unnecessary. Neither Ed nor Powell could have possibly dreamed that that carton designed in 1935, with a metallic silver-hued background and trimmed at each end in red and blue with a field of silver stars—the "All American" carton—would be as impressive and revered as to be treasured by collectors sixty years later. Any C-D kit in that one-of-a-kind carton commands a premium price and is highly prized by C-D collectors even today.

The December ads were indeed a fitting climax to the five-month-long ad campaign and the resultant increased sales, particularly in the competitively priced Dwarf line, further established C-D's industry leadership and more than justified the additional startup expenses. The trade and the modelers concurred that the innovative "All American" carton design deserved high praise and, coupled with the high quality of the contents, C-D delivered a winning combination.

Miniature Gas Model Engines Available in 1936

Name	Assembled Price	K.D. (knock-down)
Brown Jr. (Junior Motors)	$21.50	
Tlush Super Ace (Frank Tlush)	$21.50	
Forster (Forster Bros.)	$18.00	$5.50
Gwin Aero (Bunch)	$17.50	
Tom Thumb (Bunch)	$17.50	$9.85
Mighty Midget (Bunch)	$17.50	$9.85
Baby Cyclone (Aircraft Industries)	$15.75	
G. H. Q. (GHQ)	$12.50	$8.50

Special types: Fergusson Four, $75. Fergusson Twin, $35.

Gas Model Kits Available in 1936

Name	Manufacturer	Price
Lockheed Vega	(Miniature)	$25.00
Boeing F4-B4	(Miniature)	$25.00
Custom Cavalier	(Berkeley)	$15.00
Corben	(Modelcraft)	$12.75
Scorpion	(Bunch)	$12.50
Buhl "Bull Pup"	(Cyclone)	$10.00
Heath Parasol	(Rubin)	$10.00
Denny Plane Jr.	(Denny Industries)	$10.00
Buccaneer	(Berkeley)	$9.50
Super Buccaneer	(Berkeley)	$8.50

Name	Manufacturer	Price
Miss America	(Scientific)	$7.50
Red Zephyr	(Scientific)	$5.95
California Chief	(Aircraft Industries)	$7.95
GHQ Loutrel	(GHQ)	$5.00
The Scout	(Modelcraft)	$4.85
King Burd (Mid-wing designs)	(Burd)	$3.00

Speed Record Breakers of 1935

The temperament common to aviation's performance contenders in the 1930s drove them to eclipse the previous year's speed and distance records. Higher, faster, farther. The year 1935 was no exception, and before the epochal records of the year's world aircraft were relegated to history, several spectacular winged feats would be memorably recognized by C-D in miniature.

Lady Luck was not with the dashing, intrepid Roscoe Turner in 1935 in either the Bendix or the Thompson events. "Mister" Mulligan, the dazzling white streamlined high wing racer of Benny Howard, nosed out Turner in a photo finish in the Bendix by a mere 23.5 seconds. In the Thompson, he was also dealt a losing hand by fate when, as he was leading the pack in the ninth lap by a comfortable margin, suddenly the Hornet engine in his Wedell-Williams No. 57 faltered, black smoke and oil filled the cockpit, and, fortunately, Roscoe skillfully managed to make a safe forced landing and save the plane. Harold Neumann, flying "Mister" Mulligan for Benny, moved into the lead and shortly thereafter copped first place. So, Howard's Hornet-powered "Mister" Mulligan made a clean sweep of both the Bendix and the Thompson, Benny thus walking off with $17,250 in prize money, a small fortune in 1935.

Familiar with all of the racing pilot fraternity over the years through his

The C-D ad offered a choice of six Thompson Trophy winners as souvenirs and listed the location of the C-D store, which was off the main thoroughfare to the airport. C-D was the only model concern to advertise in the 1934 Cleveland National Air Races program. *E. T. Packard Collection.*

"WE"

N·X·211

The famous flier's own
story of his life and ~
his Transatlantic flight,
together with his views
on the future of aviation.

By
CHARLES A. LINDBERGH

Cover of *Lone Eagle* pulp celebrating Lindbergh's trans-Atlantic flight.

July 1929 cover of *MAN*.

Beginning in this Issue ... A Course On Airplane Designing For Model Makers

MODEL AIRPLANE NEWS

December

A MACFADDEN PUBLICATION
PRICE 15 CENTS

HOW TO BUILD—
A three foot flying scale model of the

A thrilling air mail story entitled
Eagle Jim's Kid

December 1929 Christmas cover
of *MAN*.

1932
NATIONAL AIR RACES
OFFICIAL PROGRAM
CLEVELAND   PRICE 25¢

Official program for 1932 National Air Races, featuring Hubbell cover art.

National Air Races promotional
items—collage.

Actual Photograph of Model Minutely Detailed,
Built from the Complete Cee-Dee Kit, even to the Coloring

Build and   **Fly this**

Cleveland - Designed

Great Lakes Sport Trainer

C-D dealer display card, 1930.
Author's Collection.

February 1933 issue of *Sky Birds*,
with Tinsley art.

October 1935 cover of *Bill Barnes,
Air Trails,* with Tinsley art.

CLEVELAND
MODELMAKING NEWS
& Practical Hobbies

Vol. 2, No. 7   *Winter Issue*

In this Issue:

3/4" VOUGHT CORSAIR V65 ● PACKARD PHAETON ● INDIA ELEPHANT ● 3/16" UNION PACIFIC STREAM-LINED TRAIN
and a treasure trove of other interesting features

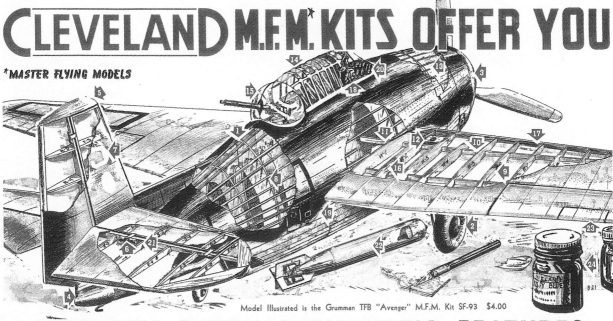

CLEVELAND M.F.M.* KITS OFFER YOU

*MASTER FLYING MODELS

Model Illustrated is the Grumman TFB "Avenger" M.F.M. Kit SF-93 $4.00

THESE TWO DOZEN OUTSTANDING FEATURES:

1. Half-shell fuselage construction—the best all-around method for constructing fuselages.

2. Shaped scale balsa wheels — fully rounded — just like the real thing.

3. Shaped balsa cowl — no more tedious whittling away. Just sand to shape.

4. Balsa tail block — avoids that unfinished-looking tail cone.

5. Printed sheet wood which is selected from light, firm balsa.

6. Moveable control surfaces where you need them.

7. Authentic insignia with which to add those finishing touches.

8. Bulkhead and stringer spacing, which affords maximum strength, without sacrificing lightness.

9. Rib spacing that keeps the airfoil section accurately uniform through the length of the wing.

10. Wing spars of balsa which give maximum strength, eliminating weakness, and a tendency to warp.

11. A good, sturdy method of joining the wing to the fuselage - no more loose and broken wings.

12. A dependable method of joining the landing gear to the wing, which eliminates the headache of broken landing gear.

13. Plenty of wood to "fill in" or cover the nose section where needed.

14. Enough celluloid to cover the entire canopy.

15. Detailed information given for making canopies for that "detailed-to-the-n-th degree"appearance.

16. An accurate scale airfoil section.

17. Smoothly cut strip balsa, which will insure a good tissue covering.

18. Plans for carving a scale pilot.

19. Detailed plans for coloring the model in exact accordance with the original plane.

20. A printed instrument panel, which is exactly like the real thing.

21. All curved parts are printed on the sheet balsa and clearly labelled, leaving no chance for an error.

22. Enough material and sufficient information to make the extras, such as torpedoes, rocket launching tubes, rockets, etc.

23. All trim-tabs, flaps, etc.authentically indicated.

24. Sufficient cement and dope of each color to color the model authentically.

Facing page: TRW artist Charles Hubbell's last issue. *Author's Collection.*

This page: The SF-93 Grumman TBF. *Author's Collection.*

JAN

10¢

DARE-DEVIL ACES

A POPULAR PUBLICATION

Frederick
blakeslee

The **WIZARD ACE**
A THREE MOSQUITOES THRILLER

The **ONE-ACE SQUADRON**
by R. SIDNEY BOWEN

This and facing page: Examples of Frederick Blakeslee's cover art. *Author's Collection.*

MODEL AIRPLANE NEWS

JULY 1949 · 25 CENTS

1929-1949 · 20TH YEAR OF CONTINUOUS PUBLICATION

NAVAL AVIATION NEWS

November 1978

Facing page: July 1949 cover of *MAN*, 20th anniversary edition.

This page: Cover featuring C-D model Curtiss (Sparrowhawk) Macon fighter. *Author's Collection.*

Above: Fulmer's hobby shop re-creation in AMA museum.

Right: Fulmer's model of 1918 Fokker DVII.

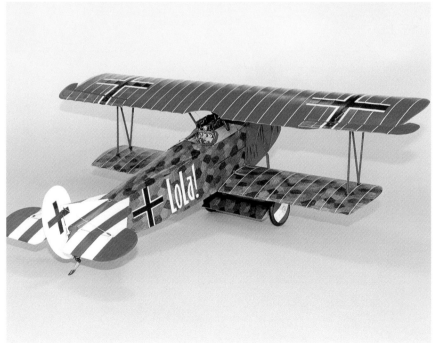

The 1976 Aviation Historical Society banquet honoring Jimmy Doolittle's 80th birthday. Artist John Desatoff. *Author's Collection.*

Overleaf: 75th anniversary issue of *MAN.*

MODEL Airplane NEWS

JANUARY 2004

THE BEST-SELLING RC FLIGHT MAGAZINE

MODEL AIRPLANE NEWS

75th ANNIVERSARY

1929-2004

Hobbico NexSTAR *Easiest trainer ever!*

First Transatlantic RC Flight! *Record-setting odyssey*

New for 2004 *50 must-have products*

modelairplanenews.com

AirAGE MEDIA

$5.99US $8.99CAN

01>

RCX.COM

0 09128 48120 3

Benny Howard's "Mister" Mulligan 1935 racer, which won both the Thompson and the Bendix. Howard flew in the Bendix and Harold Neumann flew in the Thompson. *R. S. Hirsch Collection.*

The R-54 "Rep" model of the famous Hughes H-1 land speed record holder (352 mph) in a posed in-flight scene. This photo of the model was used in many ads, and readers invariably assumed it was a photo of the real aircraft. *E. T. Packard Collection.*

close, long-term relationship with superintendent Jack Berry and his airport management staff, plus having known the flamboyant National Air Race managing director, Cliff Henderson, Ed sought out the victorious Benny Howard. "I wanted to discuss our plans for producing a C-D kit," Ed disclosed, "and there was never any problem in the past with any of the other race winners concerning their ships. In the brotherhood of air race pilots, Ed had been duly accepted. However, Howard began a litany of requirements he expected in return for a set of 'Mister' Mulligan plans, concluding with a reference to Cleveland Model and Supply as having made a lot of money off the National Air Races. In short, Howard was the only air race pilot with whom I was unable to click. He just charged off in a huff.

"My local competitor, Peerless Model Airplane Company of Lakewood, apparently had negotiated some arrangement with Ben. Their full-page ad in the November 1935 issue of *MAN* proudly proclaimed that the Peerless kit was the only kit authorized by Ben O. Howard. All other kits were copies of our well known design. I have often wondered if Benny ever learned that [in 1942] at their request I acquired Peerless for $3,500 to end their threats."

Ed, however, was able to retaliate competitively just three months later when C-D's red, white, and blue color ad on the outside back cover of the March 1936 issue of *Model Airplane News* featured the first in his series of "Rep Kits," a 20-inch span "Mister" Mulligan at 50 cents, versus the competition's $3.00. The "Rep line" was introduced to answer the modelers demand for a less expensive, lighter, less detailed scale flying model, and it went over big."

One of the other astounding aerial feats of 1935 occurred on September 13 at Santa Ana, California, when the accomplished, mysterious Howard Hughes established a new world's land plane speed record of 352.388 mph in his H-1 racer, an exceptionally streamlined (P&W R-1535), 1,000 hp, low-wing, 25-foot wingspan, retractable-geared monoplane. Designed by visionary Cal Tech engineer Dick Palmer, its elegance was characterized by the majestic sweep of the bell cowling and deep wing fillets. The aircraft's finish was unparalleled with its butt joint flush riveted fuselage and Fuller blue mirror finish plywood covered wing, representing the then state-of-the-art of a propeller-driven aircraft configuration.

Just over a year later, on January 20, 1937, modified with a set of slightly greater span wings (32-foot span for increased fuel capacity), Hughes's H-1B smashed every transcontinental speed record in existence from Los Angeles to Newark (seven hours, twenty-eight minutes). It is now displayed in all its glory at the Smithsonian's NASM, highlighted by an unbroken, almost sculptured transition from fuselage to vertical fin. Its clean lines and aerodynamic superiority attest to its qualifications to be judged as perhaps the most precise hand-built machine of all time. (Perhaps more important, Hughes's dual achievements in aviation's top speed and distance records underscored again what the Wright Brothers initiated, that there is no limit to what can be accomplished as a result of the freedom inherent in America's private enterprise system.)

Ed had written to Dick Palmer to obtain H-1 "specs" but had to seek elsewhere, for he received only details of the Fuller blue and yellow numeraled color scheme. On the outside back cover of the May 1936 issue of *MAN,* the R-54 C-D kit at 75 cents headlined the ad, with illustrations of the Hughes racer, gear retracted in full flight, and another view in a three-point static position.

While 1935 represented the year that C-D further established its supremacy with its competitively priced Dwarf line and ambitious advertising campaign (featuring a series of combination outside back-cover color ads plus center black-and-white spreads), by the end of 1936 C-D's image would undergo a major modification, which would only further enhance its already impressive status.

Air and Space

What was becoming clear to the ambitious entrepreneur was that further expansion of Ed Packard's facilities was limited by the lack of adequate space. This was beginning to be discussed by the members of the Pachasa family among themselves as well as within the entire C-D staff. Ironically, this shortcoming gained strategic importance for C-D when the September 1936 *MAN* issue appeared, containing a one-third page ad by Peerless with a photo of their "new giant factory building," located on Madison Avenue in Cleveland.

Ed had developed close, long-term relationships with his suppliers, many of whom admired the undaunted, gutsy young entrepreneur and the Pachasa family. Consequently, they favored him with the best possible quality of products or services, because they wanted to see him succeed and feel as though they had played a part in his success.

Such was his association with office furniture and store fixture dealer Al Moritz, located at 4222 Lorain Avenue. In 1932 he had supplied Ed with a solid walnut, 36-by-72-inch, 300 pound desk, chairs, and accessories for the grand sum of $48. Since the nature of his business placed him in contact with all types of enterprises, he became known for his insight and information concerning the character and financial condition present in the Cleveland West Side business world. Hence, he learned of a business occupying a building located not too far from the Pachasas on Lorain Avenue that would be moving out in the near future.

Al urged Ed to at least look at this structure and evaluate its possibilities. He had promised himself to investigate; however, the increasing number of ads in C-D's current aggressive campaign series for which he wrote all the copy (Ed never mastered the typewriter and always relied on a clerk typist to transcribe his voluminous handwritten copy), his added supervision responsibility for Jim Powell and the increasing number of draftsmen, and the challenge to locate to an engine supplier for C-D to sell for around $10 filled Ed's schedule. It would simply have to wait.

1936—On the Threshold of Becoming a Hobby House

Based on the success of the last five months of 1935's ad campaign combining back-cover color layouts with a black-and-white center spread, C-D committed for the same space in *MAN* for all twelve months in 1936, plus a lesser presence in *Popular Aviation*. Many long hours of thought, planning, evaluation, and hand-wringing went into arriving at this decision, for it represented a substantial portion of C-D's budget for the year.

However, in retrospect, 1936 would be seen as the period when the gas model derby, involving both gas models and their engines, came of age. Before the year's events were history, the marketplace would feature a representative number of gas model designs and engines offering dealers and modelers ample choice with competitive prices. Fortunately, because Ed Packard was on the leading edge of the model industry, C-D would become identified as a major force in integrating modeling and the hobby industry. From November 1936 on, C-D's image as evidenced in *MAN* would evolve into the status Ed had always dreamed of—a complete hobby house.

Far from taking their citizenship in America's democratic society for granted, the Pachasas were dedicated Americans, proud of their country. The patriotic sensibility that Ed harbored influenced his outlook and planning for C-D's destiny. His fierce dedication to aviation's future was another driving force, influenced by his direct employment in what were then the two major airframe manufacturers of the 1920s. The love of flying and aviation had become acquired by watching, knowing, and serving itinerant barnstormers and air mail pilots as they landed their pioneering aircraft in Cleveland. He had become hopelessly hooked on the romance of the age of the early birds. The realization at this point in his career that he was not able to participate in the light plane business, the next best avenue for him to pursue was to be one of aviation's best boosters.

What better way than to utilize every opportunity for C-D to demonstrate the rapidly expanding opportunities in aviation for youth than through modeling and its associated activities? An example of this deeply entrenched devotion to his cause was effectively dramatized on the outside back cover of the February 1936 issue of *MAN*. The headline emblazoned in red, white, and blue read "Help Make America First in the Air." The rest of the ad read, "Aviation is in urgent need of intelligent, well-educated men and women, and there is no better way of getting preliminary aviation training at a minimum of expense than by building the world famous Cleveland-Designed models."

The combination of Jim Powell's appealing art of a Boeing 247D pilot at the controls and an in-flight Lockheed Vega plus the compelling copy were destined to create an interest in aviation for the young modelers. Then the C-D "hard sell" was effectively presented in the accompanying center spread with many in-flight and static display photos of striking models, with one of the captions stating, "C-D kits are even better than advertised."

Designed to stimulate the action-oriented cravings of young modelers in the summer months, the July *MAN* issue utilized a clever combination of ads, with the outside back cover featuring selected SF series models, all priced over one dollar, the top of the C-D line, its headline stating: "Most Underpriced Flying Model Airplanes in America Today" and another caption blaring, "Our Kits Really Do Build Models As They Appear Here." The accompanying center-spread ad featured the bargains of the C-D line, the Reps and

Back covers of C-D catalogs were also used in advertisements promoting the attractiveness of C-D cartons to the dealer and consumer. Space was left blank for the dealer to insert his name and location (ca. 1935). The new "Master Flying Model Kit," which took all the elements of the "All American" carton and expanded them into a container suited for retailer displays as well as for liquids. These colorful cartons displayed in PX military canteens and ships' stores generated many sales among servicemen, particularly those connected with either Navy or Army aircraft. *E. T. Packard Collection.*

the Dwarfs, all priced under one dollar, with many models shown priced at 50 cents—an astute merchandising strategy to use in still-depressed 1936.

One of the most notable indications that C-D had attained a significant degree of national recognition and acceptance occurred during the last quarter of the year. Berry Brothers of Detroit, one of the most well-known manufacturers of aircraft finishes (Berryloid Finishes), announced a national contest in a full-color ad on the back cover of the October 1936 issue of *Popular Aviation.* Berryloid offered modelers an opportunity to build a ½-inch scale C-D Dwarf kit of a Waco C-6 cabin; four bottles of Berryloid finishes; a booklet,

"Specifications for Model Finishing"; and a reprint of the Waco C-6 cabin Herman R. Bollin painting on the issue's cover; all for $1.00. To qualify for fourteen cash prizes, a contestant was required to send a photo of his completed model plus a fifty-word letter on "Why I like Berryloid aircraft finishes."

The October ad was followed by another in the November issue, with the Seversky P-35 as the C-D contest model, and by the December edition featuring the Beechcraft C-17B. Berryloid was seeking to capitalize on the relationship with Cleveland Model and Supply to stimulate modelers' demands for Berryloid Finishes, perhaps to having C-D consider using Berryloid Finishes in their kits. Further, Berryloid wished to realize the benefits of their involvement with modelers as future aircraft owners or participants in the aviation industry, as well as the favorable resultant public relations with the aircraft manufacturers and fixed base operators (FBOs). The full-color ads were loaded with boldface listings of the cash prizes, the reproduction of the C-D "All American" carton, and completed with a coupon cutout with three choices.

"The Berryloid campaign undoubtedly benefited C-D more so than creating demand for their finishes," quipped Ed. "It provided us with three months of free color back cover ad recognition, further publicizing our new carton, which was represented prominently in color. We experienced some inquiries as a result and some of our C-D dealers reported modelers coming in to ask to look at one of the three different kits advertised.

"We, of course, had a fine relationship with our local supplier, S. P. Wilson, vice president and chemist of Varnish Products Company, who developed the special C-D finishes we were using, which added a further touch of realism to our models because the colors had been custom mixed to match, as closely as possible, actual aircraft color finishes. Our dopes were purchased in bulk in drums from Wilson, and with spigots installed, the C-D bottles were manually filled at the location across the street until later on, when municipal regulations forced us to comply with a series of bureaucratic requirements relating to fire hazards and resultant dangerous fumes."

The Gas Model Derby

The gas model derby in 1936 was rapidly gaining more entries of engines and kits as the year progressed. With the invasion of the gassies having had its inception on the East Coast, manufacturers were initially concentrated in that area; however, the movement gradually spread to Chicago and the rest of the Midwest. Subsequently, the West Coast realized a great concentration of activity, particularly in southern California, where year-round flying was possible. Throughout its long-term existence, C-D's greatest sales and market penetration was on the West Coast, particularly in California. (This was partially due to C-D's caveat of filling orders and shipping the same day received. This made it possible for West Coast customers to receive better service from C-D than they could expect from many local suppliers in the West.)

As the year waned, eight nationally advertised engines and some twelve gassie kits were lined up at the starting gate. Significantly, the prices of the miniature power plants ranged from $9.85 for a Mighty Midget to $21.50 for the Brown Jr., the entry that had started it all.

The lineup of the kits ranged from $3.00 for a King Burd from the Burd Company to $25.00 for a Miniature Aircraft Company–scale Lockheed Vega.

The gas model derby at this juncture certainly offered an ample, representative choice of engines to accommodate almost any modeler's budget, with the kits providing a similar wide range in price with a choice of many proven high-wing cabin designs as well as two excellent midwing monoplane types.

The extensive array of derby entrants materialized in slightly over one year; it forecast that the field would soon be experiencing a virtual glut of engines and kits. All of this activity did not include several available gas model plans and knockdown engine kits available for the more mechanically oriented modelers. As the tempo of the gas model derby escalated during 1936, new engine and model kit entrants appeared nearly every month. Therefore, C-D could not delay its entry into the competitive race much longer without risking lost sales as well as industry leadership. This was even more critical in the instance of the gassies, since many of the newer companies were either involved with the gas engine segment of the market exclusively or were entering the race with a combination package of an engine and model kit without the added investment and expense required to support an additional complete line of non-gas-powered models and accessories. Many of the new contenders, with correspondingly lower expenses and overhead, could operate on lower profit margins and concentrate their advertising and promotional dollars on the gassies only.

Agonizing nights of planning, evaluating, and finalizing his marketing strategy were routine for the entrepreneur to position C-D to the best possible entering advantage. Logically, because the end-of-the-year holiday buying season represented such a significant segment of C-D's annual sales, as well as that of the dealers, that time frame had to be the deadline; he could not miss that strategic marketing opportunity. So it was no great surprise that in the November issue of *MAN*, the now readily recognized C-D "home base" center-spread ad carried the bold declaration: "The Catalog Everyone Has Been Waiting for Is Now Ready." In his typical decisive fashion, Ed concluded that if C-D were ever to assume its rightful industry position, it was now.

Consequently, he combined his strategic move into the gas model field with the dramatic announcement of C-D as a complete hobby house effectively presented in a sixty-four-page catalog at 10 cents containing products from

November 1936 *MAN* center-spread ad announcing the No. 20 hobby catalog, listing items from more than 100 manufacturers. This hobby catalog was a lifelong interest and goal of Packard's and placed C-D in a special category in the industry. *E. T. Packard Collection.*

more than 100 suppliers, plus announcing a line of miniature engines and gas model kits. A brilliant strategy, it placed C-D in an exclusive, prestigious slot, thereby providing additional reasons for dealers and hobbyists of all types to do business with the Pachasas, because model ships, model railroads, miniature race cars, a line of ¼-inch scale solid models, and a wide assortment of accessories and hobby tools had also been included in the catalog. Well over a year's worth of planning and contacting suppliers resulted in a great array of diverse products that were professionally illustrated, described, and priced.

Concurrently, Ed and his draftsmen had been finalizing plans for the first 2-inch scale C-D gas model kits. However, since they had not been able to be ready for shipment, two other models were listed as an alternative in the November ad: a Paul Lindbergh *Popular Aviation* Rearwin Speedster kit at $7.00 and a freelance design, Scorpion kit at $12.50, which had been designed to be mated with the C-D Tom Thumb engine. C-D had a standardized Tom Thumb kit available at $9.75 or assembled at $17.50, made possible by an arrangement with Bud Warren of Bunch Motors in Los Angeles to buy two hundred units in return for C-D exclusivity on the Tom Thumb brand. Other power plant choices were listed: Baby Cyclone, Brown Jr., Forster, and the Fergusson Twin and Four Cylinder models.

The sixty-four-page catalog was an impressive effort, enhanced with cover art and many interior illustrations by Jim Powell. At a price of 10 cents, it was a great bargain, and C-D received many coupons with dimes in the mail from the November *MAN* issue ad, selling out the initial print run in sixty days.

With the continuing improvement in the nation's economy, the unemployment rate in 1936 was reduced by two million, from 18.4 to 14.5 percent, on its way to 6.4 million, a 12 percent unemployment rate, which would be the lowest until the outbreak of World War II.

As an indication of the worldwide demand for C-D models and supplies, which had increased particularly in Europe, a well-qualified agent, H. Vilen, was appointed in Stockholm, Sweden. In the period of approximately two years in which he functioned, he developed an excellent rapport, resulting in increased sales, with dealers abroad. However, after arrangements had been made for a large shipment of supplies, Vilen died suddenly and all the supplies had to be retrieved from the docks in New York after C-D coped with a great deal of frustrating bureaucracy.

With the positive surge in American business came market pressures to force raw material prices and labor rates upward, with the possibility of the announcement of price increases by manufacturers. In the February 1937 issue of *MAN*, C-D went on record, announcing the possibility of a 25 percent price increase and urging dealers and modelers to "stock up now." However, in yet another example of a bold marketing strategy, it was announced in March that the SF line, pride of C-D and the company meal ticket, would henceforth be sold as "dry kits," sans all liquids. Thus the competitive prices for its top of the line could not only be maintained but C-D could also expect an increase in the sales of their liquid supplies—cement, banana oil, and clear and colored dopes.

Speculation as to what course in gas model design would be undertaken by C-D came to an end also in the March *MAN* issue. Through the medium of two excellent Jim Powell illustrations in the center-spread ad, C-D proudly announced their entrants in the gas model derby with a pair of 2-inch scale designs with the Stinson SR-9 Reliant Gull Wing GP-66 82-inch span kit at $8.50 and the Rearwin Speedster GP-69 64-inch span kit at $4.85. Thus, the modeler had been given a choice of a larger, nearly 7-foot span model with a large enough, spacious interior cabin to be adaptable to future radio-controlled use, plus a medium-sized, slightly over 5-foot span model with a price under $5.00.

Both models were selected for the inherent stability in their respective configurations as well as excellent recognition and acceptance, with attractive design features and sturdy construction. The two designs would form the nucleus of the C-D gas-powered line for years to come, subsequently to be supplemented with various "freelance" types, the most famous of which would be known as the Playboy Senior, a perennial favorite currently as a SAM-OT (Society of Antique Modelers-Old Timer) performer and contest winner.

The model D-64 C-17B Stagger-wing, span 15⅞ inches, experienced a surge in demand after the 1936 Bendix Race, when Louis Thaden won flying the prototype with a Wright R-975 420 hp powerplant. *E. T. Packard Collection.*

When the November 1936 *MAN* ad positioned C-D as a hobby house, their new profile necessitated larger facilities. Seemingly endless hours were spent on the compiling of the sixty-four-page 1937 catalog, but Ed had managed to keep in touch with Al Moritz regarding the Lorain Avenue property he had recommended a while ago. After Ed had finally taken a tour of the multistoried building at 4508 Lorain Avenue, then occupied by the Ryan Hays Candy Company, he realized that if an acceptable deal was struck with the property owner there would still be a great deal of expense involved in the necessary modifications. However, after Ed and his family had discussed the pros and cons of the site, Al Moritz was asked to arrange a meeting with the owner, and an offer was made.

Moritz accepted the offer of $6,000, with a $1,500 downpayment, in April 1937. With the continuing success of C-D in its new home, the balance due would be paid off in approximately three years. The Pachasa family represented not only the strength of the American family but also the resourcefulness and pride of its members, enabling them to capitalize their own financial needs. It was the bedrock foundation of dedicated citizens such as this from which America would be able to recruit its sons and daughters with the will, innovation, and strength necessary to win World War II.

The headline of the September 1937 *MAN* center spread ad announced: "Overwhelming demand for C-D models has proved too great for our present quarters, so "We're Moving!" At the bottom of the ad, the new address was listed for the first time, a location that would become world famous for the next thirty years.

The unimposing structure on Lorain would be transformed into a Valhalla for modeldom and hobbyists from all over the globe (ultimately serving seventy-two countries) and contain an exhibition museum-type showroom, an

impressive engineering department, and a manufacturing and assembly operation unique among its peers, with employment at its peak periods reaching 100.

Thus in this epoch of aviation's development, Cleveland Model and Supply evolved into an estimable company with international recognition. Originally a one-man operation in 1919 and a family-run cottage industry from 1927 to 1929, the company was propelled into national prominence with the introduction of the SF-1, Great Lakes Sport Trainer, the first all-balsa production-scale flying kit. Offering the most complete line of scale flying models in the industry, Cleveland Model and Supply Company announced the expansion of its organization into a hobby house in 1937, and the company's growth necessitated its move from the confines of its humble residential facilities to a 9,000-square-foot, full-scale commercial manufacturing wholesale and retail operation.

Another view of the Lorain Avenue factory store and its many models beckoning from above. Andy Pachasa Jr. is at the counter. With its display of almost the entire line of official scale models, plus the eight-foot China Clipper, it was a virtual museum and was visited by modelers, dealers, and the curious from worldwide during its thirty years in existence. *Will Pachasa Collection.*

CHAPTER 10

The Playboy Family Takes Wing

By the latter part of 1937, when thirty-one-year-old Edward Packard, president of C-D, engineered the move from the family residence on West 57th Street to the Lorain Avenue facility, he had compiled the most impressive record of accomplishments of any model airplane company entrepreneur up to that time. In less than a decade, Cleveland Model and Supply symbolized a jarring incongruity, producing the most authentic scale flying models in quantity in the industry, with a worldwide acceptance within limited residential physical facilities—a cottage industry. It had grown to become a multi-interest hobby business.

He was a man of self-discipline who had great compassion for his fellow human beings and a strong appreciation for personal dignity and the work ethic. He had an unfettered allegiance to God, family, and country. Ed's life-long love affair with airplanes and technology of flight, served him well in attracting and motivating young people to become involved in aviation through modeling. His own plan to become a light plane builder was thwarted by his chance meeting in 1929 with Capt. Holden C. Richardson, vice president of engineering at Cleveland's Great Lakes Aircraft. His new course allowed him to develop a successful business producing kits of miniature model aircraft, whereas if he had he attempted to manufacture light planes during these tough economic times, he would most likely have lost his shirt, as did so many famous aircraft companies and auto manufacturers in the 1930s.

With the move to Lorain Avenue, business relationships within the Pachasa family would never be quite the same. Ed had, of course, moved out of the Pachasa residence after his marriage, and with his wife and two children, was striving to build his own life in his limited time away from the ever-increasing responsibilities imposed by the escalating growth of C-D. With further expansion of C-D possible by augmented facilities of the new building, each one of

The cover of the 1981 *Sport Aviation* featured the Laird Super Solution. The replica was built by dedicated volunteers with input from "Matty" Laird and is on display at the Oshkosh, Wisconsin, EAA Museum. *EAA Sport Aviation.*

The March 1991 cover of *Sport Aviation* featured Bud Davisson's No. 44 Wedell-Williams replica. *EAA Sport Aviation.*

the Pachasas, with the exception of mother Emma and the senior Andrew, would have greater responsibilities in view of more employees to supervise. Simply put, the organization would be split with the office, engineering, and financial staff reporting to Ed and the balance of the personnel (involved with production, tooling, assembly, receiving and shipping) reporting to Will. With the total employees soon numbering between forty and fifty, the close-knit family relationship that previously had been the hallmark of C-D would gradually evolve into a more formal decentralized type of organization.

The first few weeks involving the transition into the new location were a hectic, challenging experience and took its toll through reduced levels of customer service and the depletion of inventory and supplies. This was a blow to the modus operandi of C-D, for it had been an ironclad practice to process all orders within three to six hours of receipt and always shipped the same day received. Modifications to the building to accommodate power equipment; tooling; heating, cooling, and ventilation regulations; plus compliance with the strict fire department restrictions further added to the hubbub and commotion. However, management and employees benefited from the resultant synergy with a feeling of relief and satisfaction because the added space and physical improvements would prove to further motivate employee efficiency and performance. "It was my brother Will's dedicated, conscientious, and skilled supervision over the myriad details of the move that made it come off successfully in a much shorter time," commented Ed.

"With the upheaval in my normal schedule resulting from the preparation of our hobby catalog, the introduction of our first gas models, and the advanced planning for the move to Lorain Avenue, I fell behind in my annual presentation of a kit for the Thompson and Bendix Trophy winners. This was particularly the case when the National Air Races were held at Mines Field, Los Angeles, in September 1936. Consequently, it was not until the January 1937 *MAN* issue that our SF-63 kit (at $1.95) of Michel Detroyat's Caudron C-460 16⅞-inch wingspan Thompson Trophy winner was announced."

For some time the National Air Race Committee had been encouraging foreign competition for the Thompson, and it finally happened in 1936. Detroyat's French Caudron was a diminutive, 22-foot wingspan, 340 hp, 6-cylinder inline 488-cubic-inch Renault-powered retractable-geared entry. It was

The SF-63 C-D model of the French Caudron Thompson Trophy winner of 1936 (span 16⅝, $1.50) in a posed in-flight photo that appeared in several ads. *E. T. Packard Collection.*

The 1936 Los Angeles National Air Races official program. Since the race was held in Los Angeles, there was no C-D involvement. *Author's Collection.*

symbolic of the switch in the design trend of the Thompson winners—from fixed gear, mega-horsepowered, radial engine–designed racers to miniaturized, inline engine-powered, low drag, ultra-streamlined, retractable-geared designs. Both 1936 and 1937 Thompson winners were representative of this trend. (It could be argued that the 1936 results may have been altered had Roscoe Turner not cracked up his Weddell-Williams No. 25 entry in an accident near Holbrook, Arizona, resulting from carburetor icing while ferrying his racer cross-country to New York for the start of the Bendix. He skillfully dead sticked into the desert landscape; however, the plane flipped over and the fuselage broke in two. Lucky for him, Turner suffered only broken ribs and a neck injury.) To add to the challenge of the event, the Thompson course was increased from 10 laps and 150 miles, with a purse of $15,000, in 1935 to 15 laps and 150 miles, with a purse of $20,000, in 1936. In 1937 it would be bumped up to 20 laps and 200 miles with a purse of $25,000.

Beginning in 1937 the C-D ads in *MAN* would alternate between the new 3/16-inch scale, 7/8-inch-wide, two-rail track model railroad kits featured on the back cover and the center-spread ads. To his credit Ed had conceived the C-D gauge two-track system of 3/16-inch scale as the ideal size, in contrast to the popular Lionel and American Flyer 1½-inch, three-rail O-gauge. The C-D railroad concept would prove to be prophetic, for the chief designer and staff from A. C. Gilbert Company's American Flyer line visited Ed, and, ultimately, Gilbert would embrace the more realistic 7/8-inch, two-rail track system, which became identified worldwide as S-gauge. Gilbert's three-rail O-gauge would be scrapped in favor of the two-rail track system and forevermore there would be its worldwide following of Flyer fans. Lionel ultimately would acquire American Flyer. C-D realized no royalties from Gilbert and virtually no recognition until 1987, when Ed was asked to speak at the S-Gaugian's fiftieth-anniversary meeting, where he was interviewed for the July–August issue of the S Gaugian magazine.

It could be debated forever whether the investment in the engineering, tooling, and inventory, plus the added advertising expense of the C-D railroad in a model airplane magazine, was cost effective. The C-D gas models, SF, Dwarf, and Rep lines of kits had to be content to share advertising space with the model railroad kits until August 1938, when the ad campaign in *MAN* was altered to no longer include the back cover plus the center spread. A single-page ad, most often on page 3, was the strategy, and the copy concentrated on gas models, the hobby shop concept, and the scale flying line.

A vigorous economic recovery began in the summer of 1935 and witnessed commercial aviation production units increased from 1,559 in 1936 (at $12.4 million) to 2,281 in 1937 (with a $19.2 million valuation), up 54 percent over 1936. This relatively rosy economic picture since the beginning of the Great Depression (1930) provided American business a reason to press a case for price increases. Consequently, the year would be characterized by many new entries in the gas model derby, as well as price increases on existing model kits and engines. In the January *MAN* issue Irwin Ohlsson of Ohlsson Miniatures of Los Angeles announced their first Class-C engine at $17.50 and then in April hiked the price to $18.50. Frizoli's Newark-located Scientific Model Airplane Company, which early on had purchased their supplies from Ed, increased their Miss America kit to $9.50 and their Red Zephyr kit to $6.95. Comet had entered the race with their Class-C semi-scale Curtiss Robin at $4.95 and increased the price to $6.50 in April. Fred Megow introduced their Quaker Flash kit (5 foot 7 inches) at $4.95. The Ideal Company finally entered the gas model competition with their fist kit, the Air Chief at $6.00. Surprisingly, Ideal would never become a major power in the gas model fray. Then

movie actor Reginald Denny announced his Class-C Dennymite engine at $16.50, with the Denny Jr. kit at $9.50, complete with spun aluminum cowling. However, in sharp contrast to the trend of price increases, the Baby Cyclone engine price was reduced from $15.75 to $12.50. Junior Motors of Philadelphia kept their Model-B at $21.50, but to be competitive with the rest of the pack it introduced an entirely new Model-C at $17.00. C-D proudly displayed their two scale gas models, the Stinson Reliant GP-66 and the Rearwin Speedster GP-69, with attractive realistic photos; the actual models were shown for the first time on the back cover ad of the May 1937 *MAN.*

The year 1938 would see a further proliferation of engine and kit entries in the gas model competition; however, in contrast to 1937, there would be a spate of price decreases. Megow, Scientific, Comet, and Berkeley were battling it out competitively, with each company introducing several new gas models and advertising at least a half-dozen different brands of engines in stock at all times. (Scientific, in two double-spread ads in the December 1938 *MAN,*

The GP-66 Stinson Reliant plan showing the empennage structure and part of the rugged fuselage and well-engineered wing structure (1937). *E. T. Packard Collection.*

would feature four non-scale-type gas models and twelve different engines, boasting of a stock of 1,000 engines for immediate delivery.)

Behind the scenes of the frenetic activity in the marketplace, on the second floor of the Lorain Avenue building in the Engineering Department, Ed Packard and Jim Powell were exerting maximum design capability to complete the configuration of the first non-scale, freelance-type C-D gas model. It had become obvious that the two existing scale gas models were not capable of sustaining the necessary degree of competition in view of the propagation of multiple freelance types by companies like Comet, which had acquired the services of noted model designer Carl Goldberg and who had just introduced the 6-foot Class-C double elliptical wing Comet Clipper at $4.95. With his unique high-performance designs, Goldberg would recast the gas model contest design field in 1939 and thereby force major competitors to follow suit.

Scientific had retained Maxwell Bassett, regarded as the father of the gas model, who had introduced his parasol design 8-foot wingspan Miss Philadelphia at $9.95, as well as his 6-foot wingspan, low-thrust line Streamliner at $4.95. Meanwhile, Berkeley's William Effinger, known best for his Buccaneer designs, added a 6-foot wingspan version of the Custom Cavalier, a 5½-foot wingspan Standard Buccaneer and the Courier Sportster.

Finally, in the October 1938 *MAN,* C-D was able to introduce their first non-scale freelance-type design, Class-B GP-5004, 50-inch wingspan gas-model kit called the Cloudster at $2.50, and Ed breathed a sigh of relief.

The engine component of the industry was not exactly idle either. William Brown's Junior Motors Company unexpectedly startled the industry in the May *MAN* issue with the introduction of their Class-C Model D at ten dollars, apparently serving notice to their many competitors that, with their by now three engine models priced from ten dollars to $21.50, they were capable of fully meeting all comers. (Junior Motors Corporation would later advertise that fifty thousand engines had been sold.)

Before the intensely competitive year went into the record books, the miniature engine field could be characterized most aptly as a battle royal. With the Brown Junior Model D pegged at $10, the Gwinn Aero and Mighty Midget followed at $9.50 each; the Syncro Ace Special announced at a price of $9.95; the well accepted Baby Cyclone retaliated at $9.00, with the bottom rung held by the Tom Thumb at $7.50. Ohlsson Miniatures would further their market penetration with their new Class-B Model 23 at $16.50.

The economy had reacted positively to the reduction in the unemployment rate in 1936 and 1937, but the country's jobless rate in 1938 surged upward by 50 percent, from 12 to 18.8 percent. But the Depression raged on, and it was reflected in the shrinking of modelers' discretionary spending. Many dealers were cutting prices or making combination deals of an engine, gas model kit, plus a propeller thrown in to make the sale. C-D announced in the November 1938 issue of *MAN:* "Save Up to 33⅓ Percent on C-D Kits," applicable to the SF and Dwarf lines. Fortunately, while C-D's investment in the over one hundred different items comprising the hobby shop catalog was substantial, and the extensive line offered translated into sales diversification—a lifesaver. While his peers were engaged in intensive competitive manipulations, C-D could take solace that their cash registers were ringing up sales on many items not involved in the competitive industry fray.

Early in the year, in order to bolster C-D sales in New York City, the great New Jersey Bamberger Department Store, with its famous 40-foot counter hobby shop, announced that Irwin and Nathan Polk's Model Craft Hobbies, located diagonally opposite the teeming Penn Station, had been appointed as a C-D distributor. Polk Brothers advertised, "Every C-D Kit in Stock at Polks." Nathan Polk was deeply involved in the administration of the IGMAA, NAA, and the AMA, and both Irwin and Nathan served on the committees of many of the Nationals and other major gas model contests.

The 1937 Thompson had been staged at Cleveland Municipal, boasting a more challenging course with an increase from ten fifteen-mile laps in 1936 to ten twenty-mile laps and a corresponding increase in the purse, from $20,000 to $25,000. Thus, the air racers would have to plan their strategy more carefully lest they undergo blown cylinder heads or superchargers during the additional fifty miles involved.

The 1937 Cleveland National Air Races display of the Standard Oil Company, which relied on Ed Packard to provide a cavalcade of Thompson Trophy racer winners with a C-D model for each year. Suspended over the top of this diorama was the magnificent Martin 130 China Clipper eight-foot model, which had hung from Cleveland Model's Lorain Avenue store for several years. Ed never asked for or received any compensation for efforts of this type. It was a labor of love. *E. T. Packard Collection.*

SF-71 Folkert's Special with a retractable gear extended. The
model was designed so that the
modeler could build it with the
gear able to be shown retracted or
extended for exhibition purposes
at $1.50 (1937). *E. T. Packard Col-
lection.*

The 1937 Thompson trophy winner, Rudy Kling, by his Clayton-
Folkerts 16-foot wingspan 400 hp
racer. *R. S. Hirsch Collection.*

The intrepid Roscoe Turner in his 25-foot wingspan No. 29 newly built
Laird-Turner Ring-Free Meteor 1,000 hp Twin Wasp, fixed gear, midwing speedster, was a prerace favorite. Serious contenders were Earl Ortman and his 25-
foot wingspan Marcoux-Bromberg Special Twin Wasp Keith Rider R-3 and
Rudy Kling in his *Pride of Lamont* Clayton Folkers–built diminutive 16-foot-
8-inch wingspan SK-3 Menasco 6-cylinder in-line, 400 hp supercharged, retractable-geared racer.

The race results may have been quite different if Turner had not made a
quick 360-degree turn to compensate for what he thought was a cut pylon,

for he had been in the lead, averaging 262 mph. Thus, the final lap was between Ortman and Kling. In the final moments, just before the checkered flag was dropped, Kling dived his winged bullet from above and nosed out Ortman for first place by a mere fifty feet. His average speed was 256.91 mph. It was to be a short-lived victory for Rudy; he would lose his life in the following year at the Miami Air Races.

The January 1938 *MAN* center-spread ad announced the C-D 12-inch wingspan C-D Folkerts Special SF-71 at $1.95 and companion D-71 ½-inch scale kit at 65 cents, sans photo. The following February issue had a full-page C-D ad with a dramatic photo of the sleek, trim Folkerts featuring a movable retractable landing gear and an eye-catching cream with red trim color scheme.

The legion of Roscoe Turner's loyal fans had much to cheer about at the 1938 Cleveland National Air Races. The colorful Turner, astride his new Wasp 1,000 hp No. 29 Laird-Turner, 25-foot wingspan midwing speedster, had the throttle at the firewall during most of the Thompson's 30-lap, 300-mile course, turning 2,600 rpm and pulling 47 inches of manifold pressure. This time he was doubly careful not to cut a pylon and kept a comfortable margin ahead of Earl Ortman's R-3, who was in second place. His average speed of 283.416 mph placed him in the Thompson winner's circle with the $18,000 first prize, plus a $4,000 bonus Ludlum award for exceeding Detroyat's 1937 speed of 264.261 mph. It also provided the flamboyant air racer with the distinction of being the only two-time Thompson Trophy winner.

The January 1939 *MAN* page 3 C-D ad proudly offered the DSLF-72 (Deluxe Scale Flying Kit) at $2.50, and Turner's modeldom fans proved their loyalty by an enthusiastic demand for the initial run of the kit.

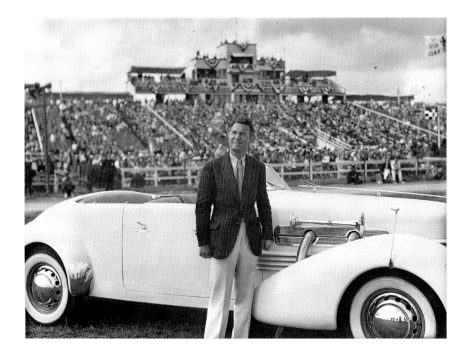

Cliff Henderson, managing director of the National Air Races, at Cleveland Municipal Airport. The model 812 Cord Phaeton he poses beside had a 289 cubic inch Lycoming engine (4.7 liter V-8) and was famed designer Gordon Buehrig's most famous automobile (he also designed the Duesenberg and Lincoln). The Cord, with a Schwitzer-Cummins supercharger, horsepower increased from 125 hp to 170 hp. Prices ranged from $1,995 to $3,600 with front-wheel drive. Cord unfortunately became a casualty of the Great Depression (1937). *Author's Collection.*

In the March 1939 issue of *MAN* the Burd Company of Baltimore would electrify the industry and please modelers with a double-spread inside-back-cover ad offering a kit of the Korda Wakefield 43-inch-span winner for the astounding price of only 29 cents.

Comet, in its new assertive stand in the industry, would begin its assault on the potential gas model contest market in its May *MAN* inside-back-cover teaser ad, stating, "Next month Comet will present on this page: Carl Goldberg's latest and greatest achievements in gas models." In the following June issue, in an inside-back-cover double-spread ad, the twin "bombshells" were unveiled—the 54-inch wingspan parasol pylon-mounted double-elliptical wing soon to be famous and aptly named Zipper at $3.95, shown with its 42-inch wingspan companion pylon-designed Mercury at $2.95. To back up Comet's and Goldberg's lofty claims, the following September's *MAN* inside-back-cover ad had the sensational headline, "Comet Models Sweep the Nationals at Detroit." In the unlimited category, the Zipper took the first nine places, operating under the AMA 20-second motor run. And so it went in all three contest categories. It was either Zipper, Mercury, or Clipper entries that walked off with the winning "hardware." Carl Goldberg and Comet had thus served notice on the model industry that the pylon-mounted, parasol-type design was here to stay. The result was that the entire industry went back to their respective drawing boards to retaliate with their own designs to meet this startling competition. (I remember an NAA meet at Benson Park, Omaha, Nebraska, in the spring of 1940. Any contestant without a Zipper, Mercury, or Clipper was simply blown away. The crowd was mesmerized by the vertical climb of the Zippers and the roll out at the top of the spiral climb at the end of the 20-second motor run, followed by the flat, hanging, thermal-seeking glide. I didn't bother flying my Super Buccaneer, powered by a Brown Junior—to be competitive I would have needed a Forster 99.)

In the configuration of the Zipper, Goldberg had utilized and parlayed his years of indoor modeling experience, which typically features parasol designs. He then transformed that acquired data and technology into the design of his parasol, pylon-mounted double elliptical, 10-foot wingspan, awe-inspiring Valkyrie—ultimately distilling its desirable characteristics, which were exploited in the 54-inch wingspan of the Zipper, approximately one half the span of the aerodynamically supreme marvel Valkyrie.

Ed Packard had not been caught unawares, for his many champion modeler friends and industry associates had kept him advised of the progress of the Zipper and other pylon-mounted designs in the year preceding the 1939 Nationals. Following the current trend in the industry of establishing a design-consultation relationship with a well-known contest-winning modeler, what could be a more logical such arrangement than one with the famous Dick Korda, 1939 Wakefield winner and a member of the hometown Cleveland Balsa Butchers model club?

The result of this relationship was announced in a December *MAN* double-page spread—"Two New Cleveland Gas Model Super Values"—Dick Korda's sensational new Champion exclusive with Cleveland (GP-5005), which generated sales of only 278 kits, not exactly a smash hit. The Champion was a 48-inch wingspan pylon-mounted Class-B gas model with a planked fuselage at $2.95. Its companion model was the Fleetster, a 42½-inch wingspan double-elliptical planform cabin design GP-5007 at $2.50. No doubt this situation forced Ed to roll up his sleeves and create a design to meet Comet's competition.

The 1939 National Air Races sounded its own death knell. First of all, it was announced that Cliff Henderson and his brother Phil had resigned from future management of the National Air Races. Participation by air-race pilots had steadily dwindled the last few years, in part because the expense of designing and building a worthy competitive air racer had escalated to approximately $50,000. The prize money was not enough to recoup even a substantial portion of such an expensive venture.

The Henderson Brothers must have known that the war clouds gathering over Europe would preclude holding future National Air Races anyway. The Spanish Civil War erupted in 1936, and Francisco Franco negotiated with Hitler, offering Spain's iron ore for German JU 52s and Dornier Do.17 bombers, which enabled the Luftwaffe's Hermann Goering to test his young Nazi airmen and

The 1938 National Air Races winner Roscoe Turner at 283 mph (new record) receiving the Thompson and Ludlum trophies from Fred C. Crawford, president of Thompson Products (later TRW). *R. S. Hirsch Collection.*

unproven Bf.109 Messerschmitt fighter. Two of the future-leading Luftwaffe aces, Werner Molders (115 victories) and Lt. General Adolph Galland (104 victories), developed their aerial strategies during the conflagration—Galland flying more than 300 sorties. At the same time the Japanese were invading mainland China, and, likewise, they had an opportunity to test their developing aircraft and to train their fledgling airmen under limited wartime conditions.

In April 1939, in anticipation of the coming conflict, Congress had appropriated $300 million, a large sum for that era, for the expansion of the U.S. Air Corps. On September 1, 1939, Hitler marched into Poland, and World War II had unofficially begun.

The outcome of the 1939 Thompson could have been predicted in advance, since two of the first three winners had placed near the top in the '38 race. Roscoe Turner, now a seasoned veteran of the classic, felt that he had a winner under him for the coming contest, so he merely arranged for a new sponsor's (Champion Spark Plugs) logo to replace his previous angel's insignia, and he was ready for the starting flag.

With his heavy hand on the throttle and brimming with confidence borne of experience, the colonel prevailed and held the lead throughout most of the race despite the fact that he again cut a pylon and had to do a "360" to recircle the missed course mark, crossing the finish line in first place at an average speed of 282.536 mph, slightly slower than his 1938 speed. Thus did the colorful Roscoe Turner become the only three-time winner of the famous Thompson classic, and he, too, announced his retirement from racing.

Tony Le Vier, famous Lockheed test pilot, in his Schoenfeldt Special, was right behind Turner in second place at 272.538 mph. Carl Ortman, a familiar performer by now in his Marcoux-Bromberg, placed third at 254.435 mph.

In the December 1939 *Model Airplane News* issue, the SF-72 16⅞-inch wingspan model of Turner's 1938 Pesco Special was reissued as the 1939 Thompson winner Miss Champion. (Actually, the SF-72 kit merely added additional decals for the Miss Champion 1939 winner, and it was advertised as the 1938–1939 Roscoe Turner Thompson winner.) Turner would later become immortalized, at least in spirit, when the racy, powerful-appearing Miss Champion went permanently on display in the museum in Indianapolis dedicated to his memory. (Later, when the museum in Indianapolis was forced to close, the Pesco Special would find a new home at the Smithsonian's NASM.)

If it had been possible to have been the proverbial fly on the wall in the C-D engineering department during the latter part of 1939, such an observer would have been able to see Jim Powell huddled around a drafting board with Ed, both of them deeply involved in launching a design-project concept that had been germinating in the entrepreneur's mind for the past year—namely, a family of three gas models with the same basic configuration, one for each class; Class A, B, and C.

The series had been christened "the Playboy Family" (long before the magazine of the same name) and the first of the series, the Playboy Junior, a 54-inch wingspan Class-B with the same wingspan as the Zipper, had been finalized, kitted as the GP-5006 at $2.50. Some initial sales had been made to dealers. Its official announcement appeared in a C-D center-spread ad in the January 1940 *MAN* issue. This marketing strategy was C-D's answer to Comet and Carl Goldberg's challenge to the industry.

The initial acceptance of the Playboy Junior was reassuring, resulting in sales of approximately 8,000 units, almost three times what the Playboy Senior would realize, a total of approximately 2,800 kits during its first year. However, with the unprecedented popularity that the Playboy Senior had garnered as a result of its continual contest-winning performances, particularly in the Society of Antique Modelers (SAM) events, it had emerged as the single most famous of the C-D designs. Hardly ever is a gas model event held involving the Old Timer designs without its representative share of Playboy Senior entries, either pylon mounted or cabin version. (The results of the 1995 SAM champs meet held in Colorado Springs attest to the continuing prowess of the Playboy design, demonstrated by the veteran contestant and gas-model designer, 75-years-old Sal Taibi, who with his Ohlsson and Rice 60-powered Playboy Senior won first place in Free Flight Class-C Fuselage and ultimately was acclaimed Gas Free Flight Power Grand Champion.)

The events involved in the behind-the-scenes planning and development

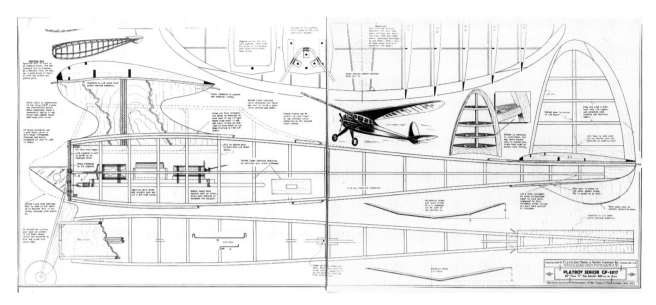

The 1940 GP-5017 C-D Playboy Senior had a span of 80 inches and originally sold for $3.95. The design could be built with either a pylon-mounted wing or a slightly lower cabin-mounted wing, which experienced modelers found flew better under windy conditions. The Senior Playboy is one of the most popular models and continues to place in various Society of Antique Modeler contests. *E. T. Packard Collection.*

that led to the Playboy Senior's successful introduction in 1940 deserve further attention. When questioned about this famous C-D design, Ed enthusiastically launched into a detailed dialogue: "Jim Powell, my artist-designer, and one of our draftsmen were completing the plan for the 54-inch Playboy Junior. I thought I had left clear instructions for them to finish the design before I had to leave to attend a meeting of the Model Industry Association in Chicago.

"When I returned from Chicago there was a deadline to meet to place the ad in *Air Trails, Flying Aces,* and *Model Airplane News.* With the model all drawn up, with the wing ribs and curved parts of the wing and empennage all laid out for printwood, there was little possibility of my making the changes to modify the wing tip, especially. So, I have always been disappointed in it, and that explains why it looks a little different from the Playboy Senior.

"My brother Will, who was in charge of our retail store on the first floor, came to me and said, 'There is a young man in the store who has been a customer who has a glider he wants to sell you.' I agreed to talk to him about the 4-foot blue-and-yellow glider, which he wanted to sell for $6.00, and he stated, 'It doesn't fly worth a darn, but it is a nice looking model.'

"I bought it immediately and told him I was going to redesign it to make it a good dollar number (I still have the model). I had been wanting and planning to introduce a large soaring glider of six-foot wingspan and perhaps this model would be a good starting point. He begged me not to produce the model because it was an absolute flop, saying it would not fly well. I said, 'I'll make it fly.'"

Ed hired the young man, J.E., as a draftsman. "I hoped to use him to help on the drawing board, and I had placed an ad for the Senior Playboy and needed someone to draw it up the way I wanted it made. So, under my direction I had him redraw the glider. My design was slightly different but most successful nevertheless." The model was introduced in 1940 as the Cleveland Condor Soaring Glider [Kit E-5019] in both 6- and 7-foot wingspan versions, which became C-D's most successful design ever with sales of over 2.5 million kits at $1.00 each.

"Getting back to the Playboy Senior plan, I stood over [J.E.] and told him everything I wanted, line-for-line, including the nice, somewhat pointed elliptical wing tips, double-elliptical stabilizer, and wing mounting pylon. I had to have him redraw the pylon, which he had drawn as a standard looking curving design. Whereas I insisted that I wanted it made into a reverse curve as a particularly curvaceous pylon to give it an additional appealing appearance instead of the usual streamlined shape.

"He drew it up while my artist, Jim Powell, was working right along with us to prepare the necessary artwork. I insisted on the polyhedral wing and specified rib spacing in order that they fit on the printwood sheets economically. I specified a slightly faired-in fuselage with a stringer shown on the top, bottom and both sides. The whole job was drawn with my absolute direction, not that of the boy draftsman."

When all was completed, C-D wound up selling approximately 2,800 kits at $3.95. At the time Ed had no idea that this design would maintain its popularity for more than fifty years and would be regarded as one of the most popular "Old Timer" designs to place regularly in SAM contests.

Ed recalled, "I did not realize it until a year or two later that he apparently went around telling modelers that this was his design. I was told that his model club friends all backed him and started spreading the word. I asked Jim Powell, who was right there during the whole project, who really designed the Playboy Senior a few years later, and his instant retort was, 'You did.'

"Powell elaborated, 'Yes, I was right there when you told him how you wanted him to draw up the various items, the parts. You even took a hand in the designing yourself, just as long as it followed through on your Playboy Family concept, and I did some of it too, along with the artwork so that you could advertise it and meet the ad deadline. This is your design, not his.'

"This is exactly as it happened, with my directing him every hour or so, something to which I had a witness, James D. Powell. It is often that a draftsman thinks he is the designer of an article instead of the man who directs him—often the chief engineer. What is most incredible about this whole Playboy episode is that most of the model industry publications have gone along with [J.E.'s] fantasy and not one of the publishers has ever bothered to substantiate it or check with the source, namely me."

How Pre-War Hype Changed C-D's Marketing Plan

In their 1940 marketing plan, Ed and Frank Lamorelle of the Carpenter Ad Agency were determined to publicize and extract maximum benefit out of the Playboy design family brand franchise exclusive to C-D. None of C-D's competitors had such unique brand identification. Comet had their Zipper A and B but chose instead the Sailplane as the name for their Class-C design. The February 1940 *MAN* ad declared the completed Playboy design series with the announcement of the 33-inch wingspan Class-A Baby Playboy at $1.00—the first $1.00 priced gas model kit offered nationally.

The resultant ad campaign would utilize the three leading national modeling publications: *Air Trails, Flying Aces,* and *Model Airplane News.* It was an ambitious schedule, perhaps the most expensively budgeted to date, with a twelve-month insertion commitment in *Flying Aces,* including three inside front covers, in addition to the usual twelve-month presence in *Model Airplane News,* with two inside front covers; plus a seven-times insertion in *Air Trails,* including a first time ever inside-front-cover ad.

Air Trails readership market penetration had been significantly improved under the bold leadership of assistant editor William Winter, noted model designer and author. In the November 1939 issue, the publication had made a switch to a 10-by-13-inch tabloid size format dictated by economies of printing resulting from the utilization of the same presses which produced Street and Smith's *PIC* picture magazine, in competition with *Life* magazine. However, the jumbo size enabled most model plans to be shown with full-size patterns, riveting dramatic cover art, and correspondingly large, more impressive ad layouts. Under Winter's direction monthly circulation increased dramatically until it peaked at 243,000 in 1944.

The C-D exposure in all three 1940 major national model magazines would be impressive, with a total of eight inside front covers, five spreads (all in *MAN* and nine full pages.

"America's Greatest Contest Line, Cleveland Outranks the Field for the Greatest Number of Money, Prize and Honor Winners" was the challenging headline of the March 1940 *MAN* full-page ad. Only C-D could make that statement, because it had been in the market since 1919 and could offer the

National Air Races promotional items included: (from top left) a 1939 window/envelope sticker, a 1936 Los Angeles sticker, a 1932 sticker; (at bottom) a 1937 sticker, a 1939 air mail envelope, a 1938 cachet. *Author's Collection.*

broadest line of scale flying, rubber endurance, glider sailplane, gassies, ³/16-inch scale railroads, ships and aircars, plus a full line of hobby supplies and equipment.

At last, via the impact of a spread layout in the April *MAN* issue, came the announcement for the 80-inch wingspan Playboy Senior, with pylon wing mount or optional cabin style, the only Class-C model offered with that option at an economical $3.95. The arresting headline of the ad, "Be Ahead of the Rest by Building the Best," was a clarion rallying call to the country's performance seeking modelers and, as will be seen, the Playboy Senior would soon live up to its C-D advertising hype. In the ad C-D came in for its share of price increases with the scale Stinson gas model increased to $11.50 and sister scale gas model Rearwin Speedster to $7.50. The C-D stable of gas models had now been increased to a total of nine.

The aerodynamically stable and attractive design of the Senior Playboy was no accident. It mirrored the twenty-some years of designing, testing, and flying models of all types, including indoor, rubber-powered endurance types, profile, scale models, and the Cloudster gas model, as well as the designing challenge of offering stable, consistently performing scale gas models, such as the Stinson and the Rearwin. Many modelers felt that the cabin option, which provided a wing-mounting position approximately 1½ inches below the pylon and two inches to the rear, was the most effective configuration for flying under windy conditions. C-D's founder had been at it since 1919, when, as an air-minded youth he had started at the entry level to modeldom. So, his experience was equally as diverse as and far exceeded the years of designing by the much heralded Carl Goldberg.

With the 1940 crescendo of the contest-gas-model euphoria, the winning ways of the Playboy Senior were not long in coming. Beginning in September and continuing for the next four months, in all three of the major modeling magazines, C-D ads proudly proclaimed the popular model's winning exploits in a series of full-page spreads and inside-front-cover ads with "The Same Model That Twice Broke the World's Record within Seven Days," realistically illustrating C-D modeler Joseph Tryczaj posing in the field with his Playboy, sixth-place winner at the Chicago Nationals. In another series of ads Trycaj was followed by C-D modeler Bill Schwab, pictured at a contest site with his Playboy and mechanic, followed by a listing of an impressive tally of contest winnings and places, first in Cleveland, first in Akron, second in Elyria, second in Toledo, and fifth in New Philadelphia.

The War Effort Becomes a Reality for America and C-D

America's entrepreneurs in modeldom, deeply involved in their respective marketing strategies, catering to the enthusiastic winged fantasies of the country's air-minded youth, could not possibly have foreseen how quickly their plans would be completely altered by the sequence of events in war-torn Europe.

With opportune timing, Gen. Hap Arnold, chief of the U.S. Air Corps, had initiated the AAC and AAF Civil Primary Flying Schools in 1938 and twenty-one private flying schools were approved, nine for primary flight training in May of 1939. After sixty-five hours of primary training, those students passing would be sent on to Randolph Field for further training.

As the conflict in Europe intensified in 1940 and heralded a greater emphasis on newly developed military aircraft designs, it was concluded that the C-D ⅞-inch railroad program would have to be curtailed. It was requiring the efforts of five employees out of the total of the normal thirty, plus supervision, development, and advertising expense. Had outside capital been feasible, perhaps the C-D railroad line would have become a success, if only by riding on the coattails of the American Flyer S-Gauge marketing program.

On May 10, 1940, Germany invaded the Low Countries, Chamberlain resigned and was replaced by Winston Churchill as prime minister in June 1940. France fell thereafter. Then the greatest challenge ever to face England's freedom raged from August 8 to September 13—six weeks, the Battle of Britain, the first "pure" air battle at a cost of 800 RAF aircraft, 420 RAF airmen, and 1,354 Nazi fighters and bombers. The strategic aerial skirmishes of the unprecedented, spectacular battle for supremacy of England's skies, a prelude to Hitler's planned invasion, would provide C-D with a never-to-be-equaled opportunistic event, replete with a cast of colorful, historically significant aircraft to duplicate as scale miniatures.

Ed had assembled an impressive aviation library over the years for his modeling research, consisting of the most prestigious hardbacks, such as a complete set of Janes *ATWA*, a complete run of aircraft yearbooks, and Angle's *Aerosphere*, plus a most extensive array of monthly aviation magazines, both domestic and foreign, many of which he also sold. Curiously, many of the foreign publications such as *The Aeroplane, Flight,* and *Aero Modeler* had more of the so-called classified data on military planes, such as plans, power plant, and armament details than was available in their American counterparts such as *Aero Digest, Aviation,* and *Flying.*

As an avid reader of *Life, Look,* and other weekly news magazines such as *Time,* plus viewing the Fox Movietone and Paramount movie newsreels, Ed became a fountainhead of information on the most current status of the progress of air power over Europe. As the war intensified, his boundless patriotism inspired Ed to offer the most current and complete line of U.S., allied and axis military scale flying wartime aircraft models. Through his network of European dealers, he had been made more aware of the significant early role of British fighters, and thus, earlier in 1940, C-D had announced 20-inch wingspan versions of the Hawker Siddeley Hurricane (R-59) and a Fairey Battle (R-67), both at an unheard-of low price of 25 cents for his European trade as well as for the U.S. market. On August 8, when the Battle of Britain began as the first "bandits," consisting of Dornier (DO) D17s, Junkers JU) 87s, JU 88s, Messerschmitt (ME)-110s and their formidable escorts of ME-109s crossed the "ditch," the United Kingdom had three formidable deterrents: a strategically deployed chain of twenty-one channels of radar and thirty different radar stations brilliantly conceived by Robert Watson-Watt, a decisive factor not yet had by the Nazis; R. J. Mitchell's ingeniously designed 1936 Mark I and II Spitfire, a descendent of his 407.5 mph Supermarine S6B Schneider Cup racer; and their most effective defense weapon, Prime Minister Sir Winston Churchill. Early on, the Luftwaffe and the courageous Royal Air Force were quite evenly matched, based on fully operational fighters; Goering's Nazi ME 109s totaled 760 with RAF Air Chief Dowding's tally at 714 Spitfires and Hurricanes. However, Ernst Udet's monstrous Nazi war machine produced only 160 more ME-109s in August due to Hitler's forced emphasis on bomber production. In contrast, Britain's Vickers (Spitfire) plants and Hawker Siddeley (Hurricane) industrial complex produced 476 fighters. Hence, initially, our future ally enjoyed a brief supremacy in the air.

At the end of September, despite having been subjected to a brutal, relentless series of devastating bombings in London, England's industrial capacity remained intact. Goering's Luftwaffe had failed for the first time, and Hitler postponed his planned invasion of the British homeland. If England had not won the Battle of Britain, the United States would have been forced into the war then.

Military experts have debated the relative merits of the Spitfire versus the ME-109. The Mark I and Mark II Spits available at that time could churn the airy-blue at 367 mph with their marvelous Rolls Royce 1,000 hp engines and their eight-wing mounted American Colt .30 caliber machine guns were matched against the ME-109's 20 mm cannon. Under conditions of negative G-forces, as in a sudden steep dive, the early Rolls carburetor would cut out while the superior fuel injection ME-109 would experience no difficulty. It would come down to the relative superiority of each pilot and his aerial strategy.

The Hawker Hurricane, typically overshadowed by its more glamorous Spitfire sister ship, was spawned in the world-famous Kingston-on-Thames establishment of the venerable English pioneer designer T. O. M. Sopwith, whose works had been acquired by Hawker-Siddeley. His ingenious, visionary designer, Sir Sidney Camm, member of Windsor Model Aero Club, who had developed Britain's fleetest biplane, the 250 mph Super Fury fighter, conceived the Hurricane in 1935. The impressive total of 4,000 blueprints needed to create the nimble contender's prototype fetched a mere £5,000 for the firm.

Mated to the all-powerful 1,050 hp Rolls "Merlin," she initially cleaved the airspace at 330 mph, but on her test hop she astonished the amazed witnessing gallery with her near-vertical climb, outside loop, and short-field takeoff performance. An initial order of 600, followed in 1936 with another 1,000, following in 1938 of which 497 were operational by September 1939 when war broke out.

A "Spit" could be flamed, but a Hurricane seldom caught fire and always seemed to hold together long enough for her pilot to parachute out ("hit the silk"). Her pilot's visibility was superior, and her undercarriage had wider tread and could take more punishment. Her defensive armor made it possible for the near impervious winged champion to ring up a record of having downed more German aircraft than all other English defenses combined in World War II.

Both the SF-73 Spitfire kit at $3.00 (27⅜-inch span) and the SF-78 Hurricane kit at $3.00 (30-inch span) were among the most consistently requested by American military personnel stationed at home and in England during World War II.

In May 1940 President Roosevelt asked Congress to approve funding for fifty thousand planes per year for our allies and our own Air Corps. The lend-lease program was initiated in March 1941, which paved the way for massive arms and aircraft shipments to the allies. Center stage was being set for Edward Pachasa to accelerate his efforts to further educate America's aviation-minded youth that he had been practicing for so many years.

"Ninety Percent of Today's Pilots Started as Model Builders" and "Four Sensational New War Planes" were the headlines in the March 1941 *MAN* ad spread and in the *Air Trails* inside front cover. The Supermarine Spitfire (SF-73 at $2.50), the Messerschmitt ME-109 (SF-74 at $2.50), the Grumman Skyrocket (SF-75 at $3.00), and the Bell Airacobra (SF-76 at $2.50) were the first warplanes in a series to be offered by C-D throughout the war years. The military aircraft shown were presented dramatically in action sequence illustrations by the talented Jim Powell, which enabled C-D to announce these fighting aircraft more quickly since the ad would not have to wait on the construction and photographing of the display models.

A follow up spread in the October *MAN* issue offered two additional warplanes, the Curtiss P-40 Tomahawk (SF-77 at $2.50) and the soon-to-be-come-scourge of the Japanese, the Lockheed P-38 Lightning (SF-85 at $3.50), referred to as the "forked tail devil."

However, a tragic turn of events occurred on November 17, 1941. Ernst Udet—a Luftwaffe brigadier general, a confidante of Luftwaffe commanding general Field Marshall Hermann Goering, a sixty-two-victory (second highest) World War I German ace and recipient of the coveted Blue Max, and the developer of the dive-bombing strategy resulting in the destructive JU 87 Stuka—despondent over failures of the Luftwaffe and the incessant bickering within the Nazi bureaucracy, shot himself in his Berlin apartment. Scrawled on the walls of his bedroom was an inscription, "Iron Man, you deserted me."

Udet's flawless aerobatic performance had been witnessed at the Cleveland 1931 and 1933 National Air Races by Ed as Udet maneuvered his own designed Flamingo biplane in low level, daring, precision aerial feats. He had been befriended by Doolittle, who was demonstrating the new Curtiss Hawk dive bomber that caught Udet's eye and resulted in his buying two export

December 1941 *MAN* spread ad that was a dramatic example of Ed Packard's role as "aviation's great recruiter" The ad was military oriented, with graphics simulating air battles and reiterating his constant slogan, "90% of Today's Pilots Started as Model Builders." This ad was placed in November, and neither Ed nor his ad agency, Carpenter, could possibly have foreseen that by the time many modelers would have had time to see this ad, that America would be attacked at Pearl Harbor. *Author's Collection.*

versions at $14,000 each, thus ushering in the era of dive bombing for the Luftwaffe with the ultimate design of the dreaded JU 87 Stuka. (C-D released a SF-49 Curtiss F11C-2 Export Hawk kit, which was based on plans that were obtained by contacting the Curtiss Wright plant in Buffalo, New York.) C-D would subsequently introduce a faithful miniature reproduction with a SF-84 Master Kit of the Stuka at $3.50.

The November 1941 C-D ad in *MAN* had the first reference to the U.S. defense program relative to material shortages, which would be a byproduct of the never before equaled American all out domestic war effort. All of the major model industry manufacturers had submitted the layouts and copy for their December 1941 and January 1942 ads in October and November of 1941, long before the date of December 7. Consequently, the editorial copy and the slant of the ads would not be reflected in most model-aviation-oriented publications until February or March of 1942 insofar as the reaction to the Japanese attack on Pearl Harbor. Little could these entrepreneurs foresee what dramatic consequences the sneak attack that ushered America into World War II would have on the hobby, the modelers, and the industry. One aspect of the catastrophic date is certain—the hobby nor its legions of dedicated young fans would ever be the same.

As 1941 became part of history and the beginning of America's entry into World War II, the market forces exerted a combination of price increases and decreases. C-D gas-model prices were increased with the Stinson advancing to $12.50, the Rearwin to $8.50, the Playboy Senior to $4.95, and the Playboy Junior to $3.00. The Brown Jr. Model E increased from $7.50 to ten dollars, and the Model D remained at $12.50; however, the shocker was a reduction from $21.50 to $16.50 for the Model B, the oldest engine on the market. The Model C simply disappeared from their ads. This was interpreted as a competitive move against Ohlsson's Custom 60 at $21.50. Ohlsson would ultimately resort to introducing another model called the Custom Special and price it at $18.50.

Many other kits and engines experienced price increases of a dollar or more, and as the inflationary pressures resulting from the scarcity of material exerted their influence, prices would increase further, not to mention the inevitable black market prices, which most always follow in the wake of such conditions.

Perhaps Ed was inspired by Churchill's oft-quoted and never-to-be-forgotten tribute to the "few"—the 420 RAF airmen who gave their all during the six-week Battle of Britain—that is indelibly stamped on the pages of history: "Never in the field of human conflict was so much owed by so many to so few." C-D was about to launch their own all-out war effort to support to their utmost any program designed to motivate and encourage America's youth to consider qualifying as potential military aviation recruits, members of the brotherhood of "the few."

CHAPTER 11

C-D Goes to War

⊕ WHEN AMERICA FOUND ITSELF engulfed in World War II as a result of that "Day of Infamy" at Pearl Harbor on December 7, 1941, a Herculean effort marshaled the heretofore untapped resources of American manpower. Since the enemy's major spearhead was air power, the total U.S. air armada had to undergo massive expansion virtually overnight. From every walk of life they came heeding the call. Some were absorbed by industry to forge the production effort. Others became the technicians and mechanics who maintained the power plants, armament, and avionics. However, the most compelling response came from those who were destined to pilot the thousands of aircraft which would comprise the ultimately invincible air force.

Undoubtedly one of America's great aviation recruiters has been the founder of C-D. In retrospect, his greatest contribution resulted when those boys and young men who had built and flown models from his authentic C-D kits during the decade prior to World War II became the recruits the Air Corps and Naval Aviation so sorely needed. Thus, Edward T. Pachasa, whose own formal education had been interrupted in the ninth grade for the needed support of his family, influenced millions of young men to rise to the challenge to join in an irresistible urge to fight and fly for victory for Uncle Sam.

An All-Out Recruiting Effort

Patriotic and *impressive* aptly described the C-D 1942 marketing campaign. As expected, it would capitalize on the powerful wave of patriotism sweeping the country, and in particular, appeal to the intense desire of America's young men to fly and fight for victory. Those who either were too young to enlist or who could not qualify to fly could have the vicarious experience of building and flying authentic wartime aircraft models.

Before the first year of America's entry into the global conflict was over, C-D would have introduced by far the most complete line of wartime models in the industry. The entire SF line by then would exceed ninety different designs.

C-D's 1942 Marketing Plan

During his relationship with the Carpenter ad agency management, he observed their annual advanced planning for their other clients as well as that for C-D. Consequently, by 1942 his marketing strategy had become more formalized, and included: advertising, new kits, additional cartons, direct mail, and graphics for point-of-sale aids.

First, the Model of the Month would feature an American, Allied, or Axis wartime aircraft currently involved in the aerial battles of the European war that would be featured in the ads for that month.

Also, a new impressive logo was designed with the letters C-D in the center of a star with the phrase "An Aviation Milestone Design" around the star.

And the Master Flying Model Kit was introduced, a new logo designated the Mark II All-American carton. Its length was the same 18½ inches, but its width of 9 inches was twice that of the original carton but only 1¾ inches deep versus the former 2⅝ inches. Appearance-wise the new carton was impressive and colorful. The basic silver hue of the original 1935 carton had been replaced by a white background with lettering done in a brilliant red combined with a blue field with white stars, the overall impression was definitely "star spangled"—most appropriate for a wartime United States. The addition of a red, white, and blue shield surmounted by an American eagle completed the patriotic image.

However, the major additional element of the design, which completely changed the character of the new carton, was the dramatic Jim Powell illustration of each particular aircraft, dominating approximately one third of the area of the nine by 18½-inch carton face. For further identification on the retailer's shelf, a reduced size of the illustration appeared on one end of the container. The utilization of the 9-inch-wide action-oriented illustration lent itself to the possibility of retailer window and counter display applications. The increased interior width provided space for four glass containers of cement, dopes, and banana oil. This feature particularly could be used to display the kit with the lid off, showing the total contents that were indeed impressive and most likely could further induce the hobbyist to make a purchase decision.

Powell's combat flight-oriented dramatic illustrations and the star-spangled carton were a winning combination, and its color scheme would make its display and sale to service personnel in Army and Navy Post Exchanges around the world even more appropriate.

In testament to the superior design of the original All-American carton, the new container used exactly the same lines of copy extolling the merits of C-D. The exception was the new copy under the red, white, and blue shield, which was included as the great recruiter's message to coincide with the needs of the wartime military:

Learn Aviation Fundamentals
Quickly and Easily By Building and
Flying Cleveland-Designed Models
They Win More Prizes, More Honors,
More Compliments Than Any Other Line
of Models in the World.
So Accurate and Authentic They Are
Considered a Preliminary Ground
School Training Course—That's Why They're
America's First Line of Models

Furthermore, the use of documented testimonials: Possibly with the exception of the combat-action-oriented illustrations dominating the C-D spread ads, the next most notable element of the ad layouts was the inclusion of one outstanding featured military flight personnel testimonial in large type, plus several others in small type around the border of the ad. The credentialed testimonials spanned all branches of the U.S. Air Force and Naval Aviation plus the Royal Air Force.

The September 1942 *MAN* ad, with a vertically read layout, was a blockbuster:

Here They Are . . . 10 Brand New War Models Added to Cleveland's Matchless Array of Realistic Sky Fighters. We Are Pleased to Present These Latest Fighting and Bombing Kits Which We Feel Will Add Greatly to Our Aviation Training Program (Note: Kits available with liquids only while they last . . . order yours now!) [This was the first reference to scarcity of materials due to wartime restrictions.]

1. The Lockheed "Hudson" SF-95 was the
    "Model of the Month   Span 49⅜ inches
2. Douglas SBD-3 "Dauntless" SF-89   Span 30⅝ inches
3. Lockheed P-38 "Lightning" SF-85   Span 38¾ inches
4. British "Spitfire" SF-73   Span 27⅝ inches
5. Republic P-47 "Thunderbolt" SF-81   Span 30¾ inches

6. German Ju.87 "Stuka" SF-84	Span 30³⁄₁₆ inches
7. North American P-51 "Mustang" SF-91	Span 27³⁄₁₆ inches
8. Vought-Sikorsky "Corsair" SF-79	Span 30³⁄₁₆ inches
9. Grumman 4F4 "Wildcat" SF-83	Span 27⅞ inches
10. Brewster F2A "Buffalo" SF-87	Span 26¼ inches

An unusual event occurred in May 1942 when Ed received a call from the owner of Peerless Model Airplane Company, a Cleveland competitor, offering the company to him as an outright sale. Thus C-D acquired most all of the drawings, files, and inventory of Peerless, and for a brief period advertised the Peerless name and drawings as a part of Cleveland Model and Supply Company.

The December *MAN* ad was a fitting climax indeed for the impressive 1942 marketing strategy, with an appropriate bold headline: "U.S. Air Power Must Lead the World." The ad signed off with the company logo, "When you build Cleveland models you're building models that pilots, bombardiers, instructors, cadets in training and mechanics of all classes in the air forces build."

The ad layout was flanked by eight specific testimonials from men in the Air Force. The spectacular horizontal spread dominated the issue with an SF-79 Vought Corsair, illustrated diving from the left, and an SF-91 P-51 Mustang, illustrated shown on the attack from the right—both dramatic, realistic, action-oriented illustrations by Powell at his best.

As a tribute, American and Allied airmen worldwide were offered a choice of any C-D kit gratis if their testimonial was published in a forthcoming C-D ad. Consequently, hundreds of letters were received from airmen from all over the world, and each letter has been kept on file in the C-D archives.

Left: 1940 No. 20 C-D Hobby Catalog. *E. T. Packard Collection.*

Right: 1942 No. 37 C-D Model Airplane Catalog. *E. T. Packard Collection.*

In perusing the leading model publications of 1942, *Air Trails, Flying Aces,* and *MAN* the C-D ads were such obvious standouts that there was simply no comparison with what the competition was showing. It was not just the professionalism of the layouts, Powell's superb illustrations, or the fact that C-D unquestionably had the most extensive line of wartime models. Most apparent was the message being conveyed loud and clear—the call by the great recruiter to America's youth to prepare to join up with Uncle Sam's air forces by building C-D models now and be ahead of the pack.

Some competitors were giving lip service to the patriotic theme and copying C-D's approach. However, the difference was significant. Ed had the following, and the airmen were sending in specific testimonials to which he was selectively referring in his ads.

The year 1942 was the first year of America's entry into World War II. Despite the attack by the Japanese on Pearl Harbor, which sank one U.S. battleship and seriously damaged seven others, the combination of quickly implemented industrial might, Yankee ingenuity, and retaliatory resolve enabled the air force to strike back in just four months. It materialized on April 18 in the form of a surprise raid on Tokyo by Jimmy Doolittle and his 16 B-25 Tokyo Raiders from their "Shangri-La" floating base, the aircraft carrier *Hornet*. In honor of his long-time friend Doolittle, who was promoted to major general for his courageous mission and awarded the Medal of Honor, Ed announced an outstanding SF-MGM 125 kit of the North American B-25 "Mitchell" shortly thereafter.

America further regained its military composure against the Japanese in June during the Battle of Midway, in which not one surface vessel exchanged a shot with another. With intelligence gained as a result of cracking the Japanese code, the Navy halted the Japanese advance in the Pacific with their SBDs (scout dive bombers), TBFs (torredo bombers), and F-4Fs (fighter carrier-based bombers), which were replacing the obsolescent TBDs, SB2Us, and Brewster "Buffalos." Admiral Yamomoto, architect of the attack on Pearl Harbor, commanded the Japanese Midway Operation with Admiral Nagumo commanding the 1st Carrier Force from the deck of his carrier *Akagi,* plus seven other carriers and their 700 aircraft. Admiral Fletcher had only three carriers plus 230 aircraft supplanted by another 98 Air Force planes based on Midway.

Midway became the most decisive naval battle of World War II. The Japanese lost four of their eight aircraft carriers. Admiral Nagumo was forced to abandon ship from his own flagship *Akagi,* and a total of 322 Japanese aircraft and 3,500 Japanese seamen were lost, versus 147 U.S. aircraft casualties, 300 seamen, and only one of the three U.S. naval carriers, the *Yorktown.*

C-D seemed to have the uncanny ability to have the right kits available to commemorate such engagements, and Midway was no exception. In their following ads, C-D could trumpet the immediate availability of the SBD

Right: An example of the authenticity of Cleveland models' Grumman TBF Avenger such as President George H. W. Bush flew as a naval pilot during World War II. This illustration exemplifies the constant effort for maximum realism in the C-D line of scale models. This is a great testimonial to the Master Model Engineer and his lifelong pursuit of scale perfection (1943). *E. T. Packard Collection.*

Below: This is the Pacific Foray battle scene of the 1944 catalog "Famous Warplane Series." *E. T. Packard Collection.*

Dauntless (SF89), replacing the obsolescent SB2U; the TBF Avenger (SF-98), the replacement for the ancient TBD and the F4F Wildcat (SF-83), the successor to the miserably performing Brewster "Buffalo" (SF-87). In this way Ed was further able to encourage his young modeling recruits to relive these historic classic air battles by building models of the American aircraft involved as well as selected enemy planes.

In August an American task force landed on Guadalcanal in the drive against the Japanese entrenched in the Solomons. The island-hopping campaign thus began and would not end until American forces were within B-29 bomber range of Tokyo.

In the European theater on November 7, as the first year of the global conflict became history, a combined force of 500 transports, 350 warships, and 400,000 men launched the allied invasion of North Africa held by German Field Marshal Erwin Rommel, commander of the Afrika Korps. The destination was Italy.

The exposure of American businesses to a wartime economy was a harsh experience for most companies. In addition to their loss of some key suppliers and vendors who had converted over their operations to supply the military and the critical availability of some raw materials that had suddenly been declared essential to the military, employers would begin to suffer from the attrition of key young employees. Those who had not already enlisted out of their obligation to serve their country would fall victim to a 1-A classification by their local draft boards. C-D would feel the pain when the youngest of the remaining Pachasa brothers, Andrew Jr., age twenty-three, left the business to become a Marine Corps supply officer stationed in Hawaii. Andrew had assisted brother Fred, manager of the first retail store on Bridge Avenue and of the company store at Lorain Avenue, but bid a sad adieu to the his family and to his many C-D customers and suppliers.

America in 1942 witnessed for the first time since World War I the inception of an accelerating trend, indigenous only to a wartime economy—the separation and departure of civilians as they joined or were drafted into the military to oppose the Axis war machine or who were tapped by officialdom in the nation's capitol to serve in strategic government positions.

1943—Increased Demand for Military Flight Personnel Training

In the United States, the second year of World War II was characterized by heightened demand for more and accelerated training aids. Production goals for mass-produced Army and Navy aircraft were being met and exceeded. However, trained pilots and trained ground support personnel were needed to make the planes operational. The buzzword became "training."

Ed, commenting on this situation, said, "It became fairly obvious to me after talking to some of the military personnel and reading about these demands publicized in the press, that to meet these requirements we must embody simplified methodology. This was similar to the Rep type kits I had introduced not too long ago, which were simplified versions of the SF line. However, I met with my brother Will and Jim Powell and put in a call to Captain Dick to get his opinion as well. Our solution involved incorporating the maximum ease of construction without sacrificing authenticity from a recognition perspective."

The resultant program, brilliantly conceived by C-D and expediently produced, was announced in the January 1943 *MAN* ad: the T warplane series of "industrial-training" models, with a consistent wingspan of three feet and at the price of $1.50 each. Initially six of the military models were introduced: T74 Me. 109; T76 Bell Airacobra; T77 Curtiss P-40; T85 Lockheed P-38; T87 RAF Hawker Hurricane; and T91 Mustang P-51.

The seven elements of for the models of the industrial-training program developed by Ed and his task force were:

1. Must be large enough so almost anyone could construct them
2. Must embody the simplest of construction methods
3. Must be durable
4. Must teach sound fundamentals
5. Must have good flight characteristics
6. Must be authentic as well as relatively inexpensive
7. Should utilize a minimum of strategically important materials

As the need for these specialized product lines developed, an additional specially designed carton was required to further differentiate the new product line at the retail level and to assist C-D in building a demand identity—all of which kept Jim Powell busy at his drawing board. With a wingspan of three feet, the resultant larger plan and necessarily longer balsa stock lengths would require a much longer carton.

Powell's design for the T line blossomed into a carton 34¾ inches in length, compared to the 18½ inches of the All American Master Scale Flying (MSF) line. As another example of his keen professionalism, the final design wisely maintained an obvious C-D family relationship. In view of its ultimate use in relation to military training or industrial orientation and training, the red, white, and blue star spangled configuration was continued. However, the most serious limitation imposed by an economical product line, with its $1.50 price tag, was the color of the natural paper stock that was used for the near-white background. The graphics maintained the eagle-crested red, white, and blue shield from the master flying model kit carton and the "Cleveland" logo was conspicuously identified in large, bold type instead of the traditional

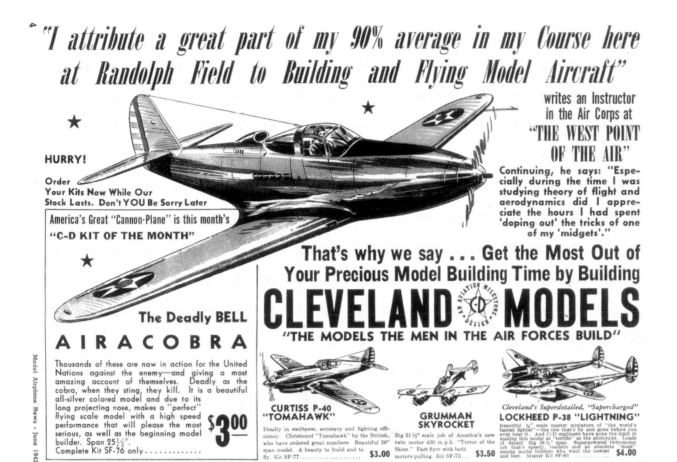

"Cleveland-Designed." The "Industrial Training Aircraft Kit" logo in red properly differentiated the carton from the SF and MSF lines.

The T line of six war-plane types quickly found its way into retail channels of distribution, as well as the suppliers to the military, gaining ready acceptance. The line was eventually expanded to eleven types and remained a popular line even after the war.

One of the most spectacular C-D ads during the war appeared in the December 1943 issue of *Air Trails Pictorial.* The spread in the large 10-by-13-inch format, with Jim Powell's dramatic art, seemed to leap out at the reader in a 3-D effect. The ad featured a large illustration of an SF-91 North American P-51 diving from the left in a combat scene in France with German ME-110s and Heinkel 111s. The right half of the spread positioned a three-quarter rear view of an SF-85 Lockheed P-38 on the attack. There were a total of twenty-four C-D models shown, all in action poses that created a dynamic ad. The headline, "Modelbuilding Helped Me Understand and Overcome Most of the Problems Encountered in Learning to Fly the 'Big Ones,'" was another testimonial by a member of the military, a Pfc. LLS, Army Air Force, Truax Field, Wisconsin. The copy enumerated how his model building experience

The June 1942 C-D kit of the month, the Bell Airacobra, with a testimonial from a Randolph Field Air Corps instructor. *Model Airplane News. Author's Collection.*

aided him in his ground school and primary flight training. Four more testimonials from the military were included and, of course, these members of the military were recipients of a free C-D model of their choice.

Wartime Bureaucratic Challenges

While entrepreneurs faced additional challenges imposed by wartime military and government bureaucracy, C-D had hedged its position involving major raw materials and supplies by investing in a commitment for twenty carloads of balsa and advanced purchase commitments for other necessities with their long-term vendors.

The additional challenge of losing key manpower to military enlistments and to the draft (brothers Will and Fred were drafted on a Friday, but on the following Monday the age requirement was increased to exempt males over twenty-eight years of age, so, fortunately for Ed, they both were able to remain at C-D) created a continuing problem of male employee replacement, and women recruits and their orientation and training required a different type of supervision. However, an even more insidious threat on businesses in the model industry was enforced by the War Production Board in Washington, D.C. Their Limitation Order L-81 had placed model airplanes in the same category with toys and games.

"Naturally, this arbitrary classification, putting us into the toy classification, angered and frustrated us," remarked Ed, "for it meant that the model industry would not have the leverage with the beltway bureaucrats to get their fair share of raw materials, often classified as 'essential.' Other well-established model manufacturers felt that we were all virtually powerless against this government edict. Outside of a relatively small amount of metal used in the manufacture of model engines and the balsa that was also used in life rafts and other military applications, the industry was not consuming any significant quantities of strategic materials. In fact, one engine manufacturer ran an ad which stated that the annual requirements of all the model engine manufacturers would consume an amount of metal equivalent to the amount used in the construction of one C-47 [military version of the DC-3]."

In his usual purposeful manner, Ed set out to oppose this arbitrary ruling that would limit the production of model engines and other such products sold by the model manufacturers to American youth. The case had to be made for the fact that our country's youth previously exposed to model building prior to World War II, as proved to the military recruiters, constituted a valuable pool of aviation-oriented, highly motivated recruits more readily trainable. It had to be forcefully demonstrated that model building was an educational aid and that the industry should be classified as "essential" and definitely not in the toy category.

The solution was found by using the clout of the Model Industry Association, in which C-D had long been a member and Ed had served on the board of directors. Thereafter, the War Production Board received a series of effective letters endorsing the educational aspect of model building from no lesser a list of aviation's military and civilian luminaries than Gen. Hap Arnold, commanding general Army Air Forces; Gill Robb Wilson, president of the National Aeronautic Association; Alexander Klemin, New York University professor and Guggenheim research professor; George Newbold, assistant to the publisher of *Aviation Magazine*; William B. Stout, Stout Research-Division Consolidated Aircraft; and Elbert K. Fretwell, chief scout executive, Boy Scouts of America.

The upshot of all this behind-the-scenes maneuvering and lobbying was that on July 14, 1943, E. B. Miller, president of the Model Industry Association received a letter from Maury Maverick, director of the Government Division, War Production Board stating: "An exception has been granted from these Limitation Orders (L-81) which allows individual manufacturers to file appeals for materials to produce a quota essential for educational purposes." (An authorization for 25,000 engines to be manufactured was received later.) This concession from the vast bureaucracy of the "arsenal of democracy" was a victory of sorts, for it differentiated the modeling industry from the toy and game business.

Periodically, however, C-D would suddenly be confronted by an unexpected material shortage from a long time supplier. To alert the distributors, dealers, and modelers, a notice was inserted in the kits as follows:

IMPORTANT NOTICE

BALSA IS A CRITICAL WAR MATERIAL AND MAY NOW BE USED ONLY IN DIRECT WAR PRODUCTION

We are called upon as patriotic Americans to make cheerfully this further contribution to our victory. Parts in this kit are, therefore, supplied with substitute materials such as pine, basswood, cardboard, etc., instead of balsa. It is a proven excellent substitute.

As the allied war machine in Europe became more powerful with additional airpower and mechanized manpower, it not only conquered the mighty, seemingly invincible Field Marshall Rommel, commander of the Afrika Korps, but also continued onward to its ultimate goal—Italy. On September 8, 1943, General Eisenhower announced the unconditional surrender of the Italian government. Italy thus became the first of the Axis powers to throw in the towel. Afterward, on December 24, Eisenhower was named leader of the allied invasion of Supreme Headquarters Army Forces Europe (SHAFE). The Allies were now poised to deliver the coup de grace to the second member of the Axis, the Nazi regime.

In an assessment of the diversity of C-D sales by the end of 1943, it became apparent that the military component had become a major source at nearly 50 percent. This included sales through dealers from whom parents and loved ones would purchase kits to be sent to their servicemen relatives. The distribution to the military post exchanges was growing rapidly, and the long term relationship with Polk Brothers, a New York–based C-D distributor, was producing a high percentage of the military orders. Total C-D sales were approaching $500,000, a stark contrast to the volume achieved a decade ago during the hectic Depression of the 1930s.

C-D Kits Score Big with the Military

C-D's 1944 marketing campaign could best be described as a "broadside," both from a sales perspective as well as from an advertising one. Ed sensed that the military liked C-D's line of wartime models, so why not give the boys more of the same but in new model types? Hence, the ad plan called for twelve spreads in *MAN*, one of which would be a vertical center spread and eight of which would be inside back cover spreads. Before the calendar year ended, some sixteen new wartime kit designs would be announced.

The first of the spreads using the inside back cover had its debut in the 1944 April *MAN* issue, with the announcement of "four brand new war models":

1. The TBF SF-93	39¾-inch span at $4.00	American
2. The Mitsubishi Zero (Zeke) SF-86	29¾-inch at $3.00	Japanese
3. The Focke-Wulf 190 SF-82	27¾-inch at $3.00	German
4. The Westland Whirlwind SF-105	33¾-inch at $3.50	British

No models in the ad were shown in the static position. All illustrations were "in-flight" situations, the entire spread alive with action-oriented aircraft. Just under the ad headline were two outstanding testimonials: one from a B-24 Liberator AAF pilot who had started model building at age eight and the other from a Navy Aviation Cadet commenting on how model building was helping him in his training syllabus.

The following May's issue of *MAN* announced the SF-97 31½-inch-span kit at $3.50, the Navy's new F6F Grismman "Hellcat" fighter designed specifically to be superior to the Japanese Zero. The Powell realistic in-flight illustration occupied one-half of the ad's left panel, with the right panel dominated by the most overwhelming testimonial C-D ever published. It was signed "Major P. J. R. AAF, A Cleveland Model Booster." The copy revealed that the major broke his back as his chute opened when he bailed out of a P-47 at 500 mph. He had previously been awarded the Distinguished Flying Cross for twenty-five successful test power dives.

An example of how the forces of inflation had affected the model industry can best be illustrated by the advertised price in a June 1944 ad for a GHQ engine at $20, which prior to the war had been offered in the $6.00 range. The ad in the September 1944 *MAN* issue was a vertically read center spread. The layout illustrated the total current SF line of twelve wartime models with the headline "The Models the Men in the Air Forces Build." In the lower page of the spread was shown the nine wartime models comprising the industrial training line. This was one of the few ads in the 1944 campaign with no testimonials. The 1944 campaign climaxed with a prestigious ad in the December issue of *MAN*, timed to capitalize on the heavy holiday demand, including the many kits anticipated to be purchased for servicemen worldwide: "Cleveland Crashes the Model Building World with the Year's Biggest Bomber Bombardment!" The headline announced four outstanding kits, consisting of the Air Force's medium and heavy bombers:

1. B-17 Flying Fortress SF-100 (72-inch span at $12.50)
2. B-25 Mitchell SF-125 (55-inch span at $8.50)
3. B-26 Martin "Marauder" SF-135 (48½-inch span at $8.50)
4. A-20 Douglas "Havoc" (Boston) SF-115 (46-inch span at $8.50)

(At C-D's ¾-inch scale, these kits were the largest in span on the market.) The SF-100 Boeing B-17 Flying Fortress kit was a monster with a 72-inch wingspan, the largest scale model kit ever produced by C-D and designed

April 1942 photo of the approximately thirty C-D employees, predominantly women. Included in the group are Andrew Pachasa (kneeling, third from right), Fred Pachasa (kneeling, fourth from right), and Kay Kreitzer, the future Mrs. Packard (standing, back row, third from left). *Will Pachasa Collection.*

The 9,000-square-foot Lorain Avenue location in wartime "dress," with the P-38 side-wall painting and the C-D truck parked in front. The front windows were closed off because the factory store had been moved to a corner location so that factory assembly operations would be housed there (1944). *Will Pachasa Collection.*

with the maximum of realistic detail. The ad also announced the largest glider-sailplane kit in the industry, the E-5022 ten-foot-wingspan Albatross at $3.50, a most economical price. The 1944 schedule of sixteen new model type introductions was challenging to the C-D organization. It kept the staff of six draftsmen drawing at maximum capacity, with overtime when needed when there were deadlines to meet.

In describing further how C-D was functioning during the war years, Ed commented, "Fortunately my brother Will, secretary-treasurer, with the responsibilities of superintendent and works manager, including planning, purchasing, and production, had developed into an extremely reliable and efficient executive. Will's duties dovetailed with those of younger brother Fred, superintendent of woodshop, receiving, and warehousing. Our average number of employees during this period was around sixty-five. However, when we were packing the 6- and 7-foot-wingspan Condor Glider-Sailplane kits, and later the 10-foot Albatross kits, it was necessary for us to use two buildings across the street. We would place a newspaper ad and had no problem hiring up to ninety women to do the packing. We used the corner two-story building and the one-story adjacent former furniture store building. At times when we were in these packing modes, we would have as much as 40,000 square feet of space in use with over 100 employees. Wartime women packers were paid 30 to 35 cents per hour, and men received 60 to 70 cents per hour.

"Our first space adjustment occurred when we discovered that we needed more space to pack the gas model kits: the Cloudster, Playboy, Stinson, and Rearwin. Because of their large size, these kits simply required more area for assembling the kit components and then packing the contents into their respective boxes. When these large kits were being packed, all other operations had to cease in order to have ample space. As a quick fix, we had to rent the

Ed Packard, president, in his modest office (1944). *Will Pachasa Collection.*

C-D office staff with Kay Kreitzer in her role as office manager (1944). *Will Pachasa Collection.*

corner store on the same side of the street, move the 'company store' there, and convert the former large ground level store into a packing department."

Every operation was planned as closely as possible and critically timed to meet shipping deadlines to satisfy C-D's caveat that orders were shipped the same day received. Hence, the company had Railway Express and U.S. Post Office trucks arriving and departing several times a day.

"A red letter day that Will and I will never forget was a day in mid-April 1944 when we received a War Department purchase order dated April 15 from the Kansas City Quartermaster Depot for a total of 30,000 kits of six types of our industrial training warplane kits. It was obviously the largest single war kit order we ever had received and fortunately it allowed us to ship in six lots of 5,000 kits each. One of the bits of information we received from dealing with the military was that the American GIs stationed in Europe would request ferry pilots to bring them Cleveland kits which ultimately would be flown across the Atlantic in the bomb bays, fuselage interiors and wherever there was room in the military AAF planes being ferried. So we learned that more C-D kits had been ferried across the Atlantic during the war than their real-life counterparts.

While C-D management was enacting the drama involving its wartime business, information was rife in the press and on the radio concerning the massive operation under way in the U.K. in preparation for what would become known as D-day, the assault on Normandy: the invasion of France en route to the liberation of Paris and thence on to the surrender of Germany. It was only a question of when. None of the Pachasas had any idea of when the war would end, and they were all so busy working long hours and often on weekends that they had little time for contemplation. So it gave them a feeling of deep pride in the U.S. military when they learned of the June 6 launch of Operation Overlord. By August 25, Paris had been liberated.

In the December 1944 issue of the *Model Industry Association Bulletin,* there was a moving tribute written by Ed concerning the death of his father, Andrew Pachasa, on November 18. It had been excerpted from a notice that Ed had mailed to his industry associates and friends, describing how instrumental the senior Pachasa had been in the early founding of C-D. It was a touching testimonial to his leadership and his being a role model for the Pachasa brothers and also to his dedication to making C-D a successful enterprise. He had reversed the role most fathers play, going into business with his sons rather than the opposite. He had always remained in the background at C-D and did not get involved with any of the customers or the day-to-day business. He quietly performed the many duties he could to simplify the various operations of both the wood and metal departments. In the initial stages of C-D's emergence, his knowledge, ingenuity, and skilled craftsmanship enabled the fledgling company to include the many finished or semifinished components in the kits that contributed to C-D's early industry leadership. After a decade at General Electric's Nela Park complex in Cleveland, where he became an accomplished machinist, in 1932 he left General Electric and entered into a full-time relationship with his sons at C-D. He remained on the company payroll until his death.

The Emergence of Edward T. Packard

Ed had long chafed under the use of the name Pachasa. This was not the true Astro-Hungarian family name, and, as were many such family names it was unpronounceable and not easily spelled in English. The family arbitrarily had settled on the Pachasa name as an Anglo-compromise.

As a dutiful and respectful son, Ed had discussed his feelings about the name with his father and promised him that he would not make a change while Andrew was still living. After having given the matter a great deal of consideration following his father's death, he was personally resigned to assume a new identity as Edward T. Packard by changing only three letters in his existing name. However, it would not be until 1958 when he complied with the necessary legal requirements. Will and other family members, however, kept the Pachasa family name, and a schism developed among the members of the family as a result of Ed's change.

With the invasion of Europe decisively launched and the liberation of Paris, 1944 was the beginning of the end for Hitler and the Nazi regime. In the South Pacific, General MacArthur had begun an invasion of the Philippines, and the Allies emerged victorious in the Battle of Leyte Gulf. It was becoming readily apparent that with the mighty allied war machine, spearheaded by its superior air power, that it was just a matter of time for victory in both the European theatre and the South Pacific.

C-D was experiencing an unprecedented market acceptance of its extensive line of MSF and Industrial Training line of war models by the military, especially at training centers. The popular priced T line of 36-inch wingspan American fighter kits at $1.50 and in particular the P-38, P-39, P-40, and P-51, as well as the British Hawker Hurricane and the German ME-109, were enjoying a sustained major demand. This phenomenon was the result of having the most complete selection of warplane models, the recognized authenticity of the plans, the high quality of the kit contents despite wartime restrictions, and even the patriotic appeal of the attractive red, white, and blue star-spangled carton.

As the final phases of military strategy evolved overseas, Edward T. Packard, accustomed to market planning at least a year in advance, attempted to forecast the demand for modeling and related hobbies after the war. There was a feeling of optimism that the American GI might return with a pent up demand for wanting to build and fly models, particularly if he had been associated with the air forces. In fact, at C-D there was a feeling that demand could exceed the prewar sales volume, so there was not too much concern for controlling inventory. It was felt that there could possibly even be a shortage of kits and related items initially, depending on the availability of critical materials. Hence, production continued unabated.

Had C-D's crystal ball been clearer, a more restrained marketing plan would have been implemented. When the American military personnel received their discharges, their leisure-time activities were less predictable because what emerged was a more experienced American citizen in contrast to the young patriot who had enlisted or been drafted. Many might have been overexposed to the subjugation of military discipline, the group-barracks lifestyle, or an austere hazardous existence under combat conditions. For some who had seen the brutality and horror of war, their adjustment to civilian life would be trying and time-consuming, and their first priority would be to seek the security and peacefulness of a domestic life. For many, the priority would include resuming relationships interrupted by the war. These deferred desires would, of course, override those of the attraction of a prewar hobby.

Another unforeseen change in the world of model building was the effect of the appearance of war-spawned, revolutionary jet-propelled aircraft. At this juncture, the "stick and tissue" method of model building had been elevated to its highest level by C-D. With the advances made during the war with new materials, particularly plastics, the question facing Packard and his contemporaries was what new direction the hobby would take.

New power options included four-cycle engines with greater displacement to propel ¼-size models, representing a trend to larger sizes to approximate more realistically the characteristics of the prototypes. Few could predict the trend to electric power, following the influence of environmentalists. No one in the industry could possibly foresee the extent to which America would become a litigious society, forcing modelers to seek the protection of an organization like the AMA. With the unpredictable urbanization of the country, former flying sites would disappear under the thrust of the developers' bulldozers, forcing greater emphasis on radio-controlled flight. Advanced technology in electronics accelerated by the war and the miniaturization of electronic components would result in smaller space requirements for receivers, greater reliability, more channels, and the resultant undreamed of greater controllability. Breakthroughs in adhesive methodology would significantly reduce construction time, and unique advances in covering materials would further simplify building techniques with greater strength and improved appearance. And perhaps the more exotic aspect of futuristic model development would include powered helicopters and ducted fans to simulate jet propulsion. It all added up to future development that could be expected to be experienced by the industry and modelers at a more rapid rate than during the prewar period.

The Fruits of Victory in 1945

Cataclysmic. Engulfing. Global. Annihilating. Ravaging. Tumultuous. Such were the impressions, observations, and evaluations of the participants in the decisive and historically significant year 1945. Its results changed the boundaries of the major countries of Europe, Asia, and the South Pacific. The world would never be the same, and from it all, America was to be regarded as the new world superpower. America's total, unconditional effort saved the free-world countries from enslavement by nazism and the domination of Japanese imperialism.

C-D's marketing plan was influenced by the events of this momentous year. Its scope and objectives were just as optimistic as postwar America was. *MAN,* the industry's articulate spokesman for modelers, would continue to be the nucleus publication for C-D's advertising, featuring a series of inside-back cover and interior spreads, following the successful strategy used in the recent wartime years. But the uncertain duration of and time of conclusion of the war also influenced C-Ds marketing plan. In the event that an allied victory in one or the both theaters of war seemed imminent, then perhaps a greater emphasis on non-wartime models, such as gas models, control-line, or endurance models, should bear increased priority.

Meanwhile, the success of the previous advertising campaign, involving documented, specific, military testimonials, was continued, and in the spread ad of the March 1945 *MAN* issue there were nine such testimonials. Packard was providing uncontested proof of the value of model building as well as recognition to the air force personnel who had put their lives on the line to defend their country.

In the spreads of the May and June *MAN* issues, a large section of the ads was devoted to the Playboy Senior at $4.50, together with the glider-sailplane Super Condor (7 feet, at $1.00) and the Albatross, (10 feet, at $3.50). These were seasonally influenced elements of the ads for Packard wanted to keep offering the lure of flight to America's youth too young to be at war.

In the South Pacific, the island-hopping strategy of the Allies was accelerated. By February 19 the marines were on Iwo Jima, and by April U.S. aircraft based there were 750 miles south of Tokyo. By June 21 Okinawa was secured at a terrible cost in lives and placed the Allies 350 miles from Japan, a milk run for American B-29s (Boeing "Superfortress").

In the European theater, the Russian forces driving from the east and the Americans aggressively charging from the west met and shook hands on April 25 at Germany's Elbe River. On April 30 it was learned that Hitler had committed suicide in a Berlin bomb shelter under the chancellery. Goering and Udet also took the easy way out instead of face defeat. On May 7, at the schoolhouse at Reims, France, Eisenhower's headquarters, the documents of the German surrender were signed.

Appropriately, in the spread of the August issue of *MAN,* C-D's ad headline urged, "Commemorate V-E Day by Building C-D Models of Planes That Fought over Europe."

On September 2, 1945, aboard the battleship USS *Missouri,* in Tokyo Bay, the Instrument of Surrender was signed by the humbled Japanese Imperial Staff and by the Supreme Commander for the Allied Powers, Gen. Douglas MacArthur and by U.S. Fleet Admiral Chester Nimitz. As if on cue, a great

The August 1945 *MAN* spread ad, with its memorable headline. Packard was again appealing to his audience's patriotism while at the same time educating modelers and others about the various military planes and their role in the conflict. *Author's Collection.*

armada of American aircraft swept across the skies—Corsairs, Hellcats, Avengers, Helldivers, Mustangs, Thunderbolts, and 462 B-29 Superfortresses—heralding the peace. The Second World War was at last over, and a monumental chapter in history was finally closed.

In a vertically read spread in the September *MAN* issue, C-D's ad reproduced an actual testimonial letter from a B-17 navigator since 1940, praising the value of C-D models in teaching and utilizing wartime recognition.

During the course of the year the air racing fraternity experienced a great loss with the death at age sixty-two of Vincent Bendix, who founded the Bendix Trophy cross-country race as a feature of the National Air Races in 1931 that was won by Jimmy Doolittle in the Laird Super Solution.

C-D had made a fortunate employee acquisition in 1939 when Kay Rita Kreitzer, a recent high school graduate, had been hired as a packer on the strength of a recommendation from a nearby business. During her first two years she willingly accepted all assignments and gradually distinguished herself as a capable employee. "Thereafter she was assigned various personnel responsibilities and exhibited an aptitude for this phase of the company operations," Ed recalled. "As a result, she became personnel manager, developing outstanding skills in the interviewing, selection, hiring and administration of employees. Since approximately 80 percent of our employees were women, especially during the war, it was most appropriate that C-D have a woman in this slot."

Not only did she excel in this position but she also became a key member of the executive management team. In 1950 she became Mrs. Packard after Ed's first marriage ended in divorce. She continued with C-D, only taking pregnancy leaves during the course of the births of their three children (Cheryl Kay, Donald Edward [named after Donald Douglas], and Nancy Lorraine). She continued holding this responsible position until C-D's move to Detroit Avenue, and then she assumed the bookkeeping duties since there were no employees then.

The youngest brother, Andrew Jr., returned from his Marine Corps tour of duty and received a C-D bonus from Ed. He resumed as manager of the company store and then left to start his own retail hobby business, Hobbyville, located at 110th and Lorain Avenue.

"In assessing our wartime business we were extremely fortunate to have had a cadre of loyal suppliers who 'moved mountains' to provide vital raw materials for us when shortages plagued the industry," Packard remarked. "Prem Gary at International Balsa Corporation in Jersey City periodically located carloads of scrap balsa remnants salvaged from a variety of sources. Doc Wilson at the Varnish Products Company in Cleveland was able to supply us with dopes and cements when there seemed to be none available. When we had to substitute veneers for printwood balsa sheets, Southern Veneer Manufacturing in Louisville, Kentucky, and J. H. Monteath Company in New York came to our rescue. And Sandusky Folding Box Corporation in Sandusky, Ohio, also bailed us out with critically needed cardboard cartons.

"Joe Zoldak graduated from West Tech High in 1930, the same school that my brothers attended. I hired him at that time, and he became woodshop superintendent and general assistant, remaining with us until he joined the military in 1943. He rejoined our staff after the war in 1946 for several more years.

"Jim Powell, our staff artist, who joined us in 1934, could tackle almost any type of design, sketching, drafting or art work. After he had been with us for approximately six years, he had a great opportunity to assume an art type responsibility with the *Cleveland Press* but still fulfilled our art, design, and drafting requirements as well. During the war he was on a special classified assignment for the Manhattan Project, involving formal art presentations. He was assigned to B-24 flight crews as a part of his responsibilities until the atom bombs were dropped and the Japanese surrendered. During this flight duty he would call me occasionally, providing me with an opportunity to request some much-needed art work for ads, carton designs, or catalog pages. Thus, his art work assignment continued on for C-D almost unbroken, even during the war. On one occasion I met him in New York with some art work assignments that he executed expediently, and I then took him to see the smash hit musical *South Pacific* during its initial performances."

From left: Col. Howard Rusk, Convalescent Training Board, Ed Packard, and Will Pachasa, vice president of C-D. Colonel Rusk is explaining photos of the facilities used for rehabilitation of service personnel recovering from war-time injuries and trauma. Ed arranged for complimentary kits to be sent for their therapy (1944). *E. T. Packard Collection.*

Packard's lifelong mission to be the catalyst for youth in their discovery of careers in aviation through model building had been fulfilled. He only had to pore over the thousands of testimonials he received from air force personnel from all over the world. While these affirmations of air force men attesting to the value of C-D models in their aviation careers were somewhat motivated by their desire to see their own name and testimonial in a C-D ad and receive a free C-D kit, Packard had received many before the U.S. involvement in the war that were not subject to the free offer. What was to become even more astounding, even to Packard himself, was that these testimonials would continue after the war and unceasingly until the company changed hands. On seeing a C-D ad, a formerly young modeler would be moved to write to Ed to buy a kit or a plan and include his own particular encounter with C-D models.

Certainly the military had ample evidence in their extensive recruitment and training of American youth to evaluate, firsthand, the difference model build-

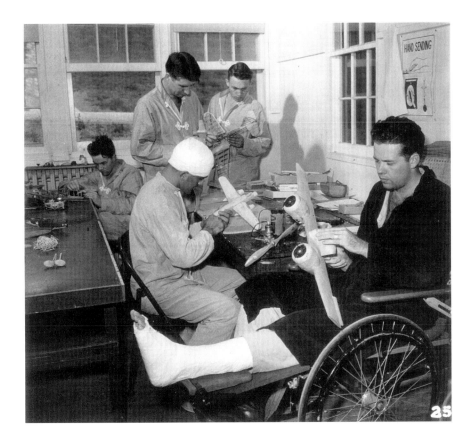

An official U.S. Army Air Force photo showing how model building was used as rehabilitation therapy for injured military personnel during World War II. In building his model, the patient temporarily forgot his condition. Patients also engaged in competitively flying their models. Ed Packard donated Cleveland models to several different military and Red Cross facilities to be used in this type of therapy. *E. T. Packard Collection*

Overleaf: Cleveland Model's 1944 No. 41 catalog cover. Printed in their red, white, and blue with the Statue of Liberty on the cover and a star-spangled bottom border, this catalog had to be one of C-D's finest efforts—that is, one of James Powell's finest efforts. Its fourteen pages featured the 36-inch Famous Warplane Series of T Industrial Training Models in five wartime battle scenes. *E. T. Packard Collection.*

ing made in aviation aptitude. The evidence overwhelmingly supported Packard's positive influence, and he felt that his lifelong philosophy had been vindicated.

However, where was the recognition by the military either to the model industry or to any of the major model manufacturers? They who had survived the bureaucratic nightmares of the war and had provided models to relieve the utter boredom the military faced in isolated bases and provided therapy to those unfortunately convalescing from war-induced afflictions never realized their deserved tribute from the military, the Civil Aeronautics Administration (CAA), the airlines, the aviation industry, or from the aviation-training schools.

In the next phase of operations, the postwar world, the commercial avenues of aviation and particularly the airlines would again benefit from these super-trained pilots who would pilot their postwar airliners to develop worldwide routes and generate greater profits for their companies. Model building's benefits to aviation would be thoroughly proved in the much-later postwar world of the 1980s and 1990s when there would be no reservoir of model builder candidates, for the legacy had not been fulfilled for the following generations; it had been abdicated to the degenerative power of the TV set.

CLEVELAND
MODELS
for
1944
No. 42

JAMES O. POWELL

CHAPTER 12

Postwar Dilemmas

⬡ THE YEAR 1946. Business as usual—hardly! As American business attempted to cope with the adjustments of the 1946 postwar economy, many of modeldom's manufacturers had to undergo the challenging transition of converting their businesses from supplying the military to fulfilling only civilian demands. Characteristic of many model engine manufacturers, their metal-machining expertise and large-capacity engine-parts production and assembly proved their increased capabilities (developed to meet the requirements of the war effort) more productive than their previous smaller-scaled operations. The challenge of the conversion involved downsizing from the mass-producing, highly automated methodology that the demands of the war effort required back to the job-shop type of operating that would suffice for postwar demand, for many would have excess capacity.

Changing product lines from wartime to peacetime merchandise created a delay in production for some model manufacturers. Consequently, some model engines came on line before others. Nevertheless, the result would be a plethora of engines that would eventually flood the postwar market, creating an intensively competitive environment that resulted in driving prices down. At the end of 1946 there were more than thirty different engines nationally advertised, and, because the supply at that time was somewhat limited, they commanded their full prices, usually around $18.50 at the high end. Conspicuous by its absence was the prime mover of the introduction of the gassies, the Brown Jr. engine.

Packard, the innovative entrepreneur, and his dedicated, creative coterie faced this challenge of unknowns with the optimism that stemmed from their wartime success. Ed and his brothers had gained additional confidence from surviving the Great Depression, which took its toll on many businesses, large and small.

Because of an accelerated advancement of technology resulting from war-time innovations and pent-up consumer demand, the economy would experience rapid rates of introductions of new consumer and commercial products and services. A single such example proved to have a revolutionary effect on the American way of life: the advent of television. As the demand by young and old for more sporting events, movies, and sitcoms developed, television's stranglehold on the lives of the consumer would have a significantly negative effect on the hobby industry. In 1946 there were only 6,000 television sets in American homes. By 1951 television's effect on Americans, initially underestimated by Hollywood, would see movie theaters closing in droves. Fifty theaters shuttered in New York City alone. By 1960, 90 percent of American homes had one or more television sets.

The First Postwar Year (1946)

Packard, in concert with the Carpenter ad agency, approached the 1946 ad schedule with spreads and full pages in *MAN* and in the 10-by-13-inch bed-sheet-sized *Air Trails Pictorial,* of which Bill Winter, famous modeler, author, and designer, had become editor in 1943. The C-D ads in the enlarged format of this publication were dramatic and unchallenged by competition.

However, there were noticeable changes in the composition and elements of C-D ads in the first postwar year, the most obvious of all was prices. While the perennially successful SF (MSF) premium line was in evidence, with its imposing choice of all the famous World War II military fighters and bombers, a competitive line of 30-inch wingspan T models at $1.00 was introduced. Well-known postwar civil aircraft designs such as the Stinson 150, Globe Swift, Culver Cadet, and Ercoupe hastened the transition for the modeler from the military types, and the line would be further expanded to meet the demand generated by the popular price.

Irwin Ohlsson, engine designer, and his partner, Harry Rice, production manager, in an unorthodox marketing ploy to steal the march on their model engine competitors, announced the acquisition of a DC-3 (NC-63122) in which they would fly to visit and service their dealers nationally. One of the first such visits by Ohlsson and Rice occurred in 1946 with a visit to Cleveland in their DC-3 to make a delivery of engine model 60s and model 23s to C-D to notify their dealers that they were in a position to deliver postwar engines and to capitalize on the incumbent publicity.

Nowhere was the postwar transition more striking than in the 1946 revival of the Thompson and Bendix Trophy events at the National Air Races held at Cleveland. Gone were the colorful racing champions of the 1930s, such as Roscoe Turner, Jimmy Doolittle, Benny Howard, and Jimmy Wedell, and their one-of-a-kind daring civil air racers.

The Ohlsson and Rice DC-3 NC-63122 delivered a shipment of Ohlsson 23 and Ohlsson 60 engines to Cleveland in a tour around the country after World War II as a promotional drive to drum up business. From left: Irwin Olhsson, Ed Packard (holding an engine), and Harry Rice, Ohlsson's partner. Rear, second from right: Fred Pachasa (ca. 1946). *E. T. Packard Collection.*

1946 National Air Races Official Directory, sixty-four pages. The first postwar National Air Race utilized all the promotional and marketing methods characterized by the prewar races and then some. The leadership was assumed by F. C. Crawford, president of Thompson Products. *Author's Collection.*

It was no longer a contest of individually designed air racers. The event had become a showcase for war surplus military fighters, since it was possible to acquire a surplus P-39, P-51, or F2-G Corsair (Vought by Goodyear) for far less than the minimum $50,000 price tag for a civil, personally designed air racer. The winners' purses could not justify that much of an investment. The advent of the military jets necessitated a separate division in each event.

With a clipped wing 1,200 hp, Allison-powered P-39Q Airacobra, Tex Johnson won the 1946 Thompson ten-lap 300-mile course at 373.9 mph. In

"AIR POWER IS PEACE POWER"

By F. C. Crawford

President, Thompson Products, Inc.
President, The National Air Races
President, The Air Foundation

WORLD WAR I hardly had ended when all but three of the seventeen companies that built our first air force went into bankruptcy. Lulled by dreams of everlasting peace, an apathetic congress and public stood by and let them fail. Our air force vanished, too. Europe took the lead in military aviation and left us far behind.

THIS MUST NEVER happen again! Today, with the jet and rocket engine, distance no longer has any meaning. New and unlimited potentialities make all nations dangerously vulnerable. From now on our only protection is an ability to strike hard and fast anywhere in the world and to bar an enemy's ravages from our own shores.

ABOVE ALL, this calls for modern air power. Planes will fight the first great battles of offense and defense if the tragedy of a major war again visits the world. Victory or crushing defeat could be a matter of days, before naval and ground strength come into play.

TO GUARANTEE this all-important air power we first of all must have an understanding, articulate public, ever ready to express its demands to our government. This public must see to it that an America at peace is always armed with a reasonable minimum of the latest military planes, and top-notch pilots to fly them. Our people must realize that obsolescence in aircraft is swift, and that the need for developing and discarding is endless. Our greatest World War II planes were outmoded three months after V-J Day by new designs, here and abroad.

OUR CITIZENS MUST foster and be willing to support a strong, aggressive aircraft industry, instantly capable of vast emergency expansion. They must be willing to pay for more great laboratories like the one on the edge of this airfield. The time is gone forever when we can again build such an industry almost from scratch during a war, as we did after Pearl Harbor!

WE MUST ENCOURAGE and promote in every possible way the creation of a great reserve of young civilian pilots, with a love for flying and basic training on which to build quickly an enlarged and invincible air force.

THE NATIONAL AIR RACES always have been a great and thrilling spectacle. But they have a very serious and constructive purpose, too. They are the public show window of our nation's progress in the air, military and civilian. They are first to reveal to

intelligent citizens whether we are going forward or slowing down in the air.

IT IS HERE and elsewhere at air meets that our Air Force shows the taxpayers what their money has bought. The new Allison service plane race, and others, are virtually military maneuvers, with the same elements of careful preparation, control and precision.

AT THESE SAME RACES, prewar, thousands of clear eyed youngsters first felt the inspiration to fly. Many of them became our pilots in the last war—the world's best! Some are now colorful race pilots, inspiring a new generation of boys. Others guide our great commercial transports.

YOU CAN BE PROUD of your country's air progress as it is traced for you here today! As a peace-loving American I hope you will do your part to assure that this progress never falters.

AGAIN, remember these four things: *An alert, expressive public! A highly developed peacetime air force —adequate, but not extravagant! A sound, progressive aircraft industry! A great reserve of youthful civilian flyers!*

America is worth that to all of us!

America must remain second to none in the air, for *"Air Power is Peace Power!"*

A message from F. C. Crawford, president of Thompson Products, Inc., with a powerful reminder that America must remain second to none in the air, for "Air Power is Peace Power." *Author's Collection.*

Today's Racing Entries
Monday, September 1, 1947

TINNERMAN TROPHY RACE
FOR P-63 AIRPLANES
TOTAL PURSE $5,500.00 and the TINNERMAN TROPHY

No.	Pilot	Airplane	Engine	No.	Pilot	Airplane	Engine
92	Joseph Kinkella	P-63	Allison	72	Ray Eiche	P-63	Allison
51	H. K. Knight	P-63	Allison	30	Charles Tucker	P-63	Allison
55	William Bour	P-63	Allison	87	A. T. Whiteside	P-63	Allison
65	Wilson V. Newhall	P-63	Allison	4	S. J. Wittman	P-63	Allison

GOODYEAR TROPHY RACE
NATIONAL FREE-FOR-ALL   MEN PILOTS ONLY
OPEN TO ENGINES OF 190 CU. IN. DISPLACEMENT
FINALS
Listen to announcement for names of Entrants

No.	Pilot	Airplane	Engine	No.	Pilot	Airplane	Engine
	Dwight Dempster	Allenbaugh Spec.	Continental	10	H. R. Salmon	Cosmic Wind	Continental
5	Paul Penrose	ARC Special	Continental	3	Tony LeVier	Cosmic Wind	Continental
52	R. W. Baker	Baker Special	Continental		Warren Siem	Loose Special	Continental
41	Charles W. Bing	Dixon	Continental	39	Mike Argandar	Nimmo Special	Continental
85	Joe Smith	Camburn Spec.	Continental	19	E. F. Robinson	Brown Modified	Continental
89	W. F. Folck	Chester Spec.	Continental	34	Al Barber	Special	Continental
81	Bill Taylor	F. & A. Special	Continental	20	Steve J. Wittman	Wittman Special	Continental
55	R. S. Thompson	Special	Continental	70	G. J. Dux	Fliteways Spec.	Continental
71	A. A. Hanes	Hanes Special	Continental	26	John Gaffrey	Special	Continental
24	Edward Honroth	Special	Continental				

THOMPSON TROPHY RACE
NATIONAL FREE-FOR ALL   MEN PILOTS ONLY
WORLD'S HIGH SPEED LAND PLANE CLASSIC
TOTAL PURSE $40,000.00 and duplicate THOMPSON TROPHIES
Including the ALLEGHENY LUDLUM AWARD
"R" Division for Reciprocating Engine Airplanes

No.	Pilot	Airplane	Engine	No.	Pilot	Airplane	Engine
50	H. L. Austell	Crosby CR4	Menasco	55	William Bour	P-63	Allison
77	Steve Beville	P-51	Packard	47	T. P. Mathews	P-38	(2) Allisons
74	Cook Cleland	Corsair	Pratt-Whitney	65	Wilson V. Newhall	P-63	Allison
94	Richard Becker	Corsair	Pratt-Whitney	18	R. G. Puckett	Corsair	Pratt-Whitney
84	Tony Jannazo	Corsair	Pratt-Whitney	66	Ivis H. Hill	P-38	(2) Allisons
15	Woody Edmondson	P-51	Allison	14	Charles C. Walling	P-38	(2) Allisons
44	Kendall Everson	P-51	Allison	64	J. E. Saum	P-38	(2) Allisons
21	M. W. Fairbrother	P-51	Packard	72	Ray Eiche	P-63	Allison
37	George Welch	P-51	Packard	40	R. R. Stevenson	P-38	(2) Allisons
61	Dale Fulton	P-51	Packard	11	Ray Demming	P-39	Allison
	Jack B. Hardwick	P-51	Packard	27	John E. Thomson	P-38	(2) Allisons
	Robert J. Harlow	P-38	(2) Allisons	30	Charles Tucker	P-63	Allison
	C. C. Brotton	P-51	Allison	87	A. T. Whiteside	P-63	Allison
45	A. L. Johnson	P-51	Packard	4	S. J. Wittman	P-63	Allison
51	H. K. Knight	P-63	Allison	82	J. L. Ziegler	P-40	Allison
3	Tony LeVier	P-38	(2) Allisons				

"J" Division for Service Jet Planes

Pilot	Organization	Residence
Lt. Col. William Dunham	56th Fighter Group (SAC) Selfridge Field, Mich.	Nez Perce, Idaho
Capt. William M. Gates	56th Fighter Group (SAC) Selfridge Field, Mich.	Ann Arbor, Mich.
Lt. Col. Robert L. Petit	12th Air Force (TAC) March Field, Calif.	Ventura, Calif.
Capt. Lewis W. Powers	12th Air Force (TAC) March Field, Calif.	Albuquerque, N. M.
Lt. Col. B. S. Preston, Jr.	4th Fighter Group (SAC) Andrews Field, Washington, D. C.	Washington, D. C.
Lt. Joseph R. Howard	4th Fighter Group (SAC) Andrews Field, Washington, D. C.	Washington, D. C.

★ **FISHER FOODS** — Cleveland's Champions of Good Living ★

The 1947 National Air Race schedule of racing entries. The Goodyear Trophy Race had, in a sense, replaced the prewar Thompson event because these entries were still the product of civilian aviation and were within the budget of the American sportsman. *Author's Collection.*

the Bendix, Hollywood movie stunt and charter pilot Paul Mantz, with a modified "wet wing" P-51C-10 Rolls Royce Merlin–powered entry, soared at 33,000 feet altitude from Van Nuys to Cleveland at 434.4 mph in four hours, forty-two minutes, thus winning first place.

Unfortunately, there was no groundswell of modelers' demand immediately after the races, as in the 1930s, much to Packard's dismay. Hence, no postwar kits of the Thompson and Bendix winners were ever offered, then or afterward. Such was the stark contrast from the modelers' unbridled enthusiasm of the thirties, which was a significant part of the C-D prewar legend.

Now that Ohlsson and Rice had fully converted their operations to civilian production, and foreseeing decreasing sales ahead, they lost no time in putting a lock on the model engine market with a startling announcement of price reductions on their line of three models: Model 60 went from $18.50 to $11.95; Model 23 from $16.50 to $9.95; and Model 19 from $14.50 to $9.95.

In his planning for the second postwar year, C-D's mentor took stock of the substantial price cuts by the leading model engine manufacturer. Although Ed's sales and marketing intuition had steered C-D on a successful course

The Bendix Trophy with names engraved on it of previous winners and photos of all the winners through 1947. Paul Mantz was shown as having won both the 1946 and 1947 events in his modified wet wing P-51. *Author's Collection.*

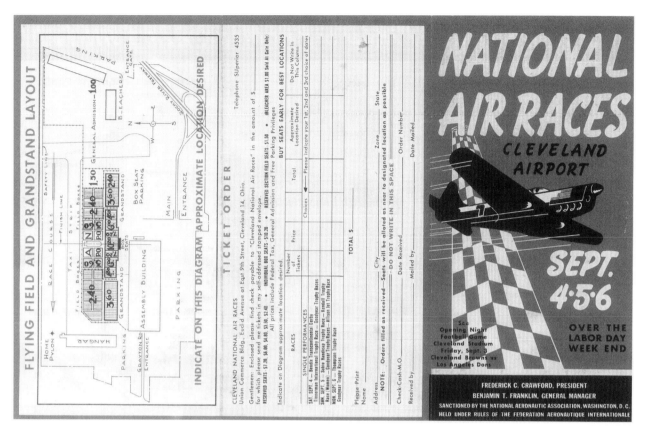

The 1947 ticket order brochure with the airfield layout and seating. *Author's Collection.*

through the nuances of the hobby market, he arrived at the Carpenter Ad Agency to talk advertising budget and, for the first time, was less than optimistic. Conferring with his associates at the Carpenter Ad Agency, Packard had to make a realistic assessment of the cost-effectiveness of the extensive ad campaign of 1946, which was ambitious for their first postwar effort and represented a significant portion of the annual C-D budget. Despite C-D's having the greatest choice of scale flying models in the industry to offer in type, size, and price, from one dollar and up, the sales were not forthcoming in proportion to the advertising. Offering an extensive line of 30-inch wingspan models for a dollar and an equally varied line of Industrial T 36-inch models at $1.50, both lines represented outstanding values for the American hobbyist. However, the dealers were simply not experiencing what should have been the resultant demand. Hence, the 1947 ad campaign was trimmed significantly to one or two spreads in both *MAN* and *Air Trails Pictorial,* with the bulk of the space in single-page and half-page insertions.

Cook Cleland, in his Corsair F-2G (by Goodyear) P&W 4360 28-cylinder Wasp-powered modified Navy fighter, whipped around the twenty-lap, 300-mile Thompson Trophy rectangular course at 396.1 mph as the winner of the event at the 1947 National Air Races. Paul Mantz repeated as the Bendix Trophy winner in his "wet wing" P-51C at 460.4 mph, having again located the right groove in the jet stream at over 30,000 feet altitude with the throttle of his Rolls Royce Merlin at the firewall most of the way. But again, no clamor from the modelers nor the dealers for kits of the National Air Race winners, so the great aerial events that made terms like "pylon polishers" and "speed brokers" synonymous with the Cleveland fall classic ceased to be a factor in C-D's postwar marketing campaign.

The Third Postwar Year (1948)

In its nineteenth year, comprising sixty-four to seventy-two pages and with front covers by famed artist Joe Kotula, picturing the latest designs in military or civil aircraft, *Model Airplane News* broke tradition with its September issue, which featured a cover photo of a young modeler with his gas model poised for launching. Thus began a tradition that this publication and many other model periodicals would follow: utilizing model scenes, although not exclusively, to more forcefully dramatize the nature of their monthly magazines.

C-D's 1948 ad schedule in *MAN* was devoid of any spreads, downsizing to 50 percent in full-page ads, with the balance in ¾-page layouts and a similar schedule in *Air Trails Pictorial*. The reduced exposure mirrored the recent trend of decreasing sales despite the extremely low prices for C-D kits that, in turn, forced employee reductions down to an average of fifteen to twenty workers. An exception in the pricing revolution was the price for the Playboy

1948 National Air Races at Cleveland Municipal Airport. Foreground is Bob Eucker's P-63 Allison–powered entry with four-bladed prop, followed by *City of Lynchburg, Virginia III* (Woody Edmondsons's Rolls Royce–powered P-51), next to a line-up of Lockheed P-80 jets. *Sid Bradd Collection.*

Senior, which had escalated to six dollars compared to its original price in 1939 of $3.95, due to the rising cost of materials and wages.

The 1948 Thompson Trophy event was won by Anson Johnson in his P-51D at 383.76 mph. In the Bendix, Paul Mantz matched the three-time honors of Roscoe Turner's Thompson winnings by clinching the event in his P-51C-10 at 447.98 mph in the winning time of four hours and thirty-three minutes.

The Fourth Postwar Year (1949)

It was to be a pivotal year for C-D's thirtieth anniversary—a year in which Packard intended to invoke the old adage, "You never know where the bottom is until you plumb for it." He had to find out how low in price he had to go in order to increase sales.

The recipient of endless advice, admonitions, and brilliant ideas, all concerned with various ways in which to simplify model construction, Ed had reached a decision. His instincts told him that this generation of model builders was of a different bent, seeking more instant gratification, much like the solutions presented on television. Some of his associates in the Model Industry Association were of the opinion that the American boy wanted a quick fix. If he were to build something like an aircraft model, it had to virtually snap together. It couldn't be a challenge, it had to be *easy.* Hence, the C-D *E-Z* line of simplified 20-inch wingspan models at 50 cents was introduced in the July *MAN* issue with much fanfare.

It was appropriate indeed for the germination of this novel approach of offering the most simple and least expensive models to occur during C-D's thirtieth anniversary and in the twentieth year of publication of *Model Airplane News.*

Since it was not a common occurrence for a modeling publication to survive twenty years, particularly when ten of those years were subject to the economic challenges of the Great Depression, *MAN* understandably promoted this achievement in the July issue, since it was July 1929 when volume 1, no. 1, debuted on the nation's newsstands as a Macfadden Publication. Therefore, this commemorative issue championed the occasion boldly on the cover and devoted an inside spread to a feature editorial complete with a montage of many of the publication's early years' cover art and minor title modifications. Outside of the fact that the magazine was called *Junior Mechanics and Model Airplane News,* beginning in 1930, and *Universal Model Airplane News,* beginning in 1932 for several months, it has not only survived but can lay claim to having the longest run with the same sort of title of any such publication.

Flying Aces, volume 1, no. 1, debuted in October 1928 but experienced several title changes after World War II and is now known as *Flying Models. Air Trails* (Street and Smith) also had its first issue published in October 1928, and after several changes of titles and ownership ceased publication as *American Aircraft Modeler* in March 1975.

The C-D E-Z System

The E-Z system featured all balsa parts accurately die-cut to exact scale, rugged yet feather light. Initially, three models were offered: the E-Z 117 Aeronca Sedan 20-inch wingspan; the E-Z 9 SE-5 20-inch wingspan; and the E-Z 108 Beechcraft Bonanza 20-inch wingspan.

If the combination of simplified assembly and a rock bottom price for C-D quality would stimulate the lethargic dealer demand, the E-Z line would seem to be the answer. Ultimately there would be nine models in the line.

The competition would also introduce simplified, low-priced lines. Shortly thereafter, in 1949–50, Comet would introduce their line of six Struct-o-Speed models at 25 cents. Monogram would follow with their line of Speedee-Bilt flying models at 75 cents each.

At the opposite end of the modeling spectrum, the C-D stable of gas models shared in the limelight and, hence, the March *MAN* issue announced the 76-inch span Luscombe Sedan at $7.50 (versus $17.50 for the venerable Stinson). Designed for free-flight, control line, or radio control (RC), it was a prudent advertising choice. The design had inherent stability, an adequate cabin interior to accommodate a radio-control receiver, and batteries, yet it incorporated scale appeal. So it met the tried-and-true specifications for which C-D had become famous.

Despite the drastic turn of events in the National Air Race insofar as the demand for models was concerned, Packard observed the keen interest what was developing in the field of Formula I racers designed and flown by such popular air racers as Art Chester, Tony Le Vier, and Steve Wittman. The only C-D new air racer initially offered postwar at one dollar was the 24-inch "IT" kit of "Fish" Salmon's Cosmic Wind Minnow, 85 hp, Continental-powered, built by Tony Levier and Associates, which was the 190 cc. winner of the 1948 Goodyear Trophy at 169.6 mph. The attractive carton in which it was offered, plus the authentically detailed plans scaled from the actual racer hangared at Cleveland, reflected the appeal of the daring miniature speedster, resulting in gratifying sales for several years. At the April 1949 San Diego Gold Cup race, another racing icon, Art Chester, famous for his Jeep and Goon designs, crashed to his death in his Formula I *Swea' Pea*.

Another tragic loss in 1949 occurred at the National Air Races when the colorful, daring Bill Odom, flying Jackie Cochran's *Beguine,* a modified P-51, crashed and burned out of a high-speed stall rounding the pylon of the second lap of the Thompson, killing the pilot and two occupants of the home in which it crashed. The accident, which took innocent lives, ended the Na-

tional Air Races at Cleveland. The "big iron" unlimiteds would not return for fifteen years, when Bill Stead would recreate the air races at Reno, Nevada. Cook Cleland, in his No. 94 chopped-wing F2G-1 P&W 4360–powered Corsair took the winner's checkered flag for the Thompson at 397.6 mph. In the Bendix, Joe DeBona set a new record of 470.13 mph in a P-51F-6C owned by Jimmy Stewart, the actor.

Thus ended the four-year attempt to revive the National Air Races. The demise was lamented by the racing fraternity and undoubtedly had a negative effect on the further development of the unlimited air racers. However, when it came to speed, the jets now took center stage.

Prefabs and Downsizing in the 1950s

As the 1950s loomed, it became apparent that the direction of C-D's marketing effort was away from the emphasis on super scale and the multiple-hobby concept. Having introduced the E-Z line, which featured all kit parts die-cut to reduce assembly time, Packard expanded the concept, and in September 1951 the Quicky line of 18-inch span knockdown models was introduced at 59 cents.

Postwar solution—the "Quicky" line of scale flying models involving no cutting, no tissue covering, and no painting. Assembly time was from thirty to sixty minutes. *E. T. Packard Collection.*

The kits were advertised with the fanfare of "no cutting, no painting" and "no tissue covering," capable of being assembled in eighteen minutes. At such a bargain price, the line set a trend, and Chuck Tracy, aviation editor of the *Cleveland Press,* directed an indoor contest in Cleveland that featured C-D Quicky kits that had been sanded down to $1/32$-inch thickness on wings and empennage. With the addition of ribs to make the wings conform to an airfoil shape, plus the substitution of a lighter balsa prop to replace the furnished plastic type, the resultant winning duration approached two minutes.

A significant downtrend in prices also appeared in the 1950s, including gas model kits and engines, with engines that had been priced at $18.50 prewar now were reduced to $11.95. However, a desirable innovation had occurred with the development of the line of class $1/2$A engines, priced at $5–6.00. This new class would mushroom into almost another new mass market, because it enabled modelers at the entry level to switch from rubber power to the gas model category with a modest investment of around ten dollars for both kit and power plant. With the typical smaller-sized wingspans in the new class and the less-potent power plants, the era of the "schoolyard" model dawned, making smaller parks, playgrounds, and nearby fields accommodating model flying.

A sign of the times and the de-emphasis on the multiple-hobby concept by C-D was evident in their thirty-two-page 1950 catalog, almost devoid of engines or other hobbies, which was in marked contrast to C-D's sixty-four-page 1939 catalog, two-thirds of which pages were for items other than aircraft models. However, in the 1955–56 issue, the most popular engines were

Richard Collins of Cleveland, Ohio, age thirteen, won the "Quicky" flying contest in 1953 with a time of 52.3 seconds. The young modeler drilled lightening holes wherever possible and used a balsa prop instead of a plastic prop. He also increased the dihedral angle of the wings. The contest was held by Charles Tracy of the *Cleveland Press. E. T. Packard Collection.*

again listed. The exception in the 1950 catalog was the outside-back cover, which introduced a craft line of C-D art-flower kits at 25 and 49 cents. This was an attempt at diversification for C-D's product line, designed to appeal to the female market. The craft lines would be marketed under the names of Profit Krafts Company and U.S. Crafts Company.

An integral part of the C-D marketing effort of the 1950s involved the advertising of most of the C-D line, which, with the exception of the specific gas model kits, and with minor modifications, gave the modeler a choice of power: rubber, CO_2, control line, free flight, or radio controlled. In 1953, as products were phased in or out, C-D began a campaign to build a demand for the C-D brand cement. Since C-D's line of dopes and other liquids had been popularly accepted over the years, cement was a logical extension of the product line.

For C-D, the 1950s witnessed a more tightly controlled marketing program, offering a select line of SF kits on a limited basis—making the high-demand SF items available periodically but not involving an inordinate amount in inventory. The strategy to maximize cash flow was inventory turnover.

As a further step to bolster C-D sales in the 1950s, Packard consulted his friends Frank Butler, then editor of *Toys and Novelties* magazine, and John Mullaney, sales manager and later publisher of *Toys*. They recommended that an experienced sales manager be hired by C-D to devote 100 percent of his time to increasing distribution and sales. After a sales manager was hired, the result was that the sales organization totaling more than a hundred representatives sold less in 1953 than Packard alone had sold in 1952.

Irwin Polk (at left) of Polks Hobbies, a distributor of C-D models, and Ed Packard discussing administrative matters of the association at the Chicago Model Industry Association trade show, ca. 1953. *Author's Collection.*

Dissolution of the Management Team

By 1958 the demand for the combined lines of C-D kits had peaked at a level requiring a complement of twelve employees or less. In comparison to the era of the 1930s and 1940s, when C-D was a booming enterprise, the 1950s represented declining demand, at least for C-D, and, in particular, it posed a limited challenge and opportunity for Ed's brother Will.

Consequently, Will confided his feelings to Ed, stating his concern for a lack of a growth opportunity for him. He felt that he must start his own enterprise for the financial security of himself and his family. For more than a quarter century, Will faithfully served with Ed, side-by-side, beginning with his working part-time after school all through high school, culminating with the responsibilities of secretary-treasurer and woodshop superintendent, including purchasing, shipping, manufacturing, and the training of many of the production workers. So in 1958 the two eldest brothers reached an agreement, and Will left the business after nearly twenty-five years of dedicated service. He would be sorely missed. Shortly thereafter, Will founded a retail hobby business in Cleveland. He ultimately expanded it into a successful wholesale hobby enterprise, Cleveland Hobby Supply Company, which currently continues to be operated by him and his family.

In considering his options at this juncture in his extended forty years of challenging entrepreneurship, Packard would have welcomed and accepted an equitable buyout offer. And there had been some along the way; however, most offers specified only selective parts of the business, such as the valuable library of plans and related assets. He was wise enough to realize that C-D had greater value as a total package, plus he wanted to avoid the hassle of spinning off the remainder of the assets. So none of these offers could be taken seriously.

Like many parent-entrepreneurs, he had harbored the hope that one of his sons, Robert or Don, would step in to fill his shoes. However, their careers evolved independently as Robert became associated with a chain of craft stores in Cleveland, and Don found a career slot in the industrial construction business in Seattle.

Relying on his ever-expanding circle of talented and dedicated C-D model engineers, Ed's most viable marketing option appeared to rest in offering model plans without kits.

PART III

Transition:
The New C-D Era

CHAPTER 13

The Origin of the Volunteer
Model Engineers

✳ AFTER THE ISSUANCE of the 1959 C-D catalog, the last in the series to list the complete C-D lines, to avoid such expense in the future Packard switched to a 4-by-11-inch format that was designed to be a self-mailer, containing a return order form.

The first in this series issued in 1960 carried the logo of Aviation Milestone Designs by Cleveland Peerless Antique Model Company (a division of Cleveland Model and Supply Company). This issue was largely devoted to listing the kits and other items being phased out, so, at the time, there were no C-D New Era Milestone Designs listed. Since there were no new designs or kits being manufactured in the early 1960s, there were no longer any full-time draftsmen employed. Ed Packard had come full circle: he had reverted to the early designing days of C-D when he personally had drawn the plans for the Great Lakes Sport Trainer SF-1.

From C-D's inception, Packard had always carried on a prolific correspondence, written as well as by telephone, with famous aviators, modelers, museum personnel, aviation journalists, writers, and artists. Of late, letters were coming in requesting kits of planes that his fans had flown or owned themselves, either civilian or military, or aircraft with which they had had a love affair or a craft that they had always wanted to own or fly but that they now began to realize would not be financially or otherwise possible.

How better to meet the unsatisfied demand that existed in the market than to expand his already extensive line so that these types that were being requested were available as plans only? Let the modelers procure their own readily available supplies if they wished to construct the model, or let them purchase and collect the plans only. There had always been a core of buffs who collected plans with no intention of ever using them for construction. (Guillow currently reports that out of 200,000 kits sold annually, 80 percent are never completely constructed.) Packard, a veteran at analyzing fickle model builders' tastes, wisely determined to capitalize on this specialized segment of the market. In essence, these elements evolved into an entirely new marketing plan, aptly called the New C-D Era Milestone designs, incorporating most of the famous Golden Era and World War I and World War II designs, which today total more than 300 different types available in seven scales: ⅜-inch, ½-inch, ¾-inch (museum scale), 1 inch and 1½ inch, 2 inches, and 3 inches (¼ size). But how could this strategy be implemented without hiring an expensive support staff?

The answer, as is often the case, came in part from the very market he served, namely his modelers, now career-oriented family types still with an unfulfilled desire for their own particular aircraft.

It was just such a situation in which Jack Tarbox, one of the C-D volunteer model engineers found himself in 1965. He had been an ardent admirer of Alfred Verville, who had designed his first plane in 1915, who then became the designer of the advanced Verville Sperry Pulitzer winning racers and who had been chief of design for the Engineering Division of the old Air Service. He also had the distinction of having designed the Buhl-Verville J4 Airster CA-3, which received the first ATC No. 1, awarded in 1927. Tarbox was involved with drawing a plan of the 1930 YPT-10 Verville Sportsman, of which four were delivered to the Air Corps (180 hp Lycoming R-680). With the assistance of Packard in the finalizing phase of the drawing, it became the SF129, the first plan in the new Milestone series, which ultimately would total over 300 new types.

Similarly, W. T. Given III, another of the dedicated volunteer model engineers, had an affection for the Waco 10. With some photos and data from Marion McClure, Waco owner, Ed finalized this design as the SF-130 Waco 10 (OX-5). However, in the No. 4 catalog, issued in 1967, there were twenty of the new design plans, starting with SF-129, the Verville Sportsman.

By 1968 Packard became aware that C-D sales were never going to return to anywhere near their prewar level, and he ceased manufacturing the kits. His mode of operation called for further drastic changes, which meant that the totally integrated operation on Lorain Avenue would no longer be necessary. Reluctantly, in 1968 he advised Broadview Savings, his mortgagor, to take over the property, bringing the world-famous C-D Lorain Avenue facility to an end.

Fortunately, Packard was able to relocate nearby on 10307 Detroit Avenue in what had originally been the White Chewing Gum factory, a historically designated city landmark where he was able to negotiate an economical lease for 7,800 square feet on one floor for the extensive C-D inventory. Little did he realize that his new location would be the home of C-D in its new role of a plans-only operation for the next quarter-century.

"Shortly after the move to Detroit Avenue in 1969, I lost a dear friend and great supporter of C-D," confided Packard. "Eugene W. Kettering, son of

Charles F. "Boss" Kettering of General Motors fame, met an untimely death. He spent many hours with me at the first C-D Hobby Shop on Bridge Avenue and West 57th Street discussing model designs, for he had a collection of over 500 scale models, then one of the largest and most valuable of such collections in the world. Before his death, he made a substantial financial contribution to the Contemporary Sciences Department of Humanities of Case Western Reserve University in Cleveland. His bequest was for the repository of original Cleveland Model drawings for safe keeping.

The New C-D Era of Aviation Milestone Designs

There is something special about the C-D volunteers that at one time consisted of a group of more than three dozen model engineers nationwide. In nearly every instance, the volunteer's relationship with the Ed Packard began with correspondence, requesting the plan of a particular aircraft. The task for that plan would then be assigned to a particularly well qualified individual. Or, in some instances, the volunteer model engineer would have been involved, on his own, in the research necessary to produce a plan for his favorite aircraft, including photos, specs, articles, and other data, incorporating a preliminary ¾-inch scale plan. After contacting Ed, the package would be sent to him, and Ed would either complete it or assign it to a more qualified volunteer.

However, it has most always been Packard himself who has finished the drawings, adding the proper documentation, necessary construction details, various rib and former patterns, photos, and the superb illustrations provided by volunteer J. Ken Sniffen. It was indeed fortunate for the success of the New C-D Era Milestone designs marketing program that Sniffen offered his services, because he was a professional artist, designer, art professor, and antique aviation buff. His passion had been World War I aircraft.

C-D had always made extensive use of graphic arts in all phases of the business from its inception; hence, there was an acute awareness of its power and influence on the modeler. This new marketing approach would obviously have to use a substitute for the photographic method previously used and adopt the use of illustrations. In 1964 the outstanding C-D staff artist and designer Jim Powell had gone because there were few new designs, kits, major catalogs, or other requirements for his varied and extensive artistic talents. Packard, long an exponent of the use of graphic arts in his business, knew it would be difficult to fill the void left by Powell's departure. However, the slot would be filled by an existing relationship from within his group of volunteer engineers.

About the same time Powell was leaving, unbeknownst to Ed, Sniffen had been collaborating with one of the earliest model engineer volunteers, Bob

Historic Model Collectors Handbook-Catalog No. 2

★ ★ ★ ★ ★ ★ ★ ★

*The Nobility of Conscientious Labor
and the Joy of Willing Service
has Made Cleveland
the Greatest Name in Modelmaking*

★ ★ ★ ★ ★ ★ ★ ★

1 Year Subs. 25c

CLEVELAND-PEERLESS

Above and facing page: Samples of Cleveland's outstanding graphic design by Ken Sniffen. *E. T. Packard Collection.*

Thompson, on various of his World War I aircraft plans. Sniffen had been a longtime C-D customer, and in the process of placing orders had developed some degree of contact with Ed. Ultimately, since there was a need to have a staff artist available to embellish the proposed New Era Plan designs with perspectives and other illustrations and the art required for period flyers and small catalogs, Ed asked Sniffen to submit sketches of proposed designs along with examples of his other artwork. There ensued a long-term relationship that continued lifelong.

As a testimonial to the creativity and engineering ability of the C-D volunteer model engineers, on every New C-D Era Milestone Designs plan, in addition to the world-famous C-D title block, in the lower lefthand corner, is listed the names of those volunteers who specifically produced that plan.

Special!

SOMETHING YOU DON'T WANT TO MISS!

A REALLY ACTIVE ANTIQUE ASSOCIATION FOR AVIATION COLLECTORS AND MODELERS! JOIN NOW! START TO ENJOY WORTHWHILE BENEFITS OF ACTIVE PARTICIPATION

Cleveland Historical Model Association

Purpose: To foster keener interest in historic old time planes of all types by collectors and modelers; to preserve plans, drawings and technical data for future generations; to encourage closer co-operation with aviation and technical museums; to encourage the building of finer, highly detailed authentic scale models for flight or museum use; to create a national contest annually to allow members to participate on an "open" basis. To these purposes, the C.H.M.A. is dedicated.

It must have your support to succeed. Please don't sit idly by, hoping others will support it as we need your comments and "votes". By becoming a member of C.H.M.A. you will receive not only a great

ADVANTAGES ENJOYED BY C.H.M.A. MEMBERS
- 1 year subscription to quarterly C.A.A.R. at $3.00 charge ($2.50 per copy after publication) SAVE 33-1/3%
- Certificates of Membership and pocket cards, soon to be available.
- Discount orders from Cleveland-Peerless Antique Model Co. 10% over $10., 20% over $20.
- Many books and back number periodicals to be made available for purchase.
- We shall do all we can to help you to make new friends nationally and internationally to exchange special plans with other members and to get acquainted with museum officials and their needs.
- Cooperation with city fathers, schools, boys clubs. To encourage younger builders.
- To be advised when hard-to-get materials sources are located, co-operatively.
- National recognition for your best models from photos you send us.
- Member privileges at Museum headquarters, to show your work to others, discuss antiques, etc.
- Receive occasional C.H.M.A. member bonus offers by Cleveland-Peerless Antique Models Co. (Note: All pics are of our own Models, as usual)

deal of clean, downright wholesome pleasure but many profitable advantages in addition for a very small sum.

Aircraft plans, photos and pictorial prints and paintings will be made available. All this is intended to encourage collection of data and relics of historic aircraft and models for museums with special emphasis on encouraging todays youngsters to follow in the footsteps of "old time" modelbuilders with its consequent character-building qualities, to help reduce juvenile delinquency and to foster finer modelbuilding for museums and personal collections. Such display models are very much in demand today as the most interesting of all displays. Did you ever see anyone who would not turn his head, then pause or stop on first viewing a well built model on public display?

OLDTIMERS
JOIN AND SAVE MONEY

You don't have to join to buy anything whatever, but this could be the wisest $5.00 you ever spent to join any group. Every time you purchase from our supporting body Cleveland-Peerless Antique Model Co., you save 10-20% on all purchases over $10. C-P deserves your full support to assist its support of C.A.A.R., to perpetuate and foster more authentic model designing for you. It's the only complete old time model airplane "hobby shop" left. Support it fully for all your hobby needs.

Membership Annual Dues $5.00.
(If also subscribing to CAAR send $8.00). Remit to C-P or C.M. Co.

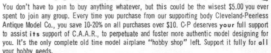

Cleveland Antique Aircraft Reports
Historical and Practical Modeling for Collectors

CLEVELAND MODELMAKING NEWS RETURNS AFTER 30 YRS. SUSPENSION!
THIS IS THE WORLD'S MOST UNUSUAL ENGINEERING SERVICE AT UNHEARD OF LOW PRICE

This new name of Cleveland Modelmaking News will better take care of todays collecting interests of most antique modelers. It is being revived, quarterly, as thousands have asked for its reinstatement for years. As formerly, you can vote on plans desired all the time. It will have from one to three large folding plans in every issue of at least one large to two smaller planes. It shall contain only aircraft hereafter, many smaller planes, mostly American shall also be included; commentary on good modeling suitable for display and museum showing; delving more deeply into the historical aspects of earlier flying; profusely illustrated with prototypes and your own good model photographs. Your name and address shall be used (by your permission only) so similarly interested members or museum officials could contact you to exchange information, or possibly to purchase your model (unless you might indicate your wish to become a donor to some museum).

Cleveland Antique Aircraft Report No. 8 shall be the first of three to appear late in 1964, perhaps irregularly until the 4th (No. 11) appears in the fall of 1965. From there on it shall appear

seasonally. Please bear with us until No. 8 appears, as there is so much yet to be accomplished. The designs to appear have not yet been selected and as in the past they will not be announced in advance for designing and production reasons. (Outside preliminary designing solicited.) If you are a qualified builder and designer please contact us, advising of designs available (if any).

Subscription $8.00 beginning with issue #8 or any desired following number. Subscribers automatically become members of Cleveland Historical Model Association for one year and their $5.00 dues absorbed. They receive 1 yr. membership benefits, discounts of 10% and 20% on all purchases from Cleveland-Peerless Antique Models Co., our sponsor. A sponsor is needed as subscriptions alone could hardly support so large an undertaking without outside help - hence discounts allowed to encourage your continued patronage of plans, supplies, etc., as no outside advertising support is to be solicited. Reports available to non-subscribers and members at $2.50 per copy after publication.

CLEVELAND-PEERLESS ANTIQUE MODEL CO.   Division of Cleveland Model Products Co.   4510 Lorain Ave. Cleveland 2, Ohio USA

LATEST CLEVELAND DESIGN, THE FIRST IN 11 YEARS! THE 1929 RED AND SILVER VERVILLE "SPORTSMAN", One Of The Cleanest Thick Wing Bipes Ever Produced. (Our Quick Sketch Does Not Do It Justice — It Is A Real Beauty!) Plans Only, Patterns Included, As No Printwood Is Available. (½" DWARF) 15½" DCC-SF129 $1.95; (¾") 23¼" SF129 $3.95; 46½" GPI½CC-SF129 $5.95.(Introductory prices to test market for future new designs.) COMING SOON: Designs No. 130 WACO-10 Straight Wing and No. 131 Eaglerock Long Wing Jobs at same prices. (½ - ¾ & 1½). Also No. 132 Rumpler C-5 (WW-I)

R. L. "Dick" Gates

From "line-boy" at the famous Cleveland Municipal Airport during the National Air Races in the 1930s, to vice president of engineering with the prestigious Kohler Company, encompasses the rise to success of R. L. "Dick" Gates, Cleveland volunteer model engineer. Dick was one of the volunteer model engineers involved in implementation of Phase 2, the New C-D Era Milestone Designs, a unique and exclusive marketing strategy that was to revitalize Cleveland Model and Supply Company, enabling it to continue as the most durable of any such enterprise in this industry.

Considering the role of Dick Gates in the life of Ed Packard, it was hard to believe that Gates, an engineering consultant deeply involved in solving complex manufacturing and organizational problems, headquartered at the Kohler Company in Sheboygan, Wisconsin, was able to find the time to participate in the implementation of C-D's Phase 2. When interviewed, it became obvious that Dick's interest in C-D's destiny was deep seated, for he immediately evolved into his alter ego of model engineer and animatedly answered the questions.

"The flying craze of the 1920s was never more evident than in Cleveland, where I grew up," he said, going on to comment that the "air-minded city" boasted one of the most advanced airports in the nation, and which was to become famous for the site of many of the National Air Races in the 1930s. "Perhaps my later obsession with aviation began with my model building at age seven."

It was opportune that he was in the grandstand at Cleveland Municipal Airport in the fall of 1929 to witness the beginning of an era of spectacular aviation progress during the National Air Races ushered in by Doug Davis, an Atlanta Travel Air dealer. As the pilot of Walter Beech's Travel Air entry, he swept the field in the Model R low-wing Wright Whirlwind 300 hp Mystery Ship, with a speed of 190.90 mph in event 26 "Free for All," a closed course race of five 10-mile laps. The event was to become the world-famous Thompson Trophy Race the following year, with the then unheard-of $10,000 purse.

Later, in 1931, at the age of eleven, Gates began his direct involvement in aviation as a candidate for line boy at the airport. A month or so before the scheduled air races, boys would apply at the various hangars for jobs. According to him, "Initially, duties began at 6 A.M. and consisted of sweeping out the hangar, emptying the waste baskets and trash containers, plus other maintenance chores. Compensation was the princely sum of 50 cents per day. As you proved yourself further each year, you began to be entrusted with more aircraft-related responsibilities, such as assisting a mechanic to soak greasy and carbon-caked parts in solvents. Then, at last, you were permitted to assist the line boy to gas up the planes. When the line boy to which you were assigned moved up, you achieved the ultimate and *you* were assigned the coveted position of line boy."

Gates went on, "In addition to having met the 1929 race winner, Doug Davis, among the other famous racing pilots I met were Charles 'Speed' Holman (1930 Thompson Trophy winner); James Wedell, designer of the famous Wedell-Williams racers; Benny Howard, 1935 Thompson and Bendix winner with the famous 'Mr. Mulligan'; Louise Thaden, 1936 Bendix winner in a Beechcraft C-17R; and, later on, the great World War I German ace [sixty victories] Ernst Udet. He was the designer of the superb aerobatic performing Flamingo in which he dazzled the spectators at the air races with his unbelievable near-ground-level stunts.

"That dashing, daredevil, the affable Col. Roscoe Turner, who became world famous as a three-time winner of the Thompson Trophy [1934, 1938, and 1939], was habitually short of cash and found it necessary to borrow funds from many of us [lineboys] to stave off the pangs of hunger at the nearby White Tower with its legendary nickel hamburgers. However, he always repaid his loans."

Model airplane contests were also staged at some of the National Air Races, and in Cleveland one of the directors was Chuck Tracy, a *Cleveland Press* journalist who had succeeded Ed Clarke and who wrote a junior aviator–type of column. Ed Packard was asked by National Air Races Executive Director Cliff Henderson to administer the contests' early models, which he accepted despite the pressures of the Depression on his cottage industry.

These contests were outstanding examples of how the construction and flying of model airplanes by youth could lead to involvement with the actual prototypes and exposure to the pilots and ground crews—in short, an aviation career opportunity. Further questions about the "line boys" at the air races prompted Dick to continue: "As was the custom with many young boys during the late twenties and early thirties, I sold newspapers in an era of no television, the introduction of national radio programming, and when the local publications were more influential in molding the opinions and mores of the American public. Earnings from this entrepreneurship of up to ten dollars per week—big wages during the Depression and at times more than my father earned when he was out of work—made it possible for me to buy inexpensive model airplane kits, such as George Wanner stick models, and then progressively master other manufacturers' types, including Paul Guillow, Megow, Comet, and Ideal, until I was capable of building a Cleveland kit."

Recalling the earlier events, Gates explained that he lived near the West 57th and Bridge Avenue location of the Pachasa residence on Cleveland's West Side and that he frequented the embryonic business of A. Pachasa and Sons, getting to know the whole family, particularly Ed and his four brothers, Will, Fred, Albert, and Andrew. "In fact, I became one of several stock boys Ed used in his business. Due to the Depression, our pay varied from eight cents to ten cents per hour, or we could take it out in trade in the form of a kit or miscellaneous supplies. All of us were in seventh heaven just to be able to be around this creative enterprise, which was on the threshold of becoming a full-blown nationally and internationally known manufacturer."

Dick graduated from his role as a C-D stock boy and began building models for display cases in the store. One of his first projects was the Cleveland Amphibion [*sic*], a semi-Profile type (FL 301) patterned after the Sikorsky S-38. "If Ed approved of the quality of your project," Gates said, "your pay would be another kit for yourself." Shortly thereafter, 1938–39, Gates opened a store and became a Cleveland dealer before going to the University of Dayton.

From the frugal earnings of his newspaper sales, plus other jobs, in 1934 Dick was able to take flying lessons and soloed in an OX-5 powered Waco 10. Two years later he realized a lifelong ambition when he qualified for his Limited Commercial (LC) License.

In 1938 he left Cleveland for the University of Dayton and was fortunate enough to remain at Wright Field during World War II. After the war he was recruited by Thompson Products at Cleveland, where he became a senior project engineer assigned to Staff Research and Development Engineering. Subsequently, he was sent to the Sterling Engine Company in Michigan, a manufacturer of diesel engines for locomotives, to troubleshoot crankshaft problems, which resulted in his being loaned to Sterling for a year. Because of his outstanding expertise, Sterling asked him to join their company permanently.

"On my trips to Cleveland I would visit my parents and always found time to drop in on Ed at the big store on Lorain," Dick revealed. More than fifteen years after World War II, Gates found that Ed was all by himself in the huge facility because his brother Will had gone to start his own retail hobby business in Cleveland. C-D sales had never returned to their prewar level; consequently, he had ceased manufacturing kits.

"In 1965, when I was on one of my many trips to Cleveland," Dick continued, "Ed approached me enthusiastically about the new plans-only program. He knew I did a lot of engineering drafting plus having drawn the plans for many of my own modeling projects, so he asked my assistance in developing the plans for a ¾-inch scale [¹⁄₁₆ size] OX-5–powered Curtiss Robin. It would become the SF-141, the seventh plan in the new series. Manufactured by Curtiss-Robertson of Anglum, Missouri, it was one of the first enclosed cabin monoplanes available for the private pilot and in 1929 at an affordable $4,000. The Robin had been a popular aircraft, it was easy to build, and had an inherent stability in its design; thus it would make an excellent scale flying model [SF-141]. Fortunately, I had access to a prototype Robin from which I could scale off not only all dimensions required but also cabin details, fitting locations, struts, rib spacing, and other important components." This was to become a standard procedure for Dick Gates on almost all of his twenty-some plans that he would ultimately draw for C-D.

Providing additional insight to the sequence of events, he described how the next design that he produced for the new program was the Stearman

Volunteer model engineer Dick Gates in the cockpit of his Waco UPF-7 during a run-up of his 225 hp Continental (ca. 1985). Gates started flying in the Cleveland area as a young man and has been an enthusiast of sport flying for many years. He also did the research and drew the plans for CD227. He was able to scale-off exact measurements from another UPF-7 while it was awaiting recovering. *Dick Gates Collection.*

Kaydet PT-17 [Navy N2-S Yellow Peril]. This was an aircraft requested by many of the former Air Corps and Navy pilots since it was used by both branches of the service as a primary trainer, the plane in which many of them first soloed. Since there were many of these craft available as surplus, it was not difficult to locate one in the process of being recovered so he could do the necessary scaling to provide the data to make this the most detailed flying scale plan of its type available on the market.

At about this time the Sterling Engine Company was acquired by the Koppers Company, so Dick was transferred to company headquarters in Pittsburgh, where he was appointed mechanical engineer on the president's staff. "In this capacity I met Robert Thompson, president of the H. P. Deucher Company, a foundry that produced castings for Koppers and who was one of Ed's most dedicated volunteer model engineers. He was the quintessential World War I aircraft buff and had several plans of allied and German types in various stages of completion. To expedite the completion of these plans, I collaborated with him by assisting in the final phases of his outstanding flying scale drawings. Consequently, C-D at present has the most complete line of World War I designs, including bombers such as the English Handley-Page 0400, the German Gotha IV, and the A.E.G.—rare plans indeed."

After being appointed chief mechanical engineer of Arco Polymers, Gates had some contact with the Kohler Company in Wisconsin, and in 1979 he was offered a permanent position with them that led to vice president of engineering, where he remained. "Since I own and fly my own Waco UPF-7," Dick noted, "a biplane designed by Waco in 1939 to meet the requirements of the Civilian Pilot Training Program [600 manufactured], when it came time for recovering, I did the usual procedure and scaled off stringer and rib spacing, fittings, and rigging details. I incorporated this wealth of data in the CD-227 plan that I drew for Ed, which is undoubtedly the most authentic scale flying UPF-7 plan available anywhere." Among the other plans Dick engineered were the Wiley Post Model A (CD-159), the Consolidated Fleet Trainer (CD-178), and, most recently, the Fairchild 22 and the Fairchild 24.

Summarizing his relationship with Cleveland Models, Dick had some final comments: "I have thoroughly enjoyed the long-term association with Ed Packard and the Pachasa family, and I am quite sure that my exposure to model building and designing models has had a significant effect on my career in engineering. No doubt it influenced me to become interested in flying and ultimately owning my own airplane. I have a good feeling about having been of some assistance to Packard and his alternative marketing program of offering the complete line of New C-D Era Milestone designs. In the process I met some of the other model engineer C-D volunteers and made some lifelong relationships that I consider a significant benefit. I hope that, through additional publicity and knowledge about the extensive line of plans that C-D has developed, Ed Packard may be the recipient of further recognition and financial success that he so richly deserves."

Dan Scherry

From model airplane builder to plant layout master model engineer—Dan Scherry is another example of how Packard's one-of-a-kind enterprise was instrumental in dramatically shaping the scope and lifelong career of a C-D volunteer. B. F. Goodrich's Chemical Group, headquartered in Independence, Ohio, can boast of having had such an accomplished engineer on their staff.

Progressing from model airplanes to industrial models came about when, in 1963, a neighbor, a heavy equipment engineer, needed a model to demonstrate a front-end loader. Scherry tackled the project, and the model enabled the engineer to sell the concept to his company. Dan's reputation spread rapidly when a local consulting engineer used one of his models in his presentations to prospective clients. Inevitably, everyone wanted to know who had built it. By 1973 news of Scherry's expertise had reached Goodrich's Chemical Group's engineering department. Engineering models were gaining widespread use on giant construction projects, and Goodrich was seeking an engineer who could translate plant layout drawings into a three-dimensional model. Dan Scherry was their man.

"Firms can quite often avoid costly mistakes," says Dan. "For, when I build a plant engineering model, the production, maintenance and safety people from the plant can come in and analyze it. Potential problems can be spotted, and the necessary design changes can be made before construction starts, which usually results in significant cost savings." He further elaborated, "Everything I know about building industrial models has been gleaned from years of experience in model-airplane work and my exposure to special engineering models."

Seeing some of Dan's outstanding C-D models, which are displayed prominently throughout his basement workshop in Wakeman, Ohio, led to asking about how it all began. "I must have been about nine during one summer as I was growing up on Cleveland's West Side," he said, "and like so many kids when out of school, I ran out of things to do." Dan thus complained to his understanding mother, who took him forthwith to a local hobby shop, purchased a model airplane kit for him, and guided him in its construction.

"I became hooked, then and there," he added, "and those first five and ten cent kits were the best small 12-inch span rubber-powered fliers I ever built."

Elaborating further, Dan explained that as his knowledge, skills, and experience in building and covering improved, he sought out the more exact, realistic 50-cent-scale C-D kits in the hobby store, "influencing me to pass up sweets and toys to save up my allowances. I can vividly recall the compelling graphics on those picturesque C-D 25-to 85-cent Dwarf kits—the Curtiss Hawks and the National Air Races–winning Travel Airs, Lairds, Gee-Bees, and Wedell-Williams. The World War I kits, such as the Fokkers, Spads, and the Sopwiths had no peers in scale models then."

He had no idea that his interest in model aviation would not only lead to a job at C-D's headquarters but would also influence his career as a professional model builder. He mused, "And to even consider the possibility of my actually designing and assisting on the plans for many of those famous scale models—yet, it happened. "The first step in further establishing my relationship with the Pachasa family occurred during the mid-forties when I landed a job as a stock boy for four summers, commuting by bicycle to West 45th and Lorain Avenue, some sixteen miles away."

Dan described C-D's operations at the time: "The layout of C-D's Lorain Avenue location at that time included two retail sales stores and a display room on the northwest corner of 45th and Lorain. The office and design department were on the second floor, the rear of which became kit-packing rooms 1 and 2. The larger retail store with the mail room, bulk stock, and shipping department was on the first floor. The variety of power equipment, including saws and routers for wood cutting and shaping, were located on the floor below. The rented warehouse on the southwest corner of 45th and Lorain had three stories with a large rope-operated elevator. The No. 3 Condor Glider assembly line was located on the second floor. Raw storage was on the third floor, and finished kits were on the first floor. The dope room was located in a two-story barn behind the Pachasa residence on West 57th Street near Bridge Avenue, which was converted from the original store and office of C-D's predecessor firm.

"I had a feeling in the 1943 to 1946 period that Ed was the big boss and to be avoided at all costs, so I never got to know him till later on in the fifties. As employees, we had no time to spend in the store and display room, but on our off times it was a place of wonderment and we would stand agape in the presence of the lineup of Thompson Trophy winners, the World War I fighters, and the Golden Era 'bipes' displayed on the cabinet tops and suspended from the ceiling. It left most of us with the feeling that we had to rush right home and begin building a model immediately."

One of the stock boy's duties was to unload carloads of balsa at a railroad siding not too far away and to truck the bales of railroad tie–size balsa timbers to the C-D woodshop, where it would be sawed into predetermined planks, blocks, strips, and sheets. Together with Ed's brother Will, he shared had the responsibility to keep the seventy-five to eighty girls on the assembly lines stocked with all manner of balsa blocks, sheet, printwood, strips, tissue, dope, wheels, music wire, and the miscellaneous items needed to make the particular kits complete.

Dan expounded on the premier line of SF kits, which originally included the appropriate bottles of dope carefully packed in the kits. "When the need arose for replenishing the dope bottles for the assembly lines, we would be dispatched to the West 57th Street location and spend the day filling one-to-eight ounce bottles with cement and colored dope from a spigot on a fifty-five-gallon drum. We soon learned that the trick was to dexterously position the dope to flow out of the spigot so that a bottle would be filling while the previously filled bottle would be capped, sealed and labeled in the nick of time to move another empty bottle in position and all the while maintain a steady flow of dope. There was no automation at this phase of production at that time."

As stock boys they also worked a half-day on Saturdays under Will's supervision, who was the warehouse superintendent. This was a critical part of C-D's success, for it was vital that the kit assembly lines be completely set up with the necessary components in readiness for the assemblers on Monday morning in order to avoid any waiting or wasted motion during the work week.

"I can vividly recall that a single assembly line made nothing but the one dollar Condor glider kits for three years. This line continued to operate week after week while the other lines switched from one kit to another. Ultimately, sales of the Condor reached 2.5 million units, the single most successful number in the entire Cleveland inventory."

Another responsibility of the stock boys was the replenishment of the supply of printwood, "for without the proper printwood the assembly line would grind to a halt. So, I can recall how we would take a load of blank sheet balsa to a printer nearby and return with large cartons of finished printwood." There were some critical logistical elements involved with producing the thousands of kits that were made daily but which few people realized when they saw the colorful, star-spangled kits for sale at the retail hobby shop.

"Occasionally, some kits would show up that had been damaged during assembly—liquids spilled inside, parts broken, or cartons torn. I would ask Will if the kit was unsaleable and, if so, could I have it. If it was okay with him, then I could consider this a bit of a 'perk' and it brightened my day. The SF-100 Boeing B-17 Flying Fortress I have to this day was acquired in 1944 thusly, since it had a broken bottle of aluminum dope inside the kit. The greatly underpriced GP69 Rearwin Speedster gas-model kit was acquired in much the same manner later on, with a $7.50 price tag on the box. I built the model, which I still have together with its original carton. Will always told us that if we were interested in some damaged item to ask him for it, because if we took it without his permission, we would be fired on the spot. As with millions of other avid modelers, I developed a passion for Cleveland models and bought kits of my favorite planes whenever they were available in expectation of building them someday."

When the new C-D Golden Era–plans concept came into being, substantially implemented by the talents of C-D model engineers such as Dan Scherry and over three dozen others, Dan was able to contribute significantly to the development of the extensive line of the more than three hundred plans that ultimately became available. "Ed Packard had a phenomenal memory for the way a certain aircraft was shaped and how the configuration of the rudder should look," Dan explained. "His files were filled with innumerable designs and it's to his credit that he had been able to make so many choices available for the buffs to enjoy."

Scherry's model engineering talent and his dedication to the C-D volunteer effort is evident in the fourteen plans in which he was either completely involved or responsible for detailing structure, drafting, or building a prototype of to determine the sequence of construction:

SF-79   1943 F4U-5 Vought Corsair
SF-180   1907 Santos-Dumont Demoiselle
SF-201   1903 Wright Flyer Commemorative Drawing
SF-211   1927 Lindbergh's NX-211 Commemorative Drawing (*Spirit of St. Louis*)
SF-226   Curtiss SB2C-4 Helldiver
SF-235   Ford 4AT-B Tri-motor (based on a 4AT-B at Island Airlines at Port Clinton, Ohio)
SF-237   Bellanca Aircruiser
SF-300   1935 Martin M-130 China Clipper (originally built in 1937 by Bob Rice)
SF-247   1928 Lockheed Air Express
SF-255   1928 Sikorsky S-38 Amphibian (subsequently acquired by Pan American Airlines and on display in their Miami facility)
SF-260   Northrop Gamma
SF-265   1933 Stinson Model "A" Low Wing Trimotor (based on the full-scale restoration at the 1982 EAA fly-in, and assisted by artist-engineer Ken Sniffen)

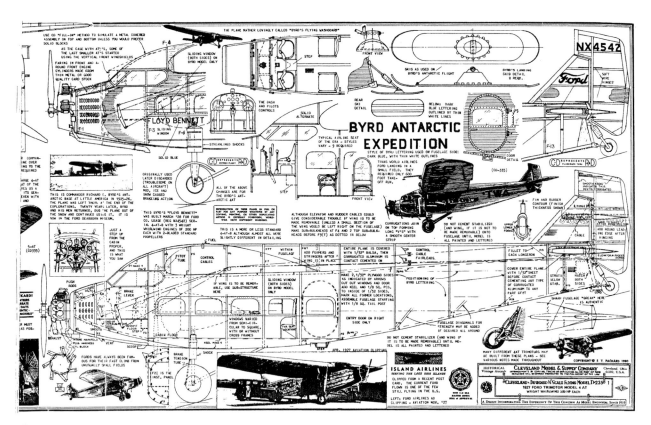

Above: Dan Scherry was instrumental in finalizing this plan for the C-D 235½-inch scale Ford Trimotor 4-AT plan (plate 1) and keeping it specifically for the 4-AT model. *E. T. Packard Collection.*

Right: Scherry's CD 165 Douglas DC-3 has United Airlines markings that are so realistic it could pass for the prototype. *Dan Scherry Collection.*

SF-285   Consolidated PBY-5 Catalina Naval Patrol Flying Boat
SF-400   1919 Curtiss NC-4 Flying Boat (original drawing by Jim Kamen)

Commenting further about his impressions and personal involvement with C-D, Dan offered, "My best-liked kit was the SF-165, the Douglas DC-3.

I remember building the SF-55, the Douglas DC-2, in the late thirties, but when the DC-3 was introduced I had to have it, for which I paid $3.50. There followed several years of collecting data and photos, and I finally decided my favorite airline markings were United Airlines' 1936 Flagship series.

"The next step was the finish, which just had to be aluminum. So, I spent some ten years on that first metal-covered model with complete interior, seats, passengers, retract gear, flaps, and, yes, U-C flying components, utilizing two .35 McCoy engines. It was completed in 1969, and I still have it. Having developed the metal covering technique, I then built several models utilizing this realistic method; SF-89 Douglas SBD Dauntless, SF-226 Curtiss Helldiver, and SF-235 Ford AT-4B Tri-motor, all of which I still have today. They all went the contest route in the late sixties and seventies. When requested, I take them occasionally to be exhibited at mall shows. At times I was my own competition, winning first, second, and third place, along with best of show.

"I fondly remember the *Cleveland Modelmaking News and Practical Hobbies* [Ed was of the opinion that offering projects other than aircraft would be advantageous to modelers, hence, trains, boats, motor cars, a cannon, and an elephant howdah appeared] authored and produced from 1933 to 1934 by Ed Packard, consisting of seven issues, which had no match then or now, and as I thumb through my collection of the copies, I can recall how much they impressed me in my developing years in the hobby."

Dan has many Cleveland kits that he hopes to build as RC types. "I have experienced that the many C-D designs command a great deal of interest and comment from other fliers and spectators who have never heard of or seen

The plan for the CD-255 Sikorsky S-38 Amphibion [*sic*] ½-inch scale was finalized to a great extent by Dan Scherry, with assistance from R. Schlenberg and E. T. Packard. *E. T. Packard Collection.*

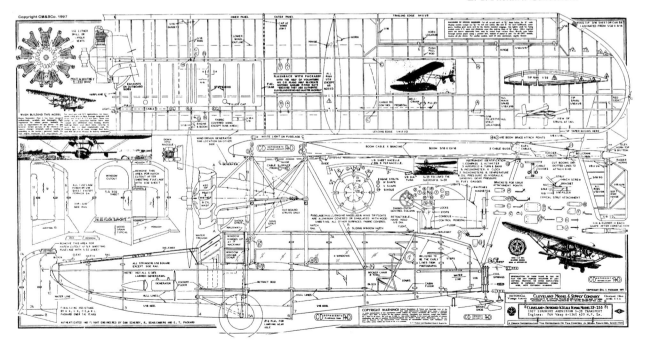

Above left: The famed *China Clipper* after it had been refurbished and recovered in aluminum sheet by C-D volunteer model engineer Dan Scherry, now on display at the Treasure Island Navy/Pan American Museum, San Francisco. Note the corrugated aluminum of the upper deck. Photo by John Underhill. *Dan Scherry Collection.*

Above right: This CD-255 Sikorsky S-38 54-inch span, ¾-inch scale aluminum-covered model is on display at Pan American's Miami, Florida, location. *Dan Scherry Collection.*

Below: This Ford 4-AT N7684 is still flying for Island Airlines, Port Clinton, Ohio, and it was used in drawing the CD-235 plan. *Dan Scherry Collection.*

such aircraft. One example is the SF-133 Alexander Eaglerock bipe, which, because of its large wing area, is a great performer. The C-D catalog is always with me when I fly or exhibit, and I share it with interested hobbyists. I have been a long-time member of AMA and was the 1993 president of the Westlake, Ohio, RC club. I have remained active in the hobby because I enjoy the satisfaction of seeing a design that I have built fly so well. I have never had a Cleveland scale flying design that has not flown well, and the C-D list of plans is the most complete that I know of for all types and historical periods."

Perhaps the most impressive model project in which Dan has been involved for C-D has been the Martin M-130 (C-D300) China Clipper. Dan described the events as follows: "On display for several years at the Lorain Avenue factory store was a ¾-inch scale, 8-foot span China Clipper that was double-tissue covered and finished in silver dope. Anyone who ever saw it at the store would never forget it because it was the largest model [8-plus feet] on display, and the China Clipper in itself is an impressive design. To commemorate the fiftieth anniversary of their three clipper models Pacific flights from San Francisco, Pan American approached Ed Packard in 1985 to have the model refurbished for them. Since Ed knew that I had perfected a method of covering with metal sheet, Ed assigned me the task. I completely refurbished the model with aluminum covering, corrugations where required, new cowlings, and new engines and props and recovered with fabric where specified. Despite its size, it was extremely lightweight. Pan American was so delighted with the detailed authenticity that I had been able to develop that the model was placed on display at their Treasure Island facility in San Francisco, California."

Dan's concluding comments are typical of such dedicated C-D volunteers: "I currently fly RC and have several Cleveland designs that I fly regularly. All the models that are pictured herein were scratch built from the 1½-inch scale Cleveland plans. It took me about ten years to perfect the metal sheet covering technique, which I have used on a Ford 4-AT Tri-motor [SF-235], a Douglas DC-3 with United Airlines markings [SF-165], and a Sikorsky S-38 [SF-255].

"I have always remembered my days at Cleveland Model and Supply as very pleasant, and it was a fun job. Airplanes have always been a part of my life and building airplane models led to my becoming a professional indus-trial-equipment model builder in charge of the engineering model depart-ment at B.F. Goodrich for more than thirty years. It was a fascinating era, and I feel fortunate to have been a part of it."

J. Ken Sniffen

From a childhood in Flatbush, Brooklyn, to art professor at the University of Wisconsin, through many interesting professional art and design positions in various assignments in several parts of the world describes the progression of the exciting career of Cleveland model volunteer artist J. Ken Sniffen.

Born shortly after the end of WWI, J. Ken Sniffen grew up at a time when, for impressionable American youngsters, model airplanes embodied the idea of romantic adventures associated with the burgeoning airline industry. Des-tined to become an artist, his imagination was especially captured by the inherent beauty of the aircraft that were the marvel of the twentieth century.

That nascent flying era was typified by the appearance of the ubiquitous, war surplus Curtiss JN-4 OX-5–powered Jenny, which the pioneering and daring barnstormers flew from the many cow pastures abundantly available in undeveloped areas throughout America.

Childhood memoirs of the colorful neighborhood of sprawling East Flatbush, Brooklyn, just beyond the hustle and bustle of New York City, at-test to the direction Sniffen's interests would carry him.

Sniffen recalls, "One of my fondly remembered haunts was an old-fash-ioned German family–type ice cream and candy shop, where small lead cast Austrian toys were fastened on top of candy filled, large glass molded animal forms. Among those four- to five-inch lead toys was a realistic, fragile ap-pearing 1909 Bleriot type monoplane with partially exposed fuselage frame-work." This was what first set this soon to be air-minded lad on his endless love affair with aeroplanes.

The world had been engulfed in cataclysmic change since Bleriot's 1909 epic flight and so had the houses, brownstones, and environs of Flatbush. However, each solitary, surviving Bleriot in the world-famous flying Shuttleworth Collection at Old Warden, Bedfordshire, England, and in the Musee de l'air at Muedon, outside Paris, continues to draw and intrigue the crowds with their fragile beauty, more so in light of the stark contrast with our contemporary space exploration orbiting vehicles.

"Aware of my air-minded inclination," Ken added, "occasional family gifts were received of delicately beautiful Japanese spruce-bodied, rubber-powered, 14-inch span flying sport models with bright colored gossamer silk–covered flight surfaces, of which framework and landing gear were of delicately soldered but strong, fine gauge wire. And, more important, they flew surprisingly well, especially when sneak launched from the second story window of the house by an avid young modeler."

By age nine or ten he began to frequent the wonderful world of Abe Berman's Candy and Newsstand store. Then, most every New York neighborhood had one or two such colorful stores, with their ice-cream-soda counters and penny-to-nickel glass candy-display cases, which usually included kazoos and penny whistles. "In the back of Berman's were cases displaying toys and those marvelous model airplane kits, priced from 10 to 25 cents. The 10 centers were starter solid models for eight to ten year old modelers, which helped in developing their basic balsa craft-building skills. The 25 centers, usually Megow or Comet stick and tissue kits of fifteen 20-inch wingspan rubber-powered types, were for the more advanced ten-to-twelve-year-old enthusiasts. In the forefront of the store were the newspapers, and included in this department," Sniffen continued, "was a veritable treasure trove, a complete assortment of the magazines of the day, mostly pulps, mainly priced at 10 to 15 cents, one thin dime, with my favorites the flying pulps, thrilling passports to the world of adventurous, daring deeds and hero worship. The millions of air enthusiasts in the crossroads and cities of America devotedly purchased and voraciously consumed these fictional adventures in the monthly issues."

Following Lindbergh's epoch-making flight in 1927, the nation's presses ground out a prolific public relations campaign for the embryonic aviation industry. In the process, such venerable publications as *Flying Aces* and *Air Trails* emerged in the fall of 1928 as two of the more durable of some-dozen flying pulps to captivate the youth of the day.

"I can see those pulps on display at Berman's in my mind's eye," Sniffen reminisced, "including titles such as *Aces, Dare-Devil Aces, War Aces, War Birds, Battle Birds, Battle Aces, Skybirds, Skyfighters, Lone Eagle, G-8 and His Battle Aces*, ad infinitum. Their rough-surfaced 120-page issues told of fearless, daredevil knights of the air, luridly illustrated with scenes of deadly dogfights engulfed by "archie" puffs from anti-aircraft batteries.

"However, it was the action-oriented full-color paintings on the covers, dramatizing the pulp's hero conquering the enemy that stopped the reader in his tracks and convinced him to part with his hard earned dime for his escape from the reality of the Depression. In reality the majority of the pulp covers depicted the aircraft as dominant, heroic steeds, battling each other with swishing wings and flashing swords of war. The heroes were in the novels, but the graphic impact was the aircraft, indubitably.

"It was those pulp magazine artists who really stirred and attracted the young, impressionistic readers. A few of them were real painters. An avid fan could recognize each artist's work or the magazine itself without seeing his signature or the publication's logo. Early on, I favored two artists: the great Frederick Blakeslee, famous for his *Dare-Devil Aces* and *Battle Aces* covers, and the remarkable Rudolph Belarski, famed for his action-oriented art on the covers of *Warbirds, Wings*, and *Aces,* as well as his realistic night battle scenes. Despite the passing of an interval of more than fifty years, I find that my evaluation and appreciation for these two has only increased. Blakeslee's story head pen-and-ink illustrations were singularly outstanding then and remain as some of the most accomplished today in that field."

Continuing, Ken recalled, "Following our selection at the newsstand we would peruse our favorite pulp at the soda counter. If we had two cents extra, Mr. Berman would serve us an egg cream, actually, a small glass of soda water with a little squirt of chocolate and a few drops of vanilla. On such occasions, Abe would advise us when a shipment of new model airplane kits had come in, and we would dash madly off to see what goodies had arrived."

When he was eleven he moved up from the Comet and Megow type kits. He received a precedent-setting Christmas present from his aunt: a Cleveland SF-2 Travel Air Mystery ¾-inch scale flying model of 21-inch wingspan, colored in red and black and modeled after the 1929 low-wing 190 mph Cleveland Air Race winning ship—a record-setting kit design for the emerging company and only the second in the long series to be of a famous line of SF C-D master kits.

He enjoyed many hours learning the detailed type of construction, including alignment and some frustration from flightless launches, resulting in minor and major crashes. After mastering the modeling technique of the simpler kits, he recalled, "Christmas rolled around again, and this time a C-D SF-34 Fokker D-VIII 21-inch World War I Fighter was under the tree. Now, resolutely determined to master the more, for me, advanced design, the project was completed more quickly and on a somewhat temperate day in late winter, voila! Five stable flights ensued with the sixth effort terminating with a shower of balsa and tissue remnants cascading from on high, the culprit being a gnarled, unyielding cherry tree in which the newly constructed D-8 had lodged itself."

But times were tough, and other C-D kits were acquired infrequently, and so his expertise only gradually improved. "However," he recalled, "with the reliable bike so prevalent in those days, a fellow could ride south toward the ocean, stopping by Mill Basin beside Old Canarsie, an environ of Jamaica Bay, along which soon was to be built the famous Floyd Bennett airfield, now a historic site, having undergone a massive change to a shopping center. I witnessed aviation history being made there by pioneer aviators like Byrd, Lindbergh, Chamberlin, and Pangborn; air shows with the daring, intrepid, Harold Johnson looping his Ford Trimotor at near ground level and thrilling events with other greats such as Wiley Post arriving from a high altitude, record-setting flight in his sleek, streamlined Lockheed Vega *Winnie Mae*, sans landing gear, which was designed to be jettisoned in flight to reduce weight and drag, center stage in front of the amazed crowd. There was an outing in a row boat in the basin with Dad, the two of us threading our way among the twenty Italian Savoia-Marchette S-55, twin hull tandem-engined flying boats, which had just completed a mass flight across the South Atlantic, led by the colorful Italian air minister, Italo Balbo. To a teenage boy in a dinky rowboat, the Italian flying boats seemed gigantic as they rode at their anchors."

As a reward, after many wash-and-polish jobs on pilot friend Andy Stinis's srikingly graceful 1933 Waco UIC cabin biplane, there came an extended, mind-boggling flight for this air-minded teenager. Buckled in the right front seat of the cabin, he witnessed the indescribable, majestic panorama of the New York City skyline, harbor, and beyond, culminating in an inspiring view of Lady Liberty—"a sight I shall never forget." He remembered, "To my everlasting delight, in his passion to document the most popular aircraft in his line of kits, Ed Pachasa produced a 1933 Waco UIC cabin model [SF-37], and I look forward to building this kit and rekindling my fond memories of Andy Stinis and that memorable flight."

As a teenager, Ken's time was shared among artwork (often drawing airplanes and boats), study, and working summers around family marine enterprises in Southern Connecticut with some C-D modeling projects interspersed. Saturday mornings were spent at Pratt Institute art classes in addition to studying art at Erasmus Hall High in Flatbush, with art assignments on the school magazine and playing in a five-piece harmonica band that won prizes on shows such as *Major Bowes Radio Amateur Hour*. Graduation came in June 1940, with World War II already in progress in Europe.

"The infamous date of the Japanese raid on Pearl Harbor, December 7, 1941," Ken continued, "found me at the Pratt Institute School of Art, deeply involved in a color-spread-class design project for Curtiss P-40 fighters with a recently constructed C-D SF-77 P-40 displayed from the ceiling. To avoid delay, I gave little regard for what branch of the service I would enter, and I promptly signed on with the Army Air Corps, returning to Pratt to await my call to arms, which came in the spring of 1942.

"Bypassing numerous assignments stateside in my service experience, my ultimate destination became the ATC [Air Transport Command] for India and the China-Burma-India theater. Eventually I came to my final destination, the twin aircraft British constructed fighter bases of Tezgoan, Kermitola near Dacca, East Bengal, India (now the capital of Bangladesh). The major undertaking assigned to us was to convert these flying fields into depart and mission return bases for B-24s, then called 109s. The Liberators' task—ferrying fifty-five-gallon drums of hundred-octane gasoline over the hump of the Himalayas into China—to keep Chenault's Flying Tigers supplied.

"The Libs arrived from North Africa showing the effects of battle fatigue but stripped of armament. At the base they were rewired to allow the pilots to jettison the bomb bay auxiliary fuel tanks. The resulting lighter weight enabled them to escape the Japanese Zeros by climbing to altitudes above the enemy's absolute ceiling."

By the end of 1944, he had painted some pinups and signatures on the capacious nose sections of the bombers and had established a flight line dope-fabric and insignia maintenance facility for control surfaces and markings on the aircraft. An unexpected human relations and intercultural experience resulted during the process of training twelve civilians for the shop, consisting of five Muslims and seven Hindus of varied castes, with ages ranging between fourteen and sixty-five. "I shared in the establishment of this group with a wonderfully adaptable and skillful Onandaga Iroquois American Indian, who demonstrated remarkable inspirational leadership."

To relieve the boredom everyone experienced, Ken ordered several C-D kits, which took three months to arrive. By then the monsoons had set in, and the contents became so moldy that they could not be completed. Nevertheless, the realism of the plans and details of construction created somewhat of a sensation in the squadron area.

Rumors of diminishing enemy military activity and of the Japanese resistance crumbling began spreading in July and early August of 1945, then persistent rumors of the A-bomb became prevalent until those final days on August 6 and 9 in 1945 when one era of warfare was ended and a new one ushered in.

In characterizing the various C-D art assignments in which he was involved, Ken related, "Bob Thompson, president of H. P. Deucher Company, a foundry, was a longtime Cleveland model fan and became an early volunteer model engineer. He was principally responsible for the extensive number of World War I New C-D Era Milestone designs, always my favorite category. Bob also produced a few outstanding World War II plans. His Curtiss SB-2C Navy Helldiver, complete in every detail, is in the Smithsonian. In our close association, I provided the necessary art in the form of illustrations for most of his World War I designs from the DH-2 on. He visited me in Oshkosh to attend the EAA Fly-In with his son, who became a commercial pilot. Bob Thompson died not long after perfecting his Curtiss SB-2C; however, his many creative contributions of more than sixty plans to the New C-D Era

Milestone designs will not be forgotten in the history of Cleveland Model and Supply. His dedication and positive spirit was a great inspiration for me."

Further describing his assignments, Ken continued, "Hundreds of camera-ready line drawings of all types of aircraft were produced for C-D from my drawing board, including catalog covers, logos, mastheads, type layouts, and settings. There were also many special semi-tech graphics, such as drawings for the control system of the 1903 Wright Flyer plan and large prints for aviation banquet presentations that had been retouched and redrawn from old archival cards and mementos.

"One of the most challenging projects was the design and production of large mailing tube labels for the 1987 60th-anniversary commemoration of the flight of the *Spirit of St. Louis* and for the 1988 85th-anniversary commemorative plan of the 1903 Wright Flyer. This latter truly remarkable plan represented over ten years of research and drawing board time by Ed.

"The professional help of Dennis Parks, archivist and friend, at the EAA Aircraft Museum in Oshkosh, has been invaluable. Dennis's insight into the complex wing-warping control system of the 1903 Wright Flyer significantly clarified the illustrations I made for that plan. His recent collaboration on the B-24 Liberator bomber with Jim Kamen of Hurley, New York, ensures that this design of such a famous World War II bomber will be properly and authentically presented." Ken and Jim have been collaborating on several C-Ds, especially on the Stinson Trimotor A, perhaps the only such remaining transport, while it was participating at Oshkosh in the EAA annual AirVenture. Ken said, "In view of my personal involvement with the 'Libs' during World War II, I will endeavor to make every effort to assist in the finalization of this plan to make it another outstanding addition to the long line of famous aircraft as exemplified by C-D."

Who is to say how much influence there was on this notable artist's career as a result of his youthful exposure to the construction of the realistic C-D model airplanes, or how this involvement would then direct him into a second career as an accomplished aircraft illustrator, not only for Cleveland Model and Supply but for his portraits of famous aviators featured in the EAA Wisconsin Aviation Hall of Fame and the International Aerobatic Association.

CHAPTER 14

The Reincarnation of the Wright Flyer and the *Spirit of St. Louis*

⧉ DURING ED PACKARD'S BOYHOOD the crude flying machines of the Wrights and Glenn Curtiss, as depicted by the wags in the then-critical press, were unreliable, flimsy, woebegone contraptions akin to man carrying kites with a doubtful future. However, to this air-minded lad living within sight of the Statue of Liberty and not far from the future home of the Teterboro airport in New Jersey, every photo, every report of extended flight duration and new records for speed and increased payloads were only more fuel for his own fanciful dreams of personal flight. At an early age he visualized his future must somehow be related to these marvelous, soaring vehicles of the air. His aspirations were realized through his employment with Glenn L. Martin and Fokker's Atlantic Aircraft Company, plus more than sixty years of involvement with C-D—a combination that exposed him to virtually every aspect of aviation. As the eighty-fifth anniversary of the Wright Brothers flight approached, he decided to commemorate the event by providing the most authentic Kittyhawk Flyer scale flying plan possible, not only for the dedicated C-D volunteer model engineers and model enthusiasts but also for numerous museums and other institutions worldwide as well. Although he had maintained a lifelong passion for information about the Wrights, his efforts had been accelerated as he approached his eighties. Hence, he forthwith dispatched an urgent letter to his devoted model engineers to send him any such relevant data, plans, or photos that might aid him in his project. He also contacted his lifelong friend at the Smithsonian's NASM, curator Paul Garber, who likewise relied on his staff, Robert C. Mikesh and Pete Jacob. Coincidentally, the American Aviation Historical Society's former secretary, aeronautical engineer Carl Friend, and Fred Clark of Cal-Tech had been involved with a group of dedicated engineers in Southern California in a project to replicate a flyable Wright Flyer. Friend had amassed a considerable data bank on many aspects of the design, construction, and the complicated wing-warping flight-control system. For example, it had been discovered that the negative dihedral of the wings was to prevent the Flyer, subject to Kittyhawk's wind gusts, from rolling into its sand dunes, providing a rather pragmatic design solution. Through the networking of artist-designer J. Ken Sniffen, who had a contact at the EAA Museum of Flight in Oshkosh in archivist Dennis Parks, he gleaned a wealth of information on the powerplant, pusher props, and wing warping. From this source Sniffen was ultimately able to develop a re-vealing perspective of the wing warping control system elements of the Flyer which contributed greatly to the visualization and construction of a scale model.

After all these years of effort, in 1987, a year in advance of the Wrights' 85th anniversary, the crowning achievement of his lifelong desire to develop the ultimate plan for the 1903 Flyer came off the press as C-D SSF-201. Em-bellished with the dramatic art of Ken Sniffen, the 17-by-44-inch layout has emerged as the most complete, authentic ¾-inch scale, 30-inch wingspan plan available for a scale flying replica. As a result, modelers, historians, mu-

This and facing page: Details from the SF-201 1903 Wright Flyer (½-inch scale), produced for the 85th anniversary commemorative plan, authenticated and engineered by C. F. Schultz, W. T. Given, R. G. Kitchell, Dan Scherry, J. Ken Sniffen, and E. T. Packard. *E. T. Packard Collection.*

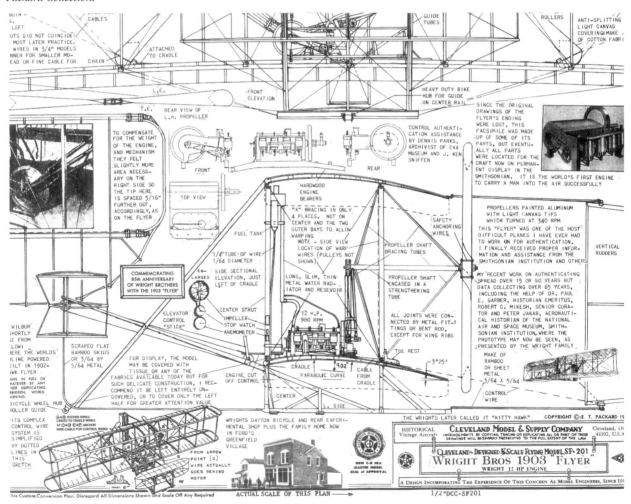

seums, and other institutions may construct and exhibit, or even fly, an authentic replica of this most historically significant canard.

Packaged in an attractive red and silver hobby tube, it represents another fitting tribute to the Master Model Engineer to be added to the great legacy he leaves. Included with the plan is an official photo of the 1903 flight, supplied by the Smithsonian's NASM. Imprinted on the label on the exterior of the hobby tube is the following most appropriate inscription:

> By their first successful 1903 historic flight, the Wrights showed mankind the way to successful powered flight after others had tried unsuccessfully to do so for ages. Thus, they opened the door to aviation and space flight as we have come to know it today.

The final product is not only a scale plan but is also designed to be a frameable pictorial document, for in addition to the plan outlines, it contains a wealth of statistics and information. The model engineers associated with producing

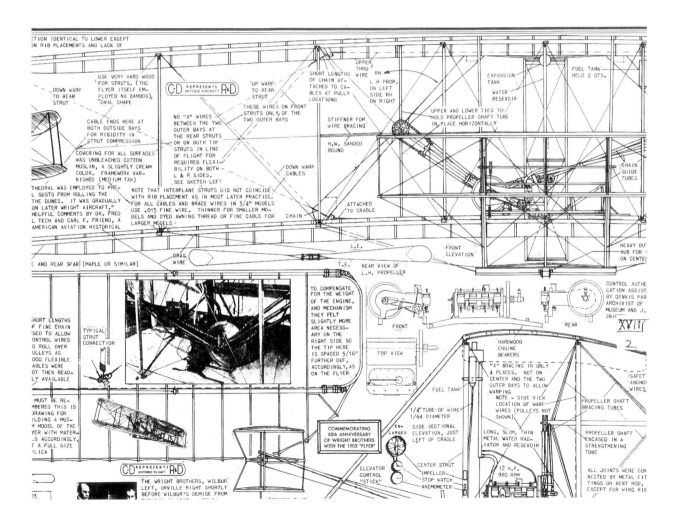

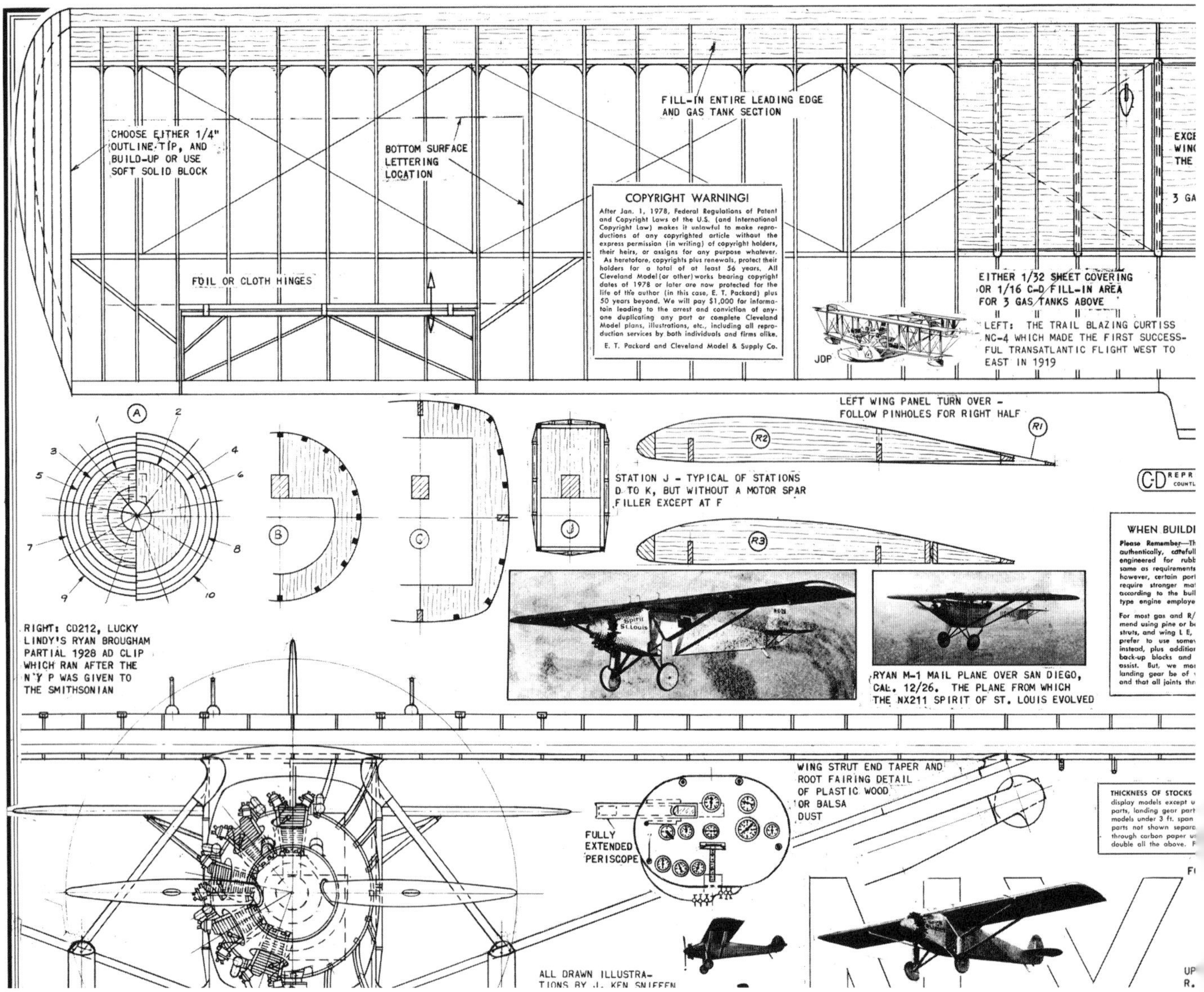

FILL-IN ENTIRE LEADING EDGE AND GAS TANK SECTION
CHOOSE EITHER 1/4" OUTLINE TIP, AND BUILD-UP OR USE SOFT SOLID BLOCK
BOTTOM SURFACE LETTERING LOCATION
COPYRIGHT WARNING!
After Jan. 1, 1978, Federal Regulations of Patent and Copyright Laws of the U.S. (and International Copyright Law) makes it unlawful to make reproductions of any copyrighted article without the express permission (in writing) of copyright holders, their heirs, or assigns for any purpose whatever. As heretofore, copyrights plus renewals, protect their holders for a total of at least 56 years. All Cleveland Model (or other) works bearing copyright dates of 1978 or later are now protected for the life of the author (in this case, E. T. Packard) plus 50 years beyond. We will pay $1,000 for information leading to the arrest and conviction of anyone duplicating any part or complete Cleveland Model plans, illustrations, etc., including all reproduction services by both individuals and firms alike.
E. T. Packard and Cleveland Model & Supply Co.
FOIL OR CLOTH HINGES
EITHER 1/32 SHEET COVERING OR 1/16 C-D FILL-IN AREA FOR 3 GAS TANKS ABOVE
LEFT: THE TRAIL BLAZING CURTISS NC-4 WHICH MADE THE FIRST SUCCESSFUL TRANSATLANTIC FLIGHT WEST TO EAST IN 1919
JDP
LEFT WING PANEL TURN OVER - FOLLOW PINHOLES FOR RIGHT HALF
STATION J - TYPICAL OF STATIONS D TO K, BUT WITHOUT A MOTOR SPAR FILLER EXCEPT AT F
RIGHT: CD212, LUCKY LINDY'S RYAN BROUGHAM PARTIAL 1928 AD CLIP WHICH RAN AFTER THE N-Y-P WAS GIVEN TO THE SMITHSONIAN
RYAN M-1 MAIL PLANE OVER SAN DIEGO, CAL. 12/26. THE PLANE FROM WHICH THE NX211 SPIRIT OF ST. LOUIS EVOLVED
WHEN BUILDI
WING STRUT END TAPER AND ROOT FAIRING DETAIL OF PLASTIC WOOD OR BALSA DUST
FULLY EXTENDED PERISCOPE
THICKNESS OF STOCKS
ALL DRAWN ILLUSTRATIONS BY J. KEN SNIFFEN

This and facing page: Details from the SF-211 plan, Lindbergh's Ryan NYP *Spirit of St. Louis* (½-inch scale) commemorating the 50th anniversary of the flight, authenticated and engineered by C. E. Steinchak and E. T. Packard. *E. T. Packard Collection.*

the actual plan were W T. Given, R. G. Kitchell, Dan Scherry, C. F. Schultz, Ken Sniffen, and, of course, Packard himself. Their names are listed on the lower border of the plan. The vital statistics of the Flyer are as follows:

> Wingspan: 41 feet; gross takeoff weight: 750 pounds; powerplant—four cylinder four-inch bore and stroke 12 hp engine developed by their mechanic, Charlie Taylor, turned at 980 rpm with bicycle chain reduction driving the propellers at 340 rpm. Patent granted #821393 in 1906; the four flights of December 17 totaled one minute, 39 seconds, with the last flight by Wilbur attaining 852 feet in 59 seconds.

In 1932 a 65-foot tall granite monument, topped by a beacon, was erected at Kittyhawk inscribed as follows:

In commemoration of the conquest of the air by the brothers Wilbur and Orville Wright. Conceived by genius, achieved by dauntless resolution and unconquerable faith.

Homage to the Spirit of St. Louis

Missing from the C-D library of original planes that were developed by Packard's cadre of volunteer model engineers is that most famous aircraft which in 1927 sparked great admiration and adulation, even frenzy: Lindbergh's *Spirit of St. Louis.*

In 1927, to mark the significant achievement, the souvenir and modeling world responded by producing all types of miniature representations of the

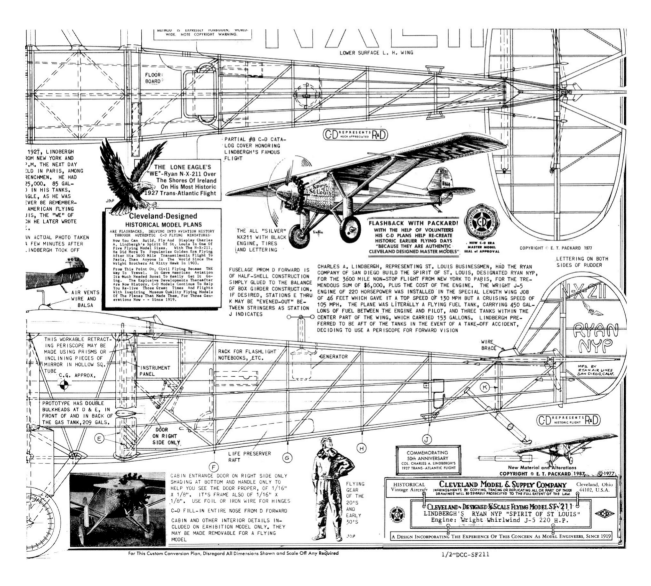

plane, facsimiles and models. At this time the fledgling A. Pachasa and Sons decided that the market was flooded with *Spirit* lookalikes and that they would not add this to their catalog. The Ideal Model Aeroplane Company in New York offered the best scale model kit for $8.50, though young Ed felt it left much to be desired.

In 1987, as the 60th anniversary of Lindbergh's historic solo flight across the Atlantic approached, Packard felt it was time to fill this obvious void in C-D's library. (A plan had been drawn up in 1977, No. 211, but Ed felt it needed to be made more authentic.) Together with volunteer model engineer C. E. Steinchak and artist Ken Sniffen, he set about designing the F-211, the most structurally authentic, museum-scale plan available for the *Spirit of St. Louis.*

PART IV

Recognition

CHAPTER 15

The AMA and
the Renaissance Man

WITH THE ENTRY OF gas-powered models in the 1933–34 contest fields, new rules and regulations were needed to distinguish a separate category from their rubber-powered predecessors. At the same time, it became apparent that a single, major, recognized national organization would have to be established so that standards of performance could ensure equitable competition. Such standards make sure that records would be official and recognized nationally as well as internationally by the FAI.

The logical umbrella seemed to be the National Aeronautics Administration (NAA), which undertook the task in 1936. Following this development, members' models received a license number (as with their prototypes), including a liability insurance policy, for one dollar. Subsequently, Charles Hampson Grant and his peers formed the IGMAA, specifically for gas-powered models, and that ultimately evolved into the present Academy of Model Aeronautics (AMA).

Fifty-nine years after Ed Packard founded what became the world-famous Cleveland Model and Supply, at the 1978 fifth annual Tournament of Champions held at Bill Bennett's Circus Circus in Las Vegas, Packard was inducted into the AMA Hall of Fame. "The event was considerably significant, in my case," recalled Packard, "for it marked the first such major industry recognition by my peers. Of course, I had been recognized for many years by my industry associates in the MIA [Model Industry Association] by serving on committees and holding offices, but it was essentially a trade association. The impressive Hall of Fame award plaque was presented to me by John Worth, president of AMA, who himself was also inducted on the very same occasion. Others receiving the award were: Phil Kraft, radio control electronics manufacturer; Leon Shulman, pioneer gas model designer and contest winner; and John Clemens, who received a Meritorious Service Award. The award provided me with a much needed feeling of recognition and acceptance by

AMA president John Worth (left) presents the Award of Hall of Fame to Edward T. Packard, 1978. *E. T. Packard Collection.*

industry associates and the impressive plaque has since occupied a place of honor in my office."

Initially headquartered in New York under the aegis of the AMA, the association's leadership chafed from years of inadequate funding and scanty staff. Fundraising drives in 1981 until 1983 yielded $300,000, sufficient for a down payment on new facilities. In 1983, forty-seven years after its founding, the AMA moved its headquarters into a beautiful new office and museum space in Reston, Virginia, a suburb of Washington, D.C. The new facility was known as the National Center for Aeromodeling (NCA).

Hurst Bowers, former Air Force colonel and dedicated aeromodeler, became its first curator. With inexhaustible energy and enthusiasm, he completely reconstituted the organization to consist of a museum, an impressive resource library, and complete membership services for the approximately 120,000 members. Bowers aimed to make the NCA the guiding light for local AMA chapters in safe contest planning and, most important, in providing adequate liability insurance.

After attending the impressive official dedication in September 1983, Packard entered into several months of negotiations with the curator to establish a representative display of C-D models, including the Playboy Senior. Packard agreed to provide the display models requested with the proviso that he be identified as the designer of the Playboy Senior. This was confirmed in writing and a bevy of C-D SF series of official museum quality display models, which had been previously exhibited in the C-D factory retail store on Lorain Avenue for many years, subsequently arrived at AMA headquarters. The result

ACADEMY OF MODEL AERONAUTICS

1810 Samuel Morse Drive   Reston, Virginia 22090   (703) 435-0750   FAX 703-435-0798

Letter from AMA curator Hurst
Bowers to Packard, confirming his
identification as the designer of
the Playboy Senior gas model and
commenting that almost all famous figures in aviation began
their careers with Cleveland
Model and Supply kits. *E. T.
Packard Collection.*

May 31, 1983

Mr. E. T. Packard
Cleveland Model and Supply Company
10307 Detroit Avenue
Cleveland, OH 44102

Dear Mr. Packard:

Thank you so much for your 10 May letter and for the kind offer
to give us your "Playboy Senior" for the A.M.A. Museum. As you so
appropriately pointed out, it will indeed be a worthy addition to
our museum in that it epitomizes the state of the art reached at that
period in the development of high performance model aircraft. You
may be assured that you will be appropriately recognized as designer
and donator of the exhibit. If you would be kind enough to send it
to us at your earliest convenience, we would be most appreciative
as we want it for our grand opening in September.

When one considers the unbelievable contribution that Cleveland
kits made to aviation, the National Center for aeromodeling would
be remiss without emphasizing this through our exhibits. Therefore, any other models and/or memorabilia that you would be willing to donate would be greatly appreciated. I'm sure you realize
better than I that almost all of the famous personages in aviation
today began their careers with your kits. We would love for them
to experience nostalgia when they visit our museum (and they will)
and seeing your models would do more to achieve this than anything
that I can imagine. Particularly the "Playboy", the "Condor"
glider, and of course, the wonderful scale models in your 3/4"
Master Series. The "China Clipper" you mentioned would also be
an outstanding exhibit.

Your mention of Roy Morahiro was most touching and brings back
memories of many of my old friends who never returned from World
War II. Like Roy, many of them were modelers.

Thank you again for your wonderful cooperation and generosity.
The "Cleveland Playboy" will be exhibited in a position of honor.

Yours truly,

Hurst G. Bowers
Curator

HGB:lmw

was a most striking array of C-D models, particularly of the Thompson Trophy winners, within display cases wherever possible, capped with a portrait
photo of Packard. Many of the models had to be repaired or refurbished, many
of which were done to perfection by Tom Yanosky, a longtime Cleveland museum quality modeler as well as being a talented, accomplished artist. In the
limited area allotted for the museum, a representative exhibition of models
from rubber powered to gas models and radio controlled types occupied every space available, including many hung vertically from the ceiling.

However, the existence of the Reston facility was to be relatively short-lived
as the governing board envisioned a facility that would be totally integrated

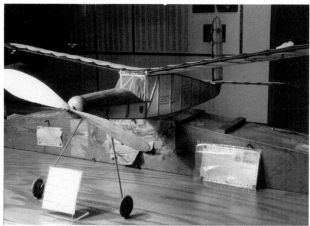

Above left: AMA curator Col. Hurst Bowers, USAF (ret.), with his "Dennyplane," a six-foot gas model that was distributed by former movie star Reginald Denny, who was in the model business during the 1930s and who during WWII made target drones for the U.S. military. *Author's Collection.*

Above right: The 1935 Wakefield Trophy winner, by Gordon Light, model editor for *Air Trails*. Note that the carton in the background was used to ship the model originally. *Author's Collection.*

Below: The AMA (Reston) exhibit, featuring Cleveland models. *Author's Collection.*

and inclusive, combining all the required functions of the AMA plus contest sites. Carrying this concept a step further, it considered that the site could be the location for the annual AMA national meet, thus eliminating the challenge and expense posed by an annual change of contest organization volunteer staff. The site could be utilized as the location for any international FAI contest, such as the Wakefield Trophy competition. All of this futuristic planning became controversial in view of the relatively short time the AMA had occupied the Reston facility. Ultimately, all of the pros and cons of the issue were laid to rest with the acquisition of 1,047 acres at Muncie, Indiana, which would place the site within four hundred miles of 60 percent of the membership and in the process reduce annual operating costs by $500,000.

Approximately two years after the 1992 move to Muncie, the AMA could finally experience the much-deserved satisfaction of its day in the sun when

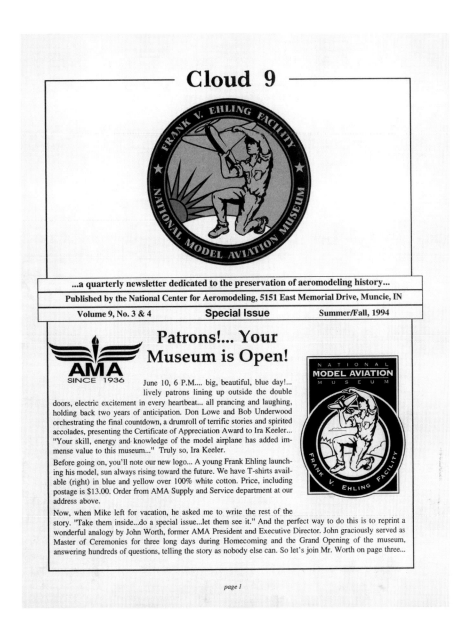

The announcement of the opening of the Frank V. Ehling Museum (1994). *Author's Collection.*

in June 1994 the Frank V. Ehling Museum rolled out the red carpet at its gala opening. Amid the audience's oohs and aahs elicited by the exhibits designed by Curator Mike Fulmer (an expert, professional C-D modeler and member of the special effects Lucasfilm's Industrial Light and Magic Division), the consensus was that at last the AMA had achieved a status comparable to that of the exhibits at the Smithsonian's NASM.

Among the many authentic replicas of the model industry's hobby shops was a colorful Cleveland Model and Supply exhibit portraying a scene replete with an array of SF models, C-D attractive cartons, *CMN&PH* issues, the famous SF Curtiss Hawk P6-E, plus other examples of the C-D line. Appropriately emblazoned above its doorway was the famous Cleveland Blue Diamond trademark, which had identified the company during its emerging

AMA Headquarters Locations

1933–40	1909 Massachusetts Ave. NW, Dupont Circle, Washington, D.C.
April 1940–December 1941	Willard Hotel, Washington, D.C.
January 1942–June 1942	718 Jackson Place NW, Washington, D.C.
July 1942–June 1965	1025 Connecticut Ave. NW, Washington, D.C.
July 1965–June 1970	1239 Vermont Ave. NW, Washington, D.C.
July 1970–February 1976	805 15th St., Washington, D.C. (shared the 6th floor with NAA)
March 1976–January 1983	815 15th St., Washington, D.C.
February 1983–June 1993	1810 Samuel Morse Dr., Reston, Virginia (own building)
May–July 1993	Frank V. Ehling Museum, International Aeromodeling Center, Muncie, Indiana
June 2001–	Muncie, Indiana

The lobby of the Ehling Museum, features the Cleveland Playboy Senior, Henry Struck's "New Ruler," and blowups of the covers of the major model aviation magazines. *Author's Collection.*

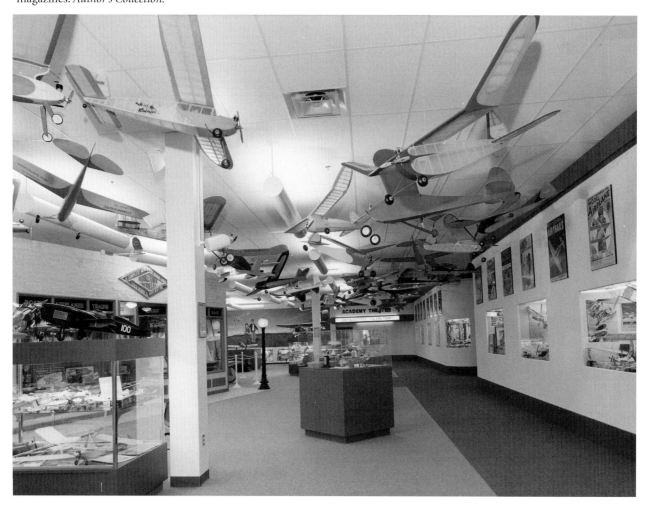

Model co-designer Ira Keeler (standing) and legendary aero-modeler Jim Noonan (seated at right) show off an 1877 Wilhelm Kress (Vienna) "Aeroveloce" design presented to Michael Fulmer along with sixteen other historical models built by Noonan during the 1915–27 era. *Author's Collection.*

years. The adjacent wall featured a near-full-size photograph of the famous C-D 1930 Austin coupe with the giant SF-2 Travel Air Model R on its roof.

The AMA, in recognition of its 60th anniversary, has established a long-term membership goal of 200,000, With this impressive site and equally impressive facilities, every indication is that this objective should be attained.

The Expertise of Thomas Yanosky

From a childhood during the Great Depression in the small coal-mining town of Colver, Pennsylvania, located on the western slopes of the Alleghenies; to designing cartographic products for the U.S. Army from 1956 to 1970, including an Erskine Hall mural of the *History of Cartography;* to a career as a professional artist in Arizona and in Virginia suburbs of Washington, D.C., briefly summarizes the progress of Tom Yanosky, expert modeler, artist, and designer.

C-D volunteer model engineer, artist, and designer Thomas Yanosky with his C-D Curtiss Command Helldiver posed against a hand-painted background of Grand Canyon No. 4 (1987). *T. R. Yanosky Collection.*

Like millions of other American youth, his passion for aviation was kindled by the Lone Eagle's epic flight of 1927. With the youthful enthusiasm engendered by the desire to emulate his new found role model, young Tom was inspired to create a miniature replica of the famous *Spirit of St. Louis.* However, during this challenging period of economic decline, with its resultant scarcity of materials, there were no retailers in this somewhat remote hamlet offering model airplane kits for sale.

Reminiscing about how this challenge was overcome, Tom recalled, "Fortunately, the town trash site was a source of all manner of wooden fruit crates and cardboard. In addition, when winemaking time came, our Italian townspeople were awash in truckloads of crated grapes. Since these colorfully branded grape crates became a prized possession for the local, eager, hobby-driven youth, fisticuffs often ensued for possession of the highly prized supply of wood. However, when necessary, I could enlist the pugilistic services of my older brother Joseph to bolster my procurement prowess. Consequently, I most always had an adequate supply of wood for model building.

"My first recognizable constructed model from the crude, primitive crate wood was the ubiquitous Curtiss Jenny. Since there were no three-views or any sort of plans then available, it was constructed from a composite of newspaper clippings, magazine photos, and my memory. As a tribute to my budding manual dexterity, my fourth grade school teacher permitted me to display the model in a corner of our classroom.

"In 1933 I began obtaining models by mail order, attracted by the colorful, appealing ads in model magazines such as *Model Airplane News, Flying Aces,* and *Popular Aviation.* I can still remember the high drama that took place when I went to the post office to pick up the ordered kit—the suspense that ensued—the opening of the kit to examine and assess the difficulty of the plan enclosed, followed by a period of imagination as I speculated on how I would build it and how high it would fly. Each such kit was a carton of dreams, dreams which only youth has the power to experience and which were a powerful force to motivate young would-be aerial chargers to accomplishment.

"Initially, I was able to afford several Comet 50-cent kits, including a Comet Dipper, Curtiss Robin, SE-5A, Monocoupe, and an Ideal Vought Corsair. As I recall, it was in 1934 when I entered Ebensburg Cambria High School that I had my first look at a Cleveland kit. It occurred at the home of a classmate, Bud Davis, who proudly showed off his SF-7 Curtiss XF8C-7 Command Helldiver, for he had become an accomplished modeler. Then and there I became hooked on Cleveland models, and I began a savings plan to accumulate the $3.50 for my own Helldiver kit. On completion, not only was it an impressive model with its spiffy wheel pants, cockpit sliding enclosure, wing-mounted machine guns, bright red speed ring, and swept back top wing, but it was a superb flyer as well. There followed the construction of the SF-15 Fokker D-VII, with its brilliant orange-and-green color scheme, complete with World War I German Latin cross insignia on wings, empennage and fuselage. Properly wound and adjusted, it was an outstanding flyer, able to right off-ground and clear the nearby utility wires.

"My modeling ability was then duly challenged by the mastering of the SF-21 Curtiss Hawk P6-E, often referred to as the "aristocrat of the Cleveland fleet." I wisely refrained from flying it and ultimately sold it to a local pilot for $3.50, just enough to buy another C-D kit."

Tom heeded his proclivity for art and in 1939 he headed for the Corcoran School of Art in Washington, D.C. A part-time position with the art department of the *Washington Post* enabled him to finance a 1-inch scale Miniature kit of the Curtiss Hawk F11C-4 at $4.50, an astronomical sum in that era. There followed the construction of the flagship of the Cleveland fleet, the SF-1 Great Lakes Sport Trainer.

Tom's artistic talent was advantageously utilized in the military in 1942 by assigning him duties as a topographical draftsman, drawing vital maps for the invasions and conflicts of the U.S. armed forces in World War II. This ultimately led to become a mapmaking career with the Army Map Service in Washington, D.C. The last thirteen years of his tenure were devoted to the research and design of military cartographic products required by the U.S.

Department of Defense. In 1964 and 1965, Tom was commissioned by the authorities of the Army Map Service (later, the Defense Mapping Agency) to research and paint a mural illustrating forty-four figures from antiquity, through the Middle Ages, and up to 1965 that, in essence, symbolized the development of the art and science of cartography through the ages. His last major project for the Department of Defense was to research, design, and create (assisted by a Navy chart designer) a large 9-by-12-foot (nine sheets) map of the entire world, which was completed in 1969, the year before his retirement.

During this same1942–70 period, Tom was also busy developing as a serious fine artist-painter and printmaker. He participated in the Washington, D.C., art community, involved in staging many exhibits, one-man shows and similar activities in its many prestigious museums and art galleries. Interspersed in this most active lifestyle when time permitted, Tom continued in his lifelong dedication to the construction of authentic aircraft models, most of which were Cleveland designs.

When a career opportunity beckoned from Arizona, he and his wife, Elizabeth, moved to this totally foreign environment. Happily, he found that the indescribable beauty and attraction of the desert landscape, the majestic grandeur of the incomparable Grand Canyon, as well as the artists and artifacts of American Indians proved to be a watershed of influence in the development of his artistic career.

Tom continued, "On our return to the east coast in 1978, we settled in picturesque Reston, Virginia, a suburb of the nation's capitol. Purely by chance I stumbled on the headquarters of the AMA, as I patronized the local post office, and I promised myself that I would have to investigate it further. In 1984, having decided to move to a smaller residence in nearby Herndon, Virginia, I called the AMA to see if there was an interest in their displaying the five-foot Sterling RC Fokker D-7 I had built, since it required a good deal of space in its protective wooden crate. Since by then the AMA was occupying their first museum headquarters in Reston, my call brought forth none other than the curator, Col. Hurst Bowers, to examine my masterpiece, with which he was thoroughly impressed. He agreed on the spot to accept it for exhibition. Thus I began a longterm relationship with Bowers and the AMA that continues to this day. Little did I know then how important this association would be in capitalizing on my artistic and modeling abilities.

"Subsequently, Bowers confided to me that he had just received from Ed Packard about twenty former ¾-inch scale exhibition models that needed to be refurbished—and would I agree to assist in this project. Initially, I chose a somewhat dusty, forlorn, shopworn Curtiss Hawk P6-E on which I lavished my attention for the better part of a year, after which Hurst Bowers graciously accepted it and placed it in an attractive showcase along with several other C-D exhibition models. I was extremely proud to have had my version of the famous C-D P6-E placed on display at this prestigious museum.

"Shortly thereafter I was contacted again by the curator inviting me to meet Ed Packard, who would be visiting the AMA to inspect the display of C-D models. I was nearly spellbound talking to this icon of modeldom as he toured the facility. Our friendship continued through years of correspondence, resulting in my acquisition of a representative number of C-D SF kits, *Cleveland Modelmaking and Practical Hobbies* issues, C-D catalogs, and an assortment of model wheels, cowlings, propellers, and various other parts. I now have my own abbreviated Cleveland Model museum. I also submitted, at his request, some sketches of proposed, revised, C-D company logos in his consideration of a possible new look for C-D. Packard was always the visionary, always looking ahead.

"To honor a retiring CEO of a mortgage banking association in Washington, D.C., Hurst Bowers asked me to construct a static 36-inch display model of a B-24J Liberator. To incorporate all of the many details of construction and armament in this project required a great deal of research which Hurst and the late Ned Kragness provided. The result was probably one of the most impressive, detailed such models. Concurrently, I had under construction an SF-7 Curtiss XF8C-7 Curtiss Command Helldiver, scratch built using Cleveland printwood. Later, at Hurst's request, I built a C-D SF-95 Lockheed Hudson Bomber, an impressive 49⅜-inch-span World War II model that was displayed along with the other Cleveland models at the museum.

"In 1990 the curator was requested to organize an exhibit of an accumulation of Jimmie Allen Flying Club memorabilia, and I was asked to assume the task. My many art exhibits and other display experiences proved to be invaluable, for to incorporate the plethora of information and accomplishments into a chronological history was a significant challenge. However, the resultant exhibit was received most enthusiastically. In 1991, similarly, I was asked to bring new life to the archival accumulation of the exploits of the well known accomplished model designer, builder and contest winner Chet Lanzo—famous for his huge Class E stick model (55-inch span, 19½-inch prop, powered with thirty-two strands of ³⁄₁₆-inch flat rubber). This task consumed the better part of a year, working when I had the time. However, when it was finally finished, Hurst felt it did justice to this famous model builder."

At this time, there was no way that Tom could know that, behind the scenes, the AMA had come to realize that the Reston facility was inadequate to properly serve this growing organization, both from a museum perspective as well as from a contest flying site. The subsequent move to Muncie, Indiana, in 1992 was, therefore, inevitable—much to the regret of Tom and his fellow modelers of the Washington, D.C., area.

However, Tom Yanosky has left his dramatic imprint on the AMA and he is most deserving of the appropriate and resultant recognition as a result of his outstanding efforts.

Michael G. Fulmer

Michael G. Fulmer—ex-Marine, pipeline welder, surveyor, high steel iron-worker, custom car fabricator, toy designer, mechanical engineer, screenwriter, special effects modeler with Lucasfilm's Industrial Light & Magic, AND the first curator of the Frank V. Ehling AMA International Center for Aeromodeling, in Muncie, Indiana—is a true renaissance man, continually reinventing his colorful life.

He was smitten early on in his model-building career with the authenticity of Cleveland models. He recalled in a nostalgic letter written to his daughters: "Between football and track and homework and general high school hell-raising, I managed to complete many Cleveland SF kits, selling the finished models to airmen and officers via the hobby shop proprietor, who took ten percent. I was the 'Prince of Printwood,' much to the chagrin of my friends who were into pre-fab 'Ukies' and free flight."

Michael G. Fulmer, special effects modeler with Lucasfilm's Industrial Light and Magic, with his mechanized robot creations C-3PO and R2-D2 from *Star Wars* (1984). *Roberto Magrath Collection.*

Above: The AMA Museum has Michael Fulmer's recreation of a 1940s hobby shop featuring Cleveland models, colorful cartons, issues of *CMN&PH,* and the original "Blue Diamond" logo. *Ruth Chin Collection.*

Left: In his model of the 1918 Fokker DVII, Michael Fulmer used C-D plans and printwood but then lavished on details such as exposed Mercedes engine, twin Spandau machine guns with charging handles, custom-made resin wheels, and cockpit instrumentation with movable controls. The authentic camouflage pattern was printed (by computer) on tissue paper; all other details were hand painted. *Roberto Magrath Collection.*

The AMA and the Renaissance Man · 275

He went on to form, with Ira Keeler, Aero/Space Model and Casting, which manufactured some of the early resin-cast kits and produced model aircraft for collectors, museums, and corporate images. Included in their fabricated model list were a few Cleveland SF models, which were in demand by connoisseurs. At this time he struck up an acquaintance with Ed Packard, and a friendship grew.

From the model-building business, Fulmer and Keeler moved into service with Lucasfilm's Industrial Light and Magic, where they produced special-effects models and props. After thirteen years in the film-making business, Fulmer left to design and construct the National Model Aviation Museum in Muncie, Indiana, for the Academy of Model Aeronautics.

Fulmer was pleased to have one of the feature exhibits be a tribute to Cleveland Model and Supply and E. T. Packard.

CHAPTER 16

Showcased and Honored

A FEW YEARS AFTER 1920, when the late Paul Edward Garber had been hired by the Smithsonian as an exhibits preparer, the curator-to-be met with Edward T. Pachasa. Garber, then in his early twenties, was also a master modeler, having founded the Capital Model Aero Club in 1913. A lifelong exchange of correspondence and communication began between the two outstanding aeromodelists.

One of the most rewarding aspects of the unique relationship between these two dedicated modelers was their agreement on a standardized ¾-inch scale (¹⁄₁₆ size) for museum scale models. Hence, all of the C-D SF series initially were of this scale until the mid-1930s, when Packard introduced the ½-inch scale Dwarf line, to offer an optional line of reduced prices to cope with the competition and the Depression.

Garber had such admiration for the authenticity of Cleveland models that he enthusiastically told Packard that "the Smithsonian will be the eastern showroom for Cleveland models." Initially, before Garber became responsible for the duties of curator in 1946, he received a copy of the plan of every new C-D SF model released. At one time there were more than sixty models in the exhibits at the Smithsonian that were either custom-built from a C-D kit or scratch-built from a C-D plan. Likewise, whenever Packard needed research or technical information regarding a certain aircraft, he relied on Garber's access to almost infinite sources of aircraft data.

Since the curator was a modeler himself, he set high standards for models to be accepted for exhibition. He was always anxious to represent within the displays the many achievements in aviation through models, and not just those of the United States. The vast collection of scale model aircraft at the now entitled NASM, which numbers nearly 1,500, was the result of his foresight in using models to represent those prototype aircraft that could not

Smithsonian curator Paul Garber inspects an exhibit of scale miniature aircraft. Through his foresight, realistic scale models were acquired to represent those aircraft that could not otherwise be part of the full-size aircraft collection. *NASM/Smithsonian Collection.*

In April 1928 the *Spirit of St. Louis* arrived at the Smithsonian, which Paul Garber had acquired for the museum from Charles Lindbergh. Before Lindbergh died, he was granted his request to once again sit in his *Spirit of St. Louis.* He sat for quite a long time before going on his way. *NASM/ Smithsonian Collection.*

otherwise be represented like the seventy-seven full-size prototypes now displayed on site and another 200 stored at the Silver Hill facility.

Perhaps the curator's two most significant accomplishments to the halls of the Smithsonian were that he brought the *Spirit of St. Louis* in 1928, which served as one of the first great aircraft attractions, and in 1948 he rescued the

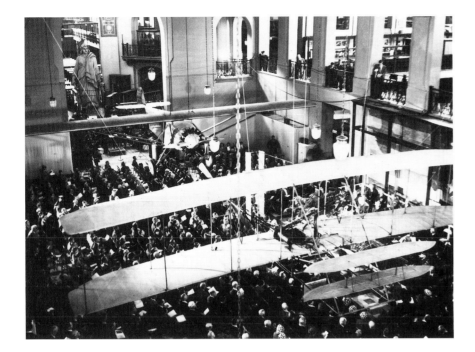

The Wrights' 1903 Flyer hanging in the Smithsonian's Arts and Industries Building, in celebration of the 45th anniversary of the famous first flight. *NASM/Smithsonian Collection.*

original Wright Flyer from London, where it had been sent for twenty years after the Wrights' controversy over the Smithsonian's claim that their Professor Langley was the first to fly.

Garber attributed his career in the NASM initially through his ability to use his hands for the repairing and making of scale models. He enthusiastically congratulated Packard on his crowning achievements of producing the two super-detailed plans of the Wright Brothers' Kittyhawk Flyer (SSF-201) and Lindy's *Spirit of St. Louis* (SSF-211) in 1987.

Paul Garber was on staff at the Smithsonian for seventy-three years and is credited with building the NASM's collection, which is the largest of its kind in the world. The nearby Suitland, Maryland, storage facility, formerly referred to as Silver Hill, has been renamed the Paul E. Garber Preservation, Restoration and Storage Facility, and there fulltime mechanics and volunteers tackle the never-ending task of restoration.

Wright-Patterson Air Force Base Museum, Dayton, Ohio

The museum at the Wright-Patterson Air Force Base in Dayton, Ohio, has the largest display of full-size American military aircraft in the country. But, significantly, the museum also acknowledges and recognized the important influence model building had on aviation design and recruitment.

Maj. (Ret.) Royal Frey—former museum staff member, avid model airplane enthusiast, and longtime Cleveland customer—arranged for a Cleveland Model and Supply exhibit in the museum that included the ¾-inch scale C-D plans

Left: The Cleveland Model and Supply display at the Wright-Patterson AFB Museum, here featuring the Curtiss F11C-2 (uncovered), Me.-109E, and Boeing B-9. Above the case is the C-D plan spread for the Curtiss F11C-2. *Author's Collection.*

Right: Paul Poberezny shown with the EAA's P-51 Mustang "Paul I," No. 4475, a Cavalier conversion with a jump seat used for VIP passengers. Paul served in WWII as a CPT instructor and U.S. Air Corps pilot and also in Korea. His logbook indicates that he has flown 270 different types of aircraft and 135 "home-builts." He received the FAA's highest civilian recognition with their Merit Award. *Sport Aviation.*

of the following aircraft: Curtiss F11-C2 uncovered, Boeing 13-9 Bomber, ME-109E; examples of model airplane magazines, such as *Flying Aces, Model Airplane News,* and *Air Trails;* and several other model airplane catalogs, such as Megows, Scientific, Berkeley, and Comet.

The display also paid tribute to Ed Packard and the role he played in hobby modeling and in the development of America's air forces in World War II.

C-D's Role in the Founding of the EAA

In 1953, when the young, relatively unknown Experimental Aircraft Association (EAA) was formally established by former Air Force pilot Paul Poberezny, it could not have occurred to him then what an influential organization it would become by its 40th anniversary. The grass roots association operated for more than a decade out of the Poberezny residence basement. Since Paul was often flying to different parts of the world as a military officer, his wife, Audrey, assumed the responsibility for EAA's day-to-day operations, serving as its office manager until 1970.

EAA's name was derived from the designation of "experimental," which the FAA applies to the homebuilt aircraft that many of its 170,000 members construct. The outstanding designs so painstakingly and laboriously built, usually from kits offered by more than 200 manufacturers, number 25,975 currently licensed in the United States. The finished aircraft operate legally under the 1949 FAA stipulation requiring the owner to have built 51 percent himself and providing that the craft is test flown for forty hours and is not used commercially.

The EAA's founder and chairman, Paul Poberezny, readily concedes, "I could honestly say that if it weren't for the serious design efforts of the Cleveland-Design models, there may never have been an EAA. It played a very important part in my life as a very early model builder. The Cleveland models were well known for their accuracy and detailed work. They offered a bit more of a challenge to the hands and minds of young people in turning out a really well built and accurate model. I still have a Howard Mike Cleveland model that I built back in 1937 at home. Though we have many plastic models today, the challenge for my age group was in the building up the model, which was like building the real thing."

For many of the early EAA members, who in their youth became accomplished model builders, there appeared to be a natural bridge between building models and constructing a man-carrying aircraft. This comparison was perhaps even more applicable in the EAA's early history, when more of the materials used were wood. Presently, the many manufacturers of the ultra modern configurations of EAA kits use elements of exotic composites consisting of graphite, epoxy, fiberglass or carbon fiber such as were used by the EAA members Burt and Dick Rutan in their successful Long-EZ and Varieze kit designs. Their advanced technology culminated in the conception and construction of their 1986 nonstop, around the world *Voyager* (for more information on this historic flight, see Web site www.dickrutan.com/page2.html) that

From left: Paul Poberezny with early EAA officers Carl Walters and Bob Nolinske in the early association headquarters, located in the founder's residence basement (ca. 1953). Poberezny was an avid C-D modeler and credits his hobby with being a major influence in the origin of the organization. *Sport Aviation.*

At the AirVenture meeting in Oshkosh in 1991, Roscoe Turner's NX-61Y original Wendell-Williams air racer, winner of the 1933 Bendix and the 1934 Thompson. Turner sold the racer in 1939 to what is now the Western Reserve Historical Society/Crawford Transportation Museum. It is the only surviving intact racer that won both the Thompson and Bendix races. *Sport Aviation.*

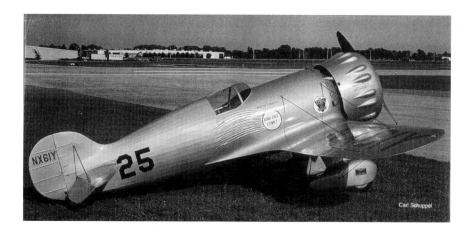

employed a "sandwich" of Hexel honeycomb surrounded by two layers of carbon fibercloth imbued with epoxies. (Graphite has half the weight of steel but is five times stronger.)

The list of accomplishments of the EAA includes the establishment of the Young Eagles program, which instills in young Americans the desire to fly through a national program that takes them aloft. Young Eagles are occasionally given rides at the EAA, using three EAA aircraft, including a Ford 4AT Trimotor, a Stinson SM88-A, and a GlaStar. The EAA also developed the annual Oshkosh fly-in, which develop into the most successful such international event. The 1995 extravaganza attracted 12,000 aircraft and 830,000 people.

Founder Paul Poberezny realized not only seeing his lifelong dream for the EAA become a reality, he has had the satisfaction of witnessing the formation of some eight hundred chapters. He oversaw the establishment and steady growth of the Young Eagles program (which now has more than one million members) and helped make the annual Oshkosh AirVenture into the most successful aviation event, internationally, with the 2004 extravaganza attracting 10,000 aircraft and more than 700,000 people. He can also take pride in having his son Tom become a member of the famous EAA Eagles Aerobatic Flight Team and, most important, to see him succeed his father as the current president of the EAA. The recognition and accolades that the EAA continually receives and so richly deserves serve to make it the most successful such aviation association worldwide.

At the August 2004 Oshkosh AirVenture, the FAA announced, effective September 1, 2004, a new type of license, "sport pilot," and a new category of aircraft, "light sport." These new categories will make it possible for a license to be earned with 20 hours of instruction versus the previously standard 40. The cost of $2,000, as compared with $6,000. The requirements for the sport pilot license include the acceptance of a valid driver's license [in place of the physical]. The new category limits the pilot to three miles visibility and a maximum altitude of 10,000 feet, 138 mph, and a stall speed of no more than 51 mph. The aircraft is limited to 1,320 pounds. The EAA anticipates that

20,000 new pilots will be licensed by 2007, versus the some 250,000 private pilots currently. The resultant kit designs costing $25,000–35,000 will create a market of $48 million by 2009.

This new type of plane and license is a tribute to the leadership of Poberezny and his many supporters and will be a boon to the progress of aviation in America.

Enshrinement in the Home Town's Aviation Hall of Fame

To attain what many feel is the most meaningful of all recognition, that by your own hometown, finally transpired for Edward T. Packard on August 31, 1990. On that date he was enshrined in Cleveland's Western Reserve Aviation Hall of Fame of the world-famous Frederick C. Crawford Auto-Aviation Museum. The occasion of Packard's induction was doubly significant, for it reunited Ed with his two remaining living brothers, Will and Andrew, all of whom had not been together for a good many years. Ed made some brief remarks expressing his deep appreciation for the honor, following which he was given a videotape of the ceremony.

The Aviation Hall of Fame is dedicated to honoring those whose personal and professional achievements contributed significantly to the progress of aviation. A purpose of the organization is to serve as a catalyst for the expanded focus upon and presentation of Cleveland's unique aviation history.

Ed Packard sits with Al Engel (right) in the Curtiss Model A607004 single float "Bumblebee" on display in the Crawford Auto-Aviation Museum, Cleveland (ca. 1986). Engel received his flight training directly from Glenn Curtiss in 1910; thereafter he became a member of the Curtiss Exhibition team along with Charles Willard and Eugene Ely. *E. T. Packard Collection.*

Above left: The 1990 enshrinement of Ed Packard into the Western Reserve Aviation Hall of Fame ceremony reunited the four living Pachasa brothers (Fred died in 1988): (from left) Ed, age 84; Will, age 79; Al, age 75; Andy, age 73. *Will Pachasa Collection.*

Above right: Ed Packard sits in the cockpit of the winning Wedell-Williams air racer, part of the Crawford Museum's permanent collection. *E. T. Packard Collection.*

ANSWER REPLY TO
HEADQUARTERS OF THE ARMY AIR FORCES
WAR DEPARTMENT
WASHINGTON, D. C.

WAR DEPARTMENT
HEADQUARTERS OF THE ARMY AIR FORCES
WASHINGTON

12 September 1943

Mr. A. G. Eaton, Chief
Schools, Hospitals & Institutions Branch
War Production Board
Temporary Building E, Room 1-301
6th and Adams Drive, S. E.
Washington, D. C.

Dear Mr. Eaton:

It has been brought to my attention by the National Aeronautic Association that the War Production Board is considering the issuance of an order which will release materials for the manufacture of a limited number of small gasoline engines to be used in model aircraft for educational purposes.

We have closely observed the development of aeromodeling in the United States and are firmly convinced that those of our American boys who participated in this activity have acquired a fundamental knowledge of aerodynamics and received an impetus which, in many cases, has carried them to the top in the field of aviation.

In view of the records established in military aviation by individuals who received their start through model building, the educational value of this activity cannot be questioned. This is, of course, particularly true at this time when so many of our young men must prepare for participation in either military aviation during the present crisis or in civil aviation following the war.

Sincerely,

H. H. ARNOLD,
General, U. S. A.,
Commanding General, Army Air Forces.

GENERAL ARNOLD'S OPINION OF THE ESSENTIALITY OF MODEL BUILDING

Enshrinement is for persons whose achievements in or major contributions to aviation or space endeavors occurred in, or who were born in the state of Ohio.

Testimonials

Significant aspects of Ed Packard's role in the history of aviation include recognition not only by prestigious aviation organizations but by important individuals as well—famous people who were avid model airplane builders and who appreciated and admired Packard's vigilance in offering the most authentic plans possible.

It is compelling to acknowledge his adulation by Maj.-Gen. Barry Goldwater, who served in the Air Transport Command during World War II and logged 12,000 hours and flew 170 different military and civil aircraft. He also served as chairman of the U.S. Senate's Armed Forces Committee for many years. Goldwater built many Cleveland models and corresponded often with Packard, even offering to write a foreword for the memoir Ed was working on.

20 December 1978

Dear Mr. Packard,

I have just completed reading the article "Model Master" in the November 1978 issue of Naval Aviation News. I am delighted to see that recognition of your invaluable service to U.S. Naval Aviation has been properly recorded for all to read. Without question many of our intrepid Naval Aviators, past and present, benefited from the pre-basic training in principles of model aircraft construction and basic aerodynamics of flight through the use of Ed Packard's Cleveland Model Aircraft plans and kits.

Speaking for myself and, I am sure, for the many thousands of Naval Aviators who cut their teeth on your model kits, we appreciate your interest and dedication in developing an aviation training media through model kits for young potential airmen. Many of us utilized that early knowledge in our aviation careers over the past decades.

Congratulations on the fine article in Naval Aviation News. I commend you and thank you for your contributions to Naval Aviation.

William H. Harris
Rear Admiral, USN (Ret.)

Mr. Ed Packard
Cleveland Model Aircraft and Supply Company
10307 Detroit Avenue
Cleveland, Ohio 44102

And both Rear Admiral William Harris and highly regarded aeronautical engineer Alexander Klemin acknowledged Cleveland Model and Supply's contribution to the motivation and development of future aviators.

United States Senate

WASHINGTON, D.C. 20510

October 30, 1978

Mr. Ed Packard
Cleveland Model and Supply Company
10307 Detroit Avenue
Cleveland, Ohio 44102

Dear Ed:

If you think my writing a foreword or an introduction to your book would help, I would be more than honored to give it a try. Having been a model builder all of my life, I think I have a little feeling for it. Let me know.

Sincerely,

Barry Goldwater

NEW YORK UNIVERSITY
COLLEGE OF ENGINEERING
UNIVERSITY HEIGHTS, NEW YORK 53

DANIEL GUGGENHEIM
SCHOOL OF AERONAUTICS

TELEPHONE: RAYMOND 9-2000

June 4, 1943

Mr. E.B. Miller
Hotel Statler
Washington, D.C.

Dear Mr. Miller:

Thank you for your letter of June 2nd. I have had a good deal to do with Boy Scouts and with students who prior to entering the University, have been engaged in model building.

It has been my experience as a teacher of Aviation for over a period of twenty years, that those young men who began their acquaintance with aircraft through model building, thereby laid a foundation of interest in skill in aircraft work which served them throughout their college careers in the study of aeronautical engineering.

I can in my classes almost pick out those boys who have model aircraft experience because their outlook is so broad, practical and enthusiastic.

I am definitely of the opinion that aircraft model kits have a tremendous educational value for boys entering universities for aeronautical engineering, or entering the air service, whether Army or Navy.

I am quite of the opinion that Governmental authority should encourage in every way and as much as possible, the manufacture of model kits.

Yours very truly,

Alexander Klemin
Guggenheim Research Professor

AK/ml

CHAPTER 17

The Changing of the Guard at C-D

✳ IN 1994, AFTER HIS MORE THAN a quarter-century of occupancy at 10301 Detroit Avenue, C-D's home address since his exodus from the famous location at Lorain Avenue in 1968, the Master Model Engineer was served notice that the designated historical city landmark site, former home of American Chicle's White Chewing Gum Company, was being remodeled and converted into a "multipurpose facility," thus forcing him to move. Facing the move, Packard knew he could not eliminate any of his historically significant largesse; hence, the bulk of his inventory was kept and moved to a nearby location at 9800 Detroit Avenue.

The following year, 1995, as Ed approached his ninetieth birthday, it became apparent that his health would force him to reduce his work schedule at C-D. He began by cutting back the number of trips into the city from his residence at North Olmsted to three days per week, the handwriting was on the wall. But this did not prove to be a solution. Late in the year the time came when he, and his wife, Kay, knew it would be best for his health to completely retire. In the interim, Kay and his capable assistant, Mildred Filsinger, kept the business operating at a minimal pace.

Finally, in 1996, Ed reluctantly placed the business up for sale. Fortunately, John Jacox, a dedicated model builder, engineer, and admirer of Packard currently in engineering management at a large aerospace company located in Indianapolis, had developed a long-time interest in the company. When Jacox became aware of the possibility that C-D would be up for sale, he traveled to Cleveland to meet with Ed (whom he had met previously when purchasing C-D memorabilia). He lost no time initiating negotiations. After a record run of continuous operation under the same ownership for seventy-seven years, the change in ownership was effective March 29, 1996.

The transition found Jacox laboriously and painstakingly sifting through the extensive inventory, files, and memorabilia accumulated and saved by

Above left: Entrepreneur John Jacox acquired Cleveland Model and Supply on March 29, 1996. He is shown with a 1934 C-D kit of the SF-1 Great Lakes Sport Trainer and a 1930–31 hobby tube for a PZL Polish Fighter. The tubes were used widely before the sales volume could justify the expense of using cardboard, lithographed cartons (1996). *James Yee.*

Above right: The 75th anniversary issue of *Model Airplane News,* which reproduced C-D's first ad of December 1929. *Author's Collection.*

Below: In 1986, at age 80, Ed Packard holds the *Packard Demoiselle,* built by C-D volunteer model engineer Dan Scherry. *E. T. Packard Collection.*

Packard before the company could be moved to Indianapolis, the new, "adopted" home for C-D. (In a respectful nod to the company's roots, Jacox arranged to preserve the (216) 961-3600 Cleveland telephone number.)

John Jacox's objective for the development of C-D was to preserve not only the Cleveland name, trademarks, and other identifying characteristics of the famous firm but to reissue a limited number of some of the SF early kits of the 1930s, as well as authentic cartons, publications, and other proprietary memorabilia.

Jacox stated, "I have a deep feeling of admiration and respect for Mr. Packard and his company, and I feel most fortunate to be in a position to recreate a great deal of the outstanding legacy of his great enterprise." C-D could not have fallen into the hands of a more concerned, dedicated, or closely protected ownership.

Epilogue

The Father of Scale Flying Modeling

❊ From the foregoing, the thousands of testimonials, and the realization of the benefits of modeling by the military in World War II, the evidence is overwhelming that the Master Model Engineer deserves the title as "aviation's great recruiter." But shouldn't we also recognize Ed Packard as the "Father of Scale Flying Modeling," if for no other reason than that he was "there" first? Who else could match his accomplishments as early as 1929 in introducing an all-balsa, simplified glued-construction scale-flying model kit nationally, which almost overnight popularized the construction and flying of scale miniatures for youth.

Though simplified in comparison with other manufacturers' kits (no nailing, no wood boiling, and no bamboo), the C-D plans featured moveable control surfaces, landing and flying wires, and innumerable other prototype details that personified scale realism. And the models were capable of outstanding flights. In contrast to other pioneer model manufacturers who were Packard's peers, Packard's designs were faithful representations of their prototypes. This contrast represented the major difference between the C-D entrepreneur and his peers—his feelings for his model engineers were visceral; he recognized them as future pilots, flight engineers and aeronautical engineers, constantly challenging their interests and abilities with the latest historically significant aircraft he offered; involving advanced construction techniques and choices for all types of powered flight.

The youthful modelers of America were regarded as "model engineers" by Packard, by which classification he appealed to them in his catalogs, in his ads, promotional brochures and on his plans. The young aeromodelers were regarded as potential aviators, and Packard set out to make each of his SF plans an educational device toward that end.

As early as 1926 Packard produced a twenty-chapter treatise, "Model Aeronautics, Construction and Flying Instructions." He subsequentially produced a 16mm motion picture dramatizing the principles of flight and model construction and flying available for libraries, schools, and model clubs.

In 1931 he launched *Cleveland Model Engineers News* that evolved into a seven-issue magazine series, *Cleveland Modelmaking and Practical Hobbies* during 1933 and 1934. This publication was never equaled then or since. It was an unparalleled, professionally produced hobby magazine that contained actual full-sized C-D SF plans for scale flying model aircraft, as well as plans for components of a model railroad, ships, autos, and other hobby projects. Many hobbies were promoted and designed to enable youth to become more versatile and more educated concerning models of other types of transportation while further developing their manual dexterity.

By the end of 1932 the C-D line had become the most extensive in the industry and included forty-five models—twenty-six scale types in the SF series and nineteen in the simplified Profile Series. Packard also introduced printwood that year, which eliminated the drudgery of tracing patterns from plans to sheet balsa. In the November 1932 issue of MAN, C-D announced the opening of their multi-hobby store at a former grocery store site at West 57 Street and Bridge Avenue, just a few doors away from the 1866 C-D headquarters. This location was one of the very first hobby stores in the entire country.

In contrast, it was not until 1934 that Joseph Ott entered into a short-lived partnership with Donald F. Duncan (Gold Seal Yo-Yos) known as Model Aircraft Products. When Duncan sold out his interest, Ott went into production in 1935 with 16-inch wingspan kits at 10 cents and 24-inch wingspan kits at 20 cents, manufactured by Western Printing (Racine, Wisconsin) under the brand name of Ace Whitman and marketed and distributed nationally by Whitman Publishing (Big Little Books). In 1937 he contracted with J. L. Wright (Lincoln Logs and Allied Toys) for his manufacturing and sales. In 1940 the Joe Ott Manufacturing Company was formed, and its products were featured in three full pages in the November 1943 issue of *MAN*. Ott left the model industry in the late forties to form a packaging and production machinery design business. Joe Ott must be accorded proper recognition, along with Comet, for conceptualizing low-priced scale-flying kits during the Depression. Ott's 10-cent kits were the introduction to modeling for millions of boys who improved their skills and gained expertise until they were able to construct the more accurate, detailed Cleveland kits.

While two of the other large model manufacturers disappeared from the industry (Bill Bishop, founder of Comet, who sold out in 1948, and Fred Megow, founder of Megows, ceasing production in 1949), Ed Packard continued his business until 1968, when he converted to a plans-only mode until 1996.

Packard as an Aero Historian

Packard embodied the rare combination of entrepreneur, historian, craftsman and marketeer. From C-D's inception he developed a regimen of recording his meetings with famous personalities, historical events and observations on 2¾-by-8½-inch paper strips (four strips per 8½-by-11-inch sheet) to be typed later by one of his office workers. Consequently, he accumulated a voluminous file of these strips typed on both sides, which represented a graphic record of his seventy-some years of involvement in aviation.

He was constantly introducing the latest civil and military aircraft in miniature plus his never equaled line of Thompson and Bendix Trophy winners. In part, his input came from his close association with Major Jack Berry, Cleveland Airport manager. Packard would receive a phone call from Berry's office advising him when any unusual aircraft had landed. However, Packard constantly purchased and subscribed to a wide variety of aviation publications such as *Janes All the World's Aircraft, Aircraft Year Book*, and *Aircraft of the Fighting Powers.* Since he sold many types of aviation and modeling magazines and maintained an extensive file of aviation clippings, he was better informed on aircraft development than most of his peers.

As a craftsman, he carved over a hundred different propellers for experimentation, built innumerable models of all types and established his reputation early on when he built a seven-foot hook and ladder fire truck entirely from memory as a present for his younger brother. It was on display in C-D's Lorain Avenue store window for years and still exists with his son Don.

As a marketeer, his ads in all of the leading modeling publications during the Thirties and Forties attest to his industry leadership. And he actually built the business under the constant threat of the Great Depression, when many famous names in all types of enterprises failed, disappeared or were acquired.

His interfacing with the leading aviation personalities was nothing short of phenomenal. The famous seemed to be attracted to him throughout his career; the list was a veritable *Who's Who* in the industry. Perhaps one of his most enduring relationships was with the late Paul Garber, curator of the Smithsonian's NASM. One aspect of these associations with aviation's notables was that they respected his consummate professionalism in seeking the ultimate replication of the maximum authenticity possible in the realism of scale miniatures. His relationship with TRW artist Charles Hubbell was an excellent example.

Suffice to say, the greatest heritage of the Master Model Engineer was his significant influence on the careers of millions of men who were motivated to seek careers in civil or military aviation or related industries. For that achievement alone he deserves national recognition from both civil and military aviation. His legacy of more than one thousand plans of all types of aircraft will enable modelers, historians, institutions, and even full-size replica builders to utilize his extensive library much as the TV industry relies on the movie industry's archives.

Despite the fact that Packard left school after the ninth grade, he ultimately was recognized by four prestigious aviation organizations: the NASM Smithsonian, the EAA (Experimental Aircraft Association), the Academy of Model Aeronautics (Hall of Fame Award), and the Crawford Auto-Aviation Hall of Fame. These organizations recognized his lifelong dedication to the development of the model airplane hobby. It could be said that throughout his ninety-three years of life, it was the boy in the man that fueled the model builder inside the successful businessman. In his heart, he was first and foremost a Master Model Engineer.

Listing of C-D Scale Model Plans

E. T. Packard dedicated his life to making accurate scale plans of museum quality so that hobbyists, collectors, replica builders, and museums could have accurate scale miniatures. Following is a list of 289 aircraft-scale flying plans compiled by Packard from his Cleveland Model catalogs between 1903 and 1947. This selection represents the most famous, the most significant, or one-of-a-kind or record-setting aircraft, from the 1903 Wright Flyer through World War I and World War II and including several early jet-powered types.

Scale: All plans listed are available in seven scales:
    ⅜"–1' (¹⁄₃₂ size)
    ½"–1' (¹⁄₂₄ size)
    ¾"–1' (¹⁄₁₆ size)
    1"–1' (¹⁄₁₂ size)
    1½"–1' (⅛ size)
    2"–1' (⅙ size)
    3"–1' (¼ size)

Key:
    AF   Air Force
    AR   Army
    CV   Civil (includes pilot, crew, and passengers)
    NV   Navy
    RC   Racer
Note: If no number follows type, it carried only its pilot; a numeral following the designation indicates pilot and crew.

C/D NO.	YEAR	MFR. NAME; TYPE; USE; CREW (INCL. PILOT)	COUNTRY OF ORIGIN	NO.
215	1917	A.E.G G-1V – Light Twin-Engine Bomber	Germany	AR-3
40	1933	AERONCA C-3 Light Sport	USA	CV-2
109	1938	AERONCA 11AC CHIEF – Light Cabin	USA	CV-2
109	1938	AERONCA L-3 Army Liaison	USA	AR-2
117	1949	AERONCA 15AC SEDAN – Light Cabin	USA	CV-2
16	1917	ALBATROS D-III – WW I Fighter	Germany	AR
160	1917	ALBATROS D-V & D-VA – WW I Fighter	Germany	AR
233	1916	ALBATROS C-III – WW I Recon./Bomber	Germany	AR-2
133	1927	ALEXANDER EAGLEROCK A-2 – Biplane OX-5	USA	CV-3
170	1929	AMERICAN EAGLE A-129 & A-229 – Biplane OX-5	USA	CV-3
169	1917	ANSALDO SVA-5 – WW I Scout/Fighter	Italy	AR
169	1917	ANSALDO SVA-9 – WW I Scout/Bomber	Italy	AR-2
11	1916	ARMSTRONG-WHITWORTH QUAD – WW I Exp. Fighter	England	AR-2
182	1929	ARROW SPORT A-2 – Sport Biplane	USA	CV
167	1914	AVRO 504 – WW I Night Bomber/Trainer	England	AR-2
64	1936	BEECHCRAFT C-17B – Neg. Stagger Biplane	USA	CV-4
108	1948	BEECHCRAFT BONANZA – Light Cabin	USA	CV-4
76	1939	BELL P-39 AROCOBRA – WW 2 Fighter	USA	AF
76S	1939	BELL P-39 – TT Race Supplement	USA	RC
189	1947	BELL X-1 – Exp. SS Jet Fighter	USA	AF
237	1931	BELLANCA AIRBUS/AIRCRUISER – Airliner	USA	CV-15
237	1931	BELLANCA Ylc-27 A&B – Army Transport	USA	AR-15
238	1930	BERLINER-JOYCE XFJ-1 – Exp. Fighter	USA	AR
39	1932	BERLINER-JOYCE P-16 – Fighter	USA	AR-2
203	1909	BLERIOT XI – 1st to Cross English Channel	France	CV
157	1919	BOEING MB3-A – Gen. Wm. Mitchell's Fighter	USA	AR
32	1928	BOEING MODEL 95 – Mailplane	USA	CV
257	1928	BOEING MODEL 100 – Sport Biplane	USA	CV
8	1929	BOEING P-12E – Biplane Fighter	USA	AR
29	1931	BOEING F4B-3 & F4B-4 – Fighter	USA	NV
23	1932	BOEING P-26 PEASHOOTER – Monoplane Fighter	USA	AR
1005	1932	BOEING B-9 – Twin Engine Monoplane Bomber	USA	AR-4
35	1933	BOEING 247 – Twin Engine Transport	USA	CV-13
60	1933	BOEING P-26A – Monoplane Fighter	USA	AR
100	1942	BOEING B-17G FLYING FORTRESS – Heavy Bomber	USA	AF-10
200	1944	BOEING B-29 SUPERFORTRESS – Heavy Bomber	USA	AF-12
185	1948	BOEING B-47 STRATOJET – Strategic Bomber	USA	AF-3
195	1952	BOEING B-52 STRATOFORTRESS – Heavy Bomber	USA	AF-6
87	1942	BREWSTER F2A BUFFALO – Fighter/Bomber WW II	USA	AF
168	1914	BRISTOL "D" BULLET – WW I Scout	England	AR
68	1917	BRISTOL F2-B "BRISFIT" – WW I Fighter	England	AR-2
236	1917	BRISTOL M1.C – WW I Fighter	England	AR
194	1928	BRISTOL BULLDOG – Fighter	England	AR

C/D NO.	YEAR	MFR. NAME; TYPE; USE; CREW (INCL. PILOT)	COUNTRY OF ORIGIN	NO.
315	1938	BRISTOL BLENHEIM – WW II Bomber	England	AR
196	1934	BROWN B-2 SPECIAL – "Miss Los Angeles" Racer	USA	RC
503	1928	BRUNNER-WINKLE BIRD – Biplane	USA	CV-3
333	1935	BUCKER BU-133 JUNGMEISTER – Sport/Trainer	Germany	CV
38	1932	BUHL BULL-PUP – Shoulder Wing Sportplane	USA	CV
206	1915	CAUDRON G-III – WW I Obs./Trainer	France	AR-2
63	1935	CAUDRON C-460 – 1936 TT Race Winner	France	RC
119	1940	CESSNA 120 – Light Cabin	USA	CV-2
33	1933	COMPER SWIFT – High Performance Sport	England	RC
56	1933	CONSOLIDATED A-11/P-30 – Attack	USA	AR-2
285	1938	CONSOLIDATED PBY5A CATALINA – Patrol	USA	NV-9
116	1947	COSMIC WIND "MINNOW" – Goodyear Racer	USA	RC
174	1923	COX-KLEMIN XS-1 – Sub Carried Observation (MARTIN MS-1 – Sub Carried Observation)	USA	NV
104	1946	CULVER "V" – Light Cabin	USA	CV-2
202	1911	CURTISS MODEL D – Al Engle's "Bumble Bee"	USA	CV
243	1913	CURTISS E – Pusher Flying Boat	USA	CV-2
4	1915	CURTISS JN4D CANUCK & Variants – Trainer	Canada	CV-2
400	1919	CURTISS NC-4 – 1st Atlantic Crossing	USA	NV-6
314	1919	CURTISS 18-T WASP – Fighter/Racer	USA	AR-2
150	1925	CURTISS R3C-1 – Pulitzer Winner	USA	RC
150	1925	CURTISS R3C-2 – Schneider Winner	USA	RC
132	1925	CURTISS P-1 HAWK – Taperwing Pursuit	USA	AR
214	1926	CURTISS 01-E FALCON – Observation/Mail	USA	AR-2
249	1927	CURTISS F7C-1 SEAHAWK – Fighter	USA	NV
44	1930	CURTISS XG6C-6 – Capt. Page's TT Racer	USA	NV
22	1931	CURTISS F9C-2 SPARROW HAWK – Dirigible Duty	USA	NV
504	1932	CURTISS XP934 SWIFT – Exp. Fighter	USA	AR
25	1932	CURTISS A-8 SHRIKE – Attack	USA	AR-2
7	1933	CURTISS COMMAND HELLDRIVER – Bomber/Fighter	USA	NV-2
21	1933	CURTISS P-6E HAWK – Pursuit	USA	AR
49	1934	CURTISS F11C-2 GOSHAWK – Fighter	USA	NV
50	1934	CURTISS EXPORT HAWK – Supplement to CD-49	USA	NV
142	1937	CURTISS S03C-1 – Scout/Observation	USA	NV-2
277	1939	CURTISS P-36A – Fighter	USA	AR
77	1939	CURTISS P-40 WARHAWK/TOMAHAWK – WW II Fighter	USA	AF
80	1941	CURTISS SBC-4 – Early WW II Dive Bomber	USA	AF-2
226	1942	CURTISS SB2C-4 HELLDRIVER – Fighter/Bomber	USA	NV-2
141	1928	CURTISS-ROBERTSON ROBIN – Cabin monoplane	USA	CV-3
187	1930	CURTISS-WRIGHT JUNIOR – Light Parasol Pusher	USA	CV-2
184	1928	DAVIS D-1 – Light Parasol	USA	CV-2
156	1915	DeHAVILLAND-2 – Box-Kite Fighter/Scout	England	AR-2

C/D NO.	YEAR	MFR. NAME; TYPE; USE; CREW (INCL. PILOT)	COUNTRY OF ORIGIN	NO.
3	1916	DeHAVILLAND-4 – WW I Fighter/Bomber	England	AR-2
148	1916	DeHAVILLAND-5 – WW I Fighter	England	AR
290	1933	DeHAVILLAND DH-85 LEOPARD MOTH – Cabin Mono.	England	CV-2
190	1936	DeHAVILLAND DH-82 TIGER MOTH – Trainer	England	CV-2
51	1937	DeHAVILLAND DH-86 COMET – MacRobertson Winner	England	RC-2
145	1942	DeHAVILLAND DH-98 MOSQUITO – WW II Bomber	England	AR-2
181	1924	DORMOY "FLYING BATHTUB" – Sport/Racer	USA	RC
250	1924	DOUGLAS DWC WORLD CRUISER – Globe Girdler	USA	AR-2
193	1926	DOUGLAS M-2 – Mailplane	USA	CV
43	1932	DOUGLAS O-38 – Observation	USA	AR-2
55	1934	DOUGLAS DC-2 – Twin Engine Airline Transport	USA	CV-17
246	1935	DOUGLAS O-46A – Observation	USA	AR-3
165	1936	DOUGLAS DC-3 – Airline Transport	USA	CV-24
165	1936	DOUGLAS C-47 – ATC Transport/Freight	USA	AR-4
89	1941	DOUGLAS SBD DAUNTLESS – Dive Bomber	USA	NV-2
89	1941	DOUGLAS A-24 – Dive Bomber	USA	AF-2
115	1942	DOUGLAS A-20 HAVOC – Medium Attack Bomber	USA	AF-3
103	1947	ERCO ERCOUPE – Light Cabin	USA	CV-2
221	1927	FAIRCHILD KR-21 – Sport Biplane	USA	CV-2
220	1930	FAIRCHILD KR-34 – Sport Biplane	USA	CV-2
219	1940	FAIRCHILD PT-19 – Primary Trainer	USA	AR-2
218	1943	FAIRCHILD PT-26 – Canopied Primary Trainer	USA	AR-2
67	1935	FAIRLEY "BATTLE" – All Purpose RAF Aircraft	England	AR-2
178	1929	FLEET MODEL 2 – Sport/Trainer	USA	CV-2
82	1941	FOCK-WULF FW.190 – WW II Fighter/Interceptor	Germany	AR
144	1915	FOKKER E-III EINDECKER – WW I Fighter	Germany	AR
14	1917	FOKKER DR.1 – WW I Triplane Fighter	Germany	AR
15	1917	FOKKER D-VII – WW I Biplane Fighter	Germany	AR
34	1918	FOKKER D-VIII – WW I Parasol Fighter	Germany	AR
71	1937	FOLKERTS SPEED KING – 1937 TT Winner	USA	RC
235	1927	FORD 4-AT – Tri-motor Transport	USA	CV-13
186	1930	FRANKLIN SPORT – Light Biplane	USA	CV-2
17	1931	GEE-BEE MODEL Z – 1931 TT Winner	USA	RC
27	1932	GEE-BEE R-1 – 1932 TT Winner	USA	RC
96	1946	GLOBE SWIFT – Light Cabin	USA	CV-2
210	1934	GLOSTER GLADIATOR – Biplane Fighter	England	AR
245	1916	GOTHA G-IV – WW I Twin Engine Bomber	Germany	AR-3
57	1929	GREAT LAKES 2T-1 – Sport/Trainer	USA	CV-2
1	1929	GREAT LAKES 2T-1A – Sport/Trainer	USA	CV-2
242	1932	GRUMMAN J2-F ⅙ DUCK – Utility Amphibian	USA	NV-2
53	1932	GRUMMAN F2F-1 Navy Fighter	USA	NV

C/D NO.	YEAR	MFR. NAME; TYPE; USE; CREW (INCL. PILOT)	COUNTRY OF ORIGIN	NO.
70	1936	GRUMMAN F3F-3 GULFHAWK – Al William's Plane	USA	CV
83	1940	GRUMMAN F4F-3 WILDCAT – WW II Fighter	USA	NV
75	1941	GRUMMAN XF5F-1 SKYROCKET – Exp. Fighter	USA	NV
93	1943	GRUMMAN TBF AVENGER – WW II Torpedo Plane	USA	NV-3
97	1943	GRUMMAN F6F HELLCAT – WW II Fighter	USA	NV
197	1945	GRUMMAN F8F BEARCAT – WW II Fighter	USA	NV
111	1948	GRUMMAN F9F PANTHER – Navy Jet Fighter	USA	NV
31	1932	HALL'S SPRINGFIELD BULLDOG – TT Racer	USA	RC
275	1916	HANDLEY PAGE 0400 (0100) – WW I Bomber	England	AR-4
163	1917	HANOVER CL.IIIA – WW I Attack/Recon.	Germany	AR-2
164	1916	HANRIOT HD-1 – WW I Fighter	France	AR
229	1917	HANSA-BRANDENBURG W-29 – Floatplane Fighter	Germany	AR-2
20	1931	HAWKER FURY – Biplane Fighter	England	AR
507	1933	HAWKER HIND – Biplane Fighter/Bomber	England	AR-2
59	1937	HAWKER HURRICANE I – WW II Fighter	England	AR
78	1938	HAWKER MK II HURRICANE – WW II Fighter	England	AR
99	1941	HAWKER TYPHOON – Bomber/Ground Attack/Fighter	England	AR
177	1928	HEATH BABY BULLET – 32 HP-178 MPH	USA	RC
26	1930	HEATH LNB-4 Light Parasol Monoplane	USA	CV
18	1931	HOWARD DGA-3 PETE – 1930 & 1931 TT Racer	USA	RC
42	1932	HOWARD DGA-4 MIKE & DGA-5 IKE – TT Racers	USA	RC
52	1935	HOWARD DGA-6 MR. MULLIGAN – 1935 TT Winner	USA	RC-2
54	1935	HUGHES H-1 – World Land Speed Record 352.388	USA	RC
183	1929	INLAND SPORT S-300 – Parasol Monoplane	USA	CV-2
84	1940	JUNKERS JU87 – WW II Dive Bomber	Germany	AR-2
225	1940	JUNKERS JU88A5 & JU88S – Fighter/Bomber	Germany	AR-2
216	1920	LAIRD SWALLOW – Early "Jenny" Replacement	USA	CV-3
46	1930	LAIRD SOLUTION – 1930 TT Winner	USA	RC
5	1931	LAIRD SUPER SOLUTION – Doolittle's TT Racer (Bendix)	USA	RC
72	1938	LAIRD-TURNER LTR-14 – 1938, 1939 TT Winner	USA	RC
305	1919	LAWSON C-2 – 1st Airliner Designed as Such	USA	CV-28
204	1908	LEVASSEUR ANTOINETTE VII – Latham's Craft	France	CV
36	1933	LINCOLN SPORT – Szekely Powered Biplane	USA	CV
247	1928	LOCKHEED AIR EXPRESS – Turner's Gilmore Spec.	USA	CV-5
24	1931	LOCKHEED VEGA – High Performance Cabin	USA	CV-5
533	1933	LOCKHEED SIRIUS – Lindy's World Explorer	USA	CV-2
65	1935	LOCKHEED MODEL 11 ELECTRA – Airline Transport	USA	CV-12
95	1939	LOCKHEED MODEL 14 HUDSON – WW II Bomber	USA	AR-5
85	1939	LOCKHEED P-38 LIGHTNING – WW II Fighter	USA	AF
90	1946	LOCKHEED F-80 SHOOTING STAR – Jet Fighter	USA	AF

C/D NO.	YEAR	MFR. NAME; TYPE; USE; CREW (INCL. PILOT)	COUNTRY OF ORIGIN	NO.
121	1950	LOCKHEED F-90 – Jet Fighter	USA	AF
241	1928	LOENING C-2 AIR YACHT – Amphibian Airliner	USA	CV-9
241	1928	LOENING OL-8 – US Navy Utility Amphibian	USA	NV-9
118	1948	LONG MIDGET MUSTANG – Goodyear Racer	USA	RC
106	1939	LUSCOMBE SILVAIRE – Cabin Monoplane	USA	CV-2
112	1949	LUSCOMBE SEDAN – Cabin Monoplane	USA	CV-2
213	1916	MACCHI M.5 – WW I Flying Boat Fighter	Italy	AR
136	1934	MACCHI-CASTOLDI – World's Speed Record 440 MPH	Italy	RC
205	1918	MARTIN MB-1 – Twin Engine Bomber	USA	AR-4
205S1	1919	MARTIN MB-1 – Passenger & Cargo Supplement	USA	CV-9
274	1927	MARTIN 74 & T4M-1 Torpedo Carrier	USA	NV-2
300	1935	MARTIN 130 CHINA CLIPPER – PAA Flying Boat	USA	CV-37
45	1934	MARTIN B-10 – Twin Engine Bomber	USA	AR-3
135	1942	MARTIN B-26 MARAUDER – WW II Medium Bomber	USA	AF-6
110	1947	McDONNELL FH-1 PHANTOM – Jet Fighter	USA	NV
122	1947	McDONNELL F1H BANSHEE – Jet Fighter	USA	NV
127	1948	McDONNELL XF-88 VOODOO – Exp. Jet Fighter	USA	NV
74	1939	MESSERSCHMITT BF109E – WW II Luftwaffe Fighter	Germany	AR
124	1947	M.I.G. 15 – Korean & Vietnam Jet Fighter	USSR	AR
86	1940	MITSUBISHI ZERO – WW II Japanese Fighter	Japan	AR
28	1932	MONOCOUPE SPORTPLANE – Light Cabin Mono.	USA	CV-2
152	1917	MORAINE-SAULNIER A1– WW I Fighter	France	AR
171	1916	NIEUPORT 17.C – Exp. Neg. Stagger Triplane	France	AR
12	1916	NIEUPORT 17.C1 – Bishop's WW I Fighter	France	AR
30	1917	NIEUPORT 28.C1 – WW I Fighter	France	AR
125	1938	NORTH AMERICAN B-25 MITCHELL – WW II Bomber	USA	AF-6
91BU	1940	NORTH AMERICAN P-51B MUSTANG – WW II Fighter	USA	AF
91DU	1940	NORTH AMERICAN P-51D MUSTANG – WW II Fighter	USA	AF
107	1947	NORTH AMERICAN NAVION – Cabin Monoplane	USA	CV-4
175.	1947	NORTH AMERICAN B-45 TORNADO – Jet Bomber	USA	AF-3
120	1947	NORTH AMERICAN F-86 SABRE – Jet Fighter	USA	AF
260	1933	NORTHROP GAMMA – Both Mail and Passenger	USA	CV-10
155	1943	NORTHROP P-61 BLACK WIDOW – Night Fighter	USA	AF-3
128	1948	NORTHROP F-89 SCORPION – All Weather Fighter	USA	AF
268	1918	PACKARD-LE PERE LUSAC-11 – WW I Fighter/Recon.	USA	AR-2
161	1917	PFALZ D-III – WW I Scout/Fighter	Germany	AR
162	1918	PFALZ D-XII – WW I Fighter	Germany	AR
94J	1936	PIPER J-3 CUB – Light Transport	USA	CV-2
94L	1936	PIPER L-4 - Army Liaison	USA	AR-2
192	1945	PIPER PA-8 SKYCYCLE – Light Sport	USA	CV
151	1927	PITCAIRN PA-5 MAILWING – Mailplane	USA	CV

C/D NO.	YEAR	MFR. NAME; TYPE; USE; CREW (INCL. PILOT)	COUNTRY OF ORIGIN	NO.
239	1941	PITCAIRN-LARSEN PA-39 – Coastal Ptl. Autogyro	USA	AR-2
217	1937	POLIKAROPV I-16 – Fighter/Ground Attack	USSR	AR
188	1923	POWELL RACER – Early Homebuilt Racer	USA	RC
6	1929	P.Z.L. P-6 PONTSWOWE – Fighter	Poland	AR
69	1937	REARWIN SPEEDSTER – Cabin Monoplane	USA	CV-2
81	1941	REPUBLIC P-47 THUNDERBOLT – WW II Fighter	USA	AF
88	1941	REPUBLIC B9F SEABEE – Amphibian Sport	USA	CV-2
113	1946	REPUBLIC F84B THUNDERJET – Jet Fighter	USA	AF
126	1946	REPUBLIC F84G THUNDERJET – Jet Fighter	USA	AF
209	1914	ROYAL AIRCRAFT FACTORY BE2C – WW I Recon.	England	AR-2
166	1916	ROYAL AIRCRAFT FACTORY RE8 – WW I Recon.	England	AR-2
9	1917	ROYAL AIRCRAFT FACTORY SE-5 – WW I Fighter	England	AR
234	1914	RUMPLER 4C TAUBE – WW I Reconnaissance	Germany	AR-2
154	1916	RUMPLER C-IV – WW I Reconnaissance	Germany	AR-2
211	1927	RYAN N.Y.P. – Lindy's Spirit of St. Louis	USA	CV
58	1936	RYAN ST. – Sport Monoplane	USA	CV-2
92	1944	RYAN FR-1 FIREBALL – Jet Fighter	USA	NV
240	1916	SALMSON S.A.L. 2A2 – Recon./General Purpose	France	AR-2
180	1907	SANTOS-DUMONT DEMOISELLE 21 – Early Homebuilt	France	CV
61	1937	SEVERSKY P-35 – Fighter	USA	AR
244	1918	SIEMANS-SCHUCKERT D-IV – WW I Fighter	Germany	AR
255	1928	SIKORSKY S-38 – Amphibian Airliner	USA	CV-14
191	1955	SMITH DSA-2 MINIPLANE – Homebuilt	USA	CV
143	1913	SOPWITH TABLOID – WW I Fighter	England	AR
137	1914	SOPWITH TABLOID– 1914 Schneider Winner	England	RC
138	1915	SOPWITH BABY – WW I Coastal Patrol	England	NV
147	1915	SOPWITH 1½ STRUTTER – WW I Reconnaissance	England	AR-2
140	1916	SOPWITH TRIPEHOUND – WW I Triplane Fighter	England	AR
139	1916	SOPWITH PUP – WW I Fighter/Trainer	England	AR
10	1916	SOPWITH 1F-1 CAMEL – WW I Fighter	England	AR
173	1917	SOPWITH 5F-1 DOLPHIN – WW I Neg. Stagger Fighter	England	AR
153	1917	SOPWITH 7F-1 SNIPE – WW I Fighter	England	AR
13	1917	S.P.A.D. XIII – WW I Fighter	France	AR
252	1937	SPARTAN 7W EXECUTIVE – Low Wing Transport	USA	CV-4
134	1920	SPERRY MESSENGER – Exp. AC Biplane	USA	AR
131	1916	STANDARD J-1 – WW I Trainer/Barnstormer	USA	AR-2
266	1927	STEARMAN C3B & C3MB – Sport/Mail Biplane	USA	CV-2
267	1931	STEARMAN C3R SPORTSTER – Business/Sport	USA	CV-2
149	1937	STEARMAN PT-17 KAYDET – WW II Primary Trainer	USA	AR-2
265	1933	STINSON A – Trimotor Airline Transport	USA	CV-10
66	1935	STINSON SR-7 – Taperwing Transport (Gullwing)	USA	CV-4
98	1938	STINSON 105 VOYAGER – Light Cabin	USA	CV-2

C/D NO.	YEAR	MFR. NAME; TYPE; USE; CREW (INCL. PILOT)	COUNTRY OF ORIGIN	NO.
114	1947	STINSON 108 STATION WAGON – Light Cabin	USA	CV-2
176	1930	STOUT SKY-CAR – Light Cabin	USA	CV-2
19	1931	SUPERMARINE S.6B – Schneider Trophy Winner	England	RC
73	1939	SUPERMARINE SPITFIRE – WW II Fighter	England	AR
102	1936	TAYLOR J-2 CUB – Light Cabin	USA	CV-2
146	1918	THOMAS-MORSE S4B & S4C – Fighter/Trainer	USA	AR
198	1925	TRAVEL AIR (BEECH) 2000 – OX-5 Biplane	USA	CV-2
198SL	1925	TRAVEL AIR (BEECH) Suppl. 1000; 3000; 4000	USA	CV-2
2	1929	TRAVEL AIR MYSTERY SHIP – '29 Thompson Cup	USA	RC
199	1929	TRAVEL AIR 6000 – Cabin Monoplane	USA	CV-6
172	1930	TRAVEL AIR TEXACO #13 – Hawk's Record Ship	USA	RC
129	1927	VERVILLE SPORTSMAN – Sleek Golden Ager	USA	CV-2
129	1927	VERVILLE PT-10C - Air Corps Trainer	USA	AR-2
208	1916	VICKERS FB5 & 9 GUN BUS – WW I Fighter	England	AR-2
207	1916	VICKERS FB12-B & E – WW I Fighter	England	AR-2
325	1919	VICKERS VIMY – 1st Transatlantic Non-stop	England	AR-2
232	1919	VOUGHT VE-7 – Recon. Float/Land Plane	USA	NV-2
232	1919	VOUGHT VE-9 – Recon./Fighter Float Plane	USA	NV-2
179	1925	VOUGHT O2U-¼ CORSAIR – Recon./Fighter	USA	NV-2
41	1933	VOUGHT V-65 CORSAIR – Biplane Fighter	USA	NV-2
79	1940	VOUGHT F4U CORSAIR - WW II Bent Wing Fighter	USA	NV
123	1948	VOUGHT F7U CUTLASS – Tailless Jet Fighter	USA	NV
158	1928	W.A.W. CORP. THUNDERBIRD – OX-5 Biplane	USA	CV-3
130	1927	WACO 10 – Sport Biplane OX-5 Powered	USA	CV-3
230	1929	WACO TAPERWING – Sport Biplane	USA	CV-3
227	1937	WACO UPF-7 – Sport Biplane	USA	CV-3
37	1933	WACO C – Cabin Biplane	USA	CV-4
228	1935	WACO D EXPORT – Waco's Export model	USA	CV-2
62	1936	WACO C-6 – Custom Cabin Biplane	USA	CV-4
248	1931	WEDELL-WILLIAMS – Turner's "Red Lion" #121	USA	RC
292	1932	WEDELL-WILLIAMS – Haizlip's TT Racer #92	USA	RC
47	1933	WEDELL-WILLIAMS – Wedell's #44 '33 TT Winner	USA	RC
48	1934	WEDELL-WILLIAMS – Turner's #57 '34 TT Winner	USA	RC
231	1936	WESTLAND LYSANDER - WW II Cooperative Craft	England	AR-2
105	1944	WESTLAND WHIRLWIND – WW II Fighter	England	AR
159	1934	WILEY POST SPORT – Ford A-1 Power Plant	USA	CV
201	1903	WRIGHT BROTHERS' "FLYER" – The 1st Airplane	USA	CV
212	1922	WRIGHT NW-1 "MYSTERY" – Schneider Entry	USA	RC

C-D Stock Prospectus and
Evaluation, 1929

P R O S P E C T U S

- - - 0 - - -

CLEVELAND MODEL AND SUPPLY COMPANY

<u>S T O C K</u>

Authorized 250 Shares No Par Common
Stock of an established value of
One-Hundred Dollars ($100.00) per
Share.

PURPOSE CLAUSE

To engage generally in the manufacturing
business, and to buy and sell either retail or wholesale; to handle any and all classes of fabric and material;
to buy and sell real estate, and the doing of all things
necessary and incidental thereto.

PURPOSE BRIEFLY IS

1. To manufacture kits for building model airplanes to 3/4 inch scale.

2. To manufacture exhibition model airplanes to 1/4 inch scale.

3. To issue on 8½ by 11, twenty pound bond paper, scale outline drawings of all the most popular present day and war time commercial airplanes. These drawings will be printed to allow clipping them together in book form. The drawings will have scales for ¼ and ¾ inch to the foot model construction.

4. To design and produce a kit for a commercial model airplane to fill the gap between the present "stick" models and the scale models which are fast becoming the vogue; this kit to be produced for Christmas sales.

5. To develop scale models to a point closely resembling the full size practice of aircraft design and construction, and still give not only ordinary but creditable flying performance.

6. To develop two universal kits which will permit the construction of practically any single motored mono or biplane complete with the exception of motor cylinders, wheels, propellors and drawings. When an order is received, the parts required to construct the special model ordered, will be selected and inserted with one of the universal kits, the box labeled accordingly, and shipped.

7. To develop a universal trimotor kit, which will be used as the kits mentioned in number 6.

8. To establish an experimental laboratory for testing thoroughly all designs and details of model construction before undertaking the actual shop work. This laboratory will include a 36 inch wind tunnel, a chemical recorder for such instruments as sensitive propellor testing devices, etc., precision scales and other instruments necessary to the successful design of scientific model airplanes.

9. To develop models for aircraft companies or clubs as a separate service apart from ordinary production.

PERSONNEL OF ORGANIZATION

Officers of The Cleveland Model and Supply Company

President	E. T. Pachasa
Vice President	Captain H. C. Richardson
Vice President- In charge of sales	H. M. Conders
Secretary	J. T. Bergeron
Treasurer	R. B. Robinette
Director of Engineering	Captain H. C. Richardson
Engineer	R. W. Germain
Shop Superintendent	William Pachasa
Attorney	J. T. Bergeron
Accountant	F. W. Gasse

- - - - - -

PROPOSED   BOARD   OF   DIRECTORS

P. W. Close-   General Manager of The Standard Oil Company of Ohio

Capt. H. C. Richardson-Formerly of the United States Navy in charge of
                          Float Designs.
                          Director of Engineering of Allied Motor Industries.
                          Vice President of The Great Lakes Aircraft Corp.

R. B. Robinette-   Vice President & Treasurer-The Tropical Paint & Oil
                            "   "   The Cleveland Chamber of Commerce

W. H. Halle-   With Halle Bros. Company.

John S. King-   Advertising

J. T. Bergeron-   Attorney

E. T. Pachasa-   President

James D. Hartshorne-   Aviation Editor The Cleveland Plain Dealer.

THE WORLD'S MOST BEAUTIFUL, LONG DISTANCE FLYING, SCALE MODEL AIRPLANE

CLEVELAND MODEL & SUPPLY COMPANY
Model Engineers
1866 West 57th Street
CLEVELAND, OHIO

Fellow Model Enthusiast,

Dear Friend:

Here is a photograph of our ¾" scale model of The Great Lakes Sport Trainer, Model 2T-1. Would you like to build a model of this little beauty, colored international orange and black? There is no denying that it is one of the world's most beautiful models, and as to its flying qualities, we-- we shall not tell you too much about it, but our models have flown over 500 feet and they were constructed from the same drawing you will use.

(CUT)

It is scientifically engineered and as near perfectly proportioned as it is mechanically possible in the ¾" scale for model flying contests. This model is not only as beautiful as the real ship, but also flies as well as the real ship. This fact can be attributed to the special new model wing section which we have developed.

Its specifications are: Span 20"   Length 15"   Height 6"
Cord 3"   and Gap 3¼". Its weight is exactly 1 ounce.

We designed this ship for you so you would have no difficulty in constructing it. On our large drawing, 34" x 44", every detail is drawn full size, with cut-out patterns for all important parts. The hardest parts are already done, for the nose blocks are partly finished and the wheels and nose spinner are made. The following is a complete list of the material you will receive in a kit for this model:

Complete wood (more than needed)	Japanese Tissue	Sandpaper
Lower nose block	Nose spinners	Ballast material
Upper " "	Propeller material	Ambroid cement
Spool #5 music wire	Snap fasteners	Clear banana oil
Spool #8 " "	Propeller shaft bearing	Black " "
Balsa wheels	Washers	Clear 15-85 dope
Rubber motor	Wing alligning material	Int.Orange" "
Windshield celluloid	Large drawing, 34" x 44"	Everything drawn full size.

This complete kit will be mailed to you immediately upon receipt of $ 4.75 plus the packing and mailing charges of twenty cents. Send for yours now.

Hoping that we may have the pleasure of sending you one of these kits within the next few days, we are,
                                        Very truly yours,

                                        CLEVELAND MODEL & SUPPLY COMPANY

S A L E S

Sales for last four years. Shows growth of Company.

Sales

1926	$ 442.79	
1927	554.18	
1928	761.92	
1929	6,599.42	full time 9 months.

Profit at least 100% on cost.

Gross Profit in 1929- $ 3,600.00

Expense

Light	$ 60.00	
Phone	125.00	
Pay Roll	400.00	
Salary	1,000.00	
General Expense	400.00	1,985.00
		$ 1,615.00

STATEMENT OF ASSETS & LIABILITIES

ASSETS

Cash		$ 204.23	
Accounts Receivable		215.52	
Inventory			
Machinery & Tools	$2,067.00		
Drafting & Equipment	290.00		
Office Furniture	75.00		
Stationery & Office Supplies			
Advertising Material	454.80		
Drawings	950.00		
Material & Finished Goods	4,085.67		
Good Will	2,000.00	$9,922.47	$10,342.22

LIABILITIES

Accounts Payable	285.82	
Back Salaries	456.40	
(Stock Sold) Advanced	700.00	
	1,442.22	
250 Shares present worth	8,900.00	$10,342.22

SUMMARY

ESTIMATED INCOME

City Sales and Direct Mail.

	Present Line	G.L.A.C.	New Waco	Robin	Ospry	Commer	Total
Jan.	700.00						$ 700.00
Feb.	800.00	1125.00					1,925.00
Mar.	900.00	1125.00	1125.00				3,150.00
Apr.	1000.00	1875.00	1875.00	650.00			5,400.00
May	1200.00	1125.00	2645.00	975.00	600.00	450.00	6,995.00
June	1200.00	375.00	1875.00	1300.00	1200.00	450.00	6,400.00
July	1000.00	162.00	750.00	325.00	300.00	450.00	2,987.00
Aug.	800.00			100.00		450.00	1,350.00
Sept.	1000.00			200.00			1,200.00
Oct.	1400.00			400.00		225.00	2,025.00
Nov.	1500.00	375.00	750.00	325.00	600.00	450.00	4,000.00
Dec.	1000.00	1125.00	2645.00	975.00	1800.00	9000.00	16,545.00
Totals	12500.00	7287.00	11665.00	5250.00	4500.00	11475.00	$ 52,677.00

ESTIMATED EXPENSE

Approximately $4000.00 per month, for the full program. This includes cost of material.

Income to January 15th - 1930 $500.00

C-D PROSPECTUS-EVALUATION (1929)

After the decision had been reached to incorporate, a practice which was so widespread in this era resulting in a cresendo of all types of business incorporations, financial assistance from his directors expedited the preparation of a prospectus. Most likely, C-D was the only model aircraft manufacturer to issue a stock prospectus, in the pre-1930's time period. The capitalization authorization was established @250 shares of No Par Common @$100 per share for a total of $25,000. (approximately $300,000 in current inflationary dollars.)

Purpose #2- The manufacture of ¼ inch scale exhibition scale models was never implemented, However, a series of accurate, impressive 1/4 inch/1/8 inch scale model plans was issued along with a binder in which C-D hoped that it would become a repository for all the C-D following plans and promotional newsletters and flyers.

Purpose #4- The concept of a series of profile scale flying models was innovative and resulted in a total of eleven different types under 20 inch wingspan; three large span models over 30 inch and four unique multi-engine types including two capable of R.O.W. flights. This profile concept has been re-invented currently with many such types offered in gas powered CL types by contemporary manufacturers.

Purpose #6-To develop two universal kits with components which could be adapted to almost any of the various designs for which kits were made. This was indeed a most laudable goal and objective. However, there is just no such standardization possible with scale aircraft for there is such a wide divergence in their designs to preclude standardization.

Purpose #8- The objective of a lab incorporating a wind tunnel as was initiated by the Wright brothers was a worthy goal. However, the testing of models versus the testing of man carrying designs is quite different due mostly to the much higher speeds which the prototypes attain. Hence, most likely it was determined the best testing was to conduct flying experiments outdoors or indoors in auditoriums and make design changes accordingly.

Purpose #9- To develop models for aircraft companies or clubs as
a separate service was never implemented with the exception of the
construction of special models for VIP's such as Rickenbacker, Billy
Bishop and Captain Richardson. The negative impact of the Great Depression
plus the difficulty of realizing profitability from such a custom type
of operation no doubt seriously jeopardized the implementation of this
objective.

Projected Sales, Expense and Profit Projections

		SALES	EXPENSE	PROFIT
1929	(9 months)	$6599 (actual)	$2999 (actual)	$3600 (actual)
	yr./2001 amount	$80000 (approx.)	$36000	$44000
1930	(est.full year)	$52677	$48000	$4677
	yr./2001 amount	$632000 (approx.)	$576000	$56000 8.9% net

1. The forecast was notable for its projection of
   a profit in the first year of operation.

2. Obviously, the objectives would have to be revised in
   light of the effects of the Great Depression which began
   in 1930. However, the actual results would show
   that C-D established itself as a successful national and
   world wide hobby manufacturer, wholesaler and retailer in
   spite of the nearly decade long depression in contrast to
   many famous aviation manufacturers which were acquired,
   consolidated, merged or simply went out of business.

National Air Race Winners and the C-D Model Kits

YEAR	THOMPSON TROPHY*	C-D KIT	BENDIX TROPHY	C-D KIT
1928 (L.A.)	—	—	—	—
1929 (Cleve.)	Doug Davis, Travel-Air R	SF-2, D-2	—	—
1930 (Chic.)	"Speed" Holman, Laird "Solution"	F-46, D-46	—	—
1931 (Cleve.)	Lowell Bayles, Gee-Bee Z	SF-17, D-17	Jimmy Doolittle, Laird "Super LC-DW500 Solution""Sky Buzzard"	SF-5, D-5
1932 (Cleve.)	Jimmy Doolittle, Gee-Bee R-1	SF-27, D-27	James Haizlip, Wedell-Williams	SF-47, D-47
1933 (L.A.)	Jimmie Wedell, No. 44 Wedell-Williams	SF-47, D-47	Roscoe Turner, Wedell-Williams	SF-47, D-47
1934 (Cleve.)	Roscoe Turner, No. 57 Wedell-Williams	SF-48, D-48	Doug Davis, Wedell-Williams	SF-47, D-47
1935 (Cleve.)	Harold Neumann, Howard's "Mr. Mulligan," Howard DGA-6	SF-52, D-52	Benny Howard, "Mr. Mulligan," Howard DGA-6	SF-52, D-52
1936 (L.A.)	Michael Detroyat, French Caudron C-460	SF-63, D-63	Louis Thaden, Staggerwing Beech C-17R	SF-64, D-64
1937 (Cleve.)	Rudy Kling, SK-3 "Jupiter"	SF-1, D-71	Frank Fuller Jr., Seversky Sev-S2	SF-61, D-61
1938 (Cleve.)	Roscoe Turner, "Pesco Special," L-RT Meteor	SF-72, D-72	Jacqueline Cochrane, Seversky Sev-S2	SF-61, D-61
1939 (Cleve.)	Roscoe Turner, "Turner Laird," L-RT Meteor	SF-72, D-72	Frank Fuller Jr., Seversky Sev-S2	SF-61, D-61

Note: SF series, ¾-inch scale; D series, ½-inch scale. Cleveland Model and Supply was the only model maker to offer all the Thompson Trophy winners.

Cleveland Model and Supply Volunteer Model Engineers

William E. Brazis	Wayne C. Love
F. L. Deemar	Marion McClure
Phillip Eagan	Earl O. Menefee
Al J. Engel	R. D. Meyers
Lynn W. Fehr	Joe Nieto
W. J. De Flourville	A. C. Olson
Fred Floyd	Gordon Plaxton
G. Ford	James D. Powell
R. L. "Dick" Gates	Rudy Profant
R. W. Geer	F. T. Roberts
W. T. Given III	Dan Scherry
W. W. Grundeman	Richard L. Schulenberg
David Hatfield	Charles F. Schultz
R. A. Hawkins	J. K. "Ken" Sniffen
Ron E. Henderson	Charles E. Steinchak
C. H. Hubbell	Don Stroble
Paul Kirk	Jack M. Tarbox
R. G. Kitchell	Robert S. Thompson
R. W. Lawson	R. P. Tilley
Les Lipsius	E. Weber

Modelers Who Made It

The following list includes some of the outstanding modelers whose hobby was responsible for motivating them to achieve success in model aviation, aviation, or related careers.

William Atwood (Los Angeles)—Builder of gas-powered cars, boats, and aircraft; was best known for designing engines with the rotary valve, particularly the Baby Cyclone.

Hurst Bowers (Maclean, Virginia)—A modeler who became an Air Force colonel; cofounded Flyline Models with Herb Clukey and became curator of the first AMA Museum in Reston, Virginia.

Peter Bowers (Seattle)—Expert modeler and designer; author and photographer with one of the largest aircraft photo collections; became a Boeing aircraft engineer; built Pietenpol Camper aircraft; designed the successful Flybaby kit that was promoted through the EAA.

William Brown (Philadelphia)—Early model builder who founded Junior Motors Corporation in Philadelphia; developed one of the first successful two-cycle miniature model engines, the Brown Jr. ($21.50) in the early 1930s, which powered Joe Kovel's gas model, ushering in the era of the gas-powered model in 1935.

Dan Bunch (Los Angeles)—Modeler who founded Bunch Motors in Los Angeles, producing miniature engines for model cars, boats, and aircraft.

Louis N. Casale (Syracuse, New York)—Modeler who became NAA Scale Model Champion in 1934, 1935, and 1936 with a scratch-built Waco Taperwing (¾-inch scale) that led to a position at Douglas Aircraft Company in 1937 in the Wind Tunnel Model Design Group; built the models used in the Disney film *Victory through Air Power* and produced the Casalaire, an all-metal 45-inch Class B or C gas model for $18.50 in 1947.

Jack Cox (Santee, South Carolina)—Exposed to the hobby of model airplane building as soon as he was permitted to use razor blades, young Jack learned about the primary aerodynamics of flight as well as typical aircraft structural components—all of which served to heighten his enthusiasm for a career in aviation. He came to the attention of the EAA's Paul Poberezny as a result of Jack's sparkling editing of the Vintage Aircraft Association's *Chapter 3* publication and his service on the staff of Wings & Wheels Transportation Museum in Santee, South Carolina. In January 1970 Jack and his wife, Golda, joined the staff of the incipient EAA at the Milwaukee suburb of Hales

Corners, Wisconsin, when membership was at the 24,000 mark. (That figure has since grown to a remarkable 170,000.) Jack served at EAA headquarters in several administrative positions, including general manager and the founder of the *Vintage Airplane* publication, while his wife filled an important slot in advertising. In 1970 he became editor-in-chief of *Sport Aviation,* the EAA's impressive, slick monthly that has become the vaunted voice of the EAA. In 1999 Jack's reluctant retirement as editor left a gaping void; however, his legacy still has "legs," and, fortunately, Jack continues to submit colorful articles and photos.

Michael G. Fulmer (Visalia, California)—Expert modeler who founded Aerospace Model and Supply; became associated with the Lucasfilm's Industrial Light and Magic organization, producing models and props for films such as *Star Wars;* as curator and designer of the AMA Museum (Muncie, Indiana) directed construction of the exhibits depicting the history of model building in America.

Paul Garber (Washington, D.C.)—Pioneer model builder and founder of the Capitol Model Aero Club in 1913; author of *Building and Flying Model Aircraft* (1928); became model editor of *U.S. Air Services* magazine; first curator of the Smithsonian's NASM.

Richard Gates (Sheboygan, Wisconsin)—Became a consulting engineer for national firms like the Kohler Company and then became a C-D volunteer model engineer, drawing several plans that were based on his measuring the actual prototype.

Carl Goldberg (Chicago)—Pioneer indoor designer, contest winner; designed and flew the 10-foot pylon-mounted gas-powered *Valkyrie* from which he scaled down the 54-inch contest-winning *Zipper* after joining Comet. He subsequently founded his own company, Carl Goldberg Products, Ltd.

Barry Goldwater (Phoenix, Arizona)—An early model builder who built many Cleveland kits and carried on a long-term correspondence with Packard. He became an Air Force colonel, having previously soloed in a Great Lakes Sport Trainer; became U.S. senator (R-Arizona), and subsequently was made an Air Force major-general.

Charles Hampson Grant (Peru, Vermont)—Grant was one of the few aeronautical engineers who achieved fame in both model aviation and prototype designing. He founded the Grant Aircraft Model League and taught modeling at his boys' camp for many years in New Hampshire. Grant revolutionized *Model Airplane News* for a decade as editor, beginning in 1932, and published a book, *Model Airplane Design and Theory of Flight.* In 1968 he received the Frank Brewer Award for the development of youth by character building and his contribution to model aviation design.

Maynard Hill—In 2003, in his late seventies, legally blind, and hearing impaired, Hill launched his gas-powered, radio-controlled 6-foot Spirit of Butts Farm TAM 5 endurance model from Cape Spear, Newfoundland. After 38 hours and 52 minutes, the TAM 5 came into view at Clifden County, Galway, Ireland, 1,882 miles across the Atlantic and was safely landed by Dave Brown, AMA president. After more than twenty years of experimenting with models, and after numerous failed extended flight attempts, Hill set a new world record.

Stanley Hiller (Palo Alto, California)—Model builder who at age twelve in 1936 had $100,000 in sales producing miniature race cars. In 1948 he received a CAA certificate for a commuter helicopter and went into production on the Hiller Helicopter.

John Jacox (Indianapolis)—Model builder who pioneered in jet propulsion for models and then as a graduate engineer joined Pratt and Whitney. He then served as chief project engineer for missile engines with a major manufacturer. In 1996 he became the new owner of Cleveland Model and Supply Company (www.clevelandairline.com).

E. M. "Matty" Laird (Chicago)—An early model builder in the Illinois Model Club, he participated in contests and later awarded prizes. He founded E. M. Laird Company in Chicago, building the Laird *Solution,* 1930 Thompson Trophy winner; *Super Solution,* 1931 Bendix Trophy winner; and the 1938–39 Turner-Laird Thompson Trophy winners.

Paul McCready (Monrovia, California)—Model builder who was motivated by building and flying the Comet Sailplane gas model; ultimately, he built the first successful man-powered aircraft, which was flown in Shafter, California, and then constructed an advanced craft that successfully flew man-powered across the English Channel.

Robert Mikesh (Washington, D.C.)—A model builder who became an Air Force colonel; postwar was associated with Paul Garber at NASM. He built an exhibition model for the NASM of the Consolidated NY-2 used by Doolittle in the famous, successful Guggenheim blind-flying project in 1929.

Irwin Ohlsson (Los Angeles)—An outstanding model builder who designed the Pacemaker gas model with which he experimented on his Ohlsson engines; founded Ohlsson Motors in Los Angeles in 1937, which became one of the most successful engine manufacturers nationally.

Paul Poberezny (Oshkosh, Wisconsin)—An early model builder who credits his building of Cleveland models as a major influence in his founding and chairmanship of the EAA. He served as a colonel in the Air Force and Air National Guard, and in 1953 he founded the EAA, which is the most successful organization of its type worldwide.

James D. Powell (Cleveland, Ohio)—An early Cleveland model builder who joined the staff of C-D as an artist and designer in 1934 and produced graphics for C-D catalogs, cartons, flyers, and magazine ads. He served as an artist for the USAF during World War II.

Burt and Dick Rutan (Mojave, California)—An outstanding team of brothers who both built models; Burt designed his own and then subsequently designed canard types for EAA home-built kits. In 1986 Burt's canard design *Voyager,* with 110-foot wingspan, piloted by Dick Rutan and Jeana Yeager, became the first aircraft to fly nonstop around the world, accomplished in nine days.

Dan Scherry (Avon Lake, Ohio)—An early Cleveland model builder who graduated to a career of building industrial-plant models and then became a C-D volunteer model engineer, drawing several plans and building models. He refurbished the Martin 130 China Clipper (8-foot) model, developing a metal covering, now on display at the U.S. Navy Museum at Treasure Island, San Francisco, California.

J. Ken Sniffen (Oshkosh, Wisconsin)—An early modeler who became a graduate of Pratt Institute, served in the USAF 1942–46, attained an MFA degree from the University of Illinois, and served as professor of art and design at the University of Wisconsin, Oshkosh. He began providing art and graphics for C-D in 1968 as a volunteer designer until 1996. He also produced line portraits of famous aviators for the Wisconsin Aviation Hall of Fame and the International Aerobatic Association. He held a private pilot's license.

Henry Struck (New York, New York)—Twice national winner of free-flight gas-powered models; designed the Kovel-Grant-Struck, modernized version of the K-G and the New Ruler; won the 1938 national rubber-powered scale event with a French Caudron. He became a draftsman for Berkeley; joined Pratt-Reed producing CG Cargo Gliders (World War II); then joined Kenyon Instrument Company manufacturing gyros, cameras, and field glasses.

Leo Weiss (New York, New York)—At age sixteen won the Texaco Trophy for gas-powered free flight and became president of Avien, Inc., manufacturer of instruments and controls for aerospace.

William Winter (Chantilly, Virginia)—A pioneer modeler who built his first models in 1927, Bill joined Street and Smith's *Bill Barnes Air Trails* staff in 1936, ultimately becoming editor of the modified title, *Air Trails.* He launched *Air Progress* from what had been an *Air Trails Annual,* which is still published. In 1950 he became editor *of Model Airplane News;* subsequently became editor and publisher of *American Aircraft Modeler.* Winter then jump-started *Model Aviation* for the AMA, for which he authored model-design articles. He authored more than twenty books. From the threshold of model building with rubber powered scale and Wakefield contenders, he designed, built, and flew all types and became an authority for RC design. He spent six years developing more than twenty electric-powered RC model designs in concert with his friend John Hunton, architect for the AMA headquarters.

References

The primary source used in the writing of this book was Edward T. Packard himself. Over the course of ten years, and in countless taped interviews and letters and conversations, he shared with me his story. In addition, in my research I was granted free use of the wealth of materials in the E. T. Packard Collection, which includes catalogs, magazines, brochures, programs, and other modeling and flight memorabilia. These materials are housed by the successor C-D company, under the ownership and care of John Jacox in Indianapolis, Indiana. I also used newspapers from the Cleveland area published during the time—*Plain Dealer, Cleveland News, Cleveland Press, Cleveland Business*—as well as modern aviation and hobbyist magazines and publications, among them *Aviation, Aero Digest, Air Trails, Flying Aces,* and *Model Airplane News.* But there were also numerous published sources that added to the story, and here I acknowledge those.

Adamson, Hans Christian. *Eddie Rickenbacker.* New York: Macmillan Co., 1946.

Aircraft Year Books. New York: Aeronautical Chamber of Commerce of America, Inc., 1919–49.

Allard, Noel. *Speed: The Biography of Charles W. Holman.* Chaska, Minn.: privately published, 1976.

Angle, Glenn D. *Aerosphere, 1939–42.* New York: Aircraft Publications, n.d.

Bruchiss, Louis. *Aircraft Armament.* New York: Aerosphere, Inc., 1945.

Christy, Joe. *Racing Planes and Pilots.* New York: Tab Books, Inc., 1982.

Cohen, Stan. *Wings to the Orient*. Missoula, Mont. Pictorial Histories Publishing, 1984.

Davis, Kenneth S. *The Hero.* Garden City, N.Y.: Doubleday, 1959.

Doolittle, J. H. "Recollections of Early Blind Flying." *Air Power History* 40, no. 4 (1993): 30–34.

Fuchida, Mitsuo, and Masatake Okumiya. *Midway.* Annapolis, Md.: U.S. Naval Institute Press, 1955.

Garber, Paul Edward. *Building and Flying Model Aircraft.* New York: Ronald Press, Playground and Recreation Association of America (Orville Wright, chair), 1929.

Glines, Carroll V. *Doolittle's Tokyo Raiders.* New York: D. Van Nostrand Co., 1964.

Gordon, Dennis. *Lafayette Escadrille Pilot Biographies.* Missoula, Mont.: Missoula Historical Society, 1991.

Hirsch, R. "Schneider Trophy Races." *Motorbooks*. N.p.: 1995.

Hood, Joseph. *The Sky Racers*. New York: Grosset & Dunlap, 1969.

Hull, Robert. *September Champions*. Harrisburg, Pa.: Stackpole Books, 1979.

Jablonski, Edward. *Atlantic Fever*. New York: Macmillan Co., 1972.

Jane, Fred T. *All the World's Aircraft*. London: Sampson Low, Maston & Co, 1912–29.

Julian, Marcel. *The Battle of Britain*. New York: Fawcett, 1967.

Juptner, Joseph P. *U.S. Civil Aircraft* 1–9.

Kimes, B. R., ed. *Packard: A History of the Motor Car and the Company*. Princeton, N.J.: Dutton, n.d.

LeMay, Curtis E. *Mission with LeMay*. New York: Doubleday & Co., 1965.

Lindbergh, Charles. *We*. New York: G. P. Putnam's, 1927.

Mason, Herbert Molloy, Jr. *The Rise of the Luftwaffe, 1918–1940*. New York: Dial Press, 1973.

Nielson, Dale. "Saga of the U.S. Air Mail Service, 1918–1927." *Air Mail Pioneer News*.

Norton, Donald V. *Larry: A Bio of Lawrence D. Bell*. Chicago: Nelson-Hall, 1981.

Queen, Ellery. *The Celebrated Cases of Dick Tracy*. New York: Chicago Tribune, Chelsea House, 1980.

Redding and Yenne. *Boeing: Planemaker to the World*. London: Crescent Pub., n.d.

Rickenbacker, Eddie. *Fighting Flying Circus*. New York: Frederick A. Stokes & Co., 1919.

———. *Rickenbacker*. Englewood Cliffs, N.J.: Prentice-Hall, 1967.

Serling, Robert J. *From the Captain to the Colonel*. New York: Dial Press, 1980.

Schmid, Wes, and Truman Weaver. *The Golden Age of Racing*. Hales Corner, Wisc.: EAA Air Museum Foundation, 1967.

Schoneberger, William A. *California Wings*. Los Angeles: Windsor Publishing, 1984.

Shamburger, Page. *Tracks Across the Sky*. Cranberry, N.J.: Barnes, 1970.